SISTERS
in the
RESISTANCE

SISTERS
—— in the ——
RESISTANCE

*How Women Fought
to Free France, 1940–1945*

Margaret Collins Weitz

John Wiley & Sons, Inc.

New York • Chichester • Brisbane • Toronto • Singapore

*To all the French women who resisted occupation,
oppression, and injustice*

Copyright © 1995 by Margaret Collins Weitz

Published by John Wiley & Sons, Inc.

Map on page xviii courtesy of the Ministère des Anciens Combattants et Victimes de
Guerre, Paris. English labels by Deborah Levinson.

Library of Congress Cataloging-in-Publication Data
Weitz, Margaret Collins.
    Sisters in the resistance : how women fought to free France, 1940–1945 /
Margaret Collins Weitz.
        p.   cm.
    Includes bibliographical references and index.
    ISBN 0-471-12676-4
    1. World War, 1939–1945—Underground movements—France.   2. World
War, 1939–1945—Women—France.   I. Title.
D802.F8W44   1995
940.53'44—dc20   95-7632
                                                                            CIP

Printed in the United States of America

10 9 8 7 6 5 4 3 2 1

Contents

Preface

"Madame. If the French army had been composed of women and not men, we Germans would never have gotten to Paris." Such were the German prosecutor's observations to Agnès Humbert at her trial. In the spring of 1941, she was arrested for Resistance activities and sentenced to five years in prison. Ten members of her group, including three women, received the death sentence.[1]

WHILE DOING RESEARCH FOR SEVERAL EARLIER BOOKS AND A NUMBER of articles on women in France, I became aware of the indispensable but little-known contributions of French women to the defense of their country. To be sure, books had been published in France about women in the French Resistance. Most were written by journalists, however, and the emphasis was on anecdote rather than analysis. More critically, these works assume a broad familiarity with French history and politics. Women's involvement in France's war-within-a-war is an important subject for the non-French-speaking public because it focuses on a complex and troubled time in France's recent past, a period receiving more and more attention. In addition, any attempt to understand postwar France better must take into account the presence of women in the French Resistance.

Although only limited information exists in archives dealing with women's Resistance activities specifically, I undertook research at all the major archives to locate what information there was (see Bibliography). I was extremely fortunate in being granted access to classified material in France's Archives Nationales (AN) and to unpublished memoirs and studies. Prefects' obligatory monthly reports on file at the AN offer valuable information on the situation in occupied France. In an effort to buttress its authority, the Vichy regime increased the number of prefects (administrative heads of a district) and demanded that they provide accurate information on the mood of the populace. The Bluet Files now available to scholars contain transcripts of postwar collaboration trials. I read many secondary sources. Again, few of these works relate specifically to women, but they are essential to a fuller understanding of occupied France. In many instances, historical records can be compared with oral testimony for possible verification—a necessary step in any historical study. This book centers on a selection of interviews from a large group of *résistants* conducted during the 1980s. In a project of this nature, the first step is to collect accounts from survivors while they still can testify. Survivors who lived through those troubled times are dying.

Oral testimony is subject to what one seeks. Paying attention to the problems of selection, reliability, verification, and motivation, I interviewed more than eighty *résistants*, mainly women. The group was chosen to obtain as wide a social, cultural, educational, geographical, and political range as possible. Spouses and children were interviewed in some instances, as were men in the Resistance. Follow-up interviews and a questionnaire helped fill in background. In a general, tacit way, those interviewed appeared to recognize that my project was designed to bring the history of women in the French Resistance to the wide English-speaking public it deserves—without bias.

A difficult problem was deciding which narratives to include, for many had to be left out. Since the primary aim of this book is to inform, rather than to commemorate, the exploits of many deserving women are not included. This was necessary in order to provide in-depth accounts, rather than a few details on many. Thus, the narratives chosen represent other women who performed many of the same tasks. It would have been all too easy to select only exceptional tales of adventure and heroism; people relish such accounts. However, to do so would have falsified the history of women in the French Resistance. The point is that women's contributions consisted of countless mundane, repetitive, everyday tasks—tasks that do not figure generally in traditional historical accounts. In occupied France, these daily activities took on new meaning and, for the women, new dangers.

Initial chapters provide a context for these narratives. Expository sections frame the narratives. I have endeavored to present a coherent overall picture, not just narratives offering readers only "the rawest of raw lumber."[2] A fair number of dates are included. Chronology is very important. Events had different imports, depending upon whether they occurred in 1940, 1941, or later. Although the Resistance covered slightly more than four years, the situation changed continually in France—at times almost daily—during that period. Assignments became much more difficult and dangerous as the war progressed and the Nazis tightened their grip.

Oral narratives vary considerably. These are not impersonal or anonymous accounts, not even in the case of women who limited themselves largely to chronological testimony: "First I did this, and then I did that." In the absence of documents, oral narratives help fill in the broader historical canvas and provide rich psychological insights. While several interviewees were critical of other Resistance members—even, in a few cases, principally deportees, of the Resistance undertaking itself—few challenged official hagiography. To cite but one example (perhaps the most obvious), it proved difficult to obtain information on sexual harassment—certainly a possibility, given the nature of Resistance work. As one would expect, the testimony of women with higher education—particularly those trained as historians—is generally more analytical and introspective. Accounts offered by women with less education were somewhat more predictable.

Interestingly, some of the women I interviewed decided later to write down and publish their experiences. Preparing for the interview may have opened the floodgates of memory. Alternatively, perhaps my insistence on the significance of *their* personal accounts encouraged them to make their memoirs available to a larger public. Whatever the reasons for the decision, their recollections can only enrich our understanding of those dark days in France's history.

Women's accounts differ frequently from traditional testimony, as if they were trying to find a new form appropriate to a unique experience. Speaking of the committed literature of World War II, writer and *résistante* Elsa Triolet maintains:

> The art of the Resistance was an *avant-garde* art: a new spirit found its way into all the arts, so much so that a new term had to be found to describe it: *engagé* [committed] art, as Sartre called it. . . . To create these works of art which attacked and undermined the Occupation, it was necessary to invent new forms and new contents in which to clothe the spirit of the Resistance. There were no rules and no theories: each artist had to create his own, forged from his own art.[3]

Lucie Aubrac's account covers nine months of her Resistance work—the nine months of her second pregnancy. Madeleine Baudoin uses the third person to detail her activities as head of a Marseilles-based attack group. While her narrator, Marianne Bardini, shares her initials, this distancing suggests that Baudoin's exceptional, nontraditional actions were those of "another."

Men and women alike found it difficult to forge their "own art," to give voice to their experiences. Writing about *Waiting for Godot*, theater critic Robert Scanlan observes that while the play is not a literal representation of Samuel Beckett's experiences in the Resistance (for which he received the croix de guerre), its imagery—and, more important, the states of mind it represents—derive clearly from these experiences: "All those who endured the war in Europe emerged transformed, and they had great difficulty expressing the magnitude of their inner tumult."[4]

Paul Fussell has described perceptively the problems inherent in writing about war: "It would seem impossible to write an account of anything without some 'literature' leaking in," he holds. For Fussell, the memoir is "a kind of fiction differing from the 'first novel' . . . only by the continuous implicit attestation of veracity or appeals to documented historical fact."[5] Oxford historian Richard Cobb chose to use works of literature rather than historical data for his portrayal of life in France during the two world wars—on the grounds that experience not shared is an almost uncrossable barrier.[6] Possible elements of "fiction" present in these women's narratives may never be discerned. But that need not be a major concern. Overall, this collective testimony more than amply attests to the Resistance roles of French women and their reactions to that experience.

From my interviews and readings, I selected those narratives that seemed to best reflect the diversity of backgrounds of the participants and to illustrate the many and varied Resistance activities of French women. Biographical data were included to help place the Resistance experience in the continuum of their lives (see Appendix).

Every effort was made to verify accounts by checking historical records or the testimony of others. The large number of narratives used for this book helped in this endeavor. One must remember that even in historical accounts, there are sometimes differing, even conflicting versions. In her biography of her brother Jean—de Gaulle's delegate and a Resistance hero and martyr—Laure Moulin calls attention to differences and discrepancies in Resistance leaders' reports of an important meeting in Lyon.[7]

When sent written transcripts of their testimony, several interviewees asked that passages be retracted (generally those presenting relatives or friends in a less-than-flattering light—which, after reflection, they did not want included)—a request I naturally granted. Others wanted to rewrite their testimony, to make it more "literary." Here we encounter the problem of the written text versus the spoken word, which often is not as grammatically "correct." While some testimony was offered in response to my questions, I chose to eliminate these interrogations and let the narrative flow unimpeded without intervening, except for some instances where clarification was required.

Unless otherwise indicated, the translations cited are mine. In most instances, I read the French publications in their original versions. During the time I worked on the book, English editions of some of the French works were published. Wherever possible, I list English translations (see Bibliography). There is no satisfactory English equivalent for the term *résistant*—that is, a member of the French Resistance—so I kept the French term. This has the advantage of indicating the sex of the person by the presence or absence of a final *e*, *résistante* being a woman in the Resistance. When dealing with couples who were both in the Resistance, I use first names to avoid confusion.

As translator of most of these interviews from the original French, I had great latitude in choosing the appropriate voice and vocabulary, searching for *le mot juste*—the appropriate word. To the extent that it is possible, I endeavored to reproduce the spirit and voice of those interviewed, as well as the informal narrative tone. Because of financial considerations, I did most of the transcriptions myself, which proved providential. Whenever I played the tapes, the voice I heard conjured up the image of the interviewee, the setting, and many details of our meetings.

At one point, the future of this book appeared most uncertain. My apartment was badly flooded when a pipe burst several floors above me. The tapes, narratives, and most of the translations on which I had spent so much time were irreparably damaged, as was my computer. I was obliged to move into a hotel while repairs were made. Fortunately, I had made copies of the original tapes and had stored them elsewhere. While the prospect of redoing much of the work was daunting, I felt strongly that what these brave women did deserved to be known. It was truly a privilege to have met these remarkable figures.

Acknowledgments

A BOOK OF THIS NATURE OWES ITS EXISTENCE TO THE SUPPORT AND contributions of many. It is a pleasure to acknowledge here my gratitude to all those who helped in one way or another, even if they are not named specifically. My heartfelt thanks go to all the former members of the French Resistance who so generously gave their time, advice, and, in many instances, warm hospitality. Without their assistance, this book would not exist. I am particularly grateful to Geneviève de Gaulle, president of ADIR, and the formerly imprisoned and deported women of that organization who agreed to be interviewed or who offered suggestions. Their journal, *Voix et Visages*, provided much pertinent information. The late Marie Granet, historian and *résistante*, kindly volunteered access to her classified documents at the Archives Nationales and later sent me all her research material, along with a copy of an unpublished study of women in the French Resistance. I can only hope that one day her book will be published in France. Essentially a testimonial, it contains the names of many *résistantes*. Lucie Aubrac not only met with me on various occasions but also came to Boston to animate the 1992 "Women and the French Resistance" conference I organized at Suffolk and Harvard Universities. Claude Bourdet of Combat generously put me in contact with many women from different Resistance movements, in addition to his own. My former mentor at Harvard, *résistant* Jean Bruneau, assembled a group in the Lyon/Grenoble area whom I would not have met otherwise. Bernard Ducamin of the Council of State helped by furnishing documentation on Vichy legislation concerning women. The extensive holdings of Harvard University's Widener Library and its interlibrary loan service furnished many rare or not readily available books. Widener's reference services were unfailingly attentive to my queries. At each of the archives and libraries where I worked—particularly at the Institut de l'Histoire du Temps Présent—helpful staff aided my research. May they be collectively thanked here.

A grant from the American Council of Learned Sciences permitted me to spend several months in France conducting interviews. Residency grants at the Rockefeller Foundation Bellagio Center and the

Camargo Foundation in Cassis allowed much-needed writing time—away from the responsibilities of teaching and chairing an interdisciplinary department. I am indebted to Stanley Hoffmann, director of the Harvard Center for European Studies, for appointing me an Affiliate of the Center. There I had the opportunity to meet permanent and visiting scholars and co-organize a 1984 conference on "Women and War."

Bernard J. Quinn, editor of *Contemporary French Civilization*, generously granted permission to reprint sections of two articles that appeared in *CFC*: "Lucie Aubrac: Femme Engagée" (vol. 15, no. 1, 1991), and "Geneviève de Gaulle: Refusing the Unacceptable" (vol. 18, no. 1, 1994). He also published the papers from the 1992 conference, *Mémoire et Oubli: Women of the French Resistance*, (vol. 18, no. 1, 1994), which I edited. Daniel J. J. Ross, director of the University of Nebraska Press, kindly permitted me to publish material that appeared in my introduction to Lucie Aubrac's *Outwitting the Gestapo* (1993). The French Ministry for Veterans and Victims of War allowed me to reproduce photos and documents from their extensive archival holdings. The Polaroid Company generously agreed to let me use portraits taken by Inge Reethof for the *Notable French Women* exhibition I curated for the French Cultural Services. I am also indebted to Mercure de France for permission to publish excerpts from Jeanne Bohec's *La Plastiqueuse à la bicyclette* (1975) and Apostolat des Éditions for granting the right to include passages from Sister Edwige Dumas's *Souvenirs de guerre: Calais 1940–45* (1978)—both in my translations. Souvenir Press of London kindly agreed to my utilizing selections from the English edition of Mathilde-Lily Carré's *I Was the Cat: The Truth about the Most Remarkable Woman Spy since Mata-Hari, by Herself* (1960). Éditions Calmann-Lévy of Paris graciously allowed me to include excerpts I translated of Simone Martin-Chauffier's book *A bientôt quand même* (1976).

Throughout the preparation and writing of this book, I have been fortunate to have the help and encouragement of colleagues and friends, including Philippe Burrin, Carole Fink, Stephen Fox, Stanley Hoffmann, Fred Marchant, Richard Marius, Karen Offen, Michelle Perrot, Robert Paxton, Lia Poorvu, Lucretia Slaughter, and my son Richard. They read sections of the manuscript or offered valuable suggestions. However, I alone bear responsibility for the finished work.

David and Catherine helped in various ways, even if they were not always certain about what their mother's project entailed. John Mulrooney of Suffolk University printed up drafts of the book. Nicole Hermann and Lucy Johnston helped with the transcriptions. I have been extremely fortunate in that Dean Michael R. Ronayne of the College of Liberal Arts and Sciences of Suffolk University supported my project from the beginning. My agent, William B. Goodman, offered wisdom and assistance at every stage. Finally, it remains for me to extend my sincere thanks to the staff of John Wiley and Sons, in particular to my dedicated editor, Hana Umlauf Lane.

Chronology

1939

July · *Code de la Famille*

September 1 · Poland invaded by the Germans

September 3 · Great Britain and France declare war on Nazi Germany

September 26 · French Communist Party and its organizations dissolved

1940

March 20 · Prime Minister Édouard Daladier resigns; new government formed by Paul Reynaud

May 10 · German offensive begins on the western front

May 18 · Marshal Philippe Pétain is brought into government

End May/ early June · British and French troops evacuated from Dunkirk

June 10 · Italy declares war on France; government leaves Paris, arrives several days later in Bordeaux

June 14 · Germans enter Paris, declared an Open City

June 16 · Pétain forms new government and orders ceasefire the following day

June 18 · From London, Charles de Gaulle issues appeal for continued resistance to French population

June 22 · French and Germans sign an armistice

June 28 · De Gaulle recognized as leader of Free French by British

July 10 · National Assembly at Vichy votes full powers to Pétain, who becomes head of state the next day, establishing the Vichy regime

July 22	First Vichy law reviewing past naturalizations, aimed largely at Jews
Mid-August	Vichy dissolves trade unions and Freemasons' organization
October 3	Vichy passes first statute on Jews
October 13	Vichy passes law regulating women working in public sector
October 30	Shortly after meeting Adolf Hitler, Pétain announces he is embarking upon "the path of collaboration"
November/ December	First clandestine newspapers appear

1941

June 22	Germany invades Soviet Union, violating August 23, 1939, pact

1942

February	Creation of what is to become the Militia, the French equivalent of the SS
February 15	Vichy declares abortion a crime against the state
March	First Jews deported from France to concentration camps
July 16–17	Close to 13,000 Jews (including almost 4,000 children) rounded up in Paris and taken to Vel' d'Hiv stadium
November 8	Allied landings in Morocco and Algeria
November 11	Germans occupy southern France, the so-called Free Zone
November 27	French scuttle their fleet in Mediterranean port of Toulon

1943

January	Three Resistance movements combine to form Mouvements Unis de la Résistance (MUR)
February 16	Compulsory labor law (STO) enacted

| Winter | *Maquis* units start to form |
| May | National Council of the Resistance (CNR) formed |

1944

January 1	Joseph Darnand appointed to head Vichy police and pursue *résistants*
March 23	Consultative Assembly in Algeria decides in favor of the vote for women
April 21	Women given right to vote in postwar France by French Committee of National Liberation (CFLN)
June 6	D day invasion of Normandy
August 15	Allied landing in southern France
August 25	Liberation of Paris

1945

| May 7 | Unconditional surrender of Germany |
| July | Trial of Pétain (death sentence commuted by de Gaulle) |

List of Acronyms

ADIR   Association des Déportées et Internées de la Résistance (organization of French women Resistance prisoners and deportees)

AFAT   Auxiliaire Féminin de l'Armée de Terre

AS   Armée Secrète

BCRA   Bureau Central de Renseignements et d'Action (French Secret Service based in London)

BOA   Bureau d'Opérations Aériennes (French organization dealing with clandestine landings and parachute drops)

CAR   Comité d'Aide aux Réfugiés

CGT   Confédération Générale du Travail (Communist-dominated labor union)

CIMADE   Comité Inter-mouvements d'Aide aux Déportés

CNR   Conseil National de la Résistance

COSOR   Comité des Oeuvres Sociales de la Résistance

CVIA   Comité de Vigilance des Intellectuels Antifascistes

FFI   Forces Françaises de l'Intérieur

FFL   Forces Françaises Libres (Free French Forces based in London

FN   Front National (Communist-led Resistance movement)

FNU   Front National Universitaire

FTP   Francs-Tireurs-Partisans (military organization of the National Front)

IS   Intelligence Service (British)

JC-MOI   Jeunesse Communiste–Main-d'Oeuvre Immigrée

JECF   Jeunesse Étudiante Chrétienne Française (French Christian Student Youth group)

LCI   landing craft

MLF   Mouvement de Libération des Femmes (Women's Liberation Movement)

MNPGD   Mouvement National des Prisonniers de Guerre et Déportés (clandestine movement of POWs and deportees)

MOI   Main-d'Oeuvre Immigrée

MPF   Mouvement Populaire des Familles

MRP   Mouvement Républicain Populaire (political party created at the Liberation by Christian Democrats)

MUR   Mouvements Unis de la Résistance (created in 1943 when the movements Combat, Libération, and Franc-Tireur were joined; MUR means "wall" in French)

NAP   Noyautage de l'Administration Publique (infiltration of public administrations, overseen by MUR)

NAP/FER   NAP within the French railway system

NAP/PTT   NAP within the French postal and telecommunications system

OCM   Organisation Civile et Militaire

OJC   Organisation Juive de Combat

PCF   Parti Communiste Français

SSA   Section Sanitaire Automobile

STO   Service du Travail Obligatoire (compulsory labor laws)

UFF   Union des Femmes Françaises (Communist-led women's organization)

Map of France (1940)

1

┼╾═╼┼

Women and the
War-within-a-War

"MY ARM WAS BADLY MANGLED, BUT I REFUSED TO LET THEM AMPU-
tate. . . . Because there were few of us to run them, I learned to operate the automatic printing machines. In the beginning, I used to
get dizzy just watching the same illustrations whizzing by. But then I
got used to it. One day my arm was caught in the press. Without
thinking, I had tried to blot out an ink smudge. My colleagues insisted that I be taken to the hospital even though it was dangerous
for all of us. The doctor who treated me knew that I was involved
in 'something,' in spite of my alibi. However, he said nothing. He
did not report me to the authorities, as other cases had been. Instead, he protected me. The nurses and female staff of the hospital
were also accomplices in keeping my presence secret. Six weeks later
[and much too soon, according to colleagues], I returned to the
shop. I was needed," Marie-Antoinette Morat insists. But that is no
longer her name.

"I lost my name during the Occupation," she explains, "because
I gave my identification papers to a Jewish girl about my age. Her
papers were stamped 'Jewish,' which meant she could be arrested at
any time and deported. And so I became—and remain—Lucienne,
now Guezennec. I was able to get false identification papers because
Combat—the Resistance movement I belonged to—could print

1

counterfeit cards and coupons of all sorts. We had commercial presses capable of publishing runs of several hundred thousand copies of our journal *Combat* and the papers of other movements.

"My family lived in northeastern France. My father was wounded fighting in World War I. The Germans invaded France in May 1940 and designated our region the 'forbidden zone,' attaching it to their Brussels command. During the exodus of those fleeing the Germans, we sheltered those in need: escaped prisoners, refugees, Jews, Allied aviators. I was in my early twenties when the Germans invaded our country. My reaction to the Occupation was anti-German. Not ideological or whatever—out-and-out anti-German. The invasion was like rape. To this day when I read about a rape trial, I am reminded of the Occupation. This was really violation—violation of my country. It was impossible to remain passive.

"At this time, I led the life of a middle-class woman with some education—but no profession. I had free time. My husband was an engineer in an armament factory. When war was declared, his mobilization assignment was to continue working at the factory, but now working day and night."

The mayor gave orders to evacuate their small town when the Germans approached; the bombings had become dangerous. Part of their house was destroyed. Since her husband had to stay at the factory, Guezennec took to the road on her bicycle. For three days she traveled by bike—partially in a train boxcar designed for horses—until she reached her parents' home in Lyon in the unoccupied zone, the center of French Resistance in the south.

"I knew deep down, viscerally, that France and we French had had it. Wild hordes, like the barbarians of old, were going to crush us and reduce us to slavery. I had scarcely gotten to my parents' place in Lyon when they asked me to take off again—and again by bike—to accompany a young cousin to the Pyrénées in southwestern France, where our two elderly grandmothers were. En route, my cousin and I heard Marshal Pétain announce that he was asking for an armistice. We broke into tears.

"Life resumed toward the end of 1940, when my husband came to Lyon and we moved in with my parents while waiting for an apartment nearby. During the following year, through gossip and contact—chance encounters—I learned that there was a certain

General Charles de Gaulle in London who was trying to reestablish French response to the Germans. The word *resistance* was not used yet. Friends who knew of my anti-German feelings asked me to do a few 'errands.' When asked to distribute a few dozen tracts, I was elated. I felt like a new Joan of Arc. At last I could do something.

"My husband was concerned about my safety, but he himself was not involved in the Resistance. For him the important thing was to continue to direct his employees and ensure the men's jobs. From the beginning of 1942 to 1943, I worked with André Bollier [Vélin], who oversaw the printing of the clandestine paper whose final name was *Combat*. I carried the lead printing plates to other underground printers. Claude Gérard from Lorraine (see chapter 7), an engineer like Bollier, worked with us. How many trips and how many bundles we made together! We wrapped the issues of *Combat* in crates or put them in valises to ship them throughout the southern zone via a distribution network that had been organized.

"In late spring 1943, Vélin asked me to work in the print shop that Combat had installed in a villa on the outskirts of Lyon. He had orders to increase the circulation of *Combat*.

"The location of the printing shop had been carefully chosen. Because of the slope of the land, half the building (a former cement factory) was below grade. This covered the noise somewhat and concealed our activities. But we still had to build a wall around the room with the presses. The 'laboratory' had been given a rather vague name: Bureau of Geodesic and Geographic Studies, suggesting a Parisian firm doing research. That way, we could get telephone service and electricity. The shop had two heavy professional presses. One enormous monster [that] Vélin put in working condition weighed five tons; there was also a newer, automated machine. The presses printed our paper *Combat*—a name that aptly described our feelings and what we were doing."

From a monthly circulation of around 40,000 in 1942, *Combat* grew to more than 200,000 issues in 1944. (One print run had more than 300,000 copies.) Combat presses helped print other clandestine papers, including *Défense de la France*, *Action*, and *La Voix du Nord*. They also printed papers such as *Témoignage Chrétien* (*Christian Witness*) when there was a breakdown in others' machines. Young Vélin, a graduate of the elite École Polytechnique (comparable to MIT), was the key figure in the success of the movement's journal. At one time, thirteen printing shops were working under his direction throughout France.[1]

The operation was plagued with problems. Supplies were rationed; there were breakdowns and electrical outages; and the humidity of the cellar meant the equipment had to be repaired constantly. Nevertheless, by using stationery with letterheads of fake German firms—along with all the stamps and seals that so delight French officialdom—the intrepid Vélin acquired for Combat the privileged status of a firm working for Germany. In short order, Guezennec learned the trade of typography—one usually requiring a long apprenticeship and one not often undertaken by women in the mid-twentieth century, and certainly not middle-class women. By now, Lucienne had gone underground, using the name of Mme Roberval. The Combat printing team worked long hours—sometimes through the night—in close quarters. Because she was the only woman in the group, Guezennec also shopped and did the cooking.

"Several of our comrades had been arrested, but we were not yet obsessed with anguish; we were unaware of the existence of concentration camps. We tried in vain to obtain news about our friends. The Red Cross never told us anything. For safety I had to leave my home and stay where I could, in different locations in Lyon or in the suburbs. The printing shop was my haven, and I think that was true for the rest of our team. When Vélin acquired photos of the camps in Germany, we brought out a special edition of Combat in November 1943, number 50. The images of the camps awakened waves of anxiety. Could our comrades who had been arrested be held in such terrible places?

"Twice in the preceding years, Vélin had been arrested by French police, brought in for questioning, but eventually released. Then he was arrested a third time in mid-March 1944, but now it was by the Gestapo. This time he was sent to Montluc prison and tortured. Yet, less than two months later Vélin managed to escape, and that very day he resumed his place at Combat, directing the printing and distribution, though on a somewhat more reduced level.

"On June 6, 1944, the Allies landed. We sensed the beginning of the end of the German occupation of France. But the Gestapo intensified its activities, at least in Lyon. Our group assumed we would soon be free to take to the *maquis*.* Vélin asked London for permission to shut down the print shop. Permission refused. Instead, we received orders to increase the number of issues of *Combat, La Marseillaise,* and various tracts. We accepted these orders without hesitation—but with full awareness of the risks we ran. You can imagine the anguish each time someone was late [for work]. At that time of the year the heat was stifling in the small, cramped room where we worked on the copy. We spoke in low tones so that no one on the outside would hear us.

"On June 17, 1944, the print shop was suddenly attacked by a large group of Milice [a French paramilitary group comparable to the Gestapo, hereafter referred to as the Militia]. We had been betrayed. 'Surrender! You are surrounded!' a loud voice ordered. Vélin was with me, along with Max [Francisque Vacher, reporter/photographer for the Lyon *Progrès*] and Dulac [Paul Jaillet, typographer for the *Progrès*]. Two machine guns were thrust into the ventilators of the composing room, where we were working on the next edition of *Combat*. Max dashed across the room. There was a burst of machine-gun fire. Max lay on the floor. There were drops of blood glistening on his chest—like stars. He did not move or make a sound; his eyes were closed. I knew he was dead.

" 'To the terraces,' Vélin cried as he pulled me along. Dulac refused to follow. We ran to the courtyard at the end of the garden. Vélin pulled me up over the wall and dragged me to the nearby street. I had trouble getting over the wall as I was still weak from my accident. A few steps and he was downed by machine-gun fire. A bullet hit me in the chest and I fell to the ground next to him. [She was also hit in the leg and foot.] Softly Vélin said to me, 'They won't take me alive.' Then, more distinctly, 'May God forgive me,' and shot himself through the heart. The next thing I remember was a German soldier trying to free me from Vélin's arm. 'It wasn't worth it,' he said to me, with pity. Thinking I would be taken away and tortured, I asked him to kill me. Instead, an ambulance arrived that took me to the Grange-Blanche clinic—the clinic I had been in when my arm was mangled.

"At the shop the unarmed Dulac was beaten and tortured. After

Maquis was the name given to the clandestine paramilitary groups that formed in isolated areas starting in the winter of 1943. The *maquis* is the coarse underbrush in parts of Corsica favored by shepherds and those in difficulty with the law (as defined in Prosper Mérimée's "Mateo Falcone," 1833).

several hours, the head of the Militia asked for volunteers, who took
their compatriot into the courtyard and shot him. He refused to
turn his back and died facing them, after straightening his worker's
smock. Then they set fire to the place. We learned of Dulac's end
from firemen who arrived on the scene. Later, German patrols came
searching and pillaging the neighborhood, terrorizing the inhabitants, who hid in their basements."

Lucienne Guezennec was the only survivor of that print-shop
crew. Thanks to the heroic efforts of other Combat members, the next
issue of Combat came out on schedule. But they lost three brave comrades and irreplaceable printing equipment; trucks, five tons of paper,
and other material it had taken months to acquire; and two hundred
rubber stamps to authorize all sorts of passes, including demobilization
papers for the many young men who had been called up for work in
Germany. The movement also lost a good deal of money. The Militia
followed their killings with theft.

"At the clinic, I was kept under armed guard. Once again the nurses
and aides did what they could to help me recover quickly. They
kept it as quiet as possible around me. When plans were made to
free me, they played a vital role. These women, like many others,
don't figure in histories of the Resistance. Yet they certainly played
their part. And then there were women who worked with me on
other projects: Simone Rieutord, Josette Bon, Mme Gros [big]—
called Madame Petit [small]—and Marie-Jeanne Bouteille. They are
but some of the women who helped.

"Less than three weeks later [and, obviously, once again not
fully recovered—in this instance from the bullet wound that just
missed her heart], friends helped me escape. My friend Marie-Jeanne
Bouteille—whom no one ever mentions in Resistance accounts—
arranged it with others. It was very carefully arranged. A nun in the
hospital distracted my guard. Then I asked to go to the toilets.
Someone had slipped me a message indicating the time I was to go
to the toilets. I could hardly stand up because of a recent operation.
And of course I was in a hospital gown. There I found clothes and
dressed. Marie-Jeanne was waiting for me at the exit. She supported
me, and the two of us walked out of the hospital, like normal visitors, at the end of visiting hours. A car waiting outside the hospital
took me to Marie-Jeanne's home, where her parents hid me. Later,

as a safety precaution, I was taken to a more distant hiding place and thus escaped torture, deportation, and death."[2]

What Lucienne Guezennec and other women did in the French Resistance to German occupation during World War II has received little attention. Yet women's participation in that war-within-a-war was considerably greater than the public roles they played in French society at that time.[3] Their contributions were critically important to every aspect of the effort of those French who sought to free their country from the Nazis and the regime of Marshal Philippe Pétain. Moreover, when women's exploits are mentioned in historical accounts, they are generally presented from a masculine perspective. Historians tend to focus on activist and traditional military undertakings such as the development of the clandestine *maquis* fighting groups that took place in the last years of the Occupation, whereas Resistance began when the Germans took over France in June 1940.

The comparative invisibility of women in French Resistance history may be attributed in part to the problems inherent in a definition of *resistance* and to the nature of women's contributions. Resistance activities were frequently differentiated by gender. Who, for example, has heard of Jean Moulin's sister? Yet Laure Moulin exists. The sister of the famed Resistance hero and martyr spent her weekends typing, decoding, and running errands for her brother. But she—like many women who participated in the French Resistance—does not figure in studies of the movement. Nor is this situation unique to France. American women veterans have also been largely marginalized. The first National Salute to Women Veterans in the United States was held in October 1989. The recently formed National Association of Women Veterans continues efforts to achieve official status and recognition. In 1994, during commemorations of D day, virtually no mention was made of the Allied women who participated in the campaign.

Unlike their male counterparts, many French women involved in Resistance activities did not seek official postwar recognition for their voluntary participation. Women did not see themselves as veterans. They simply did "what had to be done." The theme of self-effacement runs through women's testimony: "My role was very minor"; "I am not a heroine"; etc. At times their exploits are presented in apologetic or negative terms. France Pejot explained, as if somehow she had failed: "I kept getting arrested." Yet each time the young woman was arrested, she saved others, especially male leaders in her group. Given this tendency toward self-effacement, it is perhaps not surprising that women's Resistance undertakings have not been widely acknowledged. Women themselves have been slow to recognize that their contribution was an important component of France's efforts to combat German occupiers.

Utilizing narratives of women who participated in the French Resistance, this book documents the many activities of women in that clandestine war. While there is some evidence of women's participation in the Resistance in the limited archival material available, it is principally through the narratives of the participants themselves—when wartime events are placed in the wider perspective of their life cycles—that we learn of the varied activities of women members of the Resistance and come to understand the meaning of that experience for them.

+)=-=(+

Defining what constitutes *resistance* is a problem faced by all who study the efforts of some French citizens to continue the struggle against the Nazi occupiers and, as the war progressed, the Vichy regime headed by Marshal Pétain. In his 1990 study (*An Uncertain Hour*), Ted Morgan cites the *Shorter Oxford English Dictionary* definition of *resistance*: "an organized underground movement in a country occupied by enemy forces carried on with the assistance of armed fighters for the purpose of frustrating and damaging the occupying power." Both the term *organized* and the qualification of "with the assistance of armed fighters" are problematic, given the development of the French Resistance and the fact that most armed fighters did not really become involved until late spring 1944. More appropriate, perhaps, is the derivation of *resistance*, or *résistance*, from the Latin *resistere*, with the prefix *re* intensifying the verb *sistere*, resulting in a strong form of *stare* (to stand).[4] To stand fast to a position or principle well defines those French who resisted. Their inner certainty was allied with a strong sense of conscience and belief in human dignity.

Henri Michel, the doyen of Resistance historians, defines *resistance* as any action or writing in violation of the conventions of the armistice between France and Germany signed on June 22, 1940, or in opposition to the applications of these conventions—no matter where the place or who the author.[5] While historians might agree on this open, wide-ranging definition, they differ on when the term *resistance* was used in the larger sense it is now accorded. For social activist

Madeleine Baudoin, who later joined the French Communist Party (Parti Communiste Français, or PCF), one spoke of "resisting" from the beginning of the Occupation, but then in the more restricted sense of resisting German rationing and finding ways to procure more food. (The French have long used a related expression to designate efforts to get back at the system: *Je me défends*—literally, "I defend myself, i.e., stand up.")

During the Occupation, Marshal Pétain spoke frequently to the French nation as head of the government. In an August 1941 radio address, he cited the need "to conquer the *resistance* [my emphasis] of all those who oppose order," thus acknowledging that there were French people who did not accept his German-supported government. Nevertheless, it was only well into the German occupation that the term *resistance* came to be used to define opposition to the Nazis—refusal to accept the conventions of the armistice and defeat by whatever means possible. Resistance activist Lucie Aubrac did not view her first efforts in the fall of 1940 as *resistance*. It was a question of conscience. She and others refused to accept defeat.[6] This refusal was based upon firmly held views of patriotism or honor, religious or ethical principles, political views, even a desire for adventure—among other reasons.

Some historians have proposed a division between "active" and "passive" resistance. For example, in *Résistance P.T.T.*, Raymond Ruffin lists Resistance attitudes and activities in the French mail and telecommunications system under two categories: "active" and "passive." Is "failure to maintain the vehicles requisitioned by the Germans" merely "passive" resistance, as he designates it? Elsewhere I have encountered the qualification "authentic." One study has a chapter with the paradoxical title "The Resistance of the Non-Resisters," underlining the difficulty of trying to apply hard-and-fast definitions. Ultimately, I find such distinctions untenable. Research reveals that French resistance to German occupation assumed many forms, and it occurred in widely varying circumstances, vitiating any attempt to categorize neatly the Resistance acts. Thus, this book details the many and varied activities undertaken by French women—whether affiliated with a group or not.

If there were few *résistants* at the outset of the Occupation, a considerable number of French men and women belonged to different Resistance organizations by the end of hostilities. In addition to those who joined networks or movements, a far larger number helped the

Resistance in other ways. Women who sheltered someone sought by the Gestapo—a political refugee, a Jew, an Allied aviator, or a *résistant*—risked death if caught (some were executed), whereas airmen or soldiers were presumably sent to a prisoner-of-war camp. Many of these women did not necessarily "belong" to any Resistance organization. Similarly, women who remained in town, and supported *maquis* units on the sly, risked more than the men of the *maquis*, who remained hidden in the countryside—generally with some arms. Although after victory a fair number of French claimed to be members of the Resistance, they were few and far between in the early days of the Occupation. The exact number can never be known, but 220,000 men and women were officially recognized by the postwar government. These figures do not include the many women who insist they "did nothing." Resistance member and historian Marie Granet wrote several monographs on the Resistance. In her writings and in interviews with me, she stressed the difficulty inherent in any attempt to write a comprehensive history of the Resistance. There were many unknown figures involved. Some died, were overlooked, or just returned to their prewar lives without their contribution being known; this was the case with most women.[7] Resistance participants were volunteers for the most part—and amateurs. Members worked in secrecy, hence largely in isolation.

The improvised, ad hoc nature of the Resistance helped make it possible for women to participate. French women were a considerable presence in virtually all Resistance organizations. Odette Sabaté wryly recounted her father's comments when she was born (he had been badly wounded in World War I): "At least with girls, I know my children will not have to go to war." Little did he know, she observed. Communist Party member Sabaté joined the Resistance with her mother and sister, who both died during deportation.[8]

In 1944, General Charles de Gaulle created the order of Companions of the Liberation to honor those who had helped free France. Of the more than one thousand medals awarded—including five to municipalities and eighteen to fighting units—only *six* were awarded to women. The general was familiar with the activities of those who joined him in London but knew little of the exploits of the Resistance in continental France (or the Hexagon, as the country is often called, because of its shape). Further, as a career military man, he could not conceive of groups and movements composed mainly of civilians fighting the enemy in an improvised manner, their recruitment subject to

circumstantial vagaries. The very secrecy required for Resistance undertakings made it difficult to grasp their scope and nature. This secrecy was also to hinder postwar efforts to write the history of the
French Resistance. Thus, those who remained (particularly the
women) in France and resisted the occupiers—often at risk to their
lives—were in large measure overlooked.

Resistance members of both sexes had to deal with the dangers,
tribulations, and failures of clandestine action. Women who joined
underground movements have pointed out that in most instances they
shared equal rights, equal responsibilities, and equal risks. Although
not all *résistantes* shared her political vision, perhaps they instinctively
agreed with Brigitte Friang, who attributed this sharing to their common efforts to build a new society, one in which each would have full
human dignity and equality—not just worker with bourgeois, but
woman with man. In most respects, assignments were based on apti-
tude and ability. The enemy did not discriminate, either.

+━━━+

Underground movements do not leave written records. This was true
for the French Resistance. It was imperative that only what was absolutely necessary be committed to paper. There was an ever-present
need to destroy what might fall into enemy hands. Resistance accounts
are replete with incidents where compromising papers were destroyed
in whatever manner possible—burned, flushed down toilets, swal-
lowed. Even where archival materials still exist, access has been a
major problem. The French National Archives long made it difficult
for scholars to work on "delicate" subjects, such as the wartime occupation of France. Only in recent years have these archives become
more—but not completely—accessible. For example, those of the
Paris Prefecture of Police and some départements and municipalities
remain closed. In 1979, a new law extended the period of closure of
some World War II archives. This closure occurred even though interest in this period has steadily increased. A French book published
in 1994 on the "forbidden archives" renewed the debate over this
issue.

One possible reason for the increase in the number of scholars
focusing on this period is proposed by French historian Robert Frankenstein. He suggests that there is a greater need to study World War
II because, even though it was less deadly for the French than was
World War I, it wounded the nation more deeply. It was a unique

situation in that France was the only nation so humiliated—the only country conquered by the Germans to seek an armistice or to elect a government while occupied, a government that tried to implement its own policies. These circumstances led to a national psychodrama.[9] His view differs from that of André Mornet, general prosecutor of the postwar High Court and head prosecutor for Pétain's trial. Mornet entitled his memoirs of that period *Four Years to Erase from Our History*.[10] Others contend that reference to the Resistance provokes contradictory feelings among the French public. While there is admiration for the "soldiers of the night," it is coupled with a reminder of France's humiliation. There may also be feelings of guilt on the part of the many who waited, who did nothing.

Historian Henry Rousso has analyzed the difficulty the French nation has had in accepting the memory of 1940–1944—years that simultaneously brought a catastrophic defeat, a humiliating and harsh occupation, and a civil war. The collective French response to those years was a neurosis manifest in the "Vichy syndrome," as he terms it in his insightful study, *The Vichy Syndrome*.[11] After the war, the Resistance was politicized. The Communists claimed to be *the* party of the Resistance. The collaborationist policies of the Vichy regime were "forgotten" for several decades, subject to national amnesia in an effort to achieve national harmony in the postwar years. The period of national mourning, from 1944 to 1954, included a purge that obliterated France's defeat and its Vichy regime from the collective memory. Except for the period of the Algerian war (1958–1962), the French repressed events of the Vichy period until the early 1970s. Instead, they subscribed to the myth that most of the French supported the Resistance, even if they were not actively involved. Only the positive aspects of the dark years—Resistance and self-liberation—were acknowledged. Since the 1970s, however, France has been more concerned with the memory of the *années noires* (dark years). Impassioned debates now focus on the wartime record.

This *rétro* mode was renewed by the 1987 trial of Klaus Barbie and, more recently, by the indictment of previously pardoned French officials for wartime crimes against humanity—the only crime without a statute of limitation. Klaus Barbie, commonly referred to as the "Butcher of Lyon," was head of the Gestapo in that city. Several women interviewed for this book were tortured by this "monster." Barbie pursued and persecuted Jews with particular vengeance, often acting on his own initiative. One of his crimes was to arrest (without orders), on February 9, 1943, eighty-six social workers, along with those seeking help at the bureau of the Union Générale des Israélites de France (UGIF), the national organization Vichy formed to deal with Jews. In the spring of 1944, Barbie organized a raid on a Jewish children's home at Izieu. Forty-four children and seven adults caring for them were arrested and deported. None of the children survived. (In chapter 8, Sabine Zlatin speaks of the children's home, which she founded.) The raid, targeting a specifically Jewish group, was deemed a crime against humanity. In 1987, Barbie was tried in Lyon. Found guilty, he was sentenced to life in prison, where he died in 1991.[12]

Frenchman Paul Touvier was head of intelligence for the Militia in Lyon. Sentenced to death in absentia immediately after the war, he and his family hid in a series of monasteries, convents, and homes with the help of a network of conservative Catholics. The statute of limitations expired in 1967. At the urging of a prelate sympathetic to Touvier's cause, President Georges Pompidou pardoned him in 1971. Because of the continuing efforts of Resistance and Jewish groups, however, a warrant went out for his arrest ten years later, although he was not actually captured until 1989. Touvier was tried in 1993 for selecting seven men who were Jews to be shot as hostages. An eighth man initially chosen was returned to his cell because he was not Jewish. Like Barbie, Touvier was convicted and sentenced to life imprisonment, the first Frenchman to be convicted of crimes against humanity. Diary entries of recent times read at his trial recorded his continuing fascination with Nazism and hatred of Jews.[13] Because of these trials, the Holocaust has at last been brought to center stage in French historical studies of the Occupation. At the postwar trial of Pétain—and, by extension, that of his regime—there was little mention of anti-Semitism.

After 1968, however, a younger generation of French scholars and intellectuals began to examine the German occupation and the Vichy regime. In May of that year, students at the Sorbonne—the University of Paris—went on strike and occupied university buildings. Some factory workers in the region also went on strike. Both groups were protesting the shortcomings of what Stanley Hoffmann has designated as France's "stalemate society." A major event of that era was Marcel Ophuls's film *The Sorrow and the Pity* (1970). This lengthy documentary on the Occupation was produced for West German television, but authorities banned it from French television for more than a decade. In the works of these younger writers and cinéastes, new perceptions (or myths) often were substituted for earlier half-truths. Several held that many of the French willingly acquiesced—when they did not actively collaborate ("forty million *pétainistes*").[14] Non-French scholars were among the first to bring solid archival documentation (largely German, British, and American) to the debate. Time is a major factor in this renewed interest in the Occupation period. Half-century commemorations have been observed. There is an urgency to record the testimony of these witnesses.

The prime source for information on women's roles in the Resistance is oral testimony. This remains true even though these accounts may contain uncertainties, possibly errors. Yet even when archives exist, they too must be utilized with caution. As historian Antoine Prost points out, written sources themselves are not totally reliable and may in fact be traps. While working in French archives, for instance, he found two totally different police reports of the same meeting. Resistance leader Claude Bourdet notes the range of writings that have surrounded, even hemmed in the Resistance from all sides: memoirs, testimony, historical novels, fanciful accounts, pamphlets, and scholarly studies. In dealing with a period of light and darkness and obscurity, such as the Occupation, facts alone do not suffice. They must be continually called into question, interpreted and reinterpreted.

We cannot even be certain about presumed authorship. Years after the war, Simone de Beauvoir acknowledged that *she* actually wrote the accounts of the Liberation of Paris that appeared in the clandestine journal *Combat* under Jean-Paul Sartre's name. He was "too busy" to write them, she explained.[15] On the other hand, it was principally male authors and biographers who wrote up accounts of women's wartime heroism in the immediate postwar period. In a speech before ADIR (the association of French women Resistance prisoners and deportees), historian Pierre Vidal-Naquet observed: "[T]he witnesses to tragedy often have the feeling that historians do not understand them. . . . Memory does not exist independently. If it may be enriched by lies, it may also open up to truths not immediately perceived." In *Tell Me a Story*, Roger Schank claims that relating our experiences is necessary because the process creates the memory structure. To tell is to remember.[16]

Women's retrospective narratives provide important material to historians. Germaine Tillion, member of one of the earliest Resistance groups and author of an important study of Ravensbrück (the concen-

tration camp in East Germany where many French women were sent),
holds that while recollection may be partial, or contaminated with
earlier or later incidents, memory is accurate in most cases. In her
extensive research, she found that new witnesses tended to confirm
the statements of earlier ones. Tillion discerns a campaign to discredit
personal narratives that she dates from the time when the technical
means for recording testimony took a great step forward: tape recorders
for the voice, photographs and movies for images. These attempts to
suggest the unreliability of recorded testimony had a positive side in
that they put researchers on their guard. Rita Thalmann, a specialist
on German women in the Third Reich, sees efforts to denigrate oral
history as an effort to devalue women's history.[17] British historian H.
R. Kedward, author of several major studies on the Resistance, contends that no study of the Resistance can fully escape from the impact
of opinion, imagery, and representation. He insists upon the importance of oral testimony.

> Oral testimony, even fifty years after the event, suggests hypotheses,
> provides personal details, reveals local colour, facilitates insights, and
> preserves individuality in a way that historians of an under-docu-
> mented area of history cannot easily afford to ignore.[18]

There is legal precedent for using nontraditional testimony such
as that provided by Violette Rougier-Lecoq, one of the first *résistantes*.
Arrested and sentenced to death, she was sent to Ravensbrück, where
she was forced to work in below-zero temperatures with inadequate
clothing and food, like many thousands of other women. She survived
this ordeal to represent France at the 1946 British war-crimes trials
in Hamburg. The prosecution's problem was finding evidence. In
the absence of photographs and other documents, Violette Rougier-
Lecoq's sketches done in secrecy at Ravensbrück revealed the atrocious acts, the barbarities, and the cruelties that she witnessed. If the
full horrors of Ravensbrück were revealed—not only to the judges,
but to the world—it was due in no small part to her drawings.[19]

+———+

In recent years, many studies have been devoted to the problem of
memory. It is beyond the scope of this book to examine the nature of
it. Remembering is a complex act involving many components: historical events and myth, personal prejudices and beliefs, stereotypes
and hearsay. Needless to say, much attention was devoted to the prob-

lem during research investigations. History is what people report, but
we must remember that their accounts have been reworked and fil-
tered through memory. In her study of women's accounts of the French
Revolution—the other major historical event that marked modern
France—Marilyn Yalom notes:

> Certainly memory is subject to retrospective falsification, to the loss
> and confusion of facts wrought by the passage of time and, more
> important, by the distortions of a mind intent upon preserving its
> particular picture of the past.[20]

If, as some claim, there is only collective memory because the
individual is but a product of the limits society imposes, it is nevertheless the individual who remembers. Writing of France's "poisoned
memory" of the war and Occupation years, Robert Frank notes that
while individual memories of World War II are to some extent nur-
tured by the direct memory of events by those who experienced them,
the memory of all—including those who lived through that period—
is affected by the transmission of images through various media: oral
tradition, teaching, literature, cinema, radio, television, and so forth.
He also notes that television—which has played such an important
role in France in creating an official memory of World War II—offers
an almost exclusively *military* view of the Resistance, making it all the
more urgent for historians to focus on a wider assessment of the Resistance.[21]

Memory obviously plays a part in written sources as well. One
problem with oral narratives is finding the proper balance between
too much or too little credibility. Maturity and hindsight may have
colored recollections offered forty and more years after the events in
question. While a few Resistance figures interviewed were quite outspoken at times, others were too modest—a situation that obtains in
many women's testimony. This also holds true for the women's depositions available in French archives. These accounts tend to be short
and succinct, perhaps the result of an effort to be "professional" in
their depositions. In the official reports examined during research for
this book, women provide few details about *their* activities.[22] There is
a world of difference between the archival testimony and that of
women like Yvette (Barnard) Farnoux, whom I was fortunate enough
to interview at length. Her December 1945 deposition gives but the
sparsest details of her tragic love story, recounted in chapter 9.

The question naturally arises as to why a large number of French women in the Resistance were willing to offer testimony for this book—in many cases, for the first time. Why, more generally, has it taken women so long to recount or write up recollections of their wartime experiences? And why at this time?

Like their counterparts elsewhere, French women today are concerned with retrieving their history. Theirs is a history that has been largely ignored in the accounts written by men. Men were more educated in the past; they dominated and determined the discipline. A few outstanding figures were recognized from time to time at the expense of the many women less flamboyant but no less courageous and committed. Much of the history of French women—at least in the lower classes—was oral history, which has served as a precedent for the expanding use today of oral testimony. As historian Michelle Perrot points out, French women had an original and independent tradition carried on at *veillées*, evening gatherings where women met to continue their domestic chores. They helped pass the time by recounting past events. Keeping the family history has long been women's concern.

The French feminist movement of the 1970s helped women become more aware of the significance of their activities. Since then, histories, biographies, and memoirs by eyewitness participants have been published in France—as elsewhere—endeavoring to discover and recover women's past. Gradually, "women and war" became one of the themes studied, albeit somewhat timidly. In 1975, the "International Year of the Woman," the Communist-dominated Union des Femmes Françaises (UFF, Union of French Women) organized the first major colloquium on "Women in the Resistance." Even then, a participant spoke of the French Resistance as an event so far and yet so near. Like others, she had no interest in going back and plumbing her recollections; she wanted to turn the page on the past. But colleagues persuaded her to testify. Now more *résistantes* are joining that small earlier group of women who wrote memoirs. The private printing and distribution of some of these first works is consistent with many *résistantes'* not seeking official recognition for *their* contributions. At times these accounts provide previously unknown details, both complementing and correcting more traditional histories of the Resistance. They provide a collective account of women's experience during the period that has so marked twentieth-century France.

Octogenarian Lise Lesèvre was a witness at the trial of Klaus Barbie. More than forty years after the events, Lesèvre finally wrote down and published her wartime recollections (*Face à Barbie*, 1987). As she explained to me, she was trying to narrate the incommunicable to those who had not experienced it. She undertook this painful recall at the request of her surviving son. Her husband and older son were killed by the Germans, while Lesèvre survived torture by Barbie and deportation. In her book, however, Lesèvre focuses on her internment at Ravensbrück. Her account offers virtually no information about the activities that led to her deportation, although she recounted them to me at length. Admittedly, the camp experience was unique.

A major priority of women deportees today is to combat current revisionist claims that extermination camps and gas chambers did not exist.* Many former women members of the French Resistance were also concerned about the nuclear threat. Not surprisingly, then, women who have written about their activities during France's "war-within-a-war" tend to focus on the camp if that was part of their experience. Whatever their personal itinerary, they are concerned now with correcting the historical record and bearing witness. As one young woman explained:

> It is good, because it is just; because it is important for those who follow, who know of those years of sorrow and bloodshed only through brief accounts in impersonal and anonymous school texts. My mother gave me a special education. She taught me that I was personally concerned with the Germans and their disagreeable habit of visiting their neighbors—without having been invited there.[23]

Lesèvre's account touches upon another explanation for the limited testimony on women's Resistance participation: the dilemma of those who were, or subsequently became, mothers. In postwar France, children—like children elsewhere—did not want their mothers to be different. For the most part, they did not want to hear of their mothers' exploits. Mothers, in turn, found it impossible to tell their children of the horrors they had seen—and sometimes experienced. Those who had been deported had the most difficulty in recounting that nightmare. Like other women in the Resistance, Lucie Aubrac told her children nothing about that period:

"It was not easy to be the children of Resistance members, to be the children of deportees. It was not easy either to be the children of

---

*The French refer to these efforts as *négation* because the term *révision* implies adding or improving.

collaborators, to be the children of those who did nothing, who were simply afraid. So parents said nothing about that period to their children. Today those in France who are now between forty and fifty do not know that much about the Occupation. That is not true of their children. The younger generation asks questions because it has discovered racism, anti-Semitism, and genocide. Those who were too young to have known the Occupation years want to know what the Resistance was about."[24]

Like the country itself then, children of French women in the Resistance grew up largely unaware of just what their mothers had done. But as they grew older, they started asking questions. So, too, did the larger public.

The focus of this book is on metropolitan France. There were small Resistance groups in France's extensive colonial empire that included women, but since the circumstances and context differed significantly in each area, they could not be readily included without considerable introductory material. The resistance of women in France's many possessions merits a comprehensive study of its own. One example is that of architect Jeanne Scelles, then living in Algeria, who refused to obey orders from the Vichy regime. With her husband and a few friends and colleagues, she helped develop the first Resistance group there and published a newspaper, *Combat Outre-mer* (*Overseas Combat*). Scelles used her fluency in Arabic and her many contacts in Muslim circles to fight the propaganda the enemy aimed at them. Scelles and her husband were arrested in July 1941. She alone was released. Scelles succeeded in warning the other members of their group who were scheduled to meet in her office. Her husband's trial broadened support in Algeria for the Resistance. Subsequently, the Scelles were expelled from Algeria and deprived of their belongings. In metropolitan France, Jeanne Scelles continued her Resistance work. After the war, she became an Arab culture specialist and supporter of the Muslim cause.[24]

Belgian, British, American, and even Australian women were involved in the French Resistance, although obviously their numbers were smaller. Sonia Vagliano-Eloy's dual American-French nationality helped the young woman escape from occupied France and reach the United States. From there, she was finally able to join the Free French Forces (Forces Françaises Libres, FFL) of de Gaulle in London, although after much difficulty. Fluency in English served her in her dealings with Allied forces in Britain, France, and Germany. Women in other European countries, including Italy and Greece, also were active in Resistance movements. As will be seen, women partisans were more numerous in those lands than they were in France.

Through their narratives, we can better understand daily life in occupied France and the activities of women in the French Resistance. Women describe conditions and settings, and they provide many details about their everyday lives. Yet these details give texture and life to history in the broader sense. To focus only on the grand gestures—the heroic, the adventurous, the romantic—and neglect the quotidian is to distort the historical record.

2

⊹══⇥⊹

France under German
Occupation

TOWARD THE END OF THE 1930S, WHEN HITLER'S DEEDS BEGAN TO
match his designs to institute the principles of Nazism set forth in his
Mein Kampf (*My Battle*, 1925–1926), most French people continued
to believe that France was not in serious danger. This indifferent reaction may be attributed partially to the internal crises the country
had weathered after World War I, the war "to end all wars." The
interwar years in France were characterized by tensions and social
unrest. France suffered severe economic depression in the 1930s, and
the country was still trying to regain a firm financial footing.

Following an attempted rightist coup in 1934, the Popular Front,
a Left-leaning government, was installed in 1936–1937. When the
Popular Front broke up in 1937, its members followed their separate
ideological bents. Many of the Socialists were pacifists, but the Communists were not; condemning imperialist nations, they focused on
the class struggle of the workers against the ruling class as that struggle
was defined and redefined for them by the Comintern from Moscow.
The outbreak of civil war in neighboring Spain furthered dissension
among the French. French efforts to confront the growing German
aggression were met by British pressures for appeasement, the 1938
Munich accord being the most noted among these ultimately futile
efforts to keep the peace. These factors all contributed to internal

discord. Although, paradoxically, three women served as undersecretaries for the first time during the Popular Front government, French women did not gain the right to vote until the end of World War II, hence they did not yet have a voice in the political process.

In 1938, Édouard Daladier of the Radical Party put together a government that attempted to deal with the steadily deteriorating situation. Decree-laws were passed to circumvent the legislature, the elected delegates of the people. The Daladier government was convinced that Hitler could be appeased; France's ally Great Britain shared that belief even after the Germans invaded Czechoslovakia. When German troops marched into Poland on September 1, 1939, however, France and Great Britain honored their alliance and declared war on Nazi Germany two days later.

A long period of inactivity following Hitler's victories in Eastern Europe in the fall of 1939 lulled France into complacency. Rationing was not implemented and military preparations lagged. In the ensuing months, little happened except for brief French military incursions into the German Saarland and an unsuccessful Anglo-French expedition to defeat the Germans in Norway in late April 1940. This débâcle ended what the French termed the *drôle de guerre*, the phony war.

During the interwar period, the French High Command had not sufficiently studied or kept up with advances in military theory and technology. By the late 1930s, the French military was spending four times as much on fodder for horse-drawn artillery as it was on fuel for military vehicles![1] Excessive resources—and confidence—had been invested in the Maginot Line, a series of fortifications along France's eastern border. Few seemed aware of just how vulnerable a fixed fortification was; flexibility and maneuverability were now key factors in waging war. One exception was a young army officer named Charles de Gaulle, who advocated extensive use of tank units. His suggestions had been largely ignored by his countrymen—but not by their enemy. Consequently, when the German blitzkrieg overran Holland and Belgium in May 1940, the French High Command was caught off guard. There was opposition from the Allied forces, which included British troops and the belatedly called-up French reservists. Only the massive evacuation from Dunkirk saved several hundred thousand British and some French soldiers trapped by the German pincer strategy. The rest of the French army—then the world's largest—fought in retreat. The French nation was devastated, in shock. The national administration collapsed. There were no contingency plans for the possible occupation of Paris. As German troops advanced on the capital in the early days of June, perhaps close to 10 percent of the nation fled southward, along with refugees from neighboring nations. This mass exodus—consisting mainly of women, children, and the elderly—was comparable to what occurred during the barbarian invasions in the Middle Ages. Every means of transport imaginable was used—from cars to carriages and wheelbarrows, all piled high with possessions and people. German war maneuvers and strafing of refugee columns added chaos and disruption to the French military's problems and the general demoralization of the people.

When the Germans invaded France, a young woman whom we will call "Annette" (since she requested anonymity) and her widowed mother joined those making the traumatic trip southward during the exodus. Her account provides some details of that fearful flight. Along the way, mother and daughter were sheltered and fed by peasants. At times they slept on kitchen floors. Finally they arrived at "Annette's" grandmother's home, only to have trouble convincing the family maid to let them in. They were so dirty and disheveled she took them for beggars! When funds ran out, "Annette" and her mother had to return to their apartment in Paris.[2] In addition to personal reminiscences, this mass movement and its consequences is treated in novels such as Jean-Paul Sartre's La Mort dans l'âme.

Historian and sociologist Evelyne Sullerot also has vivid memories of the exodus:

"My mother was not with us when the Germans suddenly invaded France. She had gone to see my twenty-year-old brother who had been mobilized. Do you have any idea of what that means? Only twenty years between the two wars and we had lost an entire generation [of young men]. My brother was born in 1919, one year after the war ended. He had the name of a dead uncle. And now he was being called to fight in another world war. We, the younger children, had been left with our grandmother, separated from our mother. We were waiting for her in southwest France when the Germans arrived.

"They came at night. We heard strange noises and voices. It was the Germans installing guns in our garden. So it was that one night I heard that language which I came to hate to such an extent that it is impossible to express. My grandmother (who knew German) told us, 'Those are the Germans.' It was extraordinary. They entered our garden; just like that. They seemed to belong to another race. It was a Panzer division. The soldiers were very tall—almost six feet—and dressed entirely in black with skull-and-crossbones insignias. They were superb, like angels of death—completely different from our friends, our comrades, from all that we knew.

"My mother managed to join us a few days later. This was in June 1940. As it turned out, she was so anxious to rejoin us in the southwest that she traveled from the port city of La Rochelle inside a hearse—under all the flowers. A Protestant pastor arranged it. She came the rest of the way on foot. I wonder if you have any idea of the unbelievable situation in France at that moment. Ninety-nine out of every hundred French citizens were relieved that an armistice had been sought. It was frightening. Everyone had taken to the roads. We saw thousands fleeing, unbelievable scenes. All the Belgians, all of northern France had come to the southwest because they never dreamed that the Germans would penetrate that far. They had all streamed down. Food was scarce. A tomato was worth a fortune. It is difficult to imagine. People slept outdoors, on the beach. The beach was covered with families all in black. The old women were dressed in black. The peasants came with some of their livestock, with their carts, their wheelbarrows. The country was thrown into total confusion, like an anthill that had been knocked over."[3]

Career military officer Henri Frenay (who took "armistice leave" to found Combat, one of the major French Resistance movements) was very disturbed by the general mood. He found the French people "settling into defeat."[4] And Resistance martyr and historian Marc Bloch, in his moving analysis of France's *Strange Defeat* (1946), stated that he belonged to "a generation with a bad conscience"—a generation preoccupied primarily with returning to individual concerns after World War I. In Bloch's view, the French High Command capitulated long before it should have because it was ready to accept an appalling consolation: A regime it abhorred would be crushed to death in the ruins of France. This was the punishment Destiny meted out to a "guilty" nation.[5] Defeatism followed discouragement and disarray.

Paris was declared an open city and surrendered without resistance on June 14, 1940. Four days earlier, the French government itself had joined the exodus to the south and west. After a brief stop at Tours, in the château region of the Loire Valley, it reassembled in the port city of Bordeaux. Changes in cabinet and government followed. Politician Pierre Laval and several colleagues maneuvered to name Marshal Philippe Pétain head of the new French government. Although Pétain was in his eighties and had just returned from serving as French ambassador to Spain, his name inspired hope. He was the World War I victor of the Battle of Verdun. On June 17, Pétain went on national radio to inform the French public that he was offering the "gift of his person" to the French nation and asking the Germans for an end to the hostilities—the only defeated country to seek an armistice.

The following day, de Gaulle (who had been promoted temporarily to brigadier general a few weeks earlier) spoke to the French people from London via the BBC, assuring them that "the flame of French resistance must not die, and will not die." Few heard the speech and even fewer responded. Like the majority of the French, Geneviève de Gaulle heard Pétain's speech, but not that of her uncle.

"We heard the speech of Marshal Pétain on June 17, 1940, at our summer home in Brittany. My reaction was one of shame and anger. Perhaps someone was imitating the marshal. After all, there had been rumors of fifth-column activities designed to deceive the public. My conception of the hero of World War I was so different. But then my father observed that it was indeed Pétain.

"The next day, smartly uniformed 'young war gods' arrived by motorcycle in the town where we had spent the night, but they did not stop long enough to take prisoners. It was a sad day: Veterans from World War I wept. Then an excited curé came running up. He had just heard an unknown French general speaking on the BBC who urged resistance, a certain General de Gaulle. 'That's my son,' exclaimed my eighty-year-old grandmother. Already in poor health, she died a month later. The German censors forbade any mention of the name *de Gaulle*, so the obituary notice gave only her maiden name, Jeanne Maillot. Nevertheless, she was well known in the area. In spite of transportation difficulties, there was a large crowd for the funeral services—many carrying wreaths. The local gendarmes gave her military honors. Her burial became a spontaneous, collective act of Resistance."[6]

Charles de Gaulle was among a small group of French who fled to England or one of France's colonies in order to carry on the fight. Ten days later, Britain's Churchill government recognized him as head of the Free French Forces (FFL), the London-based French who vowed not to accept the armistice. De Gaulle was forced to devote considerable time trying to assert his authority, particularly vis-à-vis the United States. Throughout the war, he had to contend with power struggles among the French military who, while in agreement about continuing the fight against the Germans, were often in disagreement over the tactics to be used and the leaders to be chosen. There were tensions among de Gaulle's Free French as well as between de Gaulle and the different Resistance groups formed by those who had remained in France.

The Vichy government openly blamed the general for having, in its view, "abandoned" France. De Gaulle was, in fact, tried in absentia at a June 23 court-martial, convicted of desertion and treason, and sentenced to death. Having a French leader in exile recognized by Great Britain complicated the situation for the French remaining in metropolitan France. No other occupied country had set up a new government on home territory functioning with German approval. French citizens had been brought up to respect legal authority, and Pétain claimed to have been legally invested. This point is still debated in France today. Furthermore, the United States recognized Pétain's government by accrediting Admiral William Leahy as American ambassador to Vichy. To many French, America's recognition was further proof of the legitimacy of the Vichy regime.

Pétain and his entourage moved to the spa town of Vichy in midsummer 1940, a "temporary" situation that lasted until the liberation of France in 1944. There he presided over the demise of the Third Republic. Under Laval's leadership, the National Assembly voted itself out of existence—without debate—on July 10, 1940, and granted Pétain full powers. According to terms of the Franco-German armistice, which went into effect on June 25, France was obligated to pay exorbitant Occupation costs: the nearly two million French prisoners of war were not released.

With the armistice, France was divided into two major zones.* The occupied zone, encompassing the northern three-fifths of the country, had a larger population and greater resources than the so-

*The exceptions were the provinces of Alsace and Lorraine, which were annexed, forbidden zones in the northeast and along the coasts, and an area in the southeast that was under Italian control until 1943.

called free zone in the south, which included Vichy. The fateful word *collaborate* appears in the text of the armistice agreement: French officials and public servants were to "conform to the decisions of the German authorities and collaborate faithfully with them."

The army had fought six weeks, with high losses. Almost 100,000 died and more than 200,000 were wounded. Consequently, the vast majority of the French population tended to view the defeat with relief. France would be spared the extensive death and destruction that characterized World War I. The French people looked forward to stability, to a return to normal life. Yet the situation in France at the outset of the Occupation was far from clear. The eighty-four-year-old hero of World War I headed a new government. Although most felt that Pétain would once again outfox the Germans, some refused to accept accommodation and surrender. *Résistante* Lucie Aubrac recounts the population's confusion.

"In the beginning of the Occupation, there were few French willing to undertake risks and join the Resistance. France—unlike, say, Holland or Denmark—had a national government collaborating with the German occupiers. In France the situation was ambiguous. Moreover, it was compounded by French patriotism and nationalism. Marshal Pétain, the head of the government, was a man over eighty and a hero of the preceding war. The French respect age and authority, in addition to their fierce patriotism. It was not easy to join a Resistance group. It was voluntary—and not very glorious at that. There were no uniforms, no military preparation, and no idea of what you would be asked to do. And there was no tradition of women in the military."[7]

Like-minded individuals met to discuss the situation and determine how best to continue the struggle. The aim and nature of their efforts were in large measure determined by location. Those in the occupied zone, where collaborationists were in charge, had to deal with the German presence. There early Resistance was essentially urban, and directed against the Nazis. In the absence of uncensored information, those in the north attributed Vichy's increasingly disconcerting measures to German pressure. Even late in the war (and, for some of Pétain's supporters, to this day), the French in the northern zone accepted the myth of the grand old man playing a double game and doing his best to save France. A 1942 prefect's report from the department of Haute-Vienne claimed that Pétain's "game" was too subtle to be understood.[8] In reality, as historian Robert Paxton convincingly shows, Vichy "sought neutrality, an early peace, and a final settlement on gentle terms with Germany."[9] There was little truth to the postwar myth of Vichy's passivity. For scholar Tony Judt, Pétain embodied "the incompetence of the French High Command, the deep-rooted anti-Semitism of his class and caste, [and] the instinctive desire of many of the French to wait out the war."[10]

Pétain set about implementing what was termed a *National Redressment* or *Revolution*. His regime blamed the Popular Front coalition for France's ignominious defeat. More generally, the hated Third Republic (1871–1940) was held responsible for France's decline and decadence, decried in the literature of the period. Under the guise of patriotism, men who had not been elected to office now set about imposing their vision of France—what France specialist Stanley Hoffmann terms the "revenge of the minorities." A Vichy regime composed of traditionalists, industrialists, financiers, lawyers, technocrats, much of the Catholic hierarchy, military figures seduced by Pétain's reputation, reactionaries, and opportunists sought revenge against those they charged with France's defeat: leftists, Communists, trade unionists, civil libertarians, Freemasons, and Jews. A 1942 prefect's report from Montpellier (AN F/1C III 1156) explicitly states that those in favor of Pétain's government feared a return of the prewar regime.

Without an assembly to hinder him, Pétain instituted a series of statutes and decrees aimed at strengthening the French state. An ever-expanding administration helped implement these so-called laws signed into existence by Pétain.* Pétain's government made overtures to the Third Reich, suggesting a policy of "faithful collaboration," although initially the Germans responded lukewarmly to the marshal's invitation to walk down "the path of collaboration" together. It was in Germany's interest for France to contribute to the Reich's extensive needs. Vichy replaced the republican motto of "Liberty, Equality, Fraternity," with "Work, Family, Country" and changed the name of the French Republic to that of *l'État Français*, the French state, making it more consistent with Germany and Italy's status and underscoring the break with the Third Republic and republican traditions. The nation was to be purified and its moral tone strengthened; harmful

---

*The legal community accepted Vichy's "laws" virtually without protest.

individualism would be suppressed. In a June 25, 1940, message, Pétain convoked the nation to an intellectual and moral healing. Such broad changes were made possible by the acquiescence of a demoralized country coming to terms with defeat.

Efforts to purify the French state focused on the Jews, traditional scapegoats. In their authoritative study, *Vichy France and the Jews*, Michael Marrus and Robert Paxton show that Vichy inaugurated its own anti-Semitic policies before any German text regarding the Jews in France had been published, and without having received direct orders from the Germans. And, Paxton points out, as long as Vichy could determine the treatment of French Jews, the regime followed a Catholic and national anti-Semitic tradition.[11] The Germans wanted Jews in the occupied zone sent to the unoccupied zone. Vichy did not want them and started a rival anti-Semitic program in the hope of asserting its authority and preempting German legislation. Jews residing in France—not just the large number who fled there from Eastern Europe during the 1920s and 1930s, but also those holding French citizenship—were subject to special anti-Semitic statutes. Scarcely had the Vichy regime been installed when it set up a commission to review each case of French citizenship granted since 1927. More than fifteen thousand people had their citizenship revoked, including more than six thousand Jews who now automatically became foreigners without protection, hence vulnerable to persecution. Indigenous Jews in Algeria, who had been granted citizenship by the 1870 Crémieux decree, lost it overnight under a law enacted on October 7, 1940.

While German legislation referred to Jews by their religion, the Vichy law of October 3, 1940, defined them by race and promulgated a more restrictive definition than did the Nazis. The following day, a decree was issued permitting prefects to intern foreign Jews or assign them to forced residence. Approximately 25,000 foreign Jews ultimately were rounded up and sent to special French camps where conditions were often harsh—in some instances, worse than the Nazi concentration camps of the time. Under the Third Republic, French detention centers had been opened for foreigners judged undesirable: refugees from the Spanish Civil War; political refugees from Germany; Jews and gypsies from other countries. The history of these camps is becoming better known, and it is not an edifying chapter in French history. Madeleine Barot of the Protestant relief agency CIMADE and

Sabine Zlatin were among those who tried to help the unfortunate internees, as we learn in chapter 8.

When the war broke out, those viewed as foreign enemies—a threat to France's security—were interned. To this group were added the increasing number of foreign refugees without legal status. Austro-Hungarian Jewish writer Arthur Koestler described their precarious situation as a "new, refined form of torture," when writing of his internment (1939–1940) in the French camp of Le Vernet near the Spanish border (*Scum of the Earth*, 1941). German philosopher Hannah Arendt was imprisoned with other women at Gurs, in southwestern France. Both eventually managed to leave the country. France soon had ninety camps that, while officially described as internment centers, already were being referred to as "concentration" camps by authorities. Jews of foreign citizenship were sent either to existing camps, such as Gurs, or to new centers such as Rivesaltes, in the Pyrénées region. According to Anne Grynberg (*Camps de la honte, Camps of Shame*, 1991), there were approximately forty thousand Jews in these southern-zone camps by 1941.

Additional anti-Jewish legislation followed. Vichy passed a law in December 1942 that required Jews to have their identity and food cards stamped with the designation *Jew*. This was yet another way of keeping them under control. According to Marrus and Paxton, Vichy's aim was to limit immigration, encourage Jews in the southern zone to leave, and reduce the foreign—or what was viewed as the non-assimilable—element in French economic and cultural life. The profound indifference of Pétain and Laval to the plight of the Jews left the door open to anti-Semitic extremists. Additionally, the pursuit of Jews attracted those who sought employment and enrichment. Along with their jobs, Jews lost their property—art and jewelry, homes and businesses; ultimately, many also lost their lives.

A July 1940 decree forbade Jews—even native-born ones—from holding positions in the French national administration, in metropolitan France as well as overseas. The October 3, 1940, law virtually excluded Jews from the professions, as a 2 percent cap was placed on the number of Jews who could continue practicing medicine, law, and teaching. Those pressuring the government to enforce this legislation included the national union of students and the orders of the professions.[12] Among those who found this legislation unacceptable was Violette Morin, a student at the University of Toulouse in southwest France:

"My family was Catholic and devoted to republican traditions and values. There were few foreigners in that area. I was somewhat insular and naive about the country's policies regarding strangers. Then I went to Paris for university studies. There I worked with the Vigilance Committee of Antifascist Intellectuals (CVIA). When hostilities broke out, I transferred to the University of Toulouse to continue my studies. Now aware of the so-called Jewish problem, I was outraged to learn that several of my favorite teachers had been relieved of their teaching responsibilities. Why? Because they were Jews. This I found unacceptable. An irrepressible feeling of revolt seized me. I looked for some way to combat those who imposed such decrees and joined a Resistance group."[13]

The list of exclusions was further extended by statute on June 2, 1941. The head of Vichy's Commission for Jewish Affairs would later boast that Jewish civil servants had been eliminated from state posts they had "invaded" "in the press, in the film industry, in all areas where their functions gave them power to control and manipulate minds."[14] This was in addition to their elimination from other areas, in particular those touching the national economy. All the legislation that so affected Jews was published in the *Journal Officiel*, along with mundane matters, such as the required dimensions for sports fields— yet another example of the "banality of evil."

Efforts were concentrated on counting and controlling the Jews, along with depriving them of their goods. With unusual efficiency and utilizing the latest technology, Vichy set up a coded card index of French Jews and their property in June 1941. An earlier German order (September 1940) charged the French with registering both French and foreign Jews in the occupied zone. For the first time in seventy years, information on ethnic background was required of French citizens. The extremely detailed information gathered in these surveys— and the assiduity and thoroughness with which the French undertook them—greatly facilitated the later Nazi decision to implement the Final Solution in France. Only 2,800 of the more than seventy-five thousand Jews deported from France returned.[15] But a quarter of a million survived, according to historian Susan Zuccotti, because of the silence or benign neglect of the majority of the French population.[16] As late as 1943, when compulsory labor laws (Service du Travail Obligatoire, STO) were passed, some in France resented the exemption of Jews. Previously viewed as victims, they were now seen as privileged. Postwar emphasis has focused on the large number (three-fourths) of war survivors among Jews—most native-born—residing in France when hostilities broke out. Yet one cannot overlook the Vichy state's early initiative in excluding those deemed "undesirable," passing restrictive anti-Jewish legislation, and acquiescing to German demands to hand over non-French Jews. The rationale behind these exclusionary policies was that they would protect France's own Jewish citizens, yet they betrayed France's historic commitment to the Enlightenment and the Rights of Man.

One result of these anti-Jewish decrees was the decision of some Jews to form their own Resistance group, the Organisation Juive de Combat (OJC). Others joined various movements and groups, both Communist and non-Communist. This was more consistent with the republican tradition of seeing themselves as French citizens first and foremost. As Stanley Hoffmann has noted, the traditional prewar view was that the French Republic does not recognize minorities. In whatever group, being Jews made them doubly vulnerable if captured. On the other hand, some believed they had more reason to resist and refused to accept their fate passively.

During the Nazi occupation, French police continued their work, at times in tandem with the much smaller German police contingents and the even smaller SS group stationed in France, few of whom knew French.[17] It was French police and their helpers who rounded up the primarily foreign Jews for internment or deportation (even children, whom the Nazis had not requested) and helped pursue résistants. The biggest roundup of Jews took place on July 16, 1942. (July 16 was designated a national day of remembrance in France in 1993.) Close to thirteen thousand French and foreign Jews—including more than four thousand children—were rounded up in a carefully planned operation involving thousands of French police and auxiliaries, following minutely detailed instructions. For example, pets were to be left with concierges so they would not be "abandoned." Those without children were bused to the camp at Drancy, outside Paris, an antechamber to the German concentration and extermination camps. Children under sixteen and their parents were taken to the Vélodrome d'Hiver (or Vel' d'Hiv) in Parisian buses. In contrast to all the meticulous arrangements undertaken for the raid itself, little had been done to prepare for the more than eight thousand people crowded into the indoor racing rink in appalling conditions—oppressive heat, lack of food and water, and virtually no sanitary facilities. Teenager Annie Kriegel (shortly to join the Resistance) witnessed the roundup:

"We had been warned about it. And when I say 'we,' I mean most Jews. White Russians working at the Prefecture told their Jewish compatriots, who in turn alerted others. That day I was taking the oral examination for the *bac* at the Sorbonne. Mother appeared unexpectedly. She told me that rumors about a roundup, scheduled for that evening, were circulating in the neighborhood. She warned me not to return home. Instead, I was to try and find someone to take me in. Several people I approached could not take me in, for one reason or another. Someone suggested I go to a house that was said to be taking in Jews. So I went to an unpretentious house—at the corner of the rues Sévigné and Francs-Bourgeois in the Marais— where a woman answered the door and led me into a large room with perhaps fifty or more people. There was a heavy silence, like that in a dentist's office. I never learned who this woman was, what her affiliation was, or why she took in all those Jews. I found a spot in a corner and tried to sleep, although I was very frightened. Young girls then were not as emancipated as they are today. I had seldom been anywhere without my mother or one of my brothers, so I was very frightened.

"When I woke at dawn, I looked out the window. Things appeared calm, so I decided to return to our house. On the way there, I saw French policemen carrying suitcases from the dilapidated buildings on rue Duraigne. They were followed by entire families. A scene remains vivid: a typical French policeman, big, strong, rough-cut—crying. He was carrying suitcases and leading these families away, following orders. I kept on and then suddenly heard screams, screams like those one hears in hospital delivery rooms. It was all the human pain of both life and death. In a garage on rue de Bretagne, they were separating men and women before loading them into the buses. I sat down on a bench and thought about what I should do. There, on that bench, I left my childhood."[18]

The same might be said of the four thousand children taken to camps in Pithiviers and Beaune-la-Rolande (both near Orléans), where they and their mothers were transported after spending anywhere from three days to a week in deplorable conditions at the Vel' d'Hiv stadium. Since permission to deport the unrequested younger children had not yet arrived from Berlin, parents and children over fourteen were deported first, leaving the youngest children to fend for themselves. Annette Muller Bessmann describes her memories as a nine-year-old witness at Beaune:

> Everyone was assembled in the center of the camp. The children hung on to their mothers, pulling on their dresses. They had to separate us with rifle butts, with truncheons, with streams of icy water. It was a savage scramble, with cries, tears, howls of grief. The *gendarmes* [national police] tore the women's clothing, still looking for jewels or money. Then, suddenly, a great silence. On one side, hundreds of young children; on the other, the mothers and older children. In the middle, the *gendarmes* giving curt orders.[19]

That was the last Bessmann saw of her mother. Commenting on the testimony of Bessmann and others, historian Zuccotti terms the story of the bewildered, terrified, and abandoned children "the most horrifying, heartrending episode of the Holocaust in France, and the most shameful." Since that time, social worker Annette Monod has devoted her energies to raising the consciousness of the nation about the shocking events she witnessed that infamous day at the Vel' d'Hiv and what followed at Pithiviers. For her, bearing witness is a matter of Christian duty.

Not a single prefect and only a handful of French policemen resigned to protest anti-Jewish measures, although individual French policemen helped the Resistance in different ways. To this day, the role of the French police—which expanded considerably under Vichy—in implementing German and Vichy orders remains a delicate topic. French censors would not release *Nuit et Brouillard* (*Night and Fog*), a 1955 documentary on the Occupation, until a scene of a French policeman overseeing Jews at the Pithiviers camp was deleted from the film.[20] Between June 1940 and November 1942, French police operating in the so-called free zone hunted and pursued members of the Resistance. The police claimed they did so rightly, under orders from Pétain and Laval.[21] In January 1943, the Militia was formed. Those who joined swore to combat democracy, Jewish "leprosy," and Gaullist dissent—that is, the Resistance.

Catholics—more than 80 percent of the French population—did not have as long a tradition of resistance to persecution as did French Protestants. Catholic response to the defeat varied. In his study of the conduct of Catholics during the Occupation, Jacques Duquesne holds that for decades prior to the war, French Catholics behaved essentially as spectators of history.[22] Another observer notes that practically all of Catholic France was "anesthetized" when it came to the Jewish question. Philippe Burrin contrasts the steadfastness with which the church defended its interests and its laxity in responding to the persecution of the Jews. In 1988, Cardinal de Lubac condemned as a grave mistake the silence of Catholic authorities over the anti-Jewish legislation. Refusal to become concerned about worldly affairs was viewed as virtuous behavior by some. Catholic activists, however, did not accept the hierarchy's largely pro-Vichy position. Hearing of the projected armistice, Edmond Michelet, leader of a small group of liberal Catholics in the south, wrote what is presumed to be the first Resistance tract—reprinting texts by poet Charles Péguy—on June 17, 1940, one day before de Gaulle's call for resistance. One outcome of Catholics' participation in the Resistance was their contact with what Duquesne terms the "other": the Protestant, the Jew, the Communist, the atheist.

Education was a major component of Pétain's National Revolution. The marshal spoke to the French—as he did often—as a teacher insisting that schools must instill respect for moral and religious beliefs, particularly those beliefs that the French had held since the nation began—that is, Catholic beliefs. France's secular education system was blamed for the country's defeat. Conservatives and clerics alike saw an opportunity to change the system—one of the major achievements of the Third Republic—faulted for having instituted a clear separation between church and state. Public schools could now offer religious instruction during school hours. In early September 1940, Vichy struck down a 1901 law that required those belonging to religious orders to obtain government permission to teach. Municipalities were free to fund parochial schools. Vichy set the example by awarding Catholic schools a large grant in 1941, although stressing that it was "exceptional." After almost forty years of total prohibition, religious symbols (generally crucifixes) appeared in public schools in some regions, while busts of Pétain replaced those of Marianne—symbol of the French Republic—in public buildings. Following this and related moves, the Catholic newspaper *La Croix* urged Catholics "to express their *unreserved gratitude* to Pétain's government for revoking the iniquitous laws of the Third Republic."[23]

Vichy found that ideological commitment to the curriculum—such as adherence to the detailed instructions on the teaching of history—was more difficult to control. In practice, these directives often had the opposite result from that intended. Vichy's clericalism and demands for ideological conformity encouraged school inspectors and teachers alike to join the Resistance. With few exceptions, those in the public schools were against Pétain and his government's efforts to change their secular educational system. Early in the war, Danielle Mitterrand's father was fired for refusing to submit a list of "foreign" names to authorities. As it turned out, this freed him and his family to undertake Resistance work. Danielle Mitterrand explains:

"My parents were both teachers. They committed their lives to the republican ideals they believed in. They tried to extend the opportunities they received to others. My father [Antoine Gouze] held progressive ideas. He was freethinking, a Freemason, and nonreligious man with firmly held moral principles.

"I was enrolled in the Villefranche coed school, where my father was principal and teacher. France had surrendered and was divided into occupation zones. Then my father lost his job and, with it, our family home. [In France, the municipality was generally responsible for housing public-school teachers, whom the state provided and paid.] My father was fired because he would not give authorities the names of students who had foreign names, as required by a 1942 Vichy edict. Vichy wanted the names of Jews and other 'foreigners,' groups soon to be persecuted. As a dedicated teacher, my father believed his role was to educate the children in his classroom. Period. I left the school when he did. His colleagues gave me private lessons."[24]

Other teachers and inspectors refused to facilitate the forced-labor laws and would not submit the required lists of students eligible for mandatory work service on the coastal defenses the Germans built, or, more frequently, in German factories.

Linked to concerns with education was the cult of Pétain, the venerable father figure. The marshal spoke to the population "in the language of a father, a concerned father who at times needed to scold" his wayward children. Other variants were the adulation of Pétain in religious terms—like Christ expiating the sins of the nation—and Pétain the monarch, who would heal France.* The feast day of Saint

---

*French kings had been credited with healing powers.

Philippe became a national holiday. Double rations were issued and celebrations were held. A new act of faith was composed by the collaborationist newspaper *Le Franciste*: "Monsieur le Maréchal, I firmly believe in all the truths you teach, because you cannot err or deceive the people." An adaptation of the Lord's Prayer addressed to Pétain— "Our Father, Who is at our Head"—was circulated widely. There was even a version of the Hail Mary substituting Pétain for the Virgin. The providential savior was described in 1941 as "officiating at a great Mass for the desperate."[25] Pastoral letters urged the faithful to submit and obey the new head of government. Resistance was a crime, preached a Jesuit in a Lenten sermon at Notre Dame Cathedral. Vichy's propaganda services diffused these texts. Thus, a climate was created in which it was held that "A Catholic who disapproves of any act of Marshal Pétain commits a sin." In October 1943, the assembly of cardinals and archbishops went so far as to condemn Catholic Resistance for its deplorable "policies of personal decisions and independence," recalling the exclusive authority of the hierarchy. A recent study on the Catholic Church's role during the Occupation holds that instead of limiting itself to the Pauline doctrine of obedience to the established government, the French Church used all its authority to urge Catholics to rally behind the "legitimate" head of state and to adhere to the program of the National Revolution.[26]

As with Hitler, the new messiah was greeted with religious fervor by large, enthusiastic crowds at his many public appearances. Schoolchildren saluted his picture and expressed their loyalty in song: "Maréchal, nous voilà" ("Marshal, here we are [to follow you]"). Prefaces to historical studies of Joan of Arc, Louis XIV, or Napoleon noted the similarities between these figures and Pétain. Clubs, organizations, and programs for young people were established, the best known being the Chantiers de Jeunesse. At these obligatory camps in the southern zone, young, non-Jewish French males attended lectures and worked on outdoor projects, the emphasis being on moral and physical development. The Chantiers were set up to occupy young men who normally would have been called up for military service, following Vichy's concern for the young—which it conveniently forgot in promoting the compulsory labor of the STO. The only female presence permitted was that of the nurse. Her role, as defined by General Paul La Porte du Theil, founder of the Chantiers, reveals the conservative view of French women then widespread:

The nurses will remain in permanent contact with the young men, sharing their concerns, their difficulties, and guiding and counseling them—in a word, both sister and mother for them. [Nurses are needed in these camps] because a woman is much more kind and understanding than a man. A young man of twenty, when he feels ill, is but a child. He will be more appreciative of the maternal attentions that only a devoted nurse knows how to offer. [This implies that the nurse have] a correct attitude and appearance, and not permit any questionable conduct. [The young men must show her the respect for women] that has been lost and that we must restore in France. I well know that many women have lost [this respect] through their own fault, but it is not up to us to try them.[27]

The general's charitable stance in not throwing the first stone is undercut by his blame of women, a theme repeated in many Vichy directives: Through their vanity and selfishness (in not producing enough children), French women were responsible for the defeat. After the Liberation, women would again become public expiatory victims when women thought to have consorted with the enemy were punished.

Rural France played an important part in Vichy's ideology. Rural virtues were extolled: The land, France's sacred soil, "does not lie," proclaimed Pétain. Hitler, too, envisioned rural France playing a role by supplying Germany's ever-growing need for food and raw materials. Early in October 1940, Pétain sought to launch a family agricultural scheme destined to become the main social and economic base of France. As it turned out, the utopian peasant economy never materialized. France's pressing problems required more than "return to the soil."

The Germans in the northern zone were on their best behavior during the early days of Occupation, and most of the French population, for their part, responded in kind. A proud Rennes prefect was able to report in late 1940 that the "Christian and patriotic population behave 'correctly' toward the occupier." Over and over in these official reports, prefects in charge of *départements* (administrative districts) warned that the economic situation was the major problem of occupied France—a problem that undercut German propaganda efforts. Because the Germans controlled the press and radio in the north and Vichy in the south, it was some time before the French realized that the ever-increasing shortages were the direct result of the enormous booty of clothing, food, and raw materials being sent to Germany. The

Germans issued many requisitions and regulations, all demanding immediate attention.

Reactions to the German presence varied. Writing on the eve of
D day, a prefect from Marseilles summarized the conduct of the populace at that time:

> Industrialists and prominent businessmen concentrate on protecting
> their goods and persons until the end of hostilities, which they assume
> will usher in a new era of prosperity. Small proprietors fear the Rus-
> sians. Civil servants keep a low profile. Although they are concerned
> about their inadequate salaries, they hesitate to make their grievances
> known to the Vichy government. The clergy focuses increasingly on
> religious matters but is indignant over Allied bombings. Workers
> want the unions restored so they may enjoy a better life. Their salaries
> have not kept up with the cost of living.[28]

For most, food was *the* primary concern in France throughout the
Occupation. One can appreciate the impact of major food shortages
in a country where meals are the focus of daily life. Bread and meat
were rationed by the end of September 1940; other commodities were
added to the list of rationed products shortly thereafter. Allocations—
determined by age and activity—diminished during the Occupation
years.*

Simone de Beauvoir was among the many women for whom concerns about finding food became a major obsession during the war
years: "I watched while the coupons were clipped from my rations
books, and never parted with one too many. I wandered through the
street rummaging . . . for unrationed food stuffs, a sort of treasure hunt,
and I thoroughly enjoyed it."

The food shortage serves as a metaphor for de Beauvoir's only play,
Useless Mouths (*Les Bouches inutiles*), written during this period. De
Beauvoir wanted to convey: ". . . the daily decisions and choices each
French woman entrusted with the welfare of others had to make as
she struggled to feed her family."[29]

Escalating prices reinforced the hardship of shortages. Intercepted
telephone communications, such as this one between a grocery-store
owner and his customer, reveal the impact of shortages and price in-
creases on the population:

---

*Rationing in France did not end until 1949 because the Germans had so pillaged
and decimated French agriculture.

—Have you any coffee?

—None at all.

—Or some chicory?

—No.

—Macaroni?

—No pasta of any kind. No olive oil, either. You can't find coffee anywhere.

—This morning veal breasts went up a hundred francs. Ham, thirty francs more.

—Yes, everything is going up.

—It's difficult to know what's going on with the stores. Some sell wine for twenty-two sous, others for ten francs a liter.

The explanation behind these price variations is found in a conversation between a Paris wine merchant and his supplier in Burgundy:

PARIS: Now can we change the date on the bottles if we don't have what was ordered?

BEAUNE: Yes, without hesitation. For ordinary Burgundy, you can price it as 7.25 francs.

PARIS: And the Burgundy *fleurie?*

BEAUNE: Sell it at 13 francs, instead of the former 9.60 price. If they are going to eliminate *vin ordinaire*, we'll sell it under a château label.

PARIS: And for the wine of . . . ?

BEAUNE: Oh that, we can't discuss it over the telephone. You never know [who might be listening]. By letter, it's safer. But even then. . . .[30]

Author Gertrude Stein's companion, Alice B. Toklas, devotes a chapter in her memoir-cookbook, *The Alice B. Toklas Cook Book* (1954), to food problems during the Occupation. An excellent cook, Toklas devised new recipes for what was available under rationing. Somehow, the two women managed to continue to entertain their friends. One was Hubert de R., who was in the Resistance. To satisfy his sweet tooth, Toklas concocted a raspberry dessert that "cried for cream"—as did they, she notes. Hubert de R. enjoyed the treat. As Toklas recounts, when sitting around the fire after dinner, he said:

> "That dessert was made with gelatine, wasn't it? Where do you find gelatine these days? There is none in Savoie. My wife no longer has any." His knowing anything about gelatine surprised me. When as he was leaving I gave him twenty sheets to take to his wife, he was more grateful than the small gift justified. It was not until some time later [that] he told us for what he had wanted the gelatine. He had needed it desperately for making false papers.[31]

City dwellers "rediscovered" their country cousins. Reports from different regions reveal a growing contrast between rich and poor, between city dweller and peasant. Peasants were viewed as privileged, although this was hardly true for those with small holdings. City dwellers tended to believe the peasants received good prices for their crops and sold on the black market as well. While some did profit from the country's predicament, other peasants generously helped the Resistance with food and shelter. In his memoirs, Ephraïm Grenadou explains what he perceives as the dilemma of the French peasant. Parisians came to him and other farmers near Chartres, in the Beauce area, seeking food. The farmers preferred to sell to them—even though it was the black market—rather than have the Germans commandeer it.[32]

Simone Martin-Chauffier, a city dweller who sheltered Resistance members and Jews, had great difficulty feeding her family and her "guests." The inability to feed everyone was getting on her nerves. On one occasion, she even cooked a maggot-ridden ham friends were going to throw out; fire purifies all, she reasoned. Fortunately, she found Mme Martin, an obliging and well-provisioned peasant woman who lived near Mâcon. Unfortunately, the trip to her farm took the better part of a day, and the provisions were heavy:

> Madame Martin asked us if we could plume and dress a duck. "You'll do well to learn because while I did it this time, I won't do it again"— which suggested other ducks. I tried vainly to thank her. Mme Martin continued: "I hope you will remember who supplied you [during the war] and who didn't. You don't need to shut the door twice in the face of us peasants." She had a way of saying "us peasants," which, under the appearance of modesty, reduced city folk to their deserved place as parasites. That said, Mme Martin conspicuously added some butter, white flour, several bottles of wine—"which I presume you

appreciate more than milk"—and, surreptitiously, a cheese and small sausage. The price for all this was ridiculously low. [Mme Martin could have sold the food for much more to others not in the Resistance.]

As we got on the ferry, she asked us if we wanted to order a goose or a duck for Christmas! From that day on, Hélène [her teenaged daughter] and I returned each week. The Martins and their young son became our good friends. A visit once a week for two years creates ties. One day she told us she was certain that we would forget her once the war was over. I swore it wasn't true. Yet while I think of her often, I have only been to see her once in twenty years.[33]

Like other urban women, Martin-Chauffier came to appreciate the contribution of many peasant women. Largely apolitical, their reaction was one of patriotism, a love for *la douce France*.

Wherever they lived, the wealthy could supplement meager rations with black-market purchases. Most of the people, however, were obliged to spend a large portion of the family budget on food—when they could find it. Food prices tripled between 1939 and 1942; there was much privation. In 1938, posters had urged the population to consume more pastry because there was surplus flour; just a few years later, posters in Paris warned citizens about the health dangers of eating rats. Lucie Aubrac's hit squad killed and cooked crows. Desperate people ate cats and dogs—among other fare. At the heart of the matter was Germany's appropriation of a large part of France's extensive agricultural output.

Trials for infractions of rationing regulations increased dramatically. A woman identified only as Mme B. was sentenced to a month in prison for stealing ten potatoes and a bunch of parsley. Black marketeers, on the other hand, were generally treated with indulgence. An extensive black market developed for ration cards. This intensified the danger for the Resistance, which was forced to print false ration cards to supply its needs. Ultimately, perhaps, the food shortages and increased prices had their greatest impact on the nation's morals. Many French were forced to steal, further weakening Pétain's aim to strengthen the "true values." Occupation brought pillage, servitude, and famine.

French women stood in lengthy lines for commodities often unavailable, even with the required ration tickets. Some women hired themselves out to wait in queues. With newly acquired power and privilege, shopkeepers became feared figures. A housewife needed a large, roomy wallet for the many coupons and tickets needed for a wide range of articles: tickets for food; tickets for ersatz tobacco and wine; coupons for work clothes or even a bathing suit. In his multi-volume study of the Occupation years in France, Henri Amouroux observes that coupons were needed for shoes and detergents and soap products; for household articles made of iron; as well as for school supplies.

To add to the population's misery, the winters of the Occupation were among the coldest on record, and fuel was scarce. Because of the shortage of electricity, people often went without hot water; reading was difficult; elevators did not run. With clothing and fabrics rationed, women fashioned clothes from drapes and blankets, and everyone used newspapers to insulate garments. It was a matter of survival. As has been observed, for three years most of the French focused on surviving from day to day as best they could, obsessed with concerns about food and bombings, haunted by fears of the future, and convinced of France's impotence.

3

⊹⊱━⊰⊹

French Women under the Vichy Regime

The mother's place is at home, not in the factory. The mother's task is to protect the home; to fan the flame with her tender breath; to keep it clean and spruced up; to make it warm and welcoming for her husband when he comes home to relax after his work; to give birth to strong and healthy children. The day she undertakes this mission—which will return her halo [sic]—France will regain her full health and strength.

—*Gustave Combes*, Lève-toi et marche[1]

PRIOR TO THE WAR, FRENCH WOMEN HAD MADE ONLY LIMITED PROGRESS toward legal emancipation and securing the vote. Historically a traditional, largely Catholic country, France placed much emphasis on the domestic role of women as housewives and mothers and preservers of the family unit. Toward the end of the eighteenth century, the mistress of the household made her appearance: a woman of the upper classes who devoted herself almost exclusively to home and children. Obviously, women of the people could not afford to be totally absorbed by their families, to be homemakers. Their salaries were essential to family survival. The Vichy regime reinforced traditional concerns for family and youth; French women were held partly responsible for the country's disastrous defeat. On June 20, 1940, Pétain declared that there had been "too few children, too few arms, too few Allies." The women of France had "neglected" their duty to the state by not producing enough children. Proponents of the regime's National Revolution sometimes equated childbirth with military service. Government publications referred to the mother as the "privileged worker" who would rebuild the nation. Through childbearing, Vichy offered women an opportunity to redeem themselves. Their fecundity would ensure the future of France.

Of course, concerns with childbearing, the family, and the role of women were not new to France. The ideology of domesticity and the doctrine of separate spheres of activity were evoked continually. Nineteenth-century politicians described woman as a "domestic being," while man was the "public person." In his 1846 *Système des contradictions économiques, ou Philosophie de la misère*, philosopher—and anarchist—Pierre-Joseph Proudhon wrote that he had difficulty in justifying woman's destiny outside the family and the household. A woman could choose one of two roles—housewife or harlot. There was no halfway point.

Given their fine patriotic record in World War I, it appeared that French women's efforts—like those of women in other countries— would bring enfranchisement. Several times in the interwar period, the National Assembly voted to give women the vote—only to have the measure defeated in the more conservative Senate.

World War I affected French women in another critical way: Heavy casualties halted the family-planning movement begun at the turn of the century. A 1920 law banning contraception and one in 1923 condemning abortion effectively silenced these efforts. France needed to increase, not diminish, the birthrate. On the eve of World War II, the Family Code was instituted, providing measures to strengthen this central institution. (Birthrate policies developed during the interwar years were continued by de Gaulle and France's postwar governments.) Under Vichy, the already-stringent 1920 and 1923 laws were strengthened. Abortion was now classified as a crime against the race—that is, the state—and thus became subject to the death penalty.

Suspected abortionists were prosecuted vigorously, and some of those convicted received lengthy prison terms. At least one woman abortionist (and mother) was guillotined.* In carrying out this death

---

*A case dramatized in the film *Une Affaire de femmes* (*A Story of Women*, 1988), based upon the 1986 book.

sentence against women, Vichy went against French tradition. Even women condemned to death for collaboration had their sentences commuted to life imprisonment. Vichy regarded abortion as a national plague. Prostitution, on the other hand, was not proscribed. In fact, it continued not only to be legal but also to be regulated by the state. Nevertheless, men were urged to practice chastity and marry early to avoid resorting to prostitutes.

The 1938 Family Code favored families with three or more children when the mother remained at home. Vichy extended financial benefits: A single (family) salary was proposed. Mothers of large families received supplementary rations and preferential treatment—in food queues, for example—along with medals and pictures in local newspapers. (As part of its paternalistic concerns, women were not to receive ration tickets for cigarettes.) Fathers of large families were to receive job preference, while bachelors were penalized. France's dire situation, however, prevented many of Vichy's proposals—including those designed to favor families—from being carried out. Divorce, however, became more difficult to obtain—except for marriages between Jews and non-Jews, where divorces were expedited. A commentator of the time rejoiced that "by a providential miracle," Pétain's government—aware of the crisis in the family—had decided to pursue its policy to rejuvenate families. "The state," he held, "should strike down laws permitting divorce, against the winds and storms of public protest."[2]

Social order was dependent upon a stable and prolific French family. In 1940, Pétain wrote:

> The right of families is, in effect, prior and superior to that of the individual. The family is the essential unit; it is the foundation of the social structure; one must build upon it. If it gives way, all is lost; while it holds, everything is saved.

On another occasion, the marshal eloquently extolled the role of French mothers:

> Mothers of France, our native land, yours is the most difficult task, but also the most gratifying. You are—even before the state—the true educators. You alone know how to inspire in all that inclination for work, that sense of discipline, that modesty, that respect, that give men character and make nations strong.[3]

Historian Miranda Pollard ascribes Vichy's antifeminism to its ultraconservative and nationalist ideology. The regime subscribed to a rigid definition of masculinity and femininity that—allied with its particular views of the home and the family—underlay its search for national renovation. The regime sought to remedy the disorder and "promiscuous" *laisser aller* of the 1930s.[4]

The Vichy press embarked upon a campaign to carry out measures to strengthen and increase the family, as well as to justify the measures taken to achieve those ends. In terms almost reminiscent of Nazi propaganda, French women were told that to attract the male of the species—to ensure reproduction—women needed to be both morally and physically attractive. Sensitive to possible comparisons with Germany, Vichy claimed its natalist policy was moral and conservative, in contrast to the former's racial and secular approach. The contradiction in Vichy's repeated admonitions is obvious: French women were encouraged to make themselves more attractive; at the same time, they were implicitly condemned for their vanity and material concerns. "French women have killed France not only by their blind vanity and their obsession with themselves, but also by their shirking their national duty [i.e., bearing children]," it was claimed.[5]

The family ideology that Vichy favored made a major effort to promote what today might be called "The Joy of Housekeeping." As one article explained:

> It is possible to be a good cook and to know how to discuss literature. A woman can polish her pots and still be concerned with "higher" things. Housewives, take up your brooms and dust out the corners of your souls and hearts—as well as those of your apartments.[6]

Nevertheless, there were Vichy officials concerned about the hard lot of women workers who came to recognize the oversimplification of the state's fairy-tale image of "a happy woman surrounded by charming children who enrich her life."[7]

While Vichy made no major effort to change the policy of equal instruction for the sexes, its approach to education in general was marked by anti-intellectualism and anti-individualism. Attempts to censor school texts were hindered only by the acute paper shortage: There was little to replace the banned books. Reluctantly, Pétain's government made accommodations with reality. While it endeavored to continue the practice of separating sexes in the classroom, this became impossible because of personnel shortages in small villages and rural areas. When mixed elementary classes were set up, concerned clergy and parents protested. The diocese of Bayonne's *Bulletin* pointed out the perils of mixed classes:

What is exceptional about these "double" classes is that boys and girls are mixed together; often they share recess periods and outings. When one considers that school-leaving age has been advanced to fourteen, one immediately perceives the danger in such promiscuity. Sin inscribes itself in the body and degrades it. Do you think the wife and mother of tomorrow can be formed in this manner?

A father noted:

If French womanhood is to keep, or recapture, those feminine qualities that formerly embellished it, girls' education simply must be different from boys'. Masculine ways are not appropriate for girls.[8]

Vichy authority Robert Paxton holds that the elementary education offered girls suggests that Vichy preferred women in the kitchen, barefoot and pregnant. Conversely, a Vichy minister was to insist that the government never intended to restrict women to the home. Nevertheless, that was the general effect of the legislation the authoritarian regime introduced.

Vichy instituted compulsory home-management instruction for girls (law of March 18, 1942). The program consisted of hygiene, housekeeping, cooking, laundry, and an initiation to family psychology and morals; male students had physical education. The tacit assumption was that women would feel frustrated and develop inferiority complexes if they pursued "masculine professions."

Teachers, it has been alleged, were told to pass fewer female students, and standards were tightened. Pollard cites a 1941 Vichy publication warning fathers of the dangers of professional careers for their daughters. The author claimed that 300 Parisian female lawyers were working as prostitutes, not having found employment in the legal profession.[9] There were no women at Uriage, the best known of the sixty centers that Vichy set up to train the future leaders of the nation. Only two of these centers were designated for women interns.

Vichy set up a General Commission on the Family (Commissariat Général à la Famille, CGF) to coordinate family policies, but it was severely handicapped by the impact of German demands and the absence of all those in Germany—forced laborers, deportees, and above all, POWs. In signing the armistice, Pétain had assured the French that "now all will return to their place in the home." Instead, French POWs were sent to camps in Germany. As matters turned out, "families were separated, not strengthened, and Vichy was forced to deal with hundreds of thousands of families that could not attain the family ideal," historian Sarah Fishman points out in her study of the situation of wives of French POWs. The plight of families separated by the war highlighted Vichy's failure to put its ideological pronouncements into practice.[10] Wits dubbed the marshal's homes "abandoned homes." Jewish families, of course, were disrupted by persecution and deportation.

The Catholic Church applauded the imposition of measures intended to bolster the family and the morals of the French nation, congruent with church doctrine. Pius XI's 1930 encyclical *Casti Connubii* held that women's emancipation was detrimental to the family. To please the church, Pétain (a notorious ladies' man) had his twenty-one-year civil marriage to a divorcée annulled.* The couple was reunited in a religious ceremony that the groom did not bother to attend. Furthermore, this advocate of the family enacted a puzzling statute making it easier to recognize illegitimate children (to help his gardener, it was alleged), contravening the moral protection he promised the family. These events say much about the opportunism of Pétain and, by extension, his entourage.

Early in the war, Vichy instituted laws prohibiting a married woman from government work if her husband's salary was deemed *adequate*, a term never fully defined (law of October 11, 1940). Since a woman's place was in the home raising a family, female civil servants, principals and teachers, and some factory workers were suspended and placed on "special availability." Apart from Vichy's family policy, these measures helped with the acute unemployment problem. The legislation included provisions permitting these *same* women to undertake housework in *others'* homes to help their budget—because such work was of "little importance."[11] Yet another example of the French state's hypocritical treatment of women.

As the war progressed, the manpower shortage—reinforced by German demands for French laborers for the German war machine—forced Vichy to reverse its policies and urge women to work outside the home. The regime even went so far as to consider conscripting women for work, ordering a census of all unmarried women eighteen to forty-five deemed capable of undertaking work judged "useful to the higher interest of the nation." Germany's need for manpower increased continually, in part because the country tried to hold to *its* program of keeping German women at home: *Kinder, Kirche, Küche*

---

*He has been quoted as stating that this, his first marriage—at sixty-four, after years of cohabitation—was perhaps even too early!

(Children, Church, Kitchen). Earlier, a Vichy spokesperson had argued that women needed the protection of the home because they were "fragile; weakened by fatigue; had their nerves upset by strident noises; and were disturbed by close contact with men."[12] Now these same women were being urged to ignore all these presumed problems and spend long hours in noisy factories, sometimes near workers of the opposite sex.

Clandestine periodicals and newspapers were quick to exploit the hypocrisy inherent in Vichy's views of women and the family. While Pétain (who had no children) extolled the virtues of the family, his government did nothing to help families broken up because men were still prisoners of war, or had been sent abroad for forced labor. The first issue of the clandestine Communist paper for women, *L'Humanité de la Femme* (March 6, 1941), attacked the *femme au foyer* (woman, to the home) campaign:

> What cynicism in urging the "woman to the home" when her husband is a prisoner of war; is unemployed, wounded, or killed in the war; when her older children cannot find work.

The Catholic Church protested the February 1944 regulations under which single women and married women (without children) aged eighteen to forty-five were eligible for labor service. While recognizing that the public powers were taking all the necessary precautions to limit the social consequences of such measures, the church hierarchy drew up a proclamation insisting that the very possibility of such a mobilization was "a grave blow to the life of families and to the future of our country; to the dignity and moral sensibility of women and young girls; to their providential vocation."[13] German and French archives indicate that approximately 45,000 French women went to work in Germany—along with about 600,000 men. Many succumbed to pressure while others were deported.[14] As part of its campaign to promote the family, Vichy's ministry of propaganda produced many posters on the theme of The Family and Moral Order, once again fusing public and private spheres. Women were addressed with the patronizing and personal *tu* form of *you*, rather than the customary and polite *vous*. Captions reiterated the message that if women sincerely wanted to rebuild France, their first task should be to give her babies. The heading under an illustration of a young girl playing with a doll noted: "Now a plaything, later a mission." One series of posters focused on illustrious men [*sic*], such as Napoleon and Pasteur, who had come from large families. "A single child is a spoiled child," another poster proclaimed.

Pétain changed the paternalistic Napoleonic Code—the basis for French civil law—in women's favor when circumstances forced him to do so. The code placed a married woman under the authority of her husband, who was head of the family and could oppose her practicing a profession. Legislation passed in 1938 afforded women some autonomy. Prior to that date, a married woman could not open a bank account, cash a check, enroll in a university, or apply for a passport without their husband's approval. Yet with more than 1.5 million Frenchmen as POWs, many French women now found themselves heads of households. To address this dilemma, Vichy in September 1942 passed a law that at last eliminated married French women's legal "incapacity"—a status they formerly shared with minors, the insane, and convicted felons. Nevertheless, the husband remained the legal head of the household until 1970. As Fishman's study reveals, these were difficult times for the 800,000 wives of prisoners. While some were able to return to their families, others found themselves alone, often saddled with the dual burden of outside work and child care. As the following incidents reveal, they had much to endure.

> Andrée ran the family farm in Normandy while her husband was a prisoner of war. To help the local Resistance, she agreed to hide arms on her property until they were needed. A farmhand who had tried unsuccessfully to proposition her learned of the arms cache. With this information he became more insistent. When she rejected him again, he denounced her. Andrée was deported to the Ravensbrück camp, where she died.[15]

Résistante Agnès Humbert recounts a heartbreaking tale of another woman living on her own.

> A young war widow was mistakenly arrested and jailed in a Parisian prison. [Humbert was there for her Resistance work.] In vain the young woman tried to explain to the authorities that she had left her three-month-old baby while she went out for a moment to get some milk. He was alone, in a locked apartment. There was no concierge in the building. No one knew he was there. The police were indifferent to her days of incessant cries and screams.[16]

The Famille du Prisonnier (FP) agency was formed to help families of prisoners. Social workers were sent to determine if the family was in distress, and, if so, to help out. According to Fishman, the agency's actions were paternalistic: Married women were treated as incapable minors—as the legal code defined them. Paternalism was allied to class prejudice. Social workers for the agency (generally single, bourgeois women) thought that the problems—and they felt there were serious problems—in working-class families existed because the mothers and wives worked outside the home and lacked professional training in homemaking. Consequently, when dealing with the wives of prisoners, the agency "took over the role of husband and father, providing for the family, deciding how money should be spent, where the family should live, and whether the wife should work."[17] It oversaw the wife's conduct and the education of her children. The FP agency offered home economics courses to girls, insisting that future mothers required training for that role. Prisoners' wives were considered incapable of carrying out these duties on their own. They were subject to both class and gender discrimination.

+>=+=<+

The Vichy government endeavored to manipulate women during the war years. La mode, the French fashion industry, offered a revealing example of these efforts. As Dominique Veillon, historian at the Institut de l'Histoire du Temps Présent (IHTP), illustrates, the fashion industry also reveals the ambiguous relationships between French firms and the German occupiers. With the Occupation, immediate and pressing economic concerns arose. Could 25,000 employees of the couture industry be left unemployed? There was also the larger consideration of France's prestige and acknowledged leadership in that industry—then and in the postwar era.

Beyond concerns about the role of the fashion industry during the Occupation, one finds the view of French women as objects in the service of their country. When war was declared, couturier Lucien Lelong proclaimed, "The more French women remain elegant, the more our country will show foreigners that it is not afraid of the future." His words are echoed in various women's magazines: "Every Parisian woman is a living propaganda poster"; "The coquettish woman knows she has a role to play—to please."[18] Soldiers on leave needed to return to the front with memories of their sweethearts' and wives' optimism, courage, hope—and beauty. Exhortations to these women to "keep themselves up" were issued in the interest of the men's morale, not necessarily that of the women.

After a short period of adaptation (such as learning how to carry gas masks with style), everyday activities resumed under German occupation. For the fashion industry—as for many others—it was business as usual. When homes were no longer heated sufficiently, fashion houses responded to the challenge of the times by offering luxurious yet warm at-home apparel. Obviously, Jewish firms were soon out of business. But as the war progressed, fashion houses faced increasing difficulties with a lack of raw materials and the disruption of traditional economic networks. Firms sought exemptions from fabric rationing on the basis of their contribution to France's image as arbiter of high fashion. Freedom of artistic expression was invoked. However, this accommodation frequently entailed collaboration in varying degrees, by both couturiers and clients; the latter group expanded thanks to the black market and the female friends of the German military. To cite but one example, Réveillon, the noted furrier, agreed to make jackets for German troops on the eastern front. At the other extreme were fashion houses that totally disregarded the very detailed German regulations. Crossed lapels and pants with cuffs were forbidden, as were inside pockets and buttonholes on overcoats. This allowed garments to be reversed and worn longer.

The situation for the French fashion industry became acute when the Germans attempted to make Berlin the fashion capital of the world, threatening fashion magazines as well as couture houses. Lelong, spokesman for the industry, led a prolonged and ultimately successful counterattack—aided by the declining success of the German war machine. After the war, Lelong was acquitted on charges of collaboration. He claimed his minimal cooperation safeguarded France's cultural patrimony, although his personal record was questionable.

Dominique Veillon holds that clothing could indicate approval *or* resistance to the Vichy government and its ideology. At times, stylishness proved to be an effective psychological weapon. In Vichy's view, this was to be a time of sacrifice and penance for French women; now they had an opportunity to compensate for past indulgences. In the spring of 1941, the review *Votre Beauté* noted: "The [principal] characteristic of the National Revolution is that it is not only political and social, but also—and above all—moral. And it is here that you, women, can play a major role." Vichy condemned excessive makeup and short skirts and questioned the wearing of slacks, however practical they might be. Slacks signaled women's emancipation, which Vichy sought to curtail. The bishop of Grenoble decried women's "indecent" clothing, such as ski apparel and slacks, even though the cold in that region was a major problem.

The reactionary regime viewed women's efforts toward emancipation as leading to ambition, pride, or even intellectualism, historian Hélène Eck holds. Pronounced femininity would lead to frivolity, flirtatiousness, seduction, and, above all, infidelity. Women's presumed infidelity became an obsession, as it had in World War I. Rumors were rampant in POW camps. Now enemy troops were on home territory, reinforcing male anxiety. Linking private morality to public concerns for maintaining the social order, Vichy passed a law at the end of 1942 dealing specifically with adultery involving the wife of a POW. In these instances, adultery was a crime against the social order, hence subject to stiffer penalties. Adultery was prosecuted in order to protect the dignity of the home and the public good.

Nor was the authoritarian Vichy regime alone in its patronizing view of women. Radio France in London used the character Cunégonde from Voltaire's Candide to explain the political situation in France. The naïve young fictional character was a bit bewildered by events and did not understand what was happening under the Occupation. But she was determined to act in her country's best interests. In a series of broadcasts, she was repeatedly told that the Vichy government was the "anti-France," the accomplice of Nazi Germany.[19]

Prejudice against women wearing slacks also appears in a study of the Jewish Resistance, suggesting that the view was widespread at the time:

> A young woman came to the Refugee Aid Committee (CAR) in Lyon to volunteer her services. [The previous secretary left to seek more "active" work.] But the supervisor noticed—oh, horror—that she was wearing slacks because it was cold. Could she be a "proper" young woman since she wore slacks? He was suspicious because he was not accustomed to seeing women wear slacks.[20]

An underground paper's account of a captain's wife having an affair with a German officer while her husband was a POW noted that she wore slacks; this was yet another example of her moral turpitude.

"Masculine" style for women was criticized.* As Lucien François reported in Image de la femme et de la révolution nationale, French women and their clothing needed to adapt to their role

---

*Except for youths in the fringe groups "Swing" or "Zazou," masculine attire did not noticeably change during the years of Occupation.

in the society the Marshal wishes to build; to her place in the home; to her role as mother.

Women's bodies now reflect their rediscovered maternal role. Breasts and hips are more prominent; their form has matured.[21]

And fashion followed. Under Vichy, maternity fashions made their first appearance in France.

Enterprising as ever, the French women who were unable to patronize the couturiers made clothes from whatever fabric they could find. It was a period of recycling and improvising. Synthetic fibers first appeared during the Occupation. Nylon, an American invention, was not yet available. Resistance members had difficulty at times in ensuring the destruction of parachutes made of this new wonder fabric. Any item made of nylon would have been an obvious indication of contact with the Allies. Wood and cork were used to replace leather for shoes. Dressmakers created clothing for those women concerned with style.

Ignoring Vichy's directives, more women started wearing slacks, which allowed for needed freedom of movement and provided warmth in winter. While la femme moyenne, the average woman, made do, leading couturiers obliged their affluent clientele by designing chic bicycling ensembles.

This concern with appearance was but one aspect of women's conduct. Limited coquetry was reluctantly admitted, for such was regarded as the law of nature. The pernicious influence of American films was decried—as it still is, though now for "cultural imperialism"—while the joy of sports was celebrated (as it had been under the Popular Front). Emphasis on sports was one of the major contributions of Vichy's National Revolution to postwar French society. However, this focus was not without ulterior motives as far as women were concerned. Vichy's high commissioner of sports sought to form "young girls of robust beauty and well-hardened character; to develop strong but gracious women who will be the attraction of a fertile foyer." An eminent obstetrician was quoted to the effect that in most cases, a woman should have at least four pregnancies to ensure her "normal" health. Only maternity guaranteed women their full "flowering." A Vichy paper accused French women of "having killed France" through their blind vanity and obsessive self-interest. Once again, they were faulted for not fulfilling their national duty.

To remedy the problem, young girls could voluntarily attend one of the 380 youth centers set up for them, in lieu of the compulsory

work camps for young men of draft age. There they were to receive
"professional" training limited generally to sewing, embroidery, dressmaking, and flower arranging. In 1944, the General Commissariat for
Youth published a brochure vaunting the achievements of the youth
centers. Their young girls—ages fourteen to eighteen—were taught to
have "clean bodies, properly combed hair, and neat nails." The goal
was to "form them to become wives and mothers with pure minds and
bodies." Additionally, they were developing steadfast moral virtues
and a sense of duty and were being indoctrinated with a love of home
and children. In short, the young women were cultivating "the country's glory—the grace, taste, and finesse of French women."[22]

Throughout the Occupation, fashion magazines offered French
women two contradictory visions. Sketches and photos of high fashion
encouraged fantasies and escape from reality. This reading and reverie
distracted them from more serious thought, such as mobilizing against
the occupier. At the same time, practical examples and advice were
offered to help them cope with the steadily deteriorating daily life. In
either case, the attempt was to manipulate women. Through it all,
French women were reminded repeatedly that France would only be
reborn the day women ceased to consider the home a prison. In reality,
it was "the most beautiful of kingdoms."

In some instances, résistantes were able to use clothes, appearance,
and women's presumed vanity to advantage. Attractive young girls
served as decoys to distract police attention. Occupying forces generally felt obliged to be on their best behavior in front of "ladies."
One society woman asked for time to finish her coiffure before being
taken off to prison. The Gestapo acceded to her request, accepting
that this grande dame needed to appear her best. She continued to use
her curling iron, managing in this manner to destroy important secret
documents.[23] Résistantes who thought they were being pursued would
step aside momentarily to straighten their stockings and thus check
the situation. Ida Bourdet found that living up to the national reputation for elegance could help outwit the Germans. Because she
dressed like a "lady," the police let her stay in her home with her three
children overnight. They promised to return the next day to continue
their search. Of course, she was long gone by then, having escaped
with her children. France Pejot escaped arrest by playing up to the
Militia men who arrested her. Clandestine saboteur Jeanne Bohec
took time to buy clothes during a mission. Appearance could help in
assignments and was important for morale, she maintained. This held
true for other French women who endeavored to keep up their ap-

pearance, even those like Simone Martin-Chauffier who usually were not interested in fashionable clothes. She succumbed and invested in a good coat—without guilt or regret. The woolen coat was her "armor," which would help her look better and "resist."

Among other accommodations, Vichy had to appoint women to teach boys' classes because of the shortage of male teachers. In the teaching profession, as in others, the absence of men provided French women with professional opportunities and advancement that had not existed in prewar France. Prior to the war, only a small number of women held advanced degrees qualifying them to teach at the university level. During the war years, the number of women professors— as well as women doctors and lawyers—increased. As they had in World War I, women assumed responsibilities in a wide range of spheres—many of which heretofore were closed to them. Women rose to managerial positions in firms and factories. And it was the women by and large who ran the country's many farms during the war.

All these women had to make sacrifices and major adjustments when their husbands—some of whom had been absent as long as six years—returned to resume their "rightful" and legal places as heads of households. Young children had to adapt to life with a father whom they scarcely knew. Older children had changed greatly over the years—as had their mothers. However, the children generally had the most difficulty reverting to family life on the prewar pattern. Only about 10 percent of the POW couples failed to reestablish their marriages. This is not a large number when one considers that those who wanted to divorce during wartime were prevented from doing so by restrictive Vichy legislation that prohibited divorce during the first three years of marriage. Sarah Fishman credits wives' acquiescence for the many resumed marriages. By and large, these women were not concerned about such issues as emancipation and liberation. They still subscribed to the traditional prewar view of the woman's place in the family. Living in the nation regarded as the birthplace of *féminisme*—contemporaries or even younger than Simone de Beauvoir—these women "did not inhabit the same mental universe" as the author of *The Second Sex*, historian Karen Offen observes.[24] That a significant number of French women subscribed to conservative views of the woman's place in society puts into sharper relief the activities of women in the Resistance. Although perhaps not always cognizant of the wider implications of their commitment, they broke with tradition.

4

+═══+

Organizing Resistance in France

What we in the Resistance had not foreseen—none of us—was the full implication of our commitment. We were aware that we could be arrested, that we could be tortured. That was not a reassuring perspective at all. You never know if you will resist under torture. I could never have predicted my response. You can stand up to some things but you have no idea of your limits. If one of my children or grandchildren had been tortured in front of me, I do not know what I would have done. That is how I feel today. It is terrible to have to contemplate such possibilities, but it was like that. Then there was death. We recognized that. Death was part of our destiny.

—*Geneviève de Gaulle*, résistante[1]

FRENCH RESISTANCE STARTED WITH THE GERMAN INVASION. PATRIotic individuals who could not bear the sight of German soldiers on French soil reacted instinctively. On June 17, 1940, Mme Bourgeois was tied to a tree in her backyard and shot in front of her daughter. Her crime? Berating and harassing the German soldiers who requisitioned her home. Her daughter was ordered to leave her mother's corpse exposed for twenty-four hours before burying it in a grave the young woman was forced to dig. Three days later, a youth was caught and executed for cutting communication lines—an act of sabotage.

Individuals protested with small acts, such as wearing the French national colors and attaching "butterflies"—stickers with anti-German slogans—to mailboxes and other public places. Insignificant acts and occasional participation frequently led to full-time commitment. Yet for the first two years of the German occupation, resistance was the reaction of a small minority, sometimes in the face of indifference and even hostility. There were French people who considered such acts illegal and criminal. By the terms of the armistice, the French government accepted the responsibility of forbidding French citizens to fight the Germans—hence, the French were obligated to pursue and prosecute *résistants*.

To counteract public response, Resistance tracts insisted that the French had not only the *right* but also the *duty* to resist. Clandestine papers pointed out that the Germans had not respected the terms of the armistice, that they continually violated international conventions. Agnès Humbert served as typist and secretary for what was later to be called the Musée de l'Homme Resistance group.* She observes, "Naturally, I [as a woman] was the typist." The group's first typed tract came out on September 19, 1940. A week later, a thousand issues were run off on the museum's mimeograph machine. On December 15, the group produced the first issue of its paper, *Résistance*, which proclaimed:

> Resist! This is the cry coming from all your hearts amid the distress caused by your country's disaster. This is the cry coming from all of you who will not submit, who want to do what duty requires. Yet you feel isolated, torn by confusing ideas, opinions, and organizations. To resist is to keep your heart and head. But above all, it means acting—doing something that will bring about positive results; rational and useful acts.[2]

Women protesting food shortages—following the tradition of women who marched to Versailles demanding bread in 1789—were among the earliest public Resistance demonstrations. Throughout history, women have demonstrated and rioted for food: Nourishing the family has always been viewed as women's task. As the situation deteriorated throughout France, angry housewives marched to the offices of mayors and prefects demanding increased rations. In some in-

---

*This was one of the first Resistance groups, named for the ethnography museum where several members worked; see chapter 10.

stances, they were successful. In others, they were told to use "their womanly wiles [sic] to get more food." The clandestine press was quick to promote and report demonstrations. Tracts and newspapers supported and at times coordinated women's food strikes. At the signal of a comrade singing "La Marseillaise," Madeleine Marzin led a group of Communist-affiliated women in a 1942 protest. Like the women "incendiaries" of the nineteenth-century Commune, they rushed into a grocery store and grabbed cans and cartons of food, tossing them to the crowd of women shopping in the bustling Buci street market in Paris's sixth district.[3] Working-class women came out in force to support miners striking in the north during the early years of occupation.

In the early days, de Gaulle was comparatively isolated in London and had few followers. Initially, none of the Resistance groups in France came out in support of him. And for his part, de Gaulle was largely unaware of the development of the Resistance in metropolitan France—that is, the Resistance of the Interior (what was to become Forces Françaises de l'Intérieur, FFI), later to become part of France Combattante (Fighting France).[4] A career military man, he could not conceive of groups and movements composed mainly of civilians fighting the enemy in an improvised manner, their recruitment subject to circumstantial vagaries. The secrecy required for clandestine operations made it difficult to assess the number and nature of the résistants. This secrecy, as noted earlier, also hindered postwar efforts to write the history of the French Resistance.

U.S. president Franklin Roosevelt was opposed to the leader of the Free French, an opposition attributed in part to biased intelligence reports. Whatever the reason, the United States seemed willing to support any French commander but de Gaulle. By 1943, when the National Council of the Resistance (CNR) was established, most networks and movements on French soil had rallied to de Gaulle as leader of the French Resistance. This was due in large measure to the dedicated efforts of Jean Moulin, aided by other representatives of de Gaulle. Council members included delegates of the principal Resistance movements and, after considerable debate, representatives of the prewar political parties, including the Communists. The decision to include the parties, particularly the Communists, would be debated (and criticized) throughout the postwar years. Then, as in the 1930s, the real enemy for many French was the Soviet Union.

The French Communist Party (PCF), a partner in the Popular Front, was outlawed when Russia invaded Poland on September 19,

1939, following the Nazi–Soviet pact. The PCF was disbanded and Communist leaders who had not gone underground were rounded up and imprisoned. Until Hitler invaded Russia in June 1941, French Communists faced the dilemma of either accepting the pact or joining non-Communist groups or movements to continue the fight against the Germans, then the USSR's ally. Well-known Communist leader Charles Tillon writes in his memoirs of clandestine militants who found themselves actors or victims, or both, and urges that the historical circumstances for clandestine PCF members be remembered. For his part, Tillon chose to participate in the solitude of the Resistance, "freed from his past," because, as a banned Communist, he no longer had civil status.[5]

After Hitler attacked Russia (and Poland), the French Communist Party expanded its Resistance activities. Many of the Communists had fought in the Spanish Civil War, and their considerable experience in secrecy and clandestine operations helped in fighting the Nazis. Even so, their presence in non-Communist resistance movements— and, later, in the Resistance councils and organizations—was a source of tension. The Communists' true allegiance was always in question, a concern that surfaced over their participation in the postwar government. For their part, the Communists claimed not to have received their fair share of arms, since some Communist groups—unlike most others—had undertaken a policy of killing Germans. Most Resistance groups felt that the large number of French hostages killed in reprisals militated against such attacks. Robert Paxton holds that the issue of preemptive violence masked a deeper division between those who wanted to concentrate on chasing the Germans from French soil and those who wanted to change French society altogether.[6] Moreover, under the guise of Resistance undertakings, there was some settling of old accounts. German propaganda was quick to play upon popular fears of anarchy; it labeled résistants "anarchists," "bandits," or "Bolsheviks," thus setting the stage for the postwar myth of the Communist Party as the party of the Resistance. According to historian Stéphane Courtois, the PCF sought hegemony over the Resistance by presenting itself as the partner/adversary of de Gaulle. The Party thus contributed in a major way to the bipolarization of the Resistance between Gaullism and Communism. This division is found in the distinction the Communists made between the Resistance of the "exterior" (London, de Gaulle) and the Resistance of the "interior," which the Communists claimed to lead on "the sacred soil of the fatherland"—hence, a more legitimate Resistance.[7]

De Gaulle and other professional soldiers viewed resistance from a military perspective, underestimating *résistants'* accomplishments and capabilities. Not until March 1941 did de Gaulle's group in London mention the Resistance in France for the first time. A year later, the first *résistant* envoy from the interior managed to get to London and report on the situation in France. He was saddened by de Gaulle's lack of appreciation and interest in the Resistance within France. De Gaulle refused to have any dealings with French groups working for the British and set about organizing networks (*réseaux*), as had the British. In contrast to movements that developed independently on French soil, networks were structured organizations formed to facilitate escapes, gather intelligence, and undertake action of a military nature. Unlike Resistance movement members—who were political activists or concerned citizens—network agents were soldiers, duly enrolled. For security reasons, network agents were instructed to operate independently. In practice, this was not always possible. Agents had to improvise and at times recruited "amateurs" from Resistance movements. The formation of Resistance groups was complicated further when the United States began to establish its own networks in late 1941.

For the first two years of the Occupation, the activities of Resistance groups consisted largely in making contacts, meeting others to maintain morale and share ideas, printing tracts and papers, and laying foundations for future actions when the Allies landed. During this initial period, movements appeared and then disappeared as quickly; others were decimated by arrests. Any new, unknown colleague inevitably was regarded with suspicion (suspicions justified in some cases, for there were double agents and traitors who infiltrated and betrayed groups). In the southern zone, Resistance groups and movements increased as Vichy's true colors became more apparent.

External events also had an impact on the development of internal resistance. As seen, many French Communists joined the Resistance when the Germans invaded Poland and the Soviet Union in June 1941. In December of that year, Japan attacked the United States, which now joined the Allies. The Germans invaded the unoccupied zone in November 1942, three days after the Allied landings in North Africa—without opposition from Vichy's Armistice Army and in violation of the terms of the armistice. With all the country under occupation, some Resistance movements in the southern zone now joined with others in the northern zone.

The spring 1942 *Relève* program proved largely unsuccessful. Government head Pierre Laval conceived of the plan to encourage French workers to volunteer for work in Germany in exchange for the release of prisoners of war (one prisoner for three skilled workers). In March 1943, the STO mandatory work service for French males was instituted to fill German quotas. (The French came to view the deportation of forced laborers as *the* deportation.) This move had an immediate and dramatic effect on the previously passive population, which now opposed loved ones' being sent to Germany. Youths and men went into hiding to avoid helping the Reich. Some joined the *maquis*, small clandestine fighting units then being formed. Resistance activities increased, as Lise Lesèvre, whom we have met, explains:

"Starting in March 1943, *maquis* groups were set up in our area composed mainly of students trying to avoid forced labor in Germany. It was at this time that my family and I joined the National Service of the Maquis Schools for MUR. A group of us who knew one another well formed the Grenoble/Lyon University Committee to oppose the deportations [sending workers to Germany]. The deportations affected not only students but also workers—all young men.

"I was asked to help organize a national service for the *cadres-maquis* schools, the Périclès Service. At this time, the idea of forming *maquis* was quite new in France. Initially, we looked for several places suitable for *maquis* installations, locations that could accommodate the large number of prospective *maquis* members we foresaw would come. Indeed, they came virtually en masse when the STO law was passed."[8]

The *maquis* could not have survived without the support of the many women who procured false papers, provisions, and arms and carried them to the hidden encampments. As more young Frenchmen chose to go into hiding rather than work for the Reich, the logistics entailed in assisting them were daunting. Actress Simone Signoret was among those helping as best they could. As she observes in the interview recorded at the Caen Memorial, everyone needed tickets, fabric, food. They did what they could and didn't behave too badly, without having been aware of it.[9]

Open recruiting obviously was out of the question. Even within families, members did not always know that others were involved in Resistance groups until much later—sometimes not until after the war. Parents did not necessarily want their children to share in their dangerous undertakings. Anise Postel-Vinay's father, a noted Resistance figure, did not even tell his daughter of his own involvement. She observes:

"One never knew who among your family and friends was involved in the Resistance. My father never told me anything about *his* participation, even though he was keenly aware of the difficulty I was having in joining a group. Only much later did I learn that he and I were working for the *same* network.

"I tried to get to England to join the Free French Forces. My mother didn't want me to go over there alone, so I sought a traveling companion. It was difficult, as most young girls did not want to leave France for an unknown future. When I finally found a young woman willing to go, we couldn't find a boat. Finally I found a way to join the Resistance in France, thanks to Sophie, a philosophy professor who knew my mother.

"I undertook a number of missions of a military nature. In some respects this was ridiculous, because I knew absolutely nothing about what I was doing. For example, once I was assigned to chart all the cable sites for all the antiaircraft balloons set up around Paris. During my last mission, I was to note where bombs had landed in the city of Le Havre. While working on this mission, I was arrested and then deported."[10]

Postel-Vinay's sister also managed to join a Resistance group; she was executed by the Germans for her activities.

In addition to family connections, Resistance members were recruited through student organizations and social and professional groups. Since women were not especially prominent or well represented in these groups, they frequently encountered more difficulty in being accepted. This makes their considerable participation all the more noteworthy. Women employed in France's extensive public sector—ministries, prefectures, town halls—supplied information, false papers, and ration tickets.

Generally, few were excluded because of gender or lack of qualifications. Women could and did apply, although they were not always readily accepted at first, as will be seen. Like Anise Postel-Vinay, some went to great lengths to join. Young and ill, Madeleine Riffaud found it very difficult to join a Resistance group, but she persisted. While staying in a sanatorium, she finally made contact with a Communist Resistance operative. A period of observation followed before she was accredited. In late August 1944, she spent her twentieth birthday on the barricades with comrades during the Paris uprising. Later, the young woman wrote poetry based on her Resistance experience, and she met poet Paul Éluard.[11]

Because French women of that time were not full-fledged citizens, and thus had difficulty establishing their credentials, they paradoxically had a decided advantage in clandestine work: Their activities were less subject to public scrutiny. To cite but one example, Lucienne Welschinger and other Alsatian girls served as covers for men escaping the Germans.

> I often joined groups of men who left Strasbourg by train—generally early Sunday mornings—ostensibly for an outing in the Vosges Mountains nearby. Their real destination was much farther on. There were always two young girls in these quiet groups so as not to attract attention.

Lucienne organized this escape network with some of her friends. It was an extremely dangerous undertaking, as Alsace had been annexed by Germany. Crossing the mountains during the severe winter of 1940–1941, they encountered avalanches, which disoriented them. "But that was nothing when one is young and has a compass," she insists. Their group helped more than four hundred French and Allied prisoners of war to escape, along with Alsatian youths fleeing to avoid being forced to wear the German army uniform. Lucienne, a former Scout, views the ideal of the Resistance as being closely linked to that of scouting.[12]

Few French women held leadership positions in Resistance networks and movements. Berty Albrecht, who seconded Henri Frenay in organizing Combat, conceived of and produced the movement's first newsletter, which developed into *Combat*, the major clandestine paper in the southern zone. Lucie Aubrac helped found the Libération-Sud movement and worked on its newspaper, *Libération*. Marie-Madeleine Fourcade—the only woman to head a major network—served initially as the right hand of Commandant Georges Loustau-nau-Lacau in setting up the British Intelligence–sponsored Alliance network. He was arrested early in the Occupation, so Fourcade assumed leadership of Alliance's three thousand or so members. When the British appointed her to replace the network's captured leader, she encountered problems in establishing her authority.* Once Fourcade even traveled to Spain inside a mail sack. On another occasion, she took off her clothes and squeezed herself, headfirst, between the window bars of a room in which she was being held overnight before being taken to prison. Fourcade narrates her extraordinary activities in *Noah's Ark* (1968, 1973).

Parachuted back into France, petite explosive expert Jeanne Bohec was greeted upon landing with: "It's a child!" Although she was better qualified than most men to use the machine guns parachuted in, Bohec's efforts to join in *maquis* combats were overruled. She was informed that women were not supposed to fight when men were available. As we'll see later, this reaction was typical. It should be no surprise that there was discrimination against women in the Resistance. While participants were united principally by their common concern to overcome the Nazi occupiers, they were a very disparate group with largely conventional views. There was also anti-Semitism in the Resistance. The bitter memory of this fact was noted by philosopher and Resistance hero Vladimir Jankélévitch in remarks he left for publication after his death.[13]

While acknowledging that there was some discrimination against women in the Resistance, historian and *résistant* Henri Noguères contends that this discrimination was for the most part unconscious. It was based upon "a notion of inequality between the sexes as old as our civilization and as firmly implanted in the Resistance as it was everywhere else in France." In the years of Occupation, he holds, French women Resistance members did all those things that they alone could do—as well as what they indisputably could do better than men. And they also did—just as well as the men—all that the men did. Yet, even though women were active in all Resistance groups and were used extensively for all the routine tasks, there was not a single woman on the list of prefects or commissioners for the postwar republic. Not a single woman was named as president of one of the department liberation committees; nor was there a single woman regional head of a movement nor one among the regional and depart-

*The Germans called the network "Noah's Ark" because agents took the names of animals and birds.

ment heads of the FFI members. All of these appointments had been decided by the National Council of the Resistance.[14]

Many young women living at home quietly undertook Resistance assignments while their parents thought—or chose to think—that their daughters were attending classes or going to work. In addition to families united in their views of the situation and their desire to help, there were French families with opposing views about what course of conduct to follow in occupied France. A "frightened" Parisian grandmother from an "old Breton family" wrote the following letter to German authorities. She stated that she had always hated the British and thought—mistakenly—that her family shared her ideas:

Last Saturday I saw my granddaughters' jackets marked with "Vive de Gaulle." After questioning my loved ones—former enemies of the British—I learned that they had become convinced supporters of de Gaulle, encouraged by the Jews and by their teachers. . . . But that is not the worst. My grandson, a student at the Lycée Charlemagne, told me that the students there, along with those in other lycées,* had a stock of arms and would soon be fighting the Germans.

The distraught grandmother begged the authorities to use all their influence to stop this movement (i.e., the Resistance), which she was convinced would lead to a massacre in which French youth would perish along with the Germans. She suggested they close the schools and substitute correspondence courses.[15]

A "profoundly distressed" father wrote to his daughter in March 1943 after a visit:

How is it possible that you, my daughter, do not understand your duty as a young Frenchwoman?

The interest of our beloved country is not to see either an American or a Russian victory.

The Militia is our only true remaining strength. I have sworn [through his joining] to serve France even if it entails the sacrifice of my life. You have been listening to that vile British propaganda.[16]

Seventeen-year-old Edwige de Saint-Wexel was beaten and imprisoned for participating in a student demonstration in Paris on Ar-

*Lycées are state-supported French secondary schools equivalent to American senior high schools and the first year of college.

mistice Day in 1940.* When she returned home after three months in a filthy Parisian prison, Saint-Wexel's aristocratic father spoke to her coldly. The young woman stayed just long enough to clean up.[17] One woman confided to me that she joined the Resistance in reaction to her mother, who was having an affair with a German officer. As these examples reveal, the situation in occupied France occasionally divided parents and children. More significantly, some young women chose to contravene their parents' authority and join the Resistance. The French needed to be brought out of their isolation.

The first efforts of those who felt compelled to "do something" generally focused on information. They sought to provide the French public with accurate, truthful information. This held for both zones. In 1940, there were no television sets, transistor radios, or tape recorders. Newspapers were the principal sources of information, but they were censored in the north (and supplies were rationed). In the south, Vichy issued "guidelines" and required that certain articles be included. The radio was also censored, and obtaining sufficient power for reception was an additional problem.

The Germans broadcast much false information—such as the claim that they had landed in England—so the underground press countered with news picked up from British or Swiss radio stations. The clandestine press exposed secret agreements and detailed the extensive shipments of France's harvest and wealth to Germany—news that the occupiers tried to hide. The printing and distribution of clandestine newspapers were dangerous and difficult activities. All who worked on illegal newspapers did so at great peril. A German ordinance of December 18, 1942, decreed that anyone involved in the production or distribution of illegal newspapers would be punished by forced labor—or, in the most serious cases, with death. And they carried out their threats. Many were arrested. German efforts to suppress these papers led to mutual assistance and efforts to protect those who had gone underground—people in need of food, shelter, and forged documents.

Papers—and paper—played a crucial role in French Resistance. To help all those being persecuted in occupied France—Communists, Jews, Freemasons, political refugees, downed Allied airmen, and, later,

---

*The authorities had forbidden any public activity marking the day, but the students decided to march anyway, in part to protest the arrest of a distinguished, much-admired professor.

Resistance members—counterfeit cards and coupons were printed. The French were required to have numerous documents: identification and ration cards; coupons for fabrics, clothing, fuel, and other necessities; medical certificates and passes, such as the *Ausweis* needed to cross the demarcation line; and, later, certificates of exemption from forced labor. All were successfully copied by Resistance counterfeiters.

Former Resistance member Janine Lévy vividly recalls a train trip when her papers were checked, underscoring the importance of having authentic-looking documents. (Vichy—again acting on its own initiative—decided to have all the identity cards of Jews marked with that designation; law of December 11, 1942.)

"I remember that particular trip because of my identity card. We all had to have them. You bought them in the tobacco stores. They had a place to fill in 'name of father' and 'name of mother.' But they were not all identical, although I don't know why. Perhaps some were for Jews. Some specified 'maiden name of mother.' My card asked for 'maiden name of mother.' My father's name was a Romanian one that did not sound particularly Jewish, but my mother's maiden name was Jarnowitch. That was an abomination—grief. And so I always remember the security check on that train, the German coming in and demanding, '*Papiers, bitte.*' Then he looked at mine—for what seemed an eternity. When he finally returned it to me, what a relief!

"Upon arrival in Paris, I bought an identity card that did not have 'maiden name of mother.' I had a false 'real' card made. One of my uncles made excellent false papers. He fixed mine up. The card was authentic but the seals were not. The information could be verified, but my mother's maiden name was not required. If I were stopped in the street, it would not be obvious immediately that the seals were fake."[18]

The demand for false papers multiplied as more *résistants* were obliged to go underground and youths sought to avoid the forced labor service. Moreover, Resistance agents were obliged to change names frequently. Each change required new identity cards and coupons.

French bureaucracy has long been obsessed with official stamps, as Suzanne Borel (later the wife of Resistance leader and politician Georges Bidault) realized. Prior to the war, Borel was the first woman to pass entry exams for the French diplomatic service. However, she was not formally accepted until she swore never to seek a foreign posting; that was deemed inappropriate for a woman! During the Occupation, Borel was assigned to the Office of Information in Vichy. There she helped *résistants* acquire papers and secreted information out of the country via the diplomatic pouch. Frequently she "loaned" her modest housing to those secretly in Vichy. She recounts in her memoirs the extreme care she took to see that there were as many seals as possible on documents, even though some had no meaning whatsoever: "[T]hat is the first precaution one takes in troubled times."[19]

Défense de la France had an excellent service that supplied false papers for other groups as well. Monique Rollin and her husband, Michel Bernstein, produced many counterfeit documents for Défense. There were authentic-looking "false" identity cards, along with false "real" identity cards that had been stolen outright from municipal offices or were provided by helpful employees in those offices. These cards required photographs, seals, and information that would withstand scrutiny.* The couple also duplicated coupons and tickets for many rationed commodities. They lived in virtual seclusion in a series of small apartments where they avoided contact with neighbors and others. Windows were opened only at night. Their lodgings always smelled of burning rubber. In winter they froze and in summer they sweltered. Because Michel was Jewish (and also more suspect as a young man), Monique did all the errands and served as liaison with the outside world. She undertook the extremely dangerous task of delivering all the false documents and rubber stamps they fabricated. She concealed them in the false bottom of her shopping bag. French women carried shopping bags at all times during the Occupation; one never knew when and where food might be found. Monique shopped and prepared their meals—such as they were—in addition to doing all the work the counterfeiting operation entailed. The couple published a manual, *The Successful Counterfeiter*, which served other movements and was reissued several times.[20]

The first clandestine publications were small notes called "butterflies," attached to posts or mailboxes, and hand-lettered or typed tracts and news bulletins. Publications were very important for morale, providing psychological resistance. The French needed to be roused from the shock of defeat. Through clandestine publications, the population

---

*Towns where records had been destroyed were popular choices for birthplaces.

learned that not everyone accepted Pétain's call for collaboration with the Germans. Another function of the underground press was to insist on Germany's eventual defeat. The public needed to know of the crimes the enemy had committed through arrests and hostage executions, to be aware that Germany was bleeding France of its produce and resources. Furthermore, Resistance groups were forming in other countries; surely they should exist in France. Probably more than in any other occupied European country, the printed word in France became a major form of Resistance to the German occupiers. French culture has long given a privileged place to le discours, discourse. And, as was the case for la mode, France's prestige in the world was at stake.

Women were involved in every aspect of the French Resistance press, serving not only in the more traditional roles of typists but also as editors and authors. A few assumed the difficult jobs of linotypists and machine and press operators as news bulletins developed into professional papers with widespread distribution. Combat started as a few dozen carbon pages typed and distributed by Resistance heroine and martyr Berty Albrecht. With the acquisition of a mimeograph machine, the number of bulletins increased to several hundred. Expansion required coordination of services. Jacqueline Bernard, whose family contributed generously to the movement, helped Albrecht with the early typed copies. Her brother gave his life (see Yvette Farnoux's narrative in chapter 9). Henri Frenay appointed Jacqueline editorial secretary of Combat, a post she held until her arrest in the spring of 1944. In his memoirs, he describes her as the "sinew" of the underground press. Although she was in reality the managing editor, that title—at her suggestion—was given to different men, including famed author Albert Camus. The celebrated author, whose career was then taking off, was initially a pacifist. But he soon came to realize that one could not be a pacifist in occupied France. Unable to return to his native Algeria, he played a major role in the publication of Combat in the last years of the war and in the early postwar years. Bernard rationalized that men would command more respect in the position and be able to recruit writers more readily. Hers was the difficult, demanding job of finding editors, soliciting articles, and gathering news—all in secret. She also wrote articles. In 1941, the movement was able to locate a few printers willing to take serious risks and publish several thousand copies of the paper.

Lucie Aubrac underlines the importance of information:

"Our concern was to inform. Like the Resistance in general, our group developed from our need to inform. We simply had to tell people what was happening. The Germans gave out much misinformation. On the other hand, there was information the Germans did not want the French to know. They were pillaging and looting our country. So some of us started to print a small underground newspaper.

"As an academic, a historian by training, I felt a particular concern about information—about the truth. At that time, I was forbidden to teach my students about anything that took place after 1914! So during the winter of 1940–1941, I helped edit the clandestine newspaper *Libération-Sud* [later *Libération*]. It was difficult just to find the paper, let alone print and then distribute the issues."[21]

There is no way to determine precisely the number and circulation of clandestine journals printed during the Occupation. Many were short-lived, and it was dangerous to keep copies. The Bibliothèque Nationale holds more than a thousand clandestine newspapers published during the Occupation. Of these, more than fifty were addressed specifically to women; some were published by women themselves. The Communist press was the most active in targeting women. It well understood the importance of propaganda. The PCF was the only political organization with important women's groups prior to the war. Its archives catalogue lists dozens of illegal journals and many single-sheet tracts urging housewives to protest food shortages and join demonstrations. The most successful demonstration was a massive one that Communists organized in Marseilles on May 25, 1944. Encouraged by the women's example, the area's metalworkers and dockworkers struck in the days that followed.

In addition to papers targeted at women, underground publications raised issues of concern to women ranging from the practical to the political. The *Cahiers* (*Notebooks*) of Défense de la France, a movement with a large number of students, advocated the vote for women in its January 1944 issue—apparently the only publication to do so. "Their absence in elections prevents [French] suffrage from being truly universal," it pointed out. In April 1944, the provisional government under de Gaulle in Algiers granted French women the right to vote and to run for office.

As we have seen, the most pressing concern facing women was finding food for their families. A tract of March 1941, entitled "Why [the town of] Bourges Is without Potatoes," depicts a child complaining:

—Mother, I'm hungry.

—Here, my little one, take this picture of Marshal Pétain.

—Fewer pictures and more potatoes, please.

The answer is a wry commentary on the idolatry of Pétain, whose picture was everywhere.[22]

From the beginnings of the clandestine press, it was women who typed the tracts and printed the news bulletins (sometimes on toy presses), which were distributed with instructions for others to copy and pass on. Since only six carbons could be typed at a time, distribution was limited. Enterprising groups secured mimeographs and rotaprint machines. On occasion, new machines were purchased with false papers. More frequently, they were purchased secondhand to avoid registration. Even when presses could be acquired, it was a problem to find relatively soundproof places to hide them. The *Bulletin de Presse de la France Combattante*, the Resistance "press services" information bulletin, was typed and run off by two women hidden in an abbey. The rotaprint machine used to publish *Défense* was hidden in the basement of a Sorbonne laboratory. Courageous, feisty, eighty-four-year-old Mme Cumin allowed a *Défense* printing press—familiarly referred to as "Grandmother"—to be installed in her launderette in the Bastille district.

Transporting the lead required for printing plates was another perilous undertaking. One woman hid ninety pounds of lead in the carriage of her sleeping infant. Under the heavy load, the carriage springs scraped the wheels, almost causing a serious accident.

For greater security, typesetting often was done in separate workshops. Marlyse Guthmann allowed her apartment above a Protestant kindergarten in the Parisian suburbs to be used as a *Défense* printshop. Members—who worked there day and night—escaped across the rooftops when the Gestapo arrived one day—except for Guthmann and two friends, who were arrested and deported.[23]

A related problem was storage and distribution. Geneviève de Gaulle asked the proprietors of shops in her Paris neighborhood to conceal stock and printed newspapers. Some refused out of fear. Two of the women who agreed to help her were the owner of an art gallery (whose brother was a well-known collaborator) and the proprietor of a corner grocery shop. Both were arrested and deported for storing papers. The collaborator secured his sister's release in exchange for a few paintings. Several members of Défense daringly stole from a government office a special typewriter needed for stencils. Combat "requisitioned" supplies, including a truck. Then came the problem of distribution.

In time, the clandestine press grew to represent the range of views of the press in prewar France. There were national papers with large circulations and smaller regional journals. Some papers addressed the general public while others targeted specific political or social groups, such as Communists or militant Catholics. There were even handwritten "papers" that circulated in prison. The success of these underground publications can be measured by the many fake Resistance tracts and papers the Germans produced.

France's underground press also published books. Éditions de Minuit (Midnight Press) was founded by Pierre de Lescure and Vercors (pseudonym for Jean Bruller), author of the classic *Le Silence de la mer* (*The Silence of the Sea*, 1942). In an interview, Vercors explained the position he and his colleagues advocated:

> There were French writers who collaborated. We needed to counter them by urging silence. The idea for my book [in which a young French woman remains stoically silent each time a sympathetic German officer billeted in her home speaks to her] came from German Ambassador Otto Abetz, who had drawn up a list of forbidden authors—principally Jews, Communists, and those with a left-wing political orientation.[24]

Vercors goes on to explain that when a German officer was billeted in his home, he never greeted him. The silence became thicker, more oppressive, for, in his view, man's spiritual purity was at stake. Also at issue was the larger question of the responsibility of intellectuals in a country where they acquire the fame of pop stars. Literature can prove to be the most subversive of expressions, the most difficult to control. For Sartre, paradoxically, writers were never more free than they were during the Occupation. In "The Republic of Silence," he maintained that because an all-powerful police force tried to keep them silent, every word was like a declaration of principles. The problem with Vercors's call for silence was that collaborationist writers continued to publish and there was much German propaganda. A counterweight seemed necessary.

Paris pediatrician Robert Debré writes of the role he and his companion Dexia (Countess Elisabeth de la Bourdonnaye) played in helping publish *Le Silence*. Jean Paulhan spoke to him about the bold project of a clandestine publishing house, Éditions de Minuit, which would publish the book. All had been carefully prepared for the undertaking, but funds were lacking to set it up. Fortunately, Debré had put aside a little from his honoraria for emergencies.

> I decided to contribute these funds to the project. Paulhan brought the manuscript of *Le Silence*. It exceeded expectations; this was a masterpiece. Dexia typed the text and sewed sheets of flimsy paper folded into small pages together so the work could be secretly distributed to a few friends who shared our admiration [of the work].[25]

Women authored some of the close to thirty clandestine works published by Éditions de Minuit during the Occupation. Edith Thomas, an archivist by training, published biographies and novels prior to the war. Thomas spent the first two years of the war in a sanatorium recovering from tuberculosis. The diaries she kept during that time reveal that—in contrast to most of her compatriots—Thomas believed Pétain had a dictatorial nature. When permitted to resume work in Paris in the fall of 1941, Thomas sought to assist the Resistance. She helped co-found the Comité National des Écrivains (National Committee of Writers). Overcoming both ideological and material obstacles, the committee wrote, printed, and distributed *Les Lettres françaises* (*French Letters*), the leading journal of French intellectual resistance. The committee was formed by the PCF, which Thomas joined in 1942. Once she spent several days with a *maquis* group in the mountains and published a report on that experience in *Les Lettres françaises*. She contributed to other clandestine publications, including *L'Éternelle* and the journal *Femmes françaises* (*French Women*), published by the PCF-backed UFF. Éditions de Minuit published *Contes d'Auxois*, Thomas's collection of short stories about Resistance figures.[26]

Another prominent woman writer and Resistance member was Elsa Triolet. Her novel *The Lovers of Avignon* was brought out by Éditions de Minuit in 1943. Russian-born Triolet was harassed after the German invasion both because she was Jewish and because she was married to Communist writer Louis Aragon.* The couple fled from

---

*Triolet never formally joined the Communist Party.

Paris to the unoccupied zone, where they stayed with friends until the Germans occupied all of France and they were obliged to go underground. Triolet was among the French writers like Albert Camus, François Mauriac, and Jean-Paul Sartre who viewed writing as a political act. Of the fiction she wrote during the war, she said, "To write is my freedom, my defiance, my luxury." She sought new forms and new content to better present the spirit of the Resistance. Historian Helena Lewis notes Triolet's focus on the quotidian in her stories:

> They vividly evoke daily life under the Occupation: the mass exodus of panic-stricken Parisians fleeing south while the Germans bombarded them from the air; the newspaper columns on "how to find your loved ones"; the ration cards; the lack of heat, electricity, and water; the black marketeering; and the accidental deaths caused by rationing the gas supply.[27]

This last topic was the subject of the short story *Mille regrets* (*A Thousand Regrets*, 1942). The epilogue to her Goncourt Prize book, *A Fine of Two Hundred Francs*, recounts an actual parachute drop that brought German reprisals to a small French village. Triolet also wrote articles for *Les Lettres françaises* and helped edit and distribute the journal. Editorial duties took Triolet to Paris frequently, in spite of the dangers. On one trip, she and Aragon were arrested at the demarcation line and imprisoned for several weeks before being released. Their false identification papers withstood scrutiny. Another time, she escaped arrest on a train bound for Paris because the German soldier could not read the French clandestine materials she was carrying.

Clandestine life provided some women with the opportunity to discover their talents. Simone de Beauvoir's friend and colleague Colette Audry volunteered to plant bombs but was told she was needed instead to write articles and distribute the underground newspapers. In addition to contributing articles to underground publications, Audry began to write short stories and memoirs during the Occupation. In 1946, Camus published her first collection of short stories. The previous year, she wrote the script for and helped produce *La Bataille du Rail* (*Battle of the Rails*), the famed film about the Resistance work of French railway workers.[28]

Like secret secretaries and distributors of clandestine newspapers, most Resistance couriers were women. Liaison was central to French Resistance. Since telephone lines were not secure and mail was censored, secret messages and information had to be picked up and delivered by couriers. And since men, particularly young men, aroused suspicion in those days (most were in POW camps or at work), Resistance messengers were principally women. Doing errands, it could be assumed, was women's normal activity. During the Occupation of France, however, these daily activities often served the Resistance. Women messengers carried out extremely risky assignments, much more dangerous than many realized at the time. If caught, they were subject to the worst tortures because authorities were aware that couriers were entrusted with extremely important information. As Anne-Marie Soucelier explains:

"We had many meetings while out walking because the cafés were dangerous. You could talk discreetly on the street while checking to see if you were followed. When people say that this was *only* liaison work, they forget how dangerous it was. You could be arrested twenty times a day, because you went to twenty mail drops and each mailbox represented danger. The leaders were relatively well protected. Liaison agents risked being arrested twenty times a day, while the heads often could escape. Agents protected the leaders and said nothing—not even under torture."[29]

Liaison or courier agents linked not only those within a single town but also different towns and cities, different regions, the two major zones while the country remained divided, and *maquis* units in the countryside with the outside world. Women couriers carried compromising material between Paris and Lyon several times a week, for it was impossible to memorize lengthy messages or documents. After the Allied landings, liaison became even more difficult and dangerous. One young woman left Lyon on August 6, 1944, and finally made it to Paris (a 400-mile trip) on August 28, completing the last stretch after cycling for three and a half days.

Bicycles became *the* means of transportation during the Occupation period. Their use rose dramatically, as registration figures attest. Early on, gas became virtually unavailable. Only Germans and their supporters had access to the limited fuel resources. On occasion, the sound of a gas-driven car (as opposed to the alternative fuels some tried) warned of the approach of the Germans. A bicycle became a prized possession. By the end of the Occupation, it was virtually impossible to obtain a bicycle, new or used. In pressing circumstances, *résistants* borrowed or "recuperated" them (with the implied intention of returning them when they could). Numerous girls and young women in the Resistance covered hundreds of miles by bicycle on "Tours de France." In these circumstances, the prize was not a medal or a trophy but the food, supplies, and messages picked up and delivered to those in need.

Using a bike in Paris helped one avoid both the Métro, where there were frequent searches, and the checkpoints set up on major streets. When not circulating in towns or cities, cyclists on missions used narrow, uncomfortable back roads. The Germans did not "drag their boots there," as one young woman put it. Once she spent more than seven hours zigzagging across secondary roads to cover a distance of less than fifty miles. For the mother of nineteen-year-old Christiane, who became a liaison agent for a *maquis* in the Paris region, her daughter's life was not all that appealing, even though she herself was a *résistante*. Christiane slept without taking her things off, seldom had time to wash, ate at odd hours and in odd places, going about by bike, risking her life at every moment.[30]

German authorities allowed Dr. Geneviève Congy to ride her bike to visit patients in the Brie-Comte-Robert region northeast of Paris. Although Congy had an ailing husband (also a doctor), two young children, and two grandmothers in her charge, she carried many messages and did extensive liaison without raising suspicions, thanks to her medical visits. Seventeen-year-old Marie-Jo Chombart de Laüwe biked about her native Brittany while working for the small escape network her family helped set up to assist aviators and soldiers return to their native England in the summer of 1940. At the request of the British, the group soon extended its activities to include collecting information on the construction projects and military emplacements in the coastal region. De Laüwe enrolled in medical school in Rennes in order to have a valid pretext for repeatedly crossing the demarcation line with this vital information. The teenager spent endless hours on her bike until she and most members of the group, including her parents, were captured in 1942.[31]

One young woman who cycled about France was Australasian Nancy Wake. She considered herself French in everything but birth. Prior to the war, she worked in Paris and took frequent vacations throughout France. Her parents did not approve when she married a wealthy Marseillais. With the advent of war, the couple provided a hiding place in their chalet in the Alps. Wake started to work for the Resistance, doing liaison and helping with an escape route to Spain.

The Germans sought the young woman they called the "White Mouse." (Her husband was deported because of her Resistance activities, and did not return.) At one point, Wake escaped to London, where she trained with the British Special Operations Executive before being parachuted back to France to help a *maquis*. On one trip—to get a replacement radio—she covered almost two hundred miles by bike in seventy-two hours, acknowledging later that her legs were beginning (!) to ache because the trip included mountainous terrain. In her memoirs, Wake speaks of the help she received in her various endeavors. Describing the woman's role in France, she also notes, "I never once met a farmer who did not confer with his wife before making an important decision."[32]

The most popular recent French literary work on World War II is Régine Deforges' *Bicyclette bleue* (*The Blue Bicycle*, 1981–1985), the collective title given to a three-volume saga recounting the Resistance (and romantic) adventures of adolescent Léa Delmas. (The work's parallels with *Gone with the Wind*—the exodus of refugees fleeing an invading army, the heroine falling in love with her brother-in-law, etc.—are the subject of ongoing lawsuits; it has been translated into many languages.) Using her trusty blue bike, the fictional young heroine cycles about southwestern France delivering messages for the Resistance, as did so many French women in real life.

Madeleine Baudoin's account of the combat groups of the Communist-sponsored Francs-Tireurs-Partisans (FTP) details the activities of a number of women liaison agents, such as Georgette Guyot. To reach a member who had just been arrested, Guyot outfitted herself as a waitress in a black dress with a lace-trimmed white apron. Thus attired, tray in hand, she was able to reach the fourth floor of police headquarters.[33]

Another liaison agent graduated from the prestigious Sèvres Normal School, which prepares women for teaching careers in higher education. In a memorial volume the school published to honor graduates who gave their lives for their country in World War II, there is a profile of Corsican-born Marie Reynouard, class of 1921. Reynouard came to the conclusion that there was no point in teaching the classics if the lessons of the classics could no longer be followed—as was the case in occupied France—so she joined the Resistance. Initially arrested for distributing tracts in Grenoble, Reynouard was provisionally released from prison in Lyon. Nevertheless, she resumed clandestine activities, in particular liaison work, this time in the Marseilles region.

Arrested again, she was deported to Ravensbrück, where Reynouard, always in frail health, soon succumbed.[34]

Secret secretaries helped with liaison and the clandestine press:

> ... [A] "national liaison and secretarial" service linked the center to each region and a "regional liaison and secretarial" service linked every department and region. There were innumerable orders addressed to all the regional heads from the national headquarters; bulletins from the information service; and orders, instructions, or information. . . . It is difficult to imagine the amount of paper entailed.[35]

French women did most of the unglamorous but very necessary secretarial work required by the movements and networks. Women spent many, many hours typing important material in different locations and under difficult conditions—wearing gloves for warmth and using English keyboards (which differ from French ones). One of the many who typed for the Resistance was a PCF member named Huguette (she did not give her last name). Upon becoming an underground agent, the adolescent was asked to type reports, tracts, and stencils. Huguette found it difficult to go for long periods—sometimes several months—without news of her family, who, for their part, thought she was missing, possibly dead. Sometimes she typed at the dry-cleaning shop where her landlady worked; on other occasions, she transported the typewriter to her rooming house. There were times when Huguette typed virtually nonstop for several days. The major concern that appears in her lengthy testimony was getting food. Then there were the alerts:

> I kept on typing madly but during the alerts the only sound was that of my typewriter. I had to check from time to time to make certain no one was in hearing distance. When you type all day long, you get pains in your back—not in your fingers, as most people think. The work is also very solitary and lonely. It was much more fun, although more dangerous, when I helped a comrade move a heavy rotary printer from one location to another. Then at least I was outside and with others. When I first started to type stencils, I discovered I had no correcting liquid. I solved that problem by using nail polish.[36]

In addition to intelligence information (generally coded), arrangements for the postwar government in France were typed by unknown, volunteer secretaries. Women showed themselves to be adept at coding and decoding messages. Because girls traditionally learn languages, translation was another area where women used their skills. Women's language expertise proved extremely useful during the war years.

Gisèle Joannès stresses the necessity of remembering those insignificant but important acts that contribute to a better understanding of the Resistance as a whole, such as the secretarial work of women:

> I worked in a couture workshop. In November 1938, I was dismissed because of a strike. At the time, I was simply a card-carrying member of the CGT syndicate [the Communist-dominated union]. I was also a member of the Communist Youth organization. For my part, I typed material for publication with two fingers. During this time, I stayed in numerous places in Paris and in the provinces.

When in the provinces, Joannès took early commuting trains when she had to travel, because these trains were less subject to German checks.

> A woman who worked in the metal industry loaned me an apartment where I spent many days typing. To cover the noise, I turned up the volume of the radio as loud as possible. In addition to typing, I also did liaison. Going about the countryside, I transported food and assorted false cards—ration cards, identity cards, and blank marriage certificates.
>
> One day in November 1942, I was returning with food and false papers. To hide them, I put baby clothes on top of the package. I had to bike twelve miles with this baggage to catch my train. It was very cold and the ground was hard and hilly. A black Citroën passed me and then stopped. It was the Economic Police [which prosecuted black marketeers]. I stopped and, off guard, fell and bruised my knee, which bled copiously. The police searched my shopping bags. When they came to the package with the counterfeit papers hidden beneath the baby clothes, I started to cry and talk about my baby and my prisoner husband (neither true) and how my baby needed these clothes and I was going to use the food to make packages to send him. The police stopped searching my bags and put my things back. They asked where in town they should drop off my things.

So Joannès's bags were taken on ahead, but she still had six miles to cover by bike. During this time she was in a state of anxiety. Should she really go and claim her bags? Perhaps they had been opened and her clandestine material discovered. She decided to go nevertheless, and she picked up her baggage without difficulty, mission accomplished.[37]

Secretarial work often included coding and decoding. Laure Moulin seconded her brother Jean and helped him decipher top-secret documents.

> When Jean came to Montpellier, generally on Saturdays, he brought back coded messages that had been forwarded to him from Avignon, Marseilles, or Lyon. Sunday evening—after Mother had gone to bed—the two of us settled near the fire and he took out his messages. We used paper ruled into squares. You filled in the code agreed upon—letters horizontally and numbers vertically (like crossword puzzles). Both patience and attention were required. If you mistook a letter or a number, you had to begin all over again. The hours passed and we were both exhausted, but we simply had to complete the work before morning. Sometimes we had only an hour or two of sleep.[38]

What characterizes French women who helped in the Resistance? Some were idealists. Others were outsiders, mavericks, and perhaps, in a more profound sense, revolutionaries. Like their male comrades, they were a minority among the French population. People who involve themselves are always a minority, especially when one risks one's life. As Stanley Hoffmann has observed, those in the Resistance were men and women of character, independent, individuals—in a word, French. And Vichy was determined to crush individualism.

The Resistance transcended conventional class barriers in France by bringing together people from all social classes, although civil servants and workers were proportionately more numerous than administrators or industrialists. Those imprisoned with Geneviève de Gaulle for Resistance activities included an actress from the Comédie-Française and a pushcart peddler. Several cellmates had advanced degrees; others hardly knew how to read. All the women agreed that it was an exceptional mixture.

In *Le Convoi du 24 janvier* (1965), Charlotte Delbo provides short biographies of the 230 Frenchwomen (only a few of whom were Jewish) deported with her by cattle car to Auschwitz (the "camp of slow death") in January 1943. This group merits examination because of what it tells us about women who served in the Resistance and also because of what it reveals about the difficulty in basing generalizations on a sample like Delbo's.

None of these women were deported specifically for racial reasons—that is, because they were Jewish. Furthermore, not all were involved in Resistance work. Several had been caught in roundups;

others had been arrested when a husband or relative could not be found. This followed the German policy of collective responsibility. Two were collaborators. Delbo herself notes the problem in classifying deportees. A provisional designation of deportee was given to all who returned after the end of hostilities. Later, efforts were made to distinguish those who had been sent to Germany for forced labor from those who profited from the confusion of 1944–1945 or who were common criminals. Associations of deportees insisted that a distinction be made between those who were deported because they were Jewish or had the misfortune to be caught in a roundup and those who had been deported because of active Resistance involvement. Part of the problem here is that women were at times arrested for doing Resistance work—sometimes helping men in their families—unknown to those in the movements or networks, so their role could not always be validated.

Delbo's group ranged in age from eighteen to sixty-eight.* As to professions, forty-two were housewives, while there were about twenty each of factory workers, shop personnel, and stitchers and knitters. Particularly noteworthy are their family situations. Sixty-nine of these women were wives of men who were shot or killed by the Nazis. The same number had children under sixteen who were left behind in France. While sixteen of the mothers returned, fifty-three did not, leaving a total of seventy-five orphaned children under sixteen years of age. Finally, there were a considerable number of mothers-and-daughters, or pairs of sisters, in the group. These women were from families involved in the Resistance.

In Delbo's group, family involvement was linked to political affiliation. More than half the women in the group were either registered Communists or Communist sympathizers. Nevertheless, one cannot claim on the basis of this sampling that Communists constituted at least half the Resistance. There are a number of explanations for the high proportion of PCF members arrested.

To begin with, like Jews, Communists were known to the police, so it was much easier to keep them under surveillance. Fewer Resistance members from non-Communist groups, particularly women, had been active in politics before the war. Consequently, they were largely unknown to the authorities, who had more difficulty locating and arresting them. Second, the Communists—in spite of de Gaulle's pleas

---

*None over age forty-four survived; about a third of those under thirty-five did.

to the contrary—had a policy of killing individual German soldiers. Jews and Communists already rounded up and imprisoned were shot or deported in large numbers in retaliation for these attacks; this further distorted efforts to assess Resistance membership.

In the most recent of his works on the Jewish Resistance (*250 combattants de la Résistance témoignent*, 1991), David Diamant lists the names of 128 members for whom false identity papers were prepared. More than half of those listed are women. But here again, this sample does not really show that more women than men were active in the Jewish Resistance. There are various possible explanations for this distribution. Husbands almost automatically asked for cards for their spouses (who, to be sure, often did Resistance work), and Jewish males were the first rounded up and arrested. Although the underlying point is that there were many women in the Resistance, it is impossible to determine accurately how many were Jewish and/or Communist. Most "soldiers of the night" were not formally "registered."

Jews and Communists did not work exclusively within their own groups. PCF member Guy Besse observed that the Interfaculty Resistance Committee of the University of Lyon (formed in 1942) included Communists and Catholics—the Reds and the Blacks. The Union of Patriotic Students, formed at the end of 1943, brought together all the student Resistance movements—Communists, Catholics, Protestants, Jews, and the Women's University Union. Student groups had a significant proportion of women—up to one-third or more. Elisabeth Terrenoire summarizes the situation in her 1946 survey of women in the French Resistance, *Combattantes sans uniforme* (*Fighters without Uniform*): "You did not ask the young woman who risked her life on a dangerous liaison assignment if she were Christian or Communist. You knew she worked for the same cause you did."[39] Character was the ultimate requirement.

Those who undertook Resistance work generally did so in spite of fears for both themselves and their families. In some cases, it became necessary for *résistants* to cut themselves off completely from their families. The independence and nonconformism of some *résistants*—particularly the "difficult personalities" among the Resistance leaders—sometimes led to diverging opinions over policy and objectives. For the most part, women were not involved in these struggles. Few were leaders and interested in power per se. The need for secrecy contributed to these tensions. To be successful, Resistance groups had to observe *cloisonnement* (compartmentalization). One had to know as little as possible about others in the group in order to limit the information one could divulge under torture. The negative aspect of this policy was the difficulty in determining guilt in the event of betrayal. The best-known example is that of René Hardy, accused of being responsible for the capture and death of Jean Moulin.[40]

Women involved in the Resistance frequently had to assume the triple burden of household chores, outside job, and clandestine activities. Daily tasks were progressively more demanding during the Occupation: feeding and clothing a family when food and clothing were rationed; washing clothes when soap was difficult to find; and heating a home during the cold winter months when fuel was scarce. Women's traditional ability to improvise and adapt served them well during the Occupation. Germaine Tillion regrets that in many instances, women's lack of training and expertise required them to resort to alternatives. Nevertheless, the conventional and stereotyped view of French women then prevalent was to prove extremely useful. The Germans did not suspect them of being *terrorists* (another term they used for *résistants*)—at least not early on in the war.

+—•—+

Let us briefly consider women in resistance movements in two other countries. Italian women's presence in that country's Resistance was so pervasive that, as is the case with French women, it would be impossible to try to quantify it. Their activities were similar to those of French women: sheltering the persecuted; supplying the partisans; sabotaging products destined for Germany. Perhaps their greatest contribution to the Italian Resistance,* according to Maria de Blasio Wilhelm, was the network of *staffettas*—liaison agents who, as in France, became the vital link connecting all elements of the Italian Resistance. A representative *staffetta* was Andreini Morandi-Michelozzi, a University of Florence student from a middle-class home. Since she spoke English, she was assigned to help British prisoners of war hiding in a nearby village. She also visited captured partisans in jail and distributed *La Libertà*, the journal of the Tuscan Party of Action. The Germans went to the Morandi home after her brother Luigi killed a German soldier who discovered the hiding place of their group's clandestine radio. In prison, she was placed in a cell with Orsola Biasutti

---

*The Italian Resistance was directed against the Germans as well as Mussolini's regime.

De Cristoforo, a woman who had worked extensively to help Jews and Allied prisoners.[41]

Here again, there were women of all backgrounds, doing whatever they could. Peasant women, forced by Fascist officials to help cultivate a new field "to provide minestrone for our brave soldiers," carried out their task—planting all the seedlings upside down!

Wilhelm recounts the efforts of nuns to help the persecuted. Although the Vatican officially was neutral, religious women ran many of Italy's hospitals and prisons, proving a quiet but invaluable force in the Resistance. Among them was Sister Martha, a cloistered nun in a coastal town near Genoa. Although forbidden to communicate with the outside world, she left her cloister to help a pursued partisan whom another sister had admitted secretly. The alternative would have been his certain death. She confided in the convent's chaplain, who decided that the only way for the man to leave the convent safely was with his "wife." (Couples frequently went to the convent to offer donations and ask the sisters to pray for them.) Sister Martha volunteered for the assignment because she knew German:

> The "couple" rose and went down the road, heads bowed but occasionally greeting a passer-by. . . . Halfway to their destination, they ran into a truckload of German soldiers. Without warning, one of them took a shot at Ferruccio and hit him in the shoulder. As he bled, Ferruccio collapsed. Sister Martha threw herself on him, screaming in German: "Why have you killed my husband? What did he do to you?" The soldiers—surprised at this tirade in their own language—quickly moved off. [Ferruccio lived to participate in the liberation of Genoa, and Sister Martha returned to the cloister, never again to go out in the world.][42]

Among women in the Greek Resistance was Hélène Ahrweiler, later a specialist in Byzantine history and chancellor of the University of Paris. During the German occupation of Greece, she scribbled secret information on little slips of paper that she could swallow if necessary. She learned to write only the essential points, to distinguish the essential from the superfluous—practices that served her well in her professional career—but it took her years to learn to change her miniature handwriting back to conventional size.[43]

Eleni Fourtouni's most powerful memories of her childhood in Greece are of women involved in both political action and combat. She saw regiments of women march through her village at dawn and return at night—battle-weary, carrying their dead and wounded. And she saw women executed, their bodies dragged through the village streets. These memories prompted her to write *Greek Women in Resistance* (1986). Feminist groups that emerged after the collapse of Greece's seven-year military dictatorship in 1974 focused on publicizing the role of Greek women during the war period, including the brutal civil war (1944–1949).* Fourtouni mentions demonstrators such as Maria Karra, a young girl active in the Resistance even though her uncle, with whom she lived, disapproved.

> But I was a very determined girl, and in the end he relented. July 22, 1943. . . . Everything was ready. . . . We scattered handbills, recited poems, and sang songs of freedom. [Artillery and tanks greeted the protesters.] A young girl lay crushed at my feet. Her fair skin and blond hair were drenched in blood. . . . We saw two Germans photographing her from the tank, laughing.
>
> She was not the only victim. Fearing an even greater demonstration at their funeral, they did not let us bury our friends, and threw thousands of us in prison.[44]

Despite the dangers, many young Greek girls participated in the summer 1943 demonstration in Athens. This was one of a series of violent protests throughout Greece over the Germans' cession of Macedonia to Bulgaria as a reward for its cooperation.

+⊨━━⊨+

Heroines of the French Resistance include Berty Albrecht, the Protestant co-leader of Combat; Suzanne Buisson, secretary of the National Committee of Socialist Women; and Danielle Casanova, the Communist *pasionaria* who headed the UFF before the war. Resistance participation cut across social classes, and religious and political affiliations. For virtually the first time in French history, people from all milieus rallied behind a common cause. Traditional social barriers broke down as Resistance activities brought the French together in an effort to oust the occupiers. Those unfamiliar with French history do not fully appreciate how exceptional was the mixture in Resistance groups. Also exceptional was the contribution of women.

World War I was principally a trench war fought in northeastern

---

*Resistance in Greece was directed at both the Germans and the puppet government they established. Repression was harsh.

France between armies. By and large, the civilian population was un-involved—except for those living in the war zones. Men were at the front and women were in the rear. In contrast, during World War II, those who resisted the occupiers were civilians. With so many men away, it was inevitable that women would participate; they had to deal with survival. In a broader sense, the war was waged in people's hearts. It was not a classical war.

One must avoid stereotypes. Each woman was individual, yet cer-tain common traits emerge. For most women, commitment to the Resistance was a visceral, patriotic reaction to seeing the Germans on French soil. One woman described the German invasion as rape—the rape of her country and, by extension, of her. With the exception of women who were PCF members or Socialists, most women's commit-ment was nonpolitical. Many sought long to find a group or movement to join; Others responded spontaneously—when an opportunity arose—as with the laundress who agreed to carry messages when re-leased from prison, or the many who sheltered people in need. What they did was dependent upon various factors, including individual and local circumstances. In the words of noted Communist *résistante* Marie-Claude Vaillant-Couturier, these women were not predestined to be heroines:

> They were women and young girls like others who sought happiness and loved life. But they realized—some immediately, others little by little—what made happiness impossible: oppression, their country humiliated under the [Nazi] boot, the loss of liberty.[45]

5

+≻═━═≺+

Resistance: A Family Affair

We viewed Resistance as a family. It was the most natural thing to do. But we didn't consider security as seriously as we should have. The proof is that I was captured. They came and took my husband and my younger son as hostages. They never released them. I was brutally tortured by Klaus Barbie. I came back from deportation an invalid. My back was permanently damaged. My husband and younger son never came back. My son was only sixteen years old.

Our family was united in the Resistance. All four of us agreed to help with the Resistance. Many families participated together. But that was not the case in every family. There were instances of resistance members and collaborationists in the same family. Yes, there were even a few women in the Resistance whose sons were shot after the war because they had collaborated seriously with the enemy.

—*Lise Lesèvre, résistante*[1]

THE FAMILY HAS ALWAYS PLAYED A MAJOR ROLE IN FRENCH SOCIETY, and so, inevitably, Resistance frequently was a family affair. During the Occupation, families united in the Resistance faced the problems of dealing with daily hardships, along with anguish over events of the war and the fate of friends and colleagues who were killed or deported. Working together gave them strength.

Hélène Roederer—a young woman preparing the *agrégation* (a graduate degree) in history—came from a family actively involved in the Resistance. Her father, director of the naval steel works at Saint-Chamond, along with her mother and sister, had all joined Défense de la France, as had she. Her parents had a spacious home in the suburbs of Paris that was comparatively isolated, so Défense members used it for night meetings to plan all their activities for the following week and review security measures. Hélène had many relatives and contacts in the south of France who helped in the distribution of the newspaper *Défense de la France*. She was also able to put her group in touch with Combat and Témoignage Chrétien. After escaping to Algiers, where she was trained, Hélène Roederer was parachuted back into France. Captured carrying a machine gun with a *maquis* group she had joined in June 1944, Roederer was sent to the camps and did not survive deportation.[2]

The Germans also considered Resistance a family affair. Draconian regulations held family members responsible for the activities of a member in the Resistance. In these instances, male relatives could be—and were—shot, while women usually were deported.

Geneviève de Gaulle stresses the solidarity of the de Gaulle clan:

"For our close-knit, patriotic family, the German occupation concerned all of us. We were all more or less in the Resistance. Those who did not leave France to continue the fight distributed anti-German tracts, tore up their posters, and pulled down their swastika flags. My father became a prisoner of war, so I went to Paris to live with one of my aunts in the winter of 1940–1941. She was involved in a Resistance group affiliated with those working out of the Musée de l'Homme. Early on, the group was infiltrated. There were many arrests among the members in November 1941. My aunt was arrested for a short time, then released. But a number of our comrades were arrested and detained."

Because of her name, Geneviève was urged to keep a low profile and not undertake further Resistance activities. But she could not remain inactive while France was occupied, so she joined a small Resistance group that facilitated escape for downed British aviators.

"My activities were those of most young women my age in the Resistance: obtaining and forwarding information; making false identity cards; helping install underground escape routes to Spain. At one point, I carried mail to Spain. While there, I thought seriously about going on to London. Then I said to myself, All things considered, a woman equals a man in clandestine combat. But I was not certain that a woman equaled a man in military combat. So I decided to return to France and continue Resistance work. It seemed to be the most useful thing I could do.

"In Paris I joined Défense de la France, a movement composed mainly of young people like myself, which published an illegal newspaper with that name. The initial format was modest. We printed it on paper acquired with great difficulty on clandestine presses that had to be hidden carefully. My first assignment was to organize the distribution of *Défense* (a perilous task as the press runs increased). I recruited a group of young women to fold the papers and then put them into envelopes, which then were dropped into different mailboxes throughout Paris. Most of these young women might not be perceived as having been 'actively' involved in our movement, yet they certainly contributed to the cause, risking deportation if caught with the papers. While this was the least dangerous way of distributing the paper, it was tedious and costly. Fortunately, we eventually acquired an addressograph, so we no longer had to write out addresses by hand. The group met in my 'office' in the apartment of one of my great-aunts, not far from the church of Saint Sulpice. She was in her eighties and had decided that it would be no great loss if the Germans killed her at her advanced age.

"To mark Bastille Day in 1943, the leaders of Défense de la France decided to print up a larger format than usual. This special edition bore the line 'distributed under the enemy's nose.' We handed out the papers on several Métro lines. Two of us stayed by the doors while the other two gave out the papers as quickly as possible. Then we all jumped off at the next stop. One German officer became livid when he read the contents of the paper I handed him.

"I was also asked to serve as both editorial secretary and member of the committee of editors. I wrote two articles [under the all-too-obvious pseudonym of Gallia] about my uncle, the general, who was still not well known then. This was in 1943. His voice was known from his radio broadcasts, but people did not know what he was like or what milieu he came from. The first article was a short biography [the longest published by any Resistance paper]; the other focused on de Gaulle and French independence. I tried to explain the difficulties de Gaulle had with his allies, his real allies—the British and the Americans."

According to French historian and *résistante* Marie Granet, Geneviève's two articles were very important in informing the public about the general and his goals. De Gaulle was relatively unknown to the French public before his June 18, 1940, call to resist, and even then, few in France actually heard it. He had been promoted temporarily from colonel to brigadier general in the early days of the war and appointed to the Paul Reynaud government. His call to resist came over the BBC from London. Some thought he belonged to Action Française, a reactionary right-wing movement; moreover, had not the Vichy government tried him in absentia and condemned him to death? French citizens were intrigued by the mysterious, distant figure with a name that seemed prophetic—evoking Gaul, the oldest name for France. At the same time, there was the disturbing *de* in his name, which usually indicates an aristocrat. People were concerned about his personal ambitions and his commitment to the French Republic.[3]

"On July 20, 1943, I was arrested at one of our 'mailboxes,' a bookstore on the rue Bonaparte. We had a Gestapo informer in our group—who was French. He joined the group to make money. He was responsible for many arrests. First, I was sent to Fresnes prison. My memories of that prison are still good ones, but the interrogations were difficult. Here I can affirm that the women were treated the same as the men; we were not favored. If the Gestapo wanted some information, beatings, immersion in cold water, whatever they could imagine was used on men or women, women or men. That was not my case; I was only beaten. I did spend many nights standing up, and at one point I was put in a cell with men who had been brutally tortured. Ours was a small group, so they thought they knew everything about our activities. They did not spend a lot of time trying to get information from us. The next edition of our paper appeared right on schedule, which made those of us who were arrested very proud of our group.

"After six months, I was taken to Compiègne [outside Paris], where a section of this large prison was reserved for women. For me, it was an extraordinary discovery. There were women prisoners from all over France. You were in your cell all day by yourself or with a few others. Of course, we communicated as best we could by bang-ing Morse code on pipes or whatever. At Compiègne, there were a thousand women of every age, from every background, every social condition, every political conviction. But remember that members of the Resistance were a minority in France.

"Why did some people decide that the situation under German occupation was untenable and risk their lives and those of their families to participate in the Resistance? In my case, I was a young girl, unmarried. I had only my life to worry about. Obviously, I had a family. One never realizes how much one's family can be impli-cated. Yet I had Resistance comrades who were married and had children, very young children. Why did these men and women say, No, we cannot accept defeat? It is very difficult to explain. Georges Bernanos [the Catholic author] perhaps expressed our response when he said, 'Honor is an instinct, like love.' In one of his speeches from London, de Gaulle cited the moralist Chamfort: 'The reasonable have endured; the passionate have lived.' He went on to explain how those fighting to free France were both rational and ex-alted at the same time. The majority of the French Resistance mem-bers were like that. We had a passionate love for our country. This passion cannot be explained. Accepting the German occupation meant accepting subjugation. Then there was the passion for liberty. Some people knew what the Nazis were like—at least they had some idea of what Nazism represented. One had to resist such tyr-anny, such enslavement. That was the reason why some people did a great deal in the Resistance."[4]

RESIST, Marie Durand scratched into the stone walls of her prison cell. At eighteen, Marie was imprisoned in Aigues-Mortes, on the Mediterranean coast west of Marseilles. For twenty-seven years, from 1732 to 1759, she remained a prisoner because of her Protestant faith. Two hundred years later, members of her family were involved in the French Resistance.

Gabrielle (Cavaillès) Ferrières is a descendant of Marie Durand. Gabrielle's ancestors include a countess, Malan de Merindol, buried alive because she also had refused to repudiate her beliefs. Gabrielle Ferrières followed in that tradition by undertaking liaison during the Occupation, initially for Libération-Sud and then for Cohors, the in-telligence and sabotage network founded by her brother, Jean Cavaillès (1903–1944), a distinguished philosopher and Resistance hero captured, tortured, and executed by the Germans.

Gabrielle Ferrières recounts:

"We three children were born in different places. My father chose a military career. He taught geography in different military schools that trained officers. When he was the youngest lieutenant in France to be promoted to captain, we moved to Toulouse, where we did not attend the local elementary school. Instead, mother taught us every morning. Grandmother lived with us. She had had an eventful past. As a young bride, she accompanied her husband to New Caledonia. While she was there, an uprising occurred. She often stayed alone, surrounded by freed convicts still living on the island, while my grandfather was on missions. When he became ill, she left with him on the first available boat for Europe, even though she was about to give birth. That is how my mother came to be born on an English boat in the middle of the Indian Ocean. Grandfather never recovered his health; he died leaving Grandmother a widow of twenty-eight with four young children. Before he died, he converted to Protestantism—Calvinism—after lengthy reflection.

"About 1911, my own father became very ill as a result of his participation in military maneuvers. Shortly thereafter, my brother Paul, age four, died of typhoid. Those were difficult years indeed, with all the illnesses and deaths. Because Mother spent much of her time nursing father, I became very close to my younger brother, Jean. After his recovery, Father was posted to Bordeaux, where I attended one of the newly instituted secondary schools for girls. Then Father was sent to Paris. I attended classes at the Sorbonne and studied music at the Schola Cantorum. Jean decided to specialize in philosophy—specifically, German philosophy. He came to know, admire, and love German culture. In Paris, he joined a group of students who met to discuss politics and religion as well as philosophy. Father was next transferred to Orléans. [Military men change posts frequently.] In 1926, I became engaged to a military engineer [Marcel Ferrières] and subsequently married him. I continued music studies and my efforts to be somewhat independent. Jean, though, would sometimes criticize me for the vacuousness of my life. He would have liked to discuss his ideas with me, but I was just not up to his intellectual level.

"Mother died in May 1939. Marcel and Jean were both mobilized that summer. After the armistice, Marcel was released; Jean escaped from a prisoner-of-war camp near Anvers [Antwerp], Belgium. Nuns in an orphanage near the camp took him in and provided him with some old clothes and the names of people who could help him. Eventually, Jean made his way to southern France, across the demarcation line. He returned to his unit and had himself officially demobilized. During this time, Father became seriously ill again and died. Jean took me on as his secretary, and in September 1940 the two of us returned to Paris, where I rejoined my husband.

"Jean resumed teaching at the University of Strasbourg, now transferred to the city of Clermont-Ferrand in central France. In January 1941, Lucie Samuel [later Aubrac] came to visit him. They had known one another in Strasbourg. She introduced him to Emmanuel d'Astier de la Vigerie, who was trying to organize a Resistance movement. The three of them met in a brasserie to discuss the project, and that is where the movement Libération-Sud was born. Libération-Sud sought to counteract German propaganda and let the French people know the truth about Vichy. Libération-Sud grew into one of the three major movements in the southern zone.

"At this time, I was trying to start a family. I had just lost a child in dramatic circumstances and my health was not good. Personally, I can state that I did not really choose to join the Resistance. I simply joined my husband and brother in what they were doing. I followed both of them. It was a privilege without restrictions. So, you see, I am not one of those women who chose to become involved in Resistance work. I did not have an exceptional role. I was simply a liaison agent, a courier. My brother was head of a network and my husband directed a Resistance group. Marcel was a graduate of the École Polytechnique, and now he headed a group composed of a network of alumni. These men were part of the infrastructure of the country. They held positions in the national administrations of the railroads, mines, roads, and bridges. Given their various responsibilities, they were able to furnish him with valuable information about troop movements and work on ports, the sort of information I helped collect. In the meantime, Jean had been appointed to the University of Paris. He led the double life of Sorbonne professor and Resistance leader—until he was captured near Narbonne, waiting for the boat taking him to a rendezvous with a submarine that was to transport him to England. He was imprisoned in Montpellier [like Narbonne, in southern France].

"Marcel and I visited him in prison to see what could be done to help him. When my husband had to return to Paris, I stayed on in Montpellier. Through daily visits with Jean, I was able to deliver and exchange messages between him and his Resistance group. Finally, Jean was brought before a military tribunal and acquitted, but the prefect decided to intern him in a camp near Limoges. He described my brother as 'a suspicious individual, dangerous to the safety of the country.' I might note that while much has been written about the horror of German prison camps, little has been said about the shameful conditions in the camps that Vichy set up in France. When Marcel returned south, he brought clothes and provisions and arranged for us to see Jean so we could work out a plan for his escape. After his successful escape, Jean joined us, and the three of us continued our Resistance activities in Paris. My role was to organize meetings in our home and answer a lot of phone calls.

"A stranger—not my brother—answered on that evening of August 28, 1943, when we knocked on the door of a network apartment where we often worked with Jean. I had brought provisions for our dinner. As bad luck would have it, my husband was carrying important material with him. Marcel was in charge of economic information for the network, and Jean had asked to see some documents before they were put into code to be sent on to London. The stranger turned out to be a solitary German guard, who ordered us to sit down. Time dragged on. Our guard agreed to let us heat up the food. I turned on the gas burner and my husband threw the compromising papers into the flames. When the guard realized what we were doing, he became furious. He tried to shoot as he and Marcel struggled. More German police arrived shortly thereafter, and the three of us—Jean, Marcel, and myself—were taken to German headquarters.

"I was kept in solitary confinement at Fresnes prison in Paris for two months. What helped me during this time were the messages, the hours we spent communicating by tapping out Morse code with our soup spoons. Then I was put in a very small cell that already held four other women. That morning, the women had received a food package. I can assure you they were not about to divide it again so that I could have a share. There were no evening meals in prison, so everyone ate what had been sent in packages or saved from other meals. Discreetly, the most miserable-looking woman in the group passed me half her rations. It turned out she had been arrested for prostitution. I was reminded of what the Bible said about the prostitute. That was really a lesson for me. I had led a sheltered, bourgeois life, and here in prison I found that the prostitute was the most generous of the four women in my cell.

"At first I told my German interrogators that I knew nothing about Jean's and Marcel's activities. One of them accused me of telling nothing but lies, adding that Jean had already admitted his Resistance work. I asked why he was asking me those questions if he already knew the facts. He responded, 'You aren't worthy of your men. They, they are courageous, while you are lying to free yourself.' I answered, 'Monsieur, I just lost a baby. There is no one waiting for me outside. The only family I have are my husband and my brother, and they are both here in prison. The freedom you offer means nothing to me. You can keep me as long as you want.' Another time he queried me about my religion and acknowledged that he too was Protestant. 'Our religion teaches us that lying is a sin,' he said, 'and you have done nothing but lie.' 'When the truth is dangerous for others, you must lie,' I replied. Both Michel and Jean had tried to maintain my innocence, while I now acknowledged that I had done everything I could to help them in our Resistance undertakings. You cannot imagine what one feels in moments like that. Whatever it was going to cost me, I took pleasure in telling him that.

"My interrogator asked me to sign the deposition. When I did, he stood up and said to me, 'Madame, you are a true Frenchwoman. Would you shake my hand?' I shook his hand and something happened I will never forget. At that moment, we understood one another, my enemy and I. If only all the German soldiers had been like that. He promised to do all he could to help my husband and brother, but he said that while they would not be shot, they would be sent to a camp that was 'worse than death.'

"One day I was suddenly released, without prior notice. My outfit caused a sensation on the Métro. I was in the same summer dress I had worn to that dinner meeting five months earlier. It was now in shreds. It was winter, and I was wearing once-white sandals on my feet. Instead of a purse or luggage, I carried a bundle. Yet none of the well-dressed women who stared at me could comprehend the joy in my heart. I was still under supervised liberty, though, and had to report to Gestapo headquarters regularly. Without the warmth and generosity of friends, it would have been hard to bear those long months with virtually no news of Marcel or Jean. We did manage to get Jean's dirty laundry to wash and return. There were bloodstains, sometimes hidden messages (rolled in hems). I embroidered virtually invisible Christmas greetings on one of his handkerchiefs.

"After twenty months of captivity, mainly at Buchenwald, my husband returned in the spring of 1945. For weeks we waited anxiously and attempted to find out what had happened to Jean. Finally we learned that he had been executed in early 1944. Presumably one of our agents admitted under torture that the Cohors network was involved in sabotage as well as collection of intelligence. Jean was tried in secret and condemned to death.

"From time to time, I meet with comrades of that period, like 'Rémy' [Gilbert Renault]. We relive those days of Resistance work— so distant yet so close. There were women who worked with us, like 'Raymonde'—too many to mention. Jean called them the 'holy women' (saintes femmes). How different he found them from the Gaullist women he met while in London on a mission. He found those women cliquish, wearing crosses of Lorraine (the symbol of de Gaulle) even on their hats.

"After the war, when de Gaulle formed a government, many reactionary people said, 'Now you see de Gaulle for what he really is. He even brought Communists into his government.' They did not realize it was absolutely necessary for him to incorporate all the political parties into his government. He had to neutralize a country that was armed. Now the present [Socialist] government wants to claim the Resistance heritage.* There were people from every milieu in the Resistance, not just this or that party. I hate sectarianism of any sort."[5]

All four Lesèvre family members—Lise, her husband Georges, and their two sons, Georges and Jean-Pierre—joined the Resistance in common accord. Lesèvre extended her maternal role by helping youth in the maquis. Initially, she helped find locations suitable for maquis encampments. Once the facilities were in place, she met prospective new members at the train station and helped shepherd them to the maquis training school hidden in the mountains. She also served as a

---

*Beginning with the Communists in the immediate postwar period, who styled themselves "the party of those shot [in the Resistance]," the heritage of the Resistance has become a political issue, with various groups claiming to represent the movement.

sort of honorary godmother to maquis youth. Lesèvre viewed her work as normal, given that she was the mother of two adolescents.

Lise Lesèvre was born at the turn of the twentieth century, in a small village near Grenoble. When asked how she joined the Resistance, she said she was not certain that she and others realized that they were "joining" it. The enemy had occupied their country. The immediate reaction was a spontaneous effort of refusal—refusal to accept the German presence on French soil. But how could one fight an enemy equipped with armored vehicles and machine guns? The French had no weapons—all had been destroyed. Nevertheless, little by little, groups of friends decided to do something.

"It was quite disorganized in the beginning, what we were trying to do. We put out tracts to rouse the public, to say to people that some of us did not accept the Occupation. If they did not accept the situation either, we asked them to reflect on the matter. Besides the tracts, we spread propaganda by word of mouth. Then suddenly things became more serious. We could not leave matters there. We had to organize, so we organized quickly, very quickly, and very carefully. Resistance was under way by the end of 1940. In the beginning, we put out clandestine papers, small single sheets—not, to be sure, like what the major papers *Combat*, *Franc-Tireur*, and *Libération* soon became. As German demands increased, we had to react more vigorously, especially toward the end of 1942, when the deportations of workers to Germany (the STO) began.

"The first region we considered was in the Basses-Alpes, near Digne—a little village called Barême. The area was virtually deserted, isolated, even desolate. There were few inhabitants in the scattered villages served by an amusing little local train—a sort of Toonerville trolley—that traversed the valley. At the end of the valley were large, dry, uninhabited plateaus interspersed with gorges and gravel plains. There the first members of the *maquis* from the Lyon area were welcomed. In less than a month, the Lavanderaie camp was born. This camp was very organized and subject to strict discipline. The young men were not there to have fun, and they knew it.

"At about the same time, the Louvre *maquis* was formed. This was a school for *cadres-maquis* set up in the Isère, on the Belledonne Massif. Belledonne is a small village in the northern Alps where we had spent our previous two vacations on a modest property we owned. The villagers supported our project wholeheartedly. The mayor and his colleagues were all with us. They thought as we did—as it was dangerous to think during that terrible period. We had no problem in getting them to accept this *maquis* installation, although it was potentially very dangerous for them to welcome us. The peasants offered us their barns at higher altitudes and provided us with as much food as they could. Little by little, things were organized. Our family's modest vacation house—somewhat outside the village—became the reception center of the *maquis* school. But before they could come, we had to provide false identity cards for our travelers. We also realized they had to arrive no later than June 1943. After that, it would be virtually impossible to leave the cities. So there were group departures, but organized groups. Most of the time, the young men dressed as Boy Scouts and carried camping gear: big pots, covers, and ladles. To be sure, they had false identity cards indispensable for the long train trip with German identity checks.

"Virtually every day during that period, the future *maquisards* arrived either singly or in groups. Occasionally there was the son of a friend, whom I rushed to greet and give my *nom de guerre* so he would not call me by my real name and thus reveal it to the others. The youths usually arrived in the evening, preferably on a regular train. From the station, they would depart for the *maquis* in the mountains. Generally I was at the station to meet them—but very discreetly. Each had to give the name of the person who sent him. For those traveling alone, we had a password that changed daily. We had to be very, very careful. Identities were very complicated. The young men each had three names. The first was their real one, which they were not obliged to reveal. Nevertheless, they usually told me their real one so that I could contact their families if they were injured or arrested. I had to forget their real names and remember them only in an emergency. Then they all had a false identity card with a new name, along with the fictitious names of their supposed father and mother. When I visited the *maquis*, I used to stop someone and ask the names of his parents. This was to make certain they remembered the names on their false identity cards. For all those boys, I think, this exchange of identity was very traumatic, very difficult. I saw some with tears in their eyes when I took their real cards and gave them false ones. Their third name was a nickname—the only one we used in the *maquis*. Many kept their scouting names.* I had rabbits, bunnies, even dragons. There was a Robespierre, plus all the other major figures of the French Revolution. Each one let his imagination go."

Sessions at the school for the *cadres-maquis* lasted twenty days— twenty days of intensive work, of instruction in weapons and combat techniques. They also had physical training as well as civic instruction on the situation of the French Resistance, the meaning of their struggle, the immediate goals, and the problems faced in the future. In Lesèvre's view, things after the war did not turn out as Resistance members envisaged, but, as she notes, that is another story.

From July to October 1943, Lesèvre worked with the reception center for the school of the Louvre *cadres-maquis*, set up in the Isère near Grenoble. Her many responsibilities included reception, liaison, and social services. Working with the young people came naturally, because there were young people at home. Her oldest son was a college student; the other was younger. The young men in the *maquis* needed someone to help them, and she was able to do this work while living at home. After all, she had her own house to take care of. As she put it, one could hardly put a sign on the door proclaiming, HERE, RESISTANCE. Lesèvre had to be careful about the neighbors and continue her normal routine so they would not suspect what she was doing.

"Once I had quite a scare. An important contingent of German soldiers camped not too far from our *maquis*. The postman warned me, so I was able to alert them immediately of the danger. There were always two *maquisards* with me at the reception center we had set up in our family's summer home. I dispatched them immediately to warn their comrades and told them that none of them were to come down from their camp for any reason whatsoever, not even to get food. Normally, you see, some came down to the village each day to get food and supplies.

"That day, it was raining very, very heavily. Suddenly I saw a group of German soldiers in the field, in the barn next to the farmhouse on our property. There were arms in that barn, and not the sort of arms women use, I can assure you—several machine guns, automatic rifles, shotguns. Just the night before, a group from the Se-

---

*Prior to the war, many French youths—both boys and girls—were active in scouting groups sponsored by lay and religious organizations.

cret Army* (which had a *maquis* not far from ours) had asked me if
they could hide some arms and ammunitions for a short time until
they found a better hiding place. No one was living in the farmhouse and the barn was locked, but then those men in green could
have asked for the key or just blown the lock off. That torrential
rain might make them seek shelter, I thought. I was in a state of
terror when I saw that there were only two Germans left near the
house. They were installing a field telephone—which really upset
me. I assumed that if they were installing a telephone, that meant
they planned to stay. I went up and invited them into the house for
a warm drink. They finished their work, telephoned somewhere, and
came into the house. I served them coffee, real coffee. I always separated the good beans from the bad. They drank a generous glass of
eau-de-vie and chatted with me, speaking quite good French. We
talked about the rain and the good weather, which was late in coming that year. After warming themselves by the fire, they went toward their telephone and dismantled it. I watched as they came
back to thank me for my hospitality. That was my only act of collaboration, but I confess I was very, very frightened.

"At the end of September [1943], after the Germans took over
the Italian zone, the Périclès Service regrouped its national *maquis*
schools in the Jura region. The *maquis* were ordered to change locations. In spite of the difficulties entailed in such an operation, the
maquisards reached the Jura in small groups. Things were much
calmer there, because it is next to Switzerland. In case of catastrophe, one might just make it over the border. The Périclès *maquis*
had few arms, not even enough for practice, so they used broom-
sticks. Later, this *maquis* joined others in fighting the German attacks of April 1944. Still later, they helped the French Army liberate our territory and went on to fight in the German campaign.
That was very important, very important. . . . We thought that the
maquis would help but we never imagined they would help liberate
our country."

When the *maquis* were transferred to the Jura region, Lesèvre returned to Lyon, where she headed both the social services and the
escape sections of the *maquis* schools. It was a major undertaking, but

---

*The Secret Army (AS) was formed by combined Resistance groups inside
France. It joined France Combattante and Allied forces when they landed in France.

she was aided by some remarkable women. She planned escapes for *maquis* members who had been wounded and taken to hospitals or prisons. This was possible when they were in the hands of the French, for doctors and nurses helped. Network members needed inside co-operation. One of Lesèvre's helpers was a very young woman who could circulate freely. Another was her younger son, Jean-Pierre, then fifteen. He still wore short pants and went about unhindered. No one suspected him.

"I was captured at the Lyon train station on March 13, 1944, while on a mission. Every Monday evening, I carried our group's mail to the station. That afternoon, when I left the house to return to the station, I said good-bye to my husband and youngest son. My heart pounded when I shut the door. That door separated them from me forever. Only years later was I able to analyze my reactions to my premonition that afternoon. I was arrested with a group of travelers I did not know, with the exception of a young man who was head of the attack group. He never returned from deportation. I was sup-posed to introduce him to other members of our group. We were preparing an attack on a German center a few days later. Destroying the German center was very important—and very dangerous. This would stop SS repression in the entire area. Georges, my oldest, was scheduled to participate. He urged me to be careful when I accom-panied him to his train shortly before my arrest. [That attack never took place because the German contingent moved.] I was carrying the plans for the attack, but the Germans never knew it. They were the plans for our vacation house, I explained, and since the Ger-mans who arrested me were not architects, they never knew I had the attack plans. Now it so happened that before my arrest, I had been able to deliver the mail from our group, but I still had some mail I had been given addressed to 'Didier.' This correspondence turned out to be very compromising, because the Germans were looking for someone named 'Didier' who was the head of the Secret Army in the southeast area. For days I was questioned as 'Didier'—until they were convinced I was not 'Didier.' Then they wanted me to reveal where 'Didier' was.

"I did not know who this 'Didier' was, but I did know a liaison agent named 'Didier.' Of course, I could not betray him, because he knew so many things. This was in 1944, and affairs were going badly. There had been arrests among our members. We were meet-

ing then in the home of a spinster who let me use her apartment.
She insisted, however, that she did not want any liaison agents in
her place, so she asked me to serve as liaison agent for the other
group and carry their mail. Her ninety-two-year-old mother lived
with her, and she could not risk being arrested. So, because of the
mail I was carrying, the Germans took me for 'Didier,' one of the
leaders of the Secret Army. That was very, very grave. Since women
in the Resistance often had masculine names [and men had women's
names], they thought I was 'Didier,' a leader with the Secret Army!

" 'I have little to tell you,' I said to my interrogators. 'I am not
Didier. The documents you have belong to a friend, Louis Guérin,
who was to arrive on Monday evening.' I came up with the name
Louis Guérin because that was the name of the street across from
our home. After the war, I learned there *was* a Louis Guérin in the
Resistance! 'Perhaps they are important documents, but I don't
know what they are. Louis asked me to hold them for safekeeping
while he found a room. What I do not understand is why you have
arrested my husband and younger son. The fact that you arrested
them in our home proves their innocence. If they were guilty of
something, they would have fled.' In reality, both of them thought I
was in Paris. When I did not return, my husband and son left, then
returned, thinking I had been sent on an urgent mission. They
made two packages of the archives of the Périclès network—the history of the network from the beginning—which my husband had
hidden. Unfortunately, the neighbors with whom they were to hide
were not home. The Gestapo found them with all those documents.
For several days, during brutal interrogations and tortures, I took
comfort in the belief that they had been warned and escaped. Then
one day, when I had been returned to my cell, my husband and son
passed by, handcuffed. They smiled, and silently we mouthed, 'courage.' The horror of that moment when I saw them in chains haunts
me still."

Lesèvre describes her reaction when the first lies came tumbling
out during her interrogation:

"I saw myself on the school bench, a very young girl. I heard the
teacher telling us that lying is the most vile of defects, an unspeaka-
bly base act. Nevertheless, there are two serious situations where lying is permitted: at someone's deathbed and to the enemy.

"I kept notes about my arrest all through the deportation period. My son Georges keeps telling me I should write them up some day, because I am the only one who knows what happened. Looking over these notes, I found some extraordinary things. For example, during a questioning period a German spoke to me kindly—not the case with Barbie—and tried to reason with me. He told me how much he admired my courage. I interrupted him and asked him if what he took for courage might not simply be total ignorance, which could have been true. 'Your attitude doesn't fool anyone,' he replied. 'If you were truly innocent of what you are accused of, you would be much more frightened.' His questioning was not like that of Klaus Barbie. Barbie was not a questioner. He was a torturer; he was so busy beating you he forgot his questions, that vile beast. Anyhow, when they found that letter with the name 'Didier' on it, they were enraged. It must have been very important, although they never let me read it.

"May 4, 1944, I was taken from Montluc prison for trial. On the way, I noticed the flowers, the flowered dresses, the children. It was spring. We prisoners were invisible to those living free. No one seemed to notice the truck carrying us surrounded by guards with machine guns. The trial was grotesque, all in German. Only the verdict was in French. 'Terrorist acts against the Greater Reich. Condemned to death.' A German officer came and told me he would try to 'do something' for me. He expressed admiration for my courage and wished that more German women were like me. I can't remember his name; I have forgotten so many names from that period. I spent the night in a cell, reserved for those condemned to death, with a big French-Canadian. We spent the night laughing over stories about the Germans. He was executed the next morning, while I spent long days awaiting my turn. Instead, Barbie resumed his tortures, including the 'bathtub.'* Once they told me of a 'tragic' event. They said Georges, my oldest, had been arrested and executed. 'Marcel?' I asked in a faint voice. 'Yes, Marcel.' [Since it was not his name, she knew it was a lie.]

"After nineteen days of torture, a German doctor came to check the damage. He was particularly scandalized by the outlines of a boot on my abdomen. My back was an immense wound. Because I

---

*A form of torture in which victims' heads were repeatedly submerged into a bathtub filled with water.

was a serious case, I was put in the nurse's room for a few days. Actually, she was not a nurse at all, but a prostitute. The head of the prison came to see me. He did not appear pleased with the 'work' of his men.

"When I was more or less recovered, I was sent to the fort of Romainville (now a prison), on the outskirts of Paris, in a seventeen-car train of deportees from Lyon. Aboard, I managed to speak to Jean-Pierre briefly for what turned out to be the last time. After the war, I learned that Barbie had tortured my sixteen-year-old son. [Jean-Pierre—who dreamed of becoming a sailor—escaped being sent to Bergen-Belsen for extermination with friends' help, only to be tragically killed when his and several other ships holding many thousands of prisoners at anchor in Lübeck were bombed by the British.] Eventually I was deported to Neuenbremme, an atrocious camp where we were forced to watch others killed in an infernal Grand-Guignol spectacle [a reference to a popular horror show]. Then I was sent to Ravensbrück and later assigned to a work brigade, in a munitions factory. That was a mistake to have deportees work in munitions factories, I can assure you. We sabotaged much of the material. Those shells certainly could not have killed many of our men.

"We came back from deportation, but little was done to help us reintegrate into society. We were oddities, so we were not given much medical treatment; not much attention was paid to us. I went back to work two months after my return from deportation, for I had to earn my living. My older son had not yet completed his studies. My husband and younger son never came back. I helped dismantle our network, which entailed working with my comrades. I also helped take care of those children whose parents never returned from the camps. There were not many such children in our Resistance group, because they were mainly adolescents. Nevertheless, a few had married. I held out for eighteen months. Then I fell seriously ill. During the interrogation sessions with 'dear' Barbie, several of my vertebrae had been broken. After eighteen months, I fell. I could no longer walk. I spent two years in a hospital without ever putting my feet on the ground. They tried a bone transplant, but it did not take. My bones were in very bad shape. So they made an iron corset, which lets me walk, although with difficulty."

In the camps, Lesèvre continued her maternal role. She recounts in her "nightmare-memoirs" how she and several companions at Ravensbrück decided to prepare a snack for eight Polish Jewish children—sole survivors of a massacre—who had just been brought to the camp. From their own meager rations of bread and margarine and their weekly teaspoon of jam, the women made tarts. A piece of white paper obtained through bargaining was carefully torn to resemble lace and put over a bed plank. Lesèvre carried the "tray" of tarts, accompanied by a French woman of Polish origin to serve as interpreter. The oldest of the children was eight. On seeing Lesèvre, she broke into tears, sobbing and embracing her. The child explained that her own mother—who died in Auschwitz—used to appear in the garden on Sundays carrying a tray of tarts. The following Sunday, that young girl and the other Polish children were taken away to be killed. How were those monsters going to pay for all they had done? Lesèvre asked herself. She befriended and adopted younger women in the camp. On April 14, 1945, she was among a column of prisoners ordered to leave Ravensbrück and march, wearing wooden clogs, thirty-five miles in twenty-seven hours—on the *first* leg of the journey. The group was too large for the Germans to oversee adequately. Lesèvre managed to escape with Norante and Célia, her two "daughters," as she refers to them.

"They taught us to hate—we, the mothers who saw so many little innocents leave for their deaths. I vowed never to return to the land of the Barbarians. I was obsessed with making those monsters pay. Shortly after leaving the camps, I told a confessor that I wished our torturers the terrible punishment they merited. I fully realized that saying this would prevent the priest from giving me absolution. After some hesitation, he decided to give me absolution after all. 'The Good Lord will arrange it,' he reasoned. Upon my return, I had to learn how *not* to hate—that atrocious sentiment that they taught us there—in spite of ourselves.

"Those of us in the Resistance did all we could for France. Envisioned from a camp like Ravensbrück, France was so beautiful. When you see things from afar, they are always more beautiful than up close. Those of us who returned have had our share of deceptions, quite a number of deceptions. And I was angry with the Americans for saving Barbie when the French were ready to arrest him. Of course, he was very useful to the Americans for intelligence. Those of us who returned need to let the world know what happened during those dark days. I am eighty-two now. We who survived the camps have remained very, very close. Even if there are a few who are somewhat 'difficult,' you overlook that. We all share something that you cannot communicate to those who did not know it, who did not experience it. There is a solidarity between us—an unbreakable solidarity."[6]

6

━━━━

Young and Alone

How many girls my age—sometimes even younger—found themselves suddenly alone and having to make a decision that included what role they were going to play in the struggle, and how they were going to live. . . . One needs to remember above all that the solitude of the time had a different dimension. It was that of a child lost beyond the paths traced by adults. Today the generation gap is still referred to, but the gap was much wider and deeper then.

—Célia Bertin, résistante[1]

IN PREWAR FRANCE, GIRLS AND YOUNG WOMEN WERE GENERALLY NOT granted much independence. They could not leave for destinations unknown, to sleep they knew not where, for an undetermined length of time. However, in wartime France—with many families separated because the father was a POW or perhaps in hiding, and young girls obliged to take jobs earlier than usual because of pressing financial needs—the traditional social conventions no longer prevailed. Now young women often were accorded freedom that would have been unacceptable prior to the war.

But the freedom that some acquired through Resistance activity during the war years had its price, as Denise (Jacob) Vernay discovered. One of the many liaison agents who operated on their own,

Vernay is the sister of Simone Veil, twice a French minister and the first president of the European Parliament. Although Jewish, the Jacob family (which also included sister Madeleine and brother Jean) was not religious. Their father was a prizewinning architect whose political orientation was center right, while their mother leaned more toward the Popular Front. In 1925, their father moved from Paris to Nice to find more work. Although the Italians occupied that area early in the war, he was stymied by the increasing anti-Jewish restrictions.*

Both Denise and Simone Jacob joined the girls' secular scouting movement, the *Éclaireuses*, rather than the Jewish scouting movement. For Denise—as for other young women in the Resistance—Scout training was to prove extremely useful. Oldest of three sisters, Denise decided to go to Lyon to join the Resistance. She was able to do so thanks to one of her scouting leaders, who arranged for an interview with a movement member. In 1943, nineteen-year-old Denise was engaged as a liaison agent by the Franc-Tireur movement. The young woman assumed many pseudonyms and frequently changed addresses. She spent a long period on her own, in a city she did not know.

"You cannot imagine how much you must develop your memory when you become a liaison agent. To begin with, you have to change your identity all the time. That means different names, different addresses, different false identity cards. If stopped and questioned, you have to remember all the details of your current identity. Beyond that, there are the many messages you have to deliver. You have to commit all these to memory. It was too dangerous to have anything written down. [This policy was ignored at times, with tragic consequences.] I had to memorize the plan of the city of Lyon—a city I did not know before—along with all the names of the streets, the bridges, the districts, and other relevant details. With some agents, I had daily appointments; with others, it was every week or every month. To remember this program and the messages you transmitted, you really had to use your memory. I developed mine by memorizing poems. Like many things, it is a question of practice.

---

*In the face of continuing German anger, the Italians remained much more liberal in their treatment of the Jews living in the area under their control. The situation changed abruptly when the Germans took over in September 1943 with the sudden breakup of the Axis partnership.

"One of the most difficult aspects of my work was the solitude. I was alone in a strange city. I could not have any contact with family or friends. From early fall 1943 until late spring of the following year, I spent each day doing liaison in Lyon. Because I am blonde, I was often taken for German. That certainly helped me. Then I was advised to leave the city and change identity again. There had been a series of arrests, and I was becoming a suspicious figure to the Germans. I also learned that my family had been arrested in Nice, in what had been the Italian zone, and I felt the urge to engage in military action."

The Jacobs, along with their son, Jean, and daughters Madeleine and Simone, were arrested as Jews in 1944 and deported to a series of camps. The parents and their son did not return. Only Denise, who was deported later for Resistance work, and her two sisters survived.

+>=—=<+

When the Allies landed in Normandy in June 1944, the *maquis* for which Denise Vernay did liaison joined the fight as previously planned. The British parachuted agents and supplies to them. For some unknown reason, two radio transmitters landed more than a hundred miles from their intended destination and had been recovered by other *maquis* members. A liaison agent was needed to retrieve the transmitters. Denise Vernay volunteered for the mission and left Annecy (northeast of Lyon, in the Alps) with nothing but her bicycle and a suitcase she purchased to hold the transmitters. A helpful railway worker hid her and her bike in the baggage car for the trip to Aix-les-Bains. The next morning, she set off by bike for Mâcon to recover the transmitters. To avoid the police blockades and bombed-out roads, Vernay sometimes carried her bike across the fields in this hilly region. Her bike was in poor shape after covering so many miles: The tires looked like patchwork quilts. At times she hitchhiked. Once she let a motorcyclist pull her, but then she could not pedal fast enough. After further vicissitudes, Denise finally arrived at the town near the Saône-et-Loire *maquis* with the transmitters—only to find that the Germans had been there first, shooting and destroying in their wake. As it turned out, the transmitters had been sent to another *maquis*. Eventually she found a peasant family willing to take her to the *maquis* with the transmitters.

"With a borrowed bicycle (mine had given up the ghost), I set out with the two transmitters. There was enough equipment to fill four suitcases, all of it stamped 'Made in England'! Because of their weight, I ended up finding a gasogène-taxi [one using wood as fuel] in Mâcon to drive me to Lyon. They were just too heavy to transport by bike. This was still difficult and dangerous, and I initially told the driver I was going to pick up some books an aunt had left me. In Mâcon I stayed in an *hôtel de passe* [house of ill repute]. At least you did not have to fill out registration forms there. Finally we got to Lyon, but again I could not find a truck to take me back to Annecy, so I persuaded another taxi driver to take me to Aix-les-Bains, where a railroad crew could take them [the transmitters] the rest of the way. Just out of Lyon, we were stopped by a German roadblock and taken to Gestapo headquarters. My taxi driver did all he could to help the Germans. He even tried to hit me to show that he had not chosen to work for the Resistance, as I had. He blamed me for his arrest. I was forced to strip for the *baignoire* [bathtub] torture. I was determined not to speak; I remained silent. After more torture, they sent me on the deportation route, just forty days before the liberation of Paris. I ended up in Neuenbremme and Ravensbrück."[2]

Young women did not necessarily have to be alone to feel lonely. The theme of solitude—between hope and fear—was brought up in an interview with Célia Bertin and becomes the leitmotiv in her memoirs. Even before the war began, Bertin, a Parisian studying literature, felt isolated, different from her friends. Her beloved father, who sang patriotic songs to her when she was a child, was succumbing to depression, and relations with her mother were not good. She sought refuge in reading—until the unexpected opportunity arose to join the Resistance. The future novelist and biographer was asked to join a network in the early days of the Occupation because she knew English and could work with British intelligence agents.

"I was preparing a graduate degree in English, at the Sorbonne. I wanted to be a writer. I was very much an Anglophile and engaged to an Englishman. I was also something of a black sheep in my reactionary bourgeois family. I had Communist friends; the doctrine interested me. What I could not stand was Fascism. The Occupation was difficult to accept. By chance, Pierre de Lescure, a novelist and the father of Monique—a classmate of mine at the Sorbonne— asked his daughter if she knew someone who spoke English well. He claimed he wanted to take English lessons to 'forget' the Occupation. Actually, what he wanted was someone to help him and a small group that had formed a network to work with the British Intelligence Service (IS). Monique gave him my name.

"So Pierre de Lescure contacted me and invited me to tea at the Café de Flore. That impressed me. It was really marvelous. The Flore was frequented by writers and people from the theater and cinema, whom Pierre knew. We met several times. He asked about my reactions to the situation in France, and when he learned how I felt, he asked me to join his group.

"Naturally, I was ready and eager to help. This was in 1940. I started to do what young girls my age who had been asked to help were doing: delivering packages, carrying documents and sometimes radio transmitters. One day, I came upon a security check when leaving the Métro. I was carrying a radio transmitter in a travel bag. The Gestapo agents were searching everyone and making the men put their hands up. Inwardly terrified, I smiled at the soldier—the first and only time I smiled at a Nazi—and, struggling with my bag, I looked as if I had trouble opening the zipper. He smiled back and let me go.

"I often accompanied British agents from one location to another. That was not easy. We could not talk in public because their French was nonexistent or heavily accented. And we were posing as good friends, walking arm in arm."

In spite of the fear that tormented her, Bertin reasoned that, alone on the street or in the Métro, with her nearsighted vision and her elegant hats and high heels, no one would suspect her of being a "terrorist." Her assignments included accompanying IS radio operators to safe lodgings, where they could transmit messages. At times she carried mail—with her school notebooks—or took clean clothes and food to the IS agents. They were restricted to their quarters, but she wondered whether they always obeyed. Pierre de Lescure encouraged her to continue doing the "normal" things that young people did— attending tea dances, spending evenings at clubs—but Bertin went out less and less, preferring to focus on her Resistance work and her studies. At Lescure's insistence, for security reasons, she did not participate in the student demonstration of November 11, 1940, although she very much wanted to do so. At times, she felt overwhelmed by helplessness. Resistance work helped conquer that feeling. In the course of her assignments, Bertin kept appointments at many apartments that seemed more or less indistinguishable. At each place, she had to cope with the unknown. What would she find when she turned the key and opened the door? Who might be there? Reflecting on the period, Bertin wonders how people managed to live through that climate of growing fear, racism, shame, and hatred; it was a time when all human relations were extremely difficult.

"During this period, Pierre and Vercors founded Éditions de Minuit. . . . Once I went to the Basque country to help agents trying to cross over to Spain because they had to leave France. No, I did not hesitate, in spite of the dangers. There were dangers, but once you have made a choice, you are committed. Obviously, like others doing Resistance work, I was afraid of what I would do if I were captured and tortured. For that reason, I wanted to know as little as possible.

"Then, in June 1943, I had to leave Paris because of some disquieting incidents. Earlier, two Frenchmen in civilian clothing had come to my parents' apartment asking for me. They passed me in the stairway. The maid told them I was not there. She realized that there was something strange going on and did not tell them I had just left. But she did tell my mother about it, and my mother went to the district police commissioner and asked him why two men had come for her daughter. The commissioner advised her that I should leave home, and I did. I lived with various friends for several months.

"When I left Paris, I went to a small town in the Jura region [near the Swiss border], where a young woman of our group—whose real name I never found out—knew the mayor, a former forest ranger who was a Pétainist. She told him that the three of us [including Pierre de Lescure] wanted to spend our vacation in that region. Unfortunately, she was arrested in a train station, so Pierre and I went to the cabin of this ranger, whom I called 'Vladimir.'

"Leaving Paris, I was frightened because train stations were closely watched, so I had my shoulder-length dark-brown hair dyed and cut. Still, I was afraid I did not look different enough.

"We stayed hidden in the Jura for several months. To avoid suspicion, we went to another town to get most supplies, so that our false papers would not be questioned. Nevertheless, the baker, the postmistress, and the carpenter knew we were not 'ordinary' folk. From time to time, the baker gave me bread without the required ration coupons. During this time, I wrote the first draft of my first novel."

This enforced stay was complicated by Lescure's poor health. But it gave Bertin the time and solitude to write, something she had always wanted to do. Lescure's critical commentary was invaluable. At his suggestion, she learned to type on his portable Royal. Unlike the preceding years in Paris, and for the first time during the Occupation, Bertin was without anguish and fear, although she often still felt lonely, in spite of Lescure's presence. That interlude of calm, however, did not last long. When the Allies landed and advanced across France, the Germans retreated eastward. She and Lescure were ordered to leave. Rather than go to Switzerland, they chose to join the local *maquis*, run by the Communists: "I was a woman alone among all those men and I was treated as an equal. We were simply comrades . . . or so I thought."[3]

Later, after the region was liberated, she felt that some of her comrades resented her bourgeois origins. But, as she insists, they did not realize that she had not fought in the Resistance for four years in order to save the French bourgeoisie.[4]

Danielle Mitterrand, wife of France's former president, was one of the youngest women to receive the Medal of the Resistance. The experience had a profound impact on her life, for it was through the Resistance that she met her husband—one of a number of couples who probably never would have met but for those exceptional times. Her background was modest. France's national public-education system, the pride of the Third Republic, enabled both her parents to become teachers, to commit their professional lives to their republican ideals, and to extend the opportunities they received to others.

"My father was fired from his teaching position because he would not give authorities the names of students who had foreign names.

Fortunately, we owned a small property in the countryside near Cluny. Renting part of the house brought in a little income. We worked the garden and raised rabbits and chickens. My father did not want to have anything to do with the black market. Since I was then a student in the school where my father taught, I left when he did, but that created problems. Education was sacred to my parents. They were very concerned about my schooling, so they sent me to a boarding school in Annecy. I was not happy there, either. I really wanted to be with my parents. My parents brought me home and my father took charge of my schooling. He and his friends helped me with my studies."

Starting in March 1943, another "teacher" helped Danielle with her lessons from time to time. Monsieur "Tavernier" was in reality Henri Frenay, who rented lodgings from the Gouze family. In his memoirs, he notes that helping seventeen-year-old Danielle with her homework—particularly her philosophy lessons—was true relaxation from his responsibilities as head of the Combat movement. Furthermore, her parents impressed him. Soon he took them into his confidence and into his movement. Given his strict Catholic upbringing, Frenay notes his surprise in finding in this Freemason "an idealist of high moral value, undoubtedly without church affiliation, but authentically religious." Often his "secretary," "Mme Moulin"—Berty Albrecht—joined him. Berty's daughter, Mireille, was Danielle's age. Young Danielle was fascinated by the indomitable woman who seconded Frenay in the movement. Berty's commitment was such that she went to her last rendezvous at Mâcon because Frenay—who had been scheduled to go—had been ordered to London. She had a fatal, unfortunately accurate, premonition about the Mâcon meeting and gave young Danielle a gold brooch as a souvenir, "in case she did not return."

"My parents sheltered members of Combat. A friend of my brother Roger sent Frenay to us. Claude Bourdet and other Combat leaders stayed with us at different times. When Frenay was with us, he worked in a small gardener's hut out in the fields. I brought him lunch, and often documents and papers. Was it dangerous? This was a modest act. But every act implies acceptance or refusal. What I was doing was helping to defend my country's values. My parents never felt it necessary to discuss the risks of sheltering those pursued by the Germans. All our family actions were the natural result of the republican principles we held.

"One day, there were loud knocks on the door. When I opened it, I was pushed against a console as Gestapo men rushed in, looking for Frenay. They were surprised when my father answered them in German. My mother was in the kitchen cooking. When she realized Germans had come, she dropped incriminating papers into the cooking pot before they went into the kitchen. The German soldiers ordered her to take them to our rental apartment. It turned out that they found our address on a letter from her daughter that Berty still had with her when she was arrested. While they were searching the other place, my father happened to glance at the sheet music on the piano. Mixed in with the sheet music were the stencils my mother was typing for the next issue of *Combat*. He hid them and we covered over the typewriter. This was what might be called an automatic reflex. As it turned out, the Germans were so obsessed with finding Frenay that they did not pay that much attention to us. They didn't even leave a guard with us.[5]

"Unfortunately, they found Frenay's and Berty's things in the apartment, so they started to question my mother. One of them held a gun to her neck and threatened her. They slapped and mistreated her. My parents were very courageous. In their separate interrogations, they maintained that they were innocent landlords who were unaware of their renters' true identity. They claimed they thought the couple were a businessman and his secretary: quiet, well-behaved people who did a lot of writing and so forth. My parents had worked out this alibi in advance with Frenay and Berty in the event the Germans came. Still, the Germans were brutal with my mother, although they did not torture her. They paid no attention to me, so I slipped out and was able to warn others that my parents were about to be arrested.

"Recently I was asked to identify some of the German soldiers involved in that raid. This is impossible. The shock, the chaos was such that I have no precise, accurate recollections. Time is also a factor. I cannot even recall whether they wore uniforms or not. In the end, my parents were not arrested, as the Germans wanted to set a trap for Frenay. Not too long afterward [February 14, 1944], we noticed German troops had encircled Cluny. They were rounding up people. We wrapped a few necessities in a bundle and waited for them to come. But they never came."

Danielle Mitterrand's older sister went to Paris to pursue a career in the cinema. Asked to help Resistance members, she made her apartment available to the heads of the National Movement of POWs. At the first meeting in her apartment in March 1944, the head of the movement, "Morland" (François Mitterrand), noticed a picture of Danielle. Finding out who she was, he declared, "She is ravishing. I am going to marry her." After their introduction, marriage seemed most unlikely. Teenaged Danielle found the somewhat older Mitterrand already a man, different from her male comrades. However, a brief visit he paid to her at the family home overcame her reticence. The *petite fiancée* decided to marry on her twentieth birthday—which she did. But before that, she worked with a *maquis* while François Mitterrand continued his clandestine work. He visited her from time to time, but there were long periods of separation. The Gestapo confiscated some pictures—including one of the couple—when they raided one of Mitterrand's hideouts. Fearing for her life, he sent a comrade to warn her. Danielle interrupted her final exams for the *bac* (*baccalauréat*, the school-finishing degree at the end of the secondary studies required for university entrance) in Lyon and made her way back to Burgundy, where she went into hiding.

"The Germans evacuated Cluny as the Allies advanced. The *maquis* stationed themselves on the surrounding ridges. There was a pass at Boisclair that overlooked the route from Lyon to the Atlantic. Our *maquis* fighters would harass the German convoys from above. The Germans responded once with a bloody attack. Among the wounded was the son of the butcher. He needed to be rescued, but there was no one free to get to him. So he died a slow, agonizing, terrible death. He had been shot through the eye. When I heard of this incident, I volunteered to rescue the wounded after skirmishes. That is not a job for a young girl, I was told. But I was asked to nurse in one of the field hospitals the *maquis* set up. Why did I accept? I had not thought about it before. I just did what had to be done, what the circumstances required. You could not do otherwise.

"Originally our wounded *maquis* fighters were taken to a hospital run by nuns. The sisters were very brave. Then they had to stop caring for our wounded because the Germans threatened them. Regretfully, the nuns realized that it would be dangerous for their other patients if they continued to treat the *maquis* wounded. So we set up our own medical services.

"My friend Simone (my brother's sister-in-law) and I worked under Doctor Mazuez. We set up our hospital in a vacant château. *Maquis* members wanted us to learn how to handle arms to protect ourselves; I refused. At the very least, they wanted to give us grenades so we could alert the *maquis* in case of danger. But I refused the grenade for reasons I can't explain. Perhaps I'm 'allergic' to weapons. Then François sent for me. It was getting very dangerous, and he was worried about me. So I biked to Dijon with the escort he sent. I worked with the movement of escaped war prisoners that he headed. This group was not a *maquis;* it was a Resistance movement. While working for them, I insisted upon knowing as little as possible about their work. There are things one should not know."

A month later, Paris was liberated. But for some time, Danielle had no news of her family or her fiancé. Then Mitterrand appeared in Dijon as the city was being liberated. During their brief reunion, the couple decided to wed on October 28, 1944, the eve of her twentieth birthday. After the war, in addition to raising a family, Danielle Mitterrand worked for various humanitarian organizations. When her husband was elected president in 1981, she wanted to avoid any potential conflict of interest, so she founded her own association, France-Libertés. "My concerns since the war continue my Resistance work— defending universal values."[6]

+———+

Another young *résistante* was noted historian and professor Annie Kriegel, who joined an organized group when she was only fifteen. Through chance, she ended up in a Communist group and became a dedicated member of the party—until 1956. Kriegel brought to the Resistance a commitment to the values she was taught in a close-knit family.

"My family was traditionally of the Left. My great-grandparents were Jews from Alsace and Lorraine who left when that region was annexed by Germany after the Franco-Prussian War of 1870. My grandfather was secretary-general of the Socialist Party in the early part of this century, although I never knew him, because he died young. That is the reason my father became an orphan at ten and responsible for his family. He swore to his mother that he would not get involved in politics, that he would take care of her and his sisters. He was called up in World War I. Five years later, he returned, married, and devoted himself to his family and his work. Our family was modest, liberal, and open. Although not religious, we acknowledged ourselves as Jews. We did not observe the Sabbath or the High Holy Days. Education was a major concern. Unlike many others of that time, my mother insisted that the girls have the same education as the boys—and the same treatment. It was Mother who taught us everything: reading, writing, piano, even swimming. She had wanted to become a teacher, but her parents would not let her. I was the second child and oldest daughter, born in 1926.

"Today it is difficult to imagine a family like that. Many subjects were never discussed. Naturally, sexual matters were never mentioned. Nor were money problems mentioned. Mother took us to museums and encouraged us to read. When asked what I did in my youth, I can only answer, Read, read, read. I borrowed all the books I devoured from a prodigious, free municipal library just a few hundred yards from our home. This was in the Marais district, then the quarter of the poor and immigrant Jews, somewhat like [the Lower East Side of] New York at the end of the nineteenth century. After school, we played in the Place des Vosges, now a famed tourist site. I loved school and worked with all my heart. Greek and Latin were among my passions. Each day brought new discoveries and attractions. With school and the family—which included many relatives—I had a rich, happy childhood.

"My first political shock came in 1934, when I was just eight. I have never forgotten it. My mother was with a group of mothers waiting for their children outside school. They were crying as they listened to a dirty, unshaven man. I came over and learned he was a newly arrived German Jew. He was telling everyone about the situation in Germany. Two years later, there was the Popular Front. It was my task to go each morning and buy L'Oeuvre, the radical Socialist daily. I used to scan the news hurriedly as I brought it home.

"When war was declared, my father was mobilized again. Parisian children and young people were urged to remain in the countryside. So we stayed on that winter in Cayeux, a small beach resort on the English Channel coast where we spent vacations. They set up a temporary lycée [high school] in the village for the schoolchildren from Paris. Father joined us with the exodus and we all moved on. We went to Saint-Nazaire, because my father wanted to go to

England and eventually to the United States. He found places on
the last boat leaving. We loaded our baggage and were to return for
a night departure. In the interim, the harbor of Saint-Nazaire was
bombed, our boat was damaged, and our baggage was lost. And that
is why we spent the war years in France.

"At this time, the major event of my adolescence occurred:
That was the night Marshal Pétain announced that he was seeking
an armistice. Our family was grouped around the radio in the villa
we had rented near Saint-Nazaire, listening to Pétain. For the first
time in my life, I saw my father cry. When we asked him why he
was crying, he answered, 'My children, France is defeated.' He
stopped for a moment and then added, 'And, my children, we are
Jews.' The priority of his preoccupations was very significant. Coming from a line of Jews from Alsace-Lorraine, he was a fervent, in-
transigent patriot. He saw himself first as a Frenchman, a veteran
who had been decorated with the croix de guerre and the military
medal. He was a devoted father, always concerned about paying his
taxes on time, always anxious to show that he was a law-abiding citizen. His first concern was for France. His second concern, inevitably, was the realization that from then on, he had a new burden—
that of dealing with a situation where from henceforth his principal
identity would be that of a Jew.

"Since it had been impossible to leave the country, my father
decided we would return to Paris. So we returned and resumed life
in occupied Paris, a Paris that still appeared relatively normal. Starting in October 1940, however, the Vichy government in the unoccupied zone and the Nazis in the occupied zone (where we were)
decided to undertake a census of all Jews. All Jews had to register.
We never considered *not* obeying. Since my father was profoundly
conscious of the rights and obligations of a French citizen, he would
never have thought of disobeying the law. For that matter, everyone
knew we were Jewish. We lived in a building constructed in the
1930s for large families. Christian and Jewish families coexisted
without problems, even though we knew each others' backgrounds.
So we registered. Moreover, I do not recall any group, not a single
organization, that warned Jews *not* to register. Then the vise gradually tightened. The first stage was the roundup of a thousand prominent Jews in December 1941. One of my uncles was in that group.
He and most of the others never returned from deportation. That
roundup proved conclusively that Nazis were going to destroy the

Jews, whatever their origin. Until then—not to their credit or fore-
sightedness, it must be said—French Jews thought they would be
treated differently from foreign Jews. That day, they realized that
they shared a common destiny. This important lesson influenced the
French Jewish community in the postwar years. They realized that
they shared a common destiny whatever their background. That explains, I believe, the warm, generous welcome extended to the Jews
from France's former colonies."

Life became progressively more difficult for the Kriegel family. In
the spring of 1942 (after the January decision at the Wannsee conference to begin the Final Solution), far-reaching administrative measures were promulgated against the Jews. They could not leave their
homes between 8 P.M. and 6 A.M.; they could no longer use public
parks and gardens; they could not frequent public places such as cafés,
cinemas, restaurants, and libraries. They had to turn in bicycles and
radios; telephone service was cut off. Jews could shop for food only in
the late morning, when stores had little left, and for other items in
the late afternoon, again when stocks were depleted. After her uncle's
arrest, Kriegel's father decided not to sleep in their home. Until the
family left Paris, he spent nights in the home of the family's household
helper, narrowly escaping arrest when the concierge told the police—
who were checking identifications in the building—that no one was
home. To complicate the family's troubles, he felt obliged, because of
the tensions his presence as a Jew caused, to leave his job of twenty
years as representative for a Parisian toy firm. Now he no longer received a salary. So he decided that, while continuing preparation for
the *bac*, his oldest daughter would attend secretarial school in order
to earn a living. He chose her, rather than her older brother, because—
until that time at least—only Jewish males had been arrested. Now
the women of the family were the principal liaison with the outside
world.

"One of the scenes I remember vividly from this period was returning from school at lunchtime to see my mother sewing by the window, as she always did, but weeping. When I approached, I realized
why she was crying. She was sewing the required yellow six-pointed
stars on all our clothes. To distract her, my oldest brother put on an
act showing all the different ways he could wear his jacket while
hiding the infamous emblem with a book, a bag, a cap, and so on.

That lightened the atmosphere a bit, but things became more and more difficult. All Jews had to be home by eight o'clock in the evening. My typing lessons ended at seven forty-five. Consequently, my mother always awaited anxiously my return from class.

"Then came the big roundup of the Vélodrome d'Hiver of July 16, 1942. This was the biggest roundup of Jews yet [see chapter 2 for details]. My mother warned me. I found a place for the night in the home of an unknown woman who sheltered Jews. In the morning, when I went out and saw families being led away, I realized I should not go home then. But where could I go? To my job in an office on the avenue de l'Opéra, I decided. [Kriegel, as we saw in chapter 2, describes this moment as the end of her childhood.] Since my father was hidden nearby, he, too, escaped the roundup, as did my mother, two brothers, and sister at home. Father decided that we had to escape to the unoccupied zone.

"Two weeks later, all six of us crossed the demarcation line under extremely difficult conditions. Many of those who guided people across the lines demanded a great deal of money, and even then, they sometimes abandoned their clients. The Germans fired on anyone they saw trying to escape. That is evidently what happened to us, although my historian-brother Jean-Jacques says the German sentinel did not fire, but instead went to alert his comrades on a nearby bridge. We pretended simply to be swimming on a Loire shore. Then, hurriedly, we made for the other bank. It was very difficult; there were older people as well as youngsters—like my eight-year-old sister—trying to swim cross. Once we were on the other side, we had a family council. In disaster, my father rediscovered collective democracy. Everyone announced where he or she wanted to go. I suggested Grenoble, because I had never seen mountains. Some wanted to go to the coast, but my father decided on Grenoble, because it was in the Italian zone. This was in the summer of 1942, before the September 1943 capitulation by the Italians.

"It was in Grenoble that I joined the Resistance. My experience shows the role of chance. A philosophy teacher [Simone (Devouassoux) Debout, whose testimony is cited elsewhere] put me in touch with a group. She sensed that my situation was somewhat unusual. Sometimes I had trouble staying awake on Monday mornings. (On Sundays, I worked until two in the morning.) Luckily, I had managed to find a place in a *lycée* and a series of jobs as secretary, ending up with a newspaper, *La République du Sud-Est*. When I left class at five in the afternoon, I went to work until quite late in the evening, for I was the only one in the family who could work without too much risk. At school, I had been asked to collect for some cause—I can't remember which—and had been very successful. It was my teacher who put me in touch with the organization I joined, the Jewish Communist youth group, because she saw my organizational talents. This was the Resistance branch for the young people in MOI [Main-d'Oeuvre Immigrée], a PCF organization for foreign workers, many of whom were Jewish."

In the 1980s, Kriegel explained why, not yet sixteen, she was able to join this group. Generally speaking, the Gaullist movements accepted young recruits, but not *that* young, and their recruits were mainly male. The only organization willing to accept adolescents for active Resistance work was the Young Communists, the JC-MOI. Moreover, she was Jewish, which made her involvement almost "commonplace," she holds.

"With JC-MOI, I was responsible for various technical services: a section that printed false documents and a section that took care of the families whose children had been arrested and deported. The most important section dealt with propaganda. Texts were sent to us from Lyon, but we had to print them. All in all, we printed forty-four texts, from papers such as *Jeune Combat* (three hundred copies) to specialized appeals, sometimes running off as many as three thousand. We needed machines, paper, ink, and transportation. It may not sound like much, but it was very demanding. You had to find all those supplies, construct suitcases with false bottoms to transport things, and so forth. All these activities had to be carefully planned with the utmost precaution. The last of the technical sections dealt with weapons and disguises. One young woman, Lily, had a special flair for this sort of work. Flirtatious, she liked to disguise people and design new faces for them. We tried to get German uniforms. This section conducted TA,* penetrating German barracks to spread propaganda. These were the different areas of my Resistance work.

"During this time, I was sixteen, then seventeen years old. I had

---

Travail allemand (German work) was extremely dangerous. Young women (including Clara Malraux) who knew German—mainly Jewish—sought relationships with the occupying forces in an effort to demoralize them.

major responsibilities. And things were complicated by the fact that young girls of that time were not supposed to be on their own and living somewhat independently. My mother was very courageous and continually found excuses when my father complained about my frequent absences and tried to oversee all my movements. I would claim that there were extremely long lines at the shops. When I took out the garbage, I dashed away on a brief errand. Fortunately, I was able to convince my father of the importance of what I was doing and escape from the prison my home had become. One day, he was urgently in need of a set of identity papers for a distant cousin who had just arrived hurriedly and unexpectedly. I told him I could get them at once if he would let me leave the house. He did and I got them. Finally he realized the seriousness of my work. I could not ask him for permission, because it was his responsibility to refuse. So I knew I could not request permission for long absences.

"This dilemma also appears in an account of the Vilno [Vilnius] ghetto in Lithuania [*La partie n'est jamais nulle*, 1979]. The father explains that he cannot authorize leaves that would be contrary to his responsibility to protect his children. Nevertheless, he explains to the young people that in this case, the children are acting in complete accord with the values their parents taught them—even though they appear to be disobeying them. Remember, relations between parents and children were very different then from what they are today. Danger and misfortune brought families close together, with intense affection and love difficult to imagine today. We children did all we could to mitigate their concerns and our parents did all they could to diminish the dangers that weighed upon us. We respected each other's obligations."

The Resistance was not glamorous, Kriegel maintains. Her memories are of an overwhelming feeling of constraint tinged with tearful sadness. Resistance work was rigorous, routine, and time-consuming. Security regulations afforded members little time to themselves. Agents were required to wait one hour after a meeting before going on to the next one. During this interval, they had to keep walking, for they were forbidden to take refuge in a café or a cinema. In other words, whatever the weather—rain, snow, cold—they had to stay outside until the next meeting. Often these rendezvous were at quite distant locations. The work consisted of very repetitive assignments that required meticulous attention. It had nothing to do with the image one has of exciting adventures.

There were many arrests. From the spring of 1944 on, things broke down. Virtually all members of the Grenoble Resistance groups were arrested. Several days after the Liberation, Kriegel's leader was found riddled with bullets. A few agents stayed in town, but the majority joined the *maquis* in the countryside, where they were more protected—and productive—than in the city. During the last weeks, Kriegel went to the *maquis* frequently, guiding people who were no longer needed in the city. In particular, she carried the food ration cards they needed and performed a whole series of complicated tasks. Her other activities included rescuing children and visiting the families of those in hiding—in short, helping with everything required to maintain a clandestine micro-society.

"Now you can see why it is difficult to say that I left my studies. Rather, my studies left me. In fact, during 1943–1944, regular classes were not held in Grenoble. Everything was changing, in disorder. As for my job, I held it until at least the spring of 1944, for an important reason. My work with the newspaper offered excellent materials for our Resistance work. I collected all the information sent by the local correspondents: sporting events, matches, and so on. The paper also received a list every evening of matters that were not to be published. Scarcely an hour after the arrival of the censors' list of forbidden items, one of my comrades would pass by my ground-floor window so I could hand it to him. The 'forbidden' information was distributed to mailboxes in the evening. So my work with the paper was very important. I am not certain precisely when I stopped. I do know that I was totally involved in the Resistance during 1943 and 1944. It is difficult to remember all that happened in that period."

Kriegel had to *become* a Communist. Even when clandestine, the Communist Resistance required its members to follow a theoretical as well as a practical apprenticeship. In spite of all the demands on her time, she continued to read extensively, particularly poetry. Her brother Henri joined a Gaullist group; for his pseudonym, he transformed the family name Becker into Kerbec, prefixing it with the noble *de*. What interested him in 1943 was waging war, not reading Marx and other theorists. He did liaison between Grenoble and the *maquis* in the Vercors district until it was destroyed by the Germans in July 1944.

"My oldest brother entered the Resistance about the same time I did, but he joined a Gaullist group. He was extraordinarily courageous, a sort of daredevil. A few days before the Liberation, he was arrested and tortured. His companion was shot that day, and he himself was scheduled to be shot the following day. The next day, that was the Liberation. The Germans retreated. Freed, Henri came home in such bad shape that my mother did not recognize him at first. He was silent and covered with bruises. But his injuries proved superficial, and he enlisted in the Second Army just a few days later. He fought until 1945.

"After the Liberation, I resumed my studies. I went to Paris so that I could prepare for the École Normale Supérieure, which I entered in October 1945. While I followed the same program that I would have done under normal circumstances, obviously my perspective differed from that of most young women of that time. My experiences also affected my grades. They were below average in Latin and Greek—even though I loved the subjects—because I had been too busy to keep up with assignments. On the other hand, I received top grades in French, philosophy, and history, because I was more mature than the other students.

"My generation was barely eighteen when the war ended, but we had already acquired what might be termed an unusual accumulation of suffering. We had witnessed the death of so many of those who were close to us, those with whom we worked. That may help explain—although not excuse—the dogmatism and fanaticism in the following years. Rereading accounts of that postwar period, I am struck by the violence of those encounters. And when, appropriately, our Stalinist excesses are judged, you need to remember—not as an excuse, but as a partial explanation—that brutality was taught to us.

"I entered into the Jewish Young Communist Resistance by sheer chance. But chance can become necessity. By joining a group that was patriotic, anti-Fascist, and designed to help the Jews, I became a Communist at the same time. Consequently, like others of my age, I continued working for the Communist Party until we realized how contemptible it was. This was not what we fought for or sought. For virtually all of my generation, that moment of recognition came in 1956" [when the USSR invaded Hungary].

When she resumed her studies, Kriegel continued as a PCF militant, organizing students. In 1945, she met Guy Besse, another militant Communist, and married him two years later. The marriage did not even last that length of time. Apart from their commitment to the Party, they had little else in common. Later she married Jewish *résistant* Arthur Kriegel, a doctor. They had two boys and two girls, as had her parents. For reasons that she explains in greater detail in her autobiography, *Ce que j'ai cru comprendre* (1991), she left the Party in the mid-1950s. Finding herself with "free" time, she pursued a doctorate in history and completed her major thesis (a second thesis was also required then), the first scholarly study of French Communism. With these achievements, she received university teaching assignments and started to publish extensively—including a regular column in the conservative daily *Le Figaro*. Her travels since then have taken her to many places, including Israel, where one of her sons and his family settled.[7]

It was not easy for single mothers to undertake Resistance, yet some did. Clara Malraux, the estranged wife of noted author and statesman André Malraux, took care of their young daughter, Florence. In 1941, when he had asked for a divorce, she was stunned, facing the end of their legendary union. More ominously, she and their daughter were especially vulnerable without his protection, for Clara was Jewish. In any case, the couple did not formally divorce until after the war. As her biographer, Isabelle de Courtivron, points out, both personal and political circumstances dovetailed to make this the darkest and most despairing period of Clara's life—a period of "interior exile."

Even though mother and child had forged papers and virtually no funds, Clara unhesitatingly undertook dangerous Resistance work in southeastern France. Among her missions was socialization with German soldiers to try to identify those who were feeling particularly tired, demoralized, or discouraged. If she felt the despair was authentic, Clara Malraux would help the soldier procure false papers and find shelter so that he could eventually join a network. Since one never knew if the soldier was truly a deserter and not a member of the Gestapo, this work was fraught with peril.[8]

Until now, Clara's Resistance work has been little noted, while her famed former husband has come to symbolize the spirit of the Resistance. In fact, André Malraux spent the first three years of the Occupation writing in comfortable settings with his new companion and their two sons. He did not join the Resistance until spring 1944—inspired in part by the death of his younger brother on a mission. Yet Malraux received much attention for his flamboyant behavior as Colonel Berger, leader of the Alsace-Lorraine brigade from September 1944 to March 1945. Clara, on the other hand, is an example of a young wife who assumed care of a couple's child—with a difference. She undertook dangerous clandestine assignments much earlier than did her husband.

+▬▬◄+

Well-known feminist, historian, and sociologist Evelyne Sullerot opposed the occupiers even though she was only in her mid-teens. At one point, she and two younger siblings lived alone in the family apartment, while she carried out liaison missions. After the Allied landings, she traveled on her own to stay with an uncle—and ended up in a *maquis*. Sullerot attributes her involvement to her family milieu: Her parents gave her and their other children a precocious political education.

"My parents had a good deal of influence on what I did during the war. A young girl of fifteen is influenced much more by the milieu in which she lives than by her own ideas. My parents were both Christian—and Socialist. My mother, in particular, held strong political convictions; she was very committed, for example, to the Popular Front and the Spanish Civil War. She was committed, but she did not have the right to vote. As a child, I remember my mother listening to the radio, boiling with indignation, pounding on the tables and saying, 'And to think I can't vote.' I had an early political education, especially at the time of the Popular Front. My father had been a minister in the French Calvinist church—a minority if ever there was one. Then he studied medicine for nine years and became a psychiatrist. He became mayor of our village, where he directed a clinic for people with nervous disorders. (He did not own the clinic; my parents were not well off.) As mayor, he was very involved with Popular Front projects, such as finding work for the unemployed. All of this explains why I was aware of what was going on in the world even though I was quite young.

"The Spanish Civil War really upset my parents. My mother maintained that France had to send planes to help the republic. She talked all the time about going to see [Prime Minister] Léon Blum and telling him her views. The clinic my father directed was Protestant. The Protestant pastors, the evangelicals, were very active in Germany trying to combat Nazism. Before the war, there was a sort of network that helped Jews flee Germany. When I was little, I saw and heard these German Jews when they stayed at our house, and I read books about Nazism and the persecution of Jews. The spirit of resistance was inculcated in me at an early age, in my home.

"Even my maternal grandmother, who lived with us, was very committed to social causes. She always insisted that my mother's birth was hastened when she was struck by the police while demonstrating in the streets in favor of [Alfred] Dreyfus. The rather avantgarde visitors at our home included pacifists and conscientious objectors. Mother and Father—especially Mother—viewed the war in Spain as but a dress rehearsal of what was to come.

"The First World War affected our family profoundly. My father lost two brothers; my mother, one. My brothers were given the names of the dead. My generation was brought up with an immense black veil over it. And there were so many women wearing black. All those widows. And all those brothers and uncles who had been killed. We were born a year or two after they died. They died at twenty-one or twenty-two. It was understandable that people— Christians, and very religious ones at that, like my parents—were pacifists. But the Spanish Civil War changed their viewpoint. My mother dropped her pacifist views overnight. She became very determined, very patriotic. France *had* to fight. France had not lost almost two million youths in the previous war to become enslaved by the Nazis.

"My mother's political observations were unusually lucid. Few people I have spoken with since then realized that Pétain *volunteered* to be appointed ambassador to Franco, and that he was sympathetic toward Fascism; perhaps not toward Nazism, but certainly Fascism. Moreover, asking the enemy to set the conditions for ending hostilities when the troops were still fighting was in fact to abandon them. As a result, almost two million were taken prisoner. That was the situation at the beginning of the war.

"Our family left the southwest Atlantic coast—which the German Army now prohibited to people like us—during the summer of 1940 and settled in the town of Uzès (near Nîmes) in the south. Everyone there was in favor of Pétain, so we found ourselves quite isolated. In July 1940, France was cut in two. My mother had decided to go to whatever spot of French soil was not occupied by the Germans. It did not matter what the conditions were, just so she did not have to see the Germans. So we went to the unoccupied zone, where there were no Germans. It was absurd, because we had to live in complete poverty. We were cut off from my father in the north. The country was divided, and there was no communication between the two zones. We had no news of the other members of our family and we had no money. There we were: my seventy-six-year-old grandmother, my mother (who was not in good health), and four of us children. We had no blankets, no sheets, no books—nothing, absolutely nothing.

"When I went to school, I was told I had to have a Latin dictionary. Since we had no money to buy one, I asked people around us if someone could lend me one. But to the people in the village, we were 'those people from the north who had come to eat all our food,' as they put it. We were blue-eyed blonds, as foreign to those in the south of France as aliens from other countries. France was a rural country at that time, and the regions were very distinct. The inhabitants of the Midi really treated us like foreigners.

"So there we were, completely isolated, in a village where almost everyone was hostile to what we represented. We started listening to the BBC. My mother and grandmother listened to the broadcasts in English. We listened to their broadcasts in French all the time—even though it was forbidden. I remember that in the fall of 1940, I fell in love with Pierre Bourdan, the announcer for the program *The French Speak to the French*. But we were the only ones who listened. It took us several months to find someone else in the village who shared our sentiments.

"As 'those people from the north,' we were not welcome. In reality, my family did not come from any single region. Since Protestants are such a minority in France, they intermarry so they really do not come from any specific region. My second brother was arrested by Pétain's police in Grenoble. The Italians had occupied Grenoble, where he was studying. For the French, there was no greater shame than to be occupied by the Italians—who had not

fought. In school, his arrest was held against me. And then my sister
and I used to mark the door of the WC in the courtyard with the
cross of Lorraine [de Gaulle's symbol]. Each time they were erased,
we drew new ones. The neighbors who shared the toilets threatened
to denounce us—and they did.

"At school on Saturdays, we had to sing songs to Marshal Pétain.* One Saturday there was some special ceremony relating to
Joan of Arc. Since I came from Compiègne, the town where she was
held prisoner, I was asked to raise the flag 'in honor of Joan of Arc
and Marshal Pétain, our new Joan of Arc'! I went to the flagpole in
the center of the schoolyard before all the students and teachers and
shouted, 'Joan of Arc drove the enemy from France. When Marshal
Pétain does that, I will raise the flag, but not before.' Two hours
later, the gendarmes came and arrested me."

The charges against the sixteen-year-old were "unpatriotic remarks" and "listening to the BBC." Sullerot made no secret of listening to the forbidden British radio. Two of her classmates confirmed
the charges. During detention, the young schoolgirl had to contend
with tough women criminals who tried to steal her food (there was
little enough to eat at that time, and even less in prison) and ridiculed
her for pursuing her schoolwork.

"My philosophy teacher was wonderful. He came to prison with my
assignments and corrected my work. I passed the *bac* exam while in
prison. My examiner asked me to discuss 'liberty,' the problem of
liberty. I hesitated and told him that would be very difficult, as I myself was not free. Only then did he realize that I was with two gendarmes. So he asked me to discuss 'lying.' At my trial, the judge
dropped the accusation. He warned me: 'Since you are studying philosophy, mademoiselle, learn the virtues of silence. You must learn
to be quiet.' Later I learned that as he was sentencing me, his son
was making his way to England [to serve with the FFL]. All things
considered, the judge was very understanding; he had acted like a
father."

Only two inhabitants of Uzès came to welcome Sullerot back after
her release. One was elderly Mme Palanque, a woman of staunch re-

---

*The school week opened and closed with flag-raising ceremonies conducted
according to detailed instructions from the ministry of education.

publican convictions who had vowed to remain in her home 'for the duration'; her housekeeper did the errands. Everyone in town noticed when she left her home to visit Sullerot.* Accompanying Mme Palanque was another older woman dressed entirely in black. Sullerot did not know her. She was a World War I widow, a sales clerk in the local dry-goods store. These two women were the only villagers who had the courage to greet Sullerot when she returned from prison.

"My brother was also released from prison at this time. He went into hiding to avoid being sent to Germany. Now my poor mother no longer had to visit us both in prison. She wanted to return to our place in the north, in the occupied zone. It was easier there to work against the Germans, and much needed to be done! When we returned to Compiègne, the situation was the opposite of Uzès. Everyone was against the Germans. In 1943, my mother died. My father stayed in the clinic, which he had gotten back after the Germans occupied it for a year. That left me alone in our apartment to care for my younger brother and sister. I was seventeen and a half. I became involved in a Resistance network through childhood friends. I did liaison, transporting packages. As a young girl in charge of two younger children, I was not under suspicion. But then I became seriously ill, so we joined my father at the psychiatric clinic in the forest.

"There were twelve patients, along with eleven Jews we were hiding, at our clinic. We needed to find food for everybody. It was a tour de force. We had two sheep and a cow, but there were always problems. In those days, the animals always had some sort of problem. We had no fertilizer, insecticides, or machines. You would find the cow bloated, the rabbits dead. We spent a great deal of time caring for the livestock—the cow, the chickens, the rabbits, etc. We had to grow vegetables. Each day we had to pick off insects, like the potato bugs.

"Because of the Jews we had hidden, we could not hire just anyone to help us. Some of the Jews gave us a lot of trouble because they were not careful. Others were, for they realized we risked our lives for them. Sometimes when my sister and I brought them breakfast trays, they would complain. Then we would remind them that they were better off than the patients—who really were sick. When

*At the Liberation, seventy-three-year-old Mme Palanque became mayor of Uzès.

the Germans came from time to time, we put the Jews and others hiding with us in straitjackets and told them to shriek and howl. Since the Germans were afraid of mental illnesses, they did not stay long. At the Liberation, those we had hidden were astonished to discover who were the *real* mental patients and who were not.

"Once we hid an English aviator whom a forester had found hanging by his parachute from a tree. Later, the aviator was sent to stay with peasants in the village nearby, but we children had to visit him from time to time and serve as interpreters. He did not know a word of French. All errands were done by bicycle, as we did not own a car. It was a long way to town and back. Supplies were pulled behind the bike in a trailer-cart. Later in the war, we took in youths who had been excused from compulsory labor in Germany because they supposedly were ill. This was a very difficult situation for us. We wondered if the Germans had sent them to spy on us. Should we pity this one or that—or be suspicious? Life was complicated.

"Eventually I had to leave our clinic, as I had become quite ill with tuberculosis. My godfather, who was also a doctor, insisted I come to his home near Orléans. He was close to the countryside and could get the nourishing food I needed. I had hardly recovered when I learned that my former Resistance network in Paris had fallen into a trap. I had to go at once and warn the *maquis* linked to the network that their leaders were in the hands of the Gestapo. The *maquis* was hidden in the woods south of Orléans. I took what turned out to be the last train. There were bombings, and I had to make the last part of the trip on foot. Going across a cemetery, I saw skeletons in the trees: The tombs had been blown up. All I had carried for the two-day trip was a skirt (made from a bedspread), a blouse, sandals, and a spare pair of underpants. You could not find underpants, so my sister and I knitted them. We took apart some wonderful spreads women in the family had knitted long ago. I ended up living two months with that bare wardrobe because I joined a *maquis* group hemmed in there.

"There were two other young girls with the *maquis*. We did liaison and tried to find medicine and food; nothing very dangerous. And we waited for parachute drops. Truly, it was like a game—like games we played as Scouts. This was in the area south of Orléans known as the Sologne, where there are forests and many springs. First the British planes would shoot off a rocket, then drop contain-

ers of arms and munitions by parachute. It was a question of who
would get the supplies first—the Germans or us. That was the game.
It happened at night. Generally we were in a boat, because you had
a better vantage point on the water.

"This *maquis* was composed largely of students. Fifty-one were
shot. At the entrance to the town of La Ferté-Saint-Aubin, a monument is dedicated to them. For the most part, the young men came
from educated families. One taught me Oscar Wilde's *Ballad of Reading Gaol*—verse by verse—while we waited for parachute drops. He
also made me recite the opening section of Descartes's *Discourse*.
The *maquis* was not there simply to hide. It was trying to save the
nearby Brandt armaments factory for the Allies. The Germans
wanted to blow it up. They finally succeeded. What a fantastic
fireworks display that was!

"At that stage, we were waiting to be liberated. Paris had been
liberated but we had not. The Germans did not want to surrender
to the 'terrorists'—that is, the *maquis*. So a 'professional' French soldier was sent. We called him the 'mothball' general, as he had come
out of the cupboard, so to speak. One day, I was burying two *maquisards* with the help of the daughter of the forest ranger with whom I
lived. We were arrested. At the Kommandantur, a German soldier
(barely sixteen or seventeen) took his gun and ordered me against
the wall. I kept yelling at him that the Germans were *kaput*, and
other things, even though he did not understand a word of French. I
kept talking, thinking that as long as I talked, he would not shoot. I
said anything that came to mind, such as, 'It really bothers me to
die a virgin.' Then he was called away, and we realized we were free.
Next I developed the colic and was really sick. When all danger had
passed and I was in bed, I broke down."[9]

Through Resistance work, Catherine Roux, a modest employee in a
factory office in Lyon, found herself in Paris typing up plans for the
future government of France. Roux was born in Lyon just before World
War I ended. She had a brother and sister, both considerably older
than she. Her father—who had fought in World War I—died in the
1920s, so the children went to work at an early age. When Roux passed
her studies certificate at twelve, her mother found her a job in a factory. She worked in a number of places while continuing to take evening courses. Eventually, she was qualified to leave the factories and

workshops to do office work. At fifteen, she took a job in the office of a factory that made gas heaters. There she met someone who asked her to "help"—that is, to join the Resistance.

"From my earliest childhood, I read a great deal. When I had nothing to read, I checked garbage cans. That way, I read the *Progrès* of Lyon, a daily newspaper I dreamed of working for some day. Early on, I became interested in politics. As the years passed, I sensed the growing threats: There was Hitler; people talked of Mussolini in very favorable terms because he had drained the Pontine marshes. At fourteen, I took part in street demonstrations. In the factory, I enjoyed a privileged situation because I was the youngest employee. They let me take classes during work hours, which was exceptional. The manager was an older man—very, very kind and distinguished; he had been an artillery commander in World War I. He wrote children's tales, as I did. I gave him the address of a newspaper that had published several of my stories, and they accepted some of his. This created a different sort of relationship between us, in addition to work.

"In 1935, things were not that great. I had a very comfortable place in the office, and was not overwhelmed with work, but those who worked in the factory did so in conditions that rivaled the 1850s. In winter it was like Siberia; there was only one brazier. Frequently I went there on errands, and when I did, I replaced someone for a few minutes so he or she could warm up near the brazier. The disparity between our situations disturbed me, so I helped them to unionize; there was no union in the shop. Thus, at fifteen I had a union card. Then came 1936, an extraordinary period. We had to learn how to negotiate with management. But in the end, nothing worked, and the workers went on strike. I struck with them. The Popular Front introduced major reforms: a forty-hour workweek—which soon became forty-two—and paid vacations. I personally knew a seventy-four-year-old worker who had his first-ever paid vacation then.

"One day early on in the Occupation, a company executive asked me if I would receive mail and then bring it to him. I was very surprised, because we were not exactly friends. However, he added that it was for a good cause, so I agreed. What I did was wrong in those days, because I did not mention it to my parents. My mother had remarried, which made things difficult. My stepfather was a fine man who had been wounded eight times in World War I. He had served under Pétain, and, in his view, the marshal was incapable of doing any harm to France. So I said nothing, and the letters and packages started coming. I explained to my mother that they were to make packages for prisoners of war, a plausible excuse. I also started carrying messages to addresses of people I didn't know. After we returned from deportation, I finally met Anne-Marie Soucelier (see chapter 13). We had delivered messages to each other's addresses on numerous occasions, but we had never met until then."

With time, Roux was asked to do more for Combat—the movement she had joined when she agreed to receive parcels and do liaison—including arranging meetings at her home. That posed the major problem of what to do about her mother and stepfather. She hit on a simple solution and bought them tickets for the cinema across the street. They told all their friends what a considerate daughter they had. When they left, she signaled the waiting *résistants* by raising and lowering the shades; everyone then arrived. All the major figures in the southern zone—Jacques Soustelle, Henri Frenay, Georges Bidault—came to 8, Place Ambroise Courtois in Lyon. When the movie ended, the lights went out and everyone left. Roux opened the windows to try to get rid of all the smoke and emptied all the ashtrays. (They smoked a good deal.) Those are some of the things she insists must not be forgotten about that extraordinary period.

"At the factory, we were now helping hide young men who were scheduled to go to Germany to work. I was the liaison between our firm and the German work bureau on Garibaldi Street. I filled out identity card and cards exempting the bearers from forced labor; I imitated the boss's signature very well. I also had access to official stamps. Many activities like that were the basis of Resistance work, and you normally would not do them—they were illegal.

"In 1943, Combat needed me in Paris. Would I go? I answered yes, even though I had never been to Paris. But that wasn't a serious problem. I told my boss that I was going to work for a newspaper there. He wished me luck, signed all the papers, and wrote to the Germans to recommend that they grant me the required authorization. And that is how I went to Paris for the first time, by myself.

"The train north was very slow, eleven hours from Lyon to Paris. At Chalon-sur-Saône, I had to pass the German control. I had two large suitcases, one containing extremely compromising materials. I smiled at two young German soldiers. I was a petite blonde with a big Scout hat. It worked. They spoke French, so we talked about I-know-not-what, perhaps Wagner. In any event, my suitcases were not checked. In Paris, it was very difficult to find lodging. The Germans were everywhere. I checked my bags at the Gare de Lyon and went up and down the streets. Every hotel was full. Finally I found a room in a hotel for Chinese, and I took my bags there. Then I attended to something that had been bothering me. Each time he had been wounded, my stepfather had been treated in the American Hospital in Neuilly [a Paris suburb]. He told me how difficult it was to travel by subway. 'The gates close before you have time to get on, and so forth.' So, even though it was fairly late in the evening, I took the subway to Vincennes, the end of the line, then back to Neuilly, at the other end of the line, and then returned to the Gare de Lyon stop. After that, I was no longer afraid of the Métro. It was extraordinary to find myself suddenly alone in Paris.

"Then I made contact with my comrades Enghien and Peck, and we started work on the big project we had discussed extensively while still in Lyon. Resistance movements were very disparate. Combat, our group, helped set up the MUR, the unification of all the movements. We focused on the NAP plan (Noyautage de l'Administration Publique, working within the public administrations) to organize sabotage when the Allies landed. One of our first tasks was to contact people and see if they were favorable to working with us. One had to be extremely careful, because there had been many problems, many agents captured. Sheep in our fold turned out to be wolves. Another comrade from Lyon got me a job with *La France Socialiste*, the collaborationist newspaper of Marcel Déat. He asked me if I had a subject in mind to write about. Although I had not thought about it before, I came up with the idea of doing a sociological analysis of the Métro—the personnel, the training of new employees, and so on. This was a subject that interested me greatly. Déat accepted, so I received a journalist's card for *La France Socialiste*. This was invaluable. At the same time, I enrolled as a student at the École du Louvre, which gave me double security.

"I won't tell you I had an address, for I changed addresses weekly. Agents were continually on the run, continually moving. I think I stayed in all the garrets in central Paris, except in the sections forbidden to us: the Latin Quarter; around the Palais Royal; from the Tuileries Gardens to Place de la Concorde. Montmartre was off limits also.*

"That didn't hinder my research on the Métro, because I never had a moment's time for the project. A lovely Alsatian family, the Hartmanns, gave our group a room in their apartment, where we kept all our equipment: radio, mimeograph, typewriter. I was assigned the task of coding and decoding. Evenings, I continued work in my room. At that time, I was staying in a hotel with a very shady reputation, but you took what you could get. The room was ugly, but I had a washbasin and electricity, which was something. By chance, Jean, an agent from another movement—and a Scout from Lyon, like me—was staying in this same hotel. This was strictly forbidden by security regulations. Mme Boyoux, the proprietor, was old, widowed, and lonely. Perhaps she wasn't fully aware of the sort of hotel she was running. Each week, one of us took her out for the evening while the other one manned the hotel desk. We had to deal with very new experiences and some very unusual individuals, to say the least. To thank us, Mme Boyoux let me have a second lamp, which really helped with nighttime code work. When I was out, Jean used my room to make identity cards for his group, Ceux de la Résistance."

On December 23, 1944, Roux's chief, Marcel Peck, did not show up for a meeting on the Boulevard Raspail. Young, dynamic, enterprising, he was always on time—or he sent a message if he could not come. Roux waited half an hour—which she admits was very imprudent. Peck had been arrested (and later died under torture). Alfred Smoular, a journalist with the Havas agency, replaced him, and they finished their project, which was to help set up the future government of France. All the commissioners were named. They had been contacted and accepted, in total secrecy. Roux also typed up the plans for the Paris uprising, when the Allies came—a document seventeen pages long—and coded it.

"On February 21, 1945, I met Sévère, one of our agents. He gave me a message to be decoded that very night. We met in the gardens

---

*Not all groups adhered to these rules. After the war, it was discovered that some streets in the Latin Quarter housed a dangerous number of Resistance organizations. Part of the problem, to be sure, was that of secrecy. Addresses were carefully guarded.

of the church of Saint Julien-le-Pauvre. 'Catherine, I think I am being followed,' he said. I told him he probably should not have come.
He insisted he had been very careful and was certain no one had
followed him there. The next day, we had an appointment at the
Hartmanns' apartment to drop off some papers and meet our head,
Count Bernard de Chalvron. I was a little early—which my boss
hated. You were not supposed to be early or late. So I went into the
church of Saint Roch, where, to my astonishment, a wedding was
under way. My life had changed so completely I had forgotten that
for most of the French population, daily life continued more or less
as before, while those of us in the Resistance were truly living on
the edge. My reverie soon ended. When I got to the Hartmanns'
apartment, the Germans arrested me, as they had done with Sévère,
who had arrived before me.

"They asked me who I was and I answered, 'The governess here
to take the six-year-old for her daily walk.' I took out a governess's
veil I always carried with me. Nevertheless, they insisted on seeing
the contents of my purse. They removed everything, including the
envelope with the coded plans for the uprising. I also had other documents. Because there had been many arrests recently, I had to visit
a dozen or more drop-off points daily, on top of my regular jobs.
Sévère and I were taken to Gestapo headquarters in a Mercedes.
Somehow, I had managed to conceal my wallet in my armpit. At
the Place de l'Étoile, the Mercedes was stopped by a policeman—it
was going the wrong way or something like that. While the driver
was flashing his identity card, another policeman opened the door
on my side, so I leaned out and let my wallet drop. We arrived at
Gestapo headquarters, rue des Saussaies. I was the first to be questioned. A German named Franz, along with Roger and Geneviève
Calame [a Jewish collaborationist couple shot after the war], worked
on me. The tactic is to get as much information as possible right
away. Consequently, they were very brutal, very violent.

"They thought I was Jewish, the sister of Jean-Guy Bernard.
Now I had met Jacqueline Bernard, who is short and dark, with dark
eyes, while Jean-Guy had reddish-blond hair, blue eyes, and a light
complexion. He really could have been my brother. They brought
him from Fresnes prison. I had my period at this time, and the one
humanitarian gesture of Geneviève Calame was to let me keep my
chemise on (we wore chemises then). They threw Jean-Guy into my
arms and told me to kiss my brother. Jean-Guy told them he did not

know this young girl, and I insisted I did not know him—although I
did. He looked so different. His eyes had dark circles and his beard
was like the one Christ is portrayed with—curly and red. He was
wearing handcuffs and all his fingers were bandaged. I was one of
the last to see him alive. (See the testimony of his wife, Yvette Farnoux, in chapter 9.)

"They continued to question me, over and over again: 'Whom
were you going to meet?' 'Whom did you meet?' 'Where did the
documents come from?' 'Who are the people you know?' Finally I
collapsed and told them to leave me alone. They would not get anything out of me before three in the afternoon, when I had an appointment with my chief. 'Where?' 'Twenty-seven Place Vendôme,' I
replied, although I didn't know Paris all that well yet. They brought
me some towels so I could clean myself up. My mouth was full of
paper, which proved providential, although I had not planned it beforehand. The paper protected my teeth when I was struck. In the
bathroom, I spat out what I had been unable to swallow. I put my
clothes back on and they fixed me up. The Calame woman, Geneviève, took the silk scarf I had—you could get nice ones inexpensively
in Lyon, where they were made—and wrapped it around my disheveled hair. And so we took off for the Vendôme meeting with my
hands handcuffed behind my back. Time passed, and of course no
one came, because the Gestapo already had my chief. They said,
'That's it. We are going back to headquarters, and you will really get
it.' 'Oh please,' I said, 'let's take another turn by rue Castiglione.' I
played my role well. Once more we went around the square.

"Back at Gestapo headquarters, the questions and beatings resumed. Blows rained down; they used a lash on my back. Franz went
next door, where the Hartmann family and the others had been
held since that morning. Then Alfred Smoular spoke up and identified himself as my head, thinking he would save me; in reality, it
almost cost me my life. Franz returned to question me and then told
me my chief was next door. At this point, the elderly bailiff shoved
his watch in Franz's face. It was after midnight, the time for those
who were still among the living to be returned to Fresnes prison.
We put on our coats and were taken away. In the paddy wagon, I
was able to talk with Mme Hartmann, but once in prison, we were
separated. I was thrown into a dark basement cell. Feeling about, I
found a board with straw on it and stretched out. Things looked
very bleak. Franz had said he was looking forward to seeing me

again. I did not think I could face another day like that. I decided I
had to do something quickly. At another time, I would have to settle that with my confessor. I had a lovely blue coat with an officer's
collar that had a simple silver pin to close it. I tried to open my
veins with the pin but could not. The pin was too thin and bent
too easily. My mother always said I was clumsy; she was right. I
could not even kill myself. So I gave up but decided to keep the pin
as a sort of protection, hidden in my coat hem. Knowing it was
there was very reassuring—until it was discovered during a search
on my way to the camps.

"Next morning, they took me to the fourth floor and threw me
into a cell with four others. After having been in the dark for so
long, I could not see and was traumatized. I clung to the door.
'Come, little one, come,' a voice said. I was pulled away from the
door by a gray-haired woman who had the only bed because of her
age. I cried out because I could not lie on my back. She took off my
things. Then she took a chemise from clothes her family had sent
her and ripped it into strips. She bathed and bandaged me—neck,
back, and wrists. That was unusual, water in a French prison. It re-
vived me. I trusted Mme Odile, although I said nothing that day.
She told me she had been imprisoned during World War I because
she was caught carrying messages through the German lines in the
north of France, where she lived. This time, she had been arrested
because she was taking care of Johnny, a British aviator en route to
Spain via a network escape route. When the Germans burst into her
place, she was treating his injured leg. It was obvious, en flagrant délit. When they were taken away, Johnny wept, saying, 'I will be sent
to a prisoner-of-war camp, but you, where?' She was sixty-eight and
very courageous.

"That night, they came and knocked on our door. It is always
terrifying when they come during the night. 'Madame Roux, trial,'
they announced. I had to go to the commander's office. I could not
put on my dress, so Mme Odile put about my shoulders a plaid blanket her daughter had sent. 'Is she coming back,' she asked the interpreter, 'because I gave her my blanket?' 'Yes, she will be coming
back. This is just the preliminary trial.' So I went down to the commandant's office, a splendid room. By now they had had ample time
to examine thoroughly the contents of my purse. They wanted me
to describe Enghien, who was like a brother to me. I could not, so

they beat me and I fainted. Naturally, Mme Odile's blanket opened
up and revealed I was not dressed.

"When I regained consciousness, a man in a motorcyclist's hel-
met helped me get up. He told me that he had not been able to
come earlier but that he was *very* interested in my 'affair.' He said I
was very fortunate, for he was going to be taking care of me from
then on. Laurer—that was his name—added that he was giving me
several days to 'rest.' Back in my cell, I said nothing. Mme Odile
had warned me that the young nurse from Normandy in our cell was
not 'sure.' I had taken the place of Lulu, a Communist woman condemned to death. Her husband had been shot at Mont Valérien
[now a national monument to the Resistance], but she had been
spared because she was pregnant. Three or four days before I came,
she had labor pains. They took her to the prison infirmary, where
her son was born. She called him Pierre le Fresnois—that is, Pierre
from Fresnes prison—in the hope that someone would recognize
him in case something happened to her. They whisked her baby off
to a public orphanage. It had been a difficult birth, and Lulu had
not been treated properly. She was brought back to the cell with a
high fever. Mme Odile finally convinced the German nurse who
made daily rounds to take Lulu back to the infirmary. So I was assigned to her place. I learned all this from the tales that passed from
one cell to another—a prison tradition.

"At Sunday Mass, I exchanged a few words with Mme Hartmann, even though it was forbidden. She was beside herself because
her husband had been tortured horribly. I, too, was distraught. He
was a good man who accepted his wife's decisions. Would he have
made the decision to let us set up the office in their apartment? I
don't know. He was a dedicated patriot, but it was a very serious of-
fense to harbor a Resistance group in your home. [Madame Hartmann survived deportation but her husband did not.]

"Tuesday morning, I was called for my trial at five in the morning and again taken to rue des Saussaies. But instead of having a
trial, I was thrown into another dark cell. I heard a voice. It was
Father Riquet, a priest. His hands were bound behind his back, but
he told me to look for matches in his cassock. I lit one and shared
his piece of sugar. I had had nothing else to eat that day. There was
another prisoner there, Mme Bertier de Coligny, an aristocrat who
had been in prison for a year. 'Little one,' she said, 'here is some
advice. Tell them no matter what, but talk all the time to the Ger-

mans. They will surely kill you with blows if you don't say something, anything.'

"Finally, they came to get me and took me to a room where interrogations were conducted. Two petulant young men—real scum—were carrying the big red purse I had when arrested. They tossed out my compact ('You won't need that anymore') and my food-ration tickets ('You won't need those anymore'). They put my books on a shelf. I grabbed the anthology of French poets, which, amazingly, they let me keep. That made me wish I had grabbed my history of France as well. Laurer, my 'friend' from the other evening, entered. He sat me in a corner with a typist, who took the deposition. This was the first time since my arrest that there had been anything resembling legal or administrative procedures. Following Mme de Coligny's advice, I talked a lot. I told him I could not tell them anything about Enghien (whom they were after) because he was my lover. At that, he burst out laughing. He did not believe me. Laurer went on to tell me that he had lived in France for twenty-five years—which explained his perfect French and the job he had. He was good to me. Before I left, he offered to bring my suitcase, as I probably 'did not have much' in my cell and would need things for my 'trip.' He kept his word, and I received a suitcase full of the things I needed. For me, now, the interrogations were finished.

"I spent a few more days in prison. Maria Mertens, a laundress detained briefly in our cell, was about to be released. She had been arrested by mistake. At night, when Jeanne, the nurse from Normandy was asleep, I repeated over and over again the messages Maria was to deliver when she was freed. 'Go to my mother at such-and-such an address and tell her to go to my office and ask for this colleague and transmit what I am going to say; the Germans know this one and that one. These locations have been blown.' Altogether, I gave her eight addresses to contact, and she reached them all. This was a spontaneous but dangerous act of resistance.

"Next I was transferred to Romainville prison, on the outskirts of Paris, where I, who had never known a grandmother, discovered a group of adorable older women. There I met the wife of Colonel Reboul who had six servants in her Parisian townhouse; Mme Kahn, a woman well over eighty who walked with crutches; and Miss Zimberlin, a former English teacher who gave me lessons. I was particularly close to Mme Bernard de Laprade, who was eighty-seven. She spent long hours telling me in her rich, old-fashioned vocabulary

about her marriage and her daring decision to run away from the
Parisian home of her father, an aristocrat. When I asked her how
she got to the train station, since she had never been allowed to go
out alone in Paris before, she replied, 'Why I took a horsecab, *ma
chère petite.*' Among others, there was also Mme Marie-Thérèse de
Poix, who described to us her family château near the Loire. Each
generation of the counts of Poix, major builders since the tenth century, had added a wing to the château. There were two ageless
Breton women wrapped up in so many shawls they looked like those
nested Russian dolls. They knew and spoke only Breton. From all
these women I gained firsthand acquaintance with a France I had
known only from schoolbooks.

"Our return from the camps was what it was—that is to say,
largely ignored. Obviously, we were too small a group for the country to recognize us. While it is very, very difficult to come up with a
precise figure, there were more than two hundred thousand *résistants*
deported, men and women. People who were not *résistants* were deported with us, which complicates estimates. In any event, according to the official count, half of us came back.* We tried to resume
our lives. One thing we did—each in our own way—was to keep
alive the memory of those who did not return.

"We, the volunteers of the Resistance, had absolutely no preparation for what we did. We were not soldiers like the others. We
were thrown into the Resistance without any weapons, without any
means of defense. Young and old alike, all we had was our faith and
our enthusiasm. In my book (*Le Triangle rouge*, 1969), you will find
their names. My Resistance chief Sévère used to say, 'I don't *go* with
anyone who is not of our group. My mistress is the Resistance.' For
my part, I wanted action, not philosophy. I ignored him. He would
add, 'Perhaps all we were doing did not add up to anything. Perhaps
it just served our personal goals.' For me, the Resistance was the major event of my life."[10]

Roux's assessment holds for many women who served in the
French Resistance. That experience marked all their lives—in differing degrees. To this day, some have not attempted to sort out their

___

*For the reasons set forth in chapter 4, figures are only approximate. Six thousand
to seven thousand French women were deported to Ravensbrück, and only 50 to 60
percent returned.

reactions to the period, consciously or otherwise. A few are ambivalent about the impact of their efforts. Those who were deported sometimes are bitter about their reception upon return from the camps as well as about the failure of postwar France to live up to their ideals. A number of nondeportees had similar disappointments. Perhaps, for the young women who joined the Resistance, their postwar reactions may be attributed in part to their youth, an age of ideals—ideals that had not yet come into conflict with the larger world.

7

╬═══╬

War Is a Man's Affair

In the early battles they [the women] had fought side by side with
the men as a matter of course. It is a thing that seems natural in
time of revolution. Ideas were changing already, however. The
militiamen had to be kept out of the riding-school while the
women were drilling there, because they laughed at the women
and put them off.

—*George Orwell*, Homage to Catalonia

FROM THE ACCOUNTS THAT FOLLOW, IT IS EVIDENT THAT FRENCH
women who wanted to join military or paramilitary organizations were
not accepted readily. Charles de Gaulle was a traditional military
leader who had difficulty envisioning women in combat. When he did
finally incorporate women into the French army, it was to release men
to fight. His "*demoiselles*" (maids of honor) had to wait in the wings.
At the time de Gaulle took this step, Communists were starting to
phase out those few women who had managed to join their paramilitary groups. In every Resistance group, women had to combat stereotypes of their presumed weaknesses and shortcomings. Over and over,
they had to prove themselves—once they managed to join. Most were
assigned traditional feminine support roles, for the customary view was
that "War is a man's affair."

147

As seen, starting in late 1943, *maquis* units were formed on Ger-
man-occupied French territory, generally in rugged, out-of-the-way locations. Recruits were local inhabitants as well as those who had gone
into hiding and wanted to fight the Germans. Units were organized
along paramilitary lines. Few women were enrolled in these groups,
except for some members of the Communist Party. But many women
and young girls supplied these groups—at great risk. With the Allied
landings, the *maquis* rose up and joined regular troops. The province
of Brittany was liberated largely by local fighters. One hears of women
having joined in some of these combats, but such claims are difficult
to substantiate.

A few women are known to have joined fighting groups. In her
study of *partisanes* and gender politics in Vichy France, historian Paula
Schwartz holds that there were few *partisanes*—that is, full-time, gun-
carrying women fighters—in France.[1] For the most part, women in
combat or combat-supported positions were PCF members or women
serving in Communist Party organizations, particularly the Francs-
Tireurs-Partisans (FTP, Irregulars and Guerrillas). Communists participated in more unconventional forms of fighting—sabotage and
guerrilla attacks—which women could help carry out. Additionally,
Communist women played a crucial role as links to the leadership,
which had been forced to go underground in 1939. Nevertheless, a
report at the 1975 Communist-sponsored UFF conference on women
in the French Resistance stated specifically that "an infinitesimal number of women fought with weapons."[2]

Scarcity of weapons was one factor. *Maquis* units often trained
with broom handles while waiting to acquire weapons, as did Lise
Lesèvre's group. Unlike the situation in Italy or Greece, as we will see,
there was strong prejudice in France against women bearing arms. The
PCF did, however, use women liaison agents to deliver weapons and
hide them in places where attacks were scheduled. These women were
instructed to retrieve the valuable weapons whenever possible. This
meant that while the men with weapons at least had a plausible
chance of defending themselves, the women who carried arms hidden
in shopping bags and baby carriages were at greater risk.

For security reasons, urban fighters were to live alone, meeting
only to plan attacks. Schwartz points out that in practice, many lived
as couples, hoping to blend in with the rest of the population. While
this was deemed acceptable, the presence of women in a rural camp
was not. It was assumed that women would undermine the "legiti-

macy" of such groups because they gossip and cannot keep secrets—and because women become involved with the men. "The presence of women in rural combat groups was considered a blatant contravention of prevailing social mores," she notes. In the cities, on the other hand, the general assumption seemed to be that it was safer for members to have affairs—perhaps inevitable among those living in constant danger—with colleagues in their own organization. During the last winter of the Occupation, women helped supply the FTP combat groups but participated less and less in the action. They were assigned to the critical support areas. Orders were issued in late 1943 to phase out women in the FTP *maquis*; this was part of a larger effort to bring these groups into a single professional national military organization, with an all-male force.

Georgette (Claude) Gérard's background helps explain how she reached the unusual position of head of a *maquis*. Like many from eastern France—in her case, Lorraine—she was convinced in the 1930s that war soon would break out. Deeply regretting that women were not admitted to the army, Gérard decided to prepare for a degree in engineering so that even if she could not join the army, she could at least work in a war factory. She studied engineering while teaching math courses to support herself. With an eye to future events, she engaged in many sports, especially long hikes and bicycle trips. When war was declared, Gérard did find work briefly in a war factory before joining the exodus southward.

Eventually, Gérard found herself in Lyon, where she knew no one. But she knew about a refugee center there and went to volunteer her services. Since she was alone and had time, she bought paper and typed up Resistance tracts, which she then distributed. By the end of 1940, Gérard had managed to contact an Allied intelligence service and was scouting possible parachute landing spots and furnishing details on German troops for them. Then Gérard found some Resistance work well suited to her education and training.

"At the end of 1941, I joined Combat as assistant to the head of their paper [Vélin]. My work took me throughout the southern zone. I was responsible for printing and publishing a clandestine paper that rapidly reached a print run of 100,000 copies a month, later double that. Then I was arrested by Vichy police. A printer had turned me in. Fortunately, I was not held long. Three weeks later, I was arrested and released—again. Now I realized I had to leave the area. Combat assigned me to the Dordogne region [southwestern France] to help organize the Secret Army (AS) there. I went from village to village, setting up sections, ensuring liaison, planning arms raids and sabotage. This was the first time I had been in that part of France. I tried to enlist reserve officers for the AS; they all refused. To inspire confidence, I didn't let on that I was really in charge. I pretended to represent a male leader.

"When the Resistance movements joined to become MUR* in January 1943, I became regional head for the *maquis* in seven departments [regions]. Because of my experience, Combat offered me several assignments, but I chose this one. Until August 1944, I was the only chief; after that date, I was co-leader. There was so much to do. Everything had to be organized. I was helped by a male military commander who took the name 'Pierrette' [a woman's name; Gérard's Resistance pseudonym, Claude, is unisex]. He handled the military aspects; I was in charge of the organization. By November 1943, the total number in the *maquis* under me was close to five thousand, divided into camps of 120 at most. All were hidden in the forests. Arms were parachuted in by the British. We experienced more difficulty getting plastic explosives for sabotage. Close to half the fighters were Communists. I got along well with them.

"My responsibilities required me to be on the move continually in the central regions of France—to say nothing of frequent trips to Paris and Lyon, where our national meetings were held. By now, the Gestapo was hot on my trail. For safety reasons, I never spent more than one night in the same place. The Militia sent a few men to infiltrate our groups. All in all, there were several thousand arrests among the AS and the *maquis* in the region where I worked. My assistant, Pierrette, was arrested in December 1943.

"When the FFI was formed early in 1944, *maquis* groups were incorporated into it. Because I was too well known, I was sent to head a section of the French intelligence network. Germans arrested me in May 1944 and put me in prison in Limoges. I was recognized and arrested as a *maquis* leader—not as head of an intelligence network. The *least* I can say is that I was very badly treated. If I am alive today, it is because of the Liberation. French forces surrounded and attacked the prison before the departing Germans could massacre us."[3]

---

*Mouvements Unis de la Résistance (MUR); *mur* means "wall" in French.

As one of two women known to have headed a *maquis* group—and by far the largest one, with several thousand men under her command—Commandant Gérard's experience was atypical. She was able to assume this position in part because *maquis* were paramilitary groups formed in enemy-occupied territory in secrecy and under difficult conditions.

Among French women seeking to free their country were a small group who managed to get to London and join de Gaulle's FFL. Since few—either men or women—sought to join de Gaulle in London in the early days, one would assume the welcome mat would have been out for those who wanted to sign on with his fledgling group. Such was not the case, however, for French women who wanted to join the FFL. And, once accepted, they had difficulty convincing their supervisors they could do something other than the usual women's tasks: secretarial and administrative work, nursing, and chauffeuring.

+————+

Jeanne Bohec of Brittany was trained as a chemist and wanted to put this expertise at her country's service. She had grown up in Breton villages, a tomboy and a Scout. She did well in math classes in her Catholic *lycée*. After graduating from school, she became an assistant chemist in a gunpowder factory in Brest, a seaport town. The workday lasted ten hours and the salary was very modest, but she was helping her country. When the Germans invaded France in the spring of 1940, the lab was moved into a tunnel to protect it from the bombings.

When Bohec learned that German forces were approaching, she went to England by boat—on June 18, 1940. It was a spur-of-the-moment decision. She was twenty-one. She had little money and not even a coat with her. When questioned upon her arrival in England, she claimed to be able to speak English—although that was not quite accurate. Bohec wanted to use her considerable knowledge of nitrates. But authorities did not know what to do with her, as the British women's auxiliary had no policy on accepting refugees, and de Gaulle's FFL did not yet accept women. For some months, she lived with an English family, where she babysat and improved her English—all the while becoming more frustrated in her desire to "do something."

Finally realizing that French women also wanted to volunteer, de Gaulle authorized the formation of a women's corps toward the end of 1940.* On January 6, 1941, Bohec was among the first five women accepted into the auxiliary. By the end of the war, there were about four thousand in the corps. The French women volunteers unit was modeled on the Auxiliary Territorial Service (ATS) of the British army. The women in the FFL contingent ranged in age from seventeen to fifty-plus. They came from every region, colony, and social class. From what she observed, Bohec was not certain that all her compatriots fully accepted the discipline of the corps. FFL women replaced the gas masks they were issued with personal effects, using the mask's canvas bag as a handbag. Several young women provoked gossip because they appeared overly interested in men.

This assessment of women in the corps is seconded by Raymonde Teyssier-Jore, a volunteer from New Caledonia. Some of her group wore silk rather than regulation wool stockings. Teyssier-Jore had her uniform tailored, because it was too large. This was against regulations, but she suggests that the French women officers closed their eyes to such infractions, perhaps deciding it was best to accept what might be innate coquetry. When de Gaulle was scheduled to visit, the women knocked themselves out preparing their uniforms, equipment, and quarters for inspection. But all the general appeared to notice was the absence of bidets in British bathrooms.

Upon completion of basic training, the women were assimilated into the French forces and assigned to secretarial duties or nursing. Because there were too many nurses, Teyssier-Jore was assigned to the automobile service, i.e., chauffeuring. She had many adjustments to make, since she had never before been in a large city—let alone London—and had never seen snow. In addition to coping with male officers' skepticism about women's ability, she bore the extra burden of being one of the few black women. At times, she even regretted risking her life—as she did on later assignments in North and sub-Saharan Africa—for the colonial French.[4]

For her part, Bohec finally was allowed to undertake what the military then considered a man's job. But to do it, she had to insist.

---

*Originally called the *Corps Féminin*, the name was changed within a year. *Corps* means "body" as well as "formation," and the possible meaning of "feminine body" provoked unwanted humor.

"They tried to train me as a nurse's aide," Bohec narrates. "I hated it. I had chemistry and scientific training and had worked with gunpowder. I hadn't escaped France and joined up just to fold bandages." She took stenographic lessons—following the British method—but continued to demand a job appropriate to her skills. At last, Bohec was promoted to corporal and assigned to a lab where she was the only woman. This was in 1942. The work was fascinating but hard—and still not the active participation she sought. Bohec's top-secret assignment was to find the best ways of undertaking sabotage with chemicals that could be purchased readily in drugstores. To this day, the formulas remain secret. The work was dangerous: All the chemists working on the project were hospitalized for burns at one time or another.

Then she was asked to teach the fundamentals of explosives to French agents being dropped into France. While the British were sending women agents, the French intelligence service, the BCRA, was not. Why, she asked, not teach those already in France? The BCRA said no, no women. But Bohec insisted: "I kept banging my head against the wall. But then I am from Brittany, and Bretons are stubborn. So I asked and asked, to the point where they finally said all right. I was the first woman to be taken by the BCRA and sent to France." Since this was another top-secret assignment, Bohec could not share the exciting news with her friends. Training was intensive and rigorous. First she attended Sabotage School, where there were seven in the class—Bohec and six men. They learned how to fire guns, including machine guns; how to become accomplished thieves; how to conduct sabotage. Subjects included "silent killing":

> This training left me skeptical about my own chances against a strong, determined man, but perhaps someone caught off guard would find it hard to overpower me. In any case, the training gave us confidence in our potential and a combative spirit that would be essential to us.

During parachute training, Bohec again found herself the only woman in the group. Petite, she had to have a specially made parachute harness and boots. On their first jump, she led her classmates out of the plane. The training took place in England, with British instructors.

> The English were fine. The only discrimination came from the men in the BCRA, who initially didn't want women involved. I believe this is because France is a Latin country. Even today, it is difficult for women to get equal treatment. Men go to war; women stay home.

Upon completion of her training, Bohec was promoted to second lieutenant and assigned on a mission to her native Brittany. Her equipment included a purse fitted with a secret compartment. Somehow, it didn't seem right, so she crocheted one for herself. She was disappointed also with the "ladies'" handgun she was issued. She threw away her cyanide capsule, deciding that God would help her keep quiet if tortured. Then it was off to France, when weather finally permitted her to parachute on the third attempt: "I was scared, but less than you might expect. There were so many things to think about that you didn't have time to be afraid."

The *maquis* member who met her after she landed did not expect agent "Râteau" to be a woman—and a young one at that: "What's going on? They're sending us children now!" Bohec, however, was *not* involved in child's play. A male colleague who parachuted into France with her was arrested and shot three weeks later.

Bohec went to Paris to meet other operatives in the Galilée network. This was her first trip to the capital—where she ended up settling after the war. Back in Brittany, she bought a bicycle so she could circulate freely; she cycled to all the neighboring villages to teach *maquis* units how to handle weapons and explosives. She somehow found time to have a suit and a dress made: "Dressing, sleeping, and eating properly are also elements of clandestine life." She worked with the FFI and gave courses in sabotage and clandestine warfare to *maquis* fighters. And she participated in sabotage missions.

In preparation for the Allied landings, Bohec was assigned to sever a major railway line—part of the "Green Plan" to disrupt as many railway lines as possible in Normandy. The detonator somehow had been left out of the armament drop, so she fashioned one herself. With four of her students, she drove through back roads and stopped near the station: "The others covered me as I placed the charges in the switches and attached them. I drove the detonator deeply into the explosives and joined them with a detonating fuse. Finally, I put in a thirty-minute delayed-action mechanism."

Then the group waited: "Half an hour can seem an eternity." When nothing happened after thirty minutes, it looked like failure. "Then there was an incredible explosion that rocked the countryside. Dogs began to bark. . . . My heart beat loudly."

Bohec subsequently joined up with the major Breton *maquis* near Saint-Marcel and served as their decoder. By the summer of 1944, local women were working with the *maquis*, serving as couriers and nurses; others prepared and delivered warm meals. When the BBC gave the signal for the general uprising of the *maquis* on August 3, 1944, Bohec wanted to get a machine gun and join in the attack on the Germans. The local FFI agreed, but *not* the team that had been parachuted in. They maintained, "No, this is not a woman's affair." Yet that was not the way her *maquis* companions felt: "I was considered a comrade—one of them. It was the men in uniform, the professional army. They couldn't accept the idea of a woman carrying a gun."[5]

The regular army did not trust women in war. It still subscribes to ancestral traditions, she holds. The Resistance—the army of the shadows—was something totally new, born of the circumstances. Thus, it sometimes allowed women to fight.[6]

+➤━◄+

Dr. Suzanne Vallon joined the FFL after she and her husband were spirited out of France and taken to London, via Gibraltar. In 1940, she joined a network with her husband, Louis, after he returned from a POW camp. Vallon insists that she had no active role in the group. She just "helped" in the meetings in their home. This brought her into contact with a number of important Resistance members. After indiscretions committed by several network agents, the Gestapo was on their trail and the Vallons were ordered to England. There she did not receive the field posting she sought because her husband was assigned to FFL headquarters in London. Her commanding officer would not let her go elsewhere—on her own. When she finally became a regimental doctor, she found that those in the field accepted her. If war was a man's affair for the administrators, that was not true on the battlefields. Anyone qualified to help was welcome.

"The trip to England was extraordinary. Originally, my husband and other Resistance figures were scheduled to be picked up by a British plane. They were going to find other means of transport for me. There were several unsuccessful attempts to land, but atmospheric conditions were never right. Besides, the German patrols along the coast were heavy, so it was decided that the two of us would get to England by boat. Like tourists on vacation, we went to Marseilles. It was summer: July 14, 1941—Bastille Day, to be precise. Our rendezvous was on a beach at the nearby resort of Cassis. This was a perfectly plausible outing, and, from a tourist's point of view, not at all unpleasant. That night, we stayed hidden in the bushes with a member of the local Resistance. Our hand baggage was light, but it did contain a gun. A small boat run by a Polish refugee picked us up and took us to our meeting place with the British boat that would take us to Gibraltar. There was a terrible storm en route. To my shame, I must confess I was terribly seasick, so when we met up with the boat, I was tossed like a parcel into the larger British vessel.

"On the British boat, we found ourselves amid peace and prosperity again. It was extraordinary. The British officers were so hospitable. The crew were dressed as fishermen and the boat was filled with fishnets. As we approached Gibraltar, we were told to stay in our cabins for a time. When allowed on deck again, we had quite a surprise. All the fishing gear and the fishermen had disappeared. In their place were British sailors and officers—and guns. The crew changed like that all the time—camouflaged as a fishing boat, then a military ship. We were amazed by life in Gibraltar after all the difficulties of daily life in occupied France—food shortages and all that. Seeing German flags flying everywhere over French public buildings was unbelievably distressing. In Gibraltar, we could talk openly, while in France we spoke freely only to people we knew very, very, very, very well. The British questioned us about our identities and our plans. We protested, because they separated us for the questioning. Over and over, I repeated that I was en route to join General de Gaulle—not the British army. Perhaps it was wounded national pride. After two days, we were given total freedom and taken to London.

"There I decided I really wanted to do something. Since I was a doctor by training, I joined de Gaulle's Free French Forces and asked to be sent to treat the troops as soon as possible. Because I was a physician, I did not have to stay in the barracks-like accommodations for French women with the FFL. They decided—fortunately, very, very quickly—that it made no sense to restrict me to military clinics. I was qualified for a medical assignment with the troops, and that is what I demanded. I was commissioned second lieutenant, the starting rank in the FFL. The head doctor for the FFL in London—a man not much older than I was, but much more conservative—said, 'Since your husband is here, you will remain in London.' There was no longer any question of my leaving to serve the troops. He was a general and I had to obey. With my snappiest salute (which I learned on my own), I answered, 'At your orders, general.'

"My husband also sought a more active assignment and eventually was sent abroad on various missions. [De Gaulle chose Louis Vallon to direct all the specifically nonmilitary matters of the French intelligence service (BCRA).] With his comings and goings, 'my' general decided it would be appropriate for me to be assigned to active duty. I was sent to Tunisia just as the Anglo-American-French forces were moving toward Tunis, the capital. I was welcomed fraternally by the officers, most of them career military men. I will always remember the head doctor of the division, who took me aside and apologized, saying the conversations in the canteen were not always appropriate for 'young women.' 'First,' I told him, 'I am not all that young; second, my ears are not all that pure. I will not be embarrassed by whatever they talk about.' In the end, everything worked out; they were good comrades. Another officer told me, 'I am telling you straightaway that for me you are just a medical officer like the others.' 'Fine,' I said. 'That is all I ask. I want to be like everyone else and not receive special treatment. I am not here as a woman but as a medical officer. Ask what you want of me for your medical needs. I want to be treated like a man.' And that is how it was until the end. I never had any problems because I was a woman. They never forbade me to do certain things. Nor did I receive unwanted attention because I was a woman. I was simply a military doctor, and that was all I asked.

"My field of specialty is ophthalmology. During those few months in London, I had the title of Ophthalmologist of the Free French Forces in Great Britain, a very pompous-sounding position that meant nothing because I could not do much of anything except go around and inspect our troops. If their problems were minor, they did not need me. I sent the serious cases to British hospitals, where they were always treated well. My contacts with my British colleagues were very cordial, but I begged for active duty because I simply was not doing much.

"However, even in Tunisia I could do little more because I was an ophthalmologist: They had all the help they needed for medical treatment. The staff was mainly British, with a few French. Each nationality treated the other's patients when needed. The main thrust was to treat the wounded. So I continued to ask for more active duty. Finally I was assigned to a Pierce ambulance. In the beginning of the war, specially fitted Pierce ambulances were sent to France with British personnel. In Tunisia, there were a few French nurses with the British medical personnel, but no French doctors. Our medical team soon developed a special Franco-English language for our own use. The atmosphere was very friendly among the ambulance group, and we still hold reunions.

"At one point, I was sent to Algeria* for an internship in anesthesia. I *did* learn something then. Early in my medical studies, I had had training in anesthesia, but procedures had evolved rapidly since then. When I returned to Tunisia, there still was not much for me to do. At last I was assigned to a medical battalion that had ambulances working behind the lines—just behind the lines. There I did whatever needed to be done in the way of emergency treatment. I did triage—determining priorities for the ambulances, deciding who should be evacuated first.

"I debarked in Italy shortly after the beginning of the Italian campaign. Then we landed on the Provençal coast with the first soldiers. During our long wait at anchor, one of my former medical-student colleagues asked me to go with him on another boat that was about to land. At first I said, 'No, I cannot. My post is here.' Then I thought about it and decided I would leave with him after all. I wrote a letter to my commanding officer at our port of embarkation, excusing myself for deserting in order to return to France. At first he was furious, but there was not much he could do. I had gone.

"As it turned out, our boat landed when Toulon was being taken, and doctors were badly needed. Unfortunately, there were many wounded, many victims. We went up the Rhône Valley with the troops. When we got to Alsace, we stayed some time at a medical station because, once again, there were many wounded, many victims. I was the only woman doctor with the division, and there were few French women nurses.

"By sheer chance, I rendezvoused with my husband, who had been sent to France on an assignment. He left shortly thereafter for Algeria, but I stayed in France. The war was far from finished. I had been promoted to captain—yes, I was promoted.

"Then we went down again through the Alps region. Fierce

---

*At that time, Algeria was a French department; Morocco and Tunisia were colonies.

battles were raging near the Franco-Italian border. Many, many wounded needed attention. There were also some wounded German prisoners. Naturally, we treated them like the others. Some of them claimed to be Austrians or even Alsatians in order to be treated better. Whether it was true or not, they made these claims because they had heard that the French killed wounded prisoners. Obviously, that was absurd. Our humanitarian concerns, the medical instincts, were against killing.

"I was in the south of France in 1945 when the armistice was signed. When it was announced, obviously we were all very happy the war was over. The only exceptions were a few career officers, most quite young, who were appalled at the dismal prospect of ending their careers in a small, quiet garrison town. Even though the war was over, there were still serious consequences of the war— unhappy people, disorganized families. For my part, I returned to Paris and resumed civilian life without too much regret, although— all things considered—it was very difficult to resume a calm, regular, modest life. Actually, I was ambivalent at first about returning to civilian life. Then, by a stroke of good fortune, I was one of several French medical specialists chosen to go to the United States for a period of training in rehabilitation. We learned about the new techniques developed while we were at war. I was lucky in every respect to be part of America's welcome for the returning GIs. I crossed on a boat with many GIs and a few families—after waiting quite a while, as few boats had women's accommodations.

"In the end, I really did not do very much, but at least I had a satisfying role, from a moral point of view, that provided me with the illusion that I was doing something. I ran some risks, but those were nothing in comparison with the risks of those who stayed in France and joined the Resistance. They operated under the very eyes of the Gestapo and could be attacked at any moment. The risks I ran were nothing like those of men and women who faced possible arrest and torture by the Gestapo. After the war, I had something of a guilty conscience, but I really had tried as much as I could to do something. The important thing was that I did do something. Perhaps it is an inferiority complex about risking less than if I had stayed in France. But you never know, and, ultimately, it does not matter. Fate decided it would be thus.

"Before the war, I wanted an active professional life, just like a man. It is true the path had been traced by other women before

me—but not by that many. The majority of my high-school classmates did not have professional careers. In my case, my family
helped. My parents were open-minded and realized that it would be
best to let me do what I wanted to do. What *they* wanted, though,
was for me to be like my mother—that is, a woman who did not
work unless it was financially necessary. A woman's career was marriage and children, taking care of the home. That was what my
mother had always done, and very well at that. She was much better
than I in managing a home. It is, I guess, a question of temperament. I wanted an interesting profession just so I would not have to
live that sort of routine life. My work during the war was a continuation of my efforts to lead—the phrase sounds slightly ridiculous
now—a full and interesting life. There were some difficulties from
time to time, but they were not all that hard to overcome because I
had a professional mentality.

"The profession of regimental doctor is difficult for a woman—
or it was at that time. You worked under much pressure, and you
had to decide which cases needed to be treated first. It was very demanding physically. If the same situation were to arise now—
although I fervently hope it never does—I think there certainly
would be more women."[7]

Both Suzanne Vallon and Jeanne Bohec had training that the
Resistance military forces eventually used, yet both encountered problems convincing the Free French in London to let them use their skills.
It was even more difficult for young women without professional training to join the FFL, but they persisted. Sonia Vagliano-Eloy overcame
many obstacles before becoming one of de Gaulle's "*demoiselles*."

In her family, there was a precedent for serving the country. Her
mother was an American who had been decorated by Marshal Pétain
himself for work on the front in 1917–1918. One of four children in
a bourgeois family, Vagliano-Eloy learned English as a young girl and
visited England and the United States. The Parisian was but seventeen
when she took part in the student demonstration on Armistice Day
in 1940. The young people marched down the Champs-Élysées, defying a German interdiction. She was among those arrested. Bowing
to family pressure, she left the capital with her mother in late January
1941—on the last train for American citizens. Her father feared that
his wife might be interned. In addition, their daughter was obliged to

sign in each week at the neighborhood police headquarters—the condition for her release after arrest. This concerned her parents but not Vagliano-Eloy; she found it flattering.

"In Lisbon, I went to the British consulate, never doubting for a moment—in my naïveté—that I would be given a visa for England. My mother had given her consent. My appointment was with an important figure. I was eighteen years old, but, petite and blonde, I looked younger. Furthermore, in order to qualify for the exit train, my passport listed me as fifteen. The consul laughed in my face and told me to return in five years."

She encountered the same difficulties in the United States, so while waiting, she tried to prepare herself and enhance her background by taking political-science courses at Smith College, and, later, by doing volunteer work for the FFL delegation in New York. Her flying lessons were interrupted by the bombing of Pearl Harbor. All this time, her letters to the FFL in London went unanswered. She was angry with de Gaulle. He invited the military, engineers, workers, sailors, and aviators to join him—everyone but French women! Great Britain forbade entry to "nonessential" people, and the United States refused exit visas to women under twenty-five who wanted to go to countries at war. Laying siege to the New York FFL delegation, Vagliano-Eloy finally was accepted in late 1942.

"In early August 1943, my orders finally arrived. I was to leave for England with four friends. But my Free French boss wanted me to stay in the New York office and continue doing paperwork. What a bitter deception! Exasperated, I slipped my leave order into a stack of documents that my somewhat negligent supervisor signed one day. Two weeks later, I was on my way. The Liberty ship took twenty-four days to cross the Atlantic, and German submarines attacked almost daily. Ten ships in our convoy were lost. During the interminable nights, I fought the same panic I had experienced when we had to go down into the shelters during the 'phony war.' "

In London at last, Vagliano-Eloy could not locate the barracks of the FFL women's section. Finally she found Moncorvo House. It was too late in the day, she was told. Exhausted by her efforts—and the

long sea voyage—she fainted in front of the building.* Regaining consciousness, she was upbraided by adjutant P., a highly made-up woman
who made life miserable for her—as she did for all under her command. Vagliano-Eloy signed her formal engagement, "for the duration
of the war plus three months." A sympathetic woman captain allowed
her to sign up for the entry exam for liaison officer. Her fondest hope
was to be sent back to France on secret missions. Among her qualifications were an excellent memory and a native command of English.

Vagliano-Eloy spent a week on kitchen duty before being sent for
training with the British in Guilford, where they marched, drilled, and
did military exercises. Returning to London, she learned she had been
accepted to liaison officer's school. She met Lieutenant Ford, who led
the women's section of this group. British, but living in France, Ford
signed up with the French army in 1939 and ended up with de Gaulle
on the disastrous Dakar expedition. Decorated, Ford was now the senior woman with the FFL.

+⟩━━⟨+

Because she was young—and without relatives in London—Sonia
Vagliano-Eloy had to continue staying at the Moncorvo House barracks. Incensed that Vagliano-Eloy had been accepted for liaison officer training, officer P. (now a lieutenant, but *not* accepted for the
training program) assigned her the worst possible chores, such as sort-
ing the garbage. She was obliged to study under very difficult conditions. Her schedule was so tight she bought a bike to travel between
the dormitory and her classes, but she hid her bike for fear of the
vengeful lieutenant. She did manage to attend fascinating meetings
where future liaison missions were discussed and planned:

"My uncle came to town. Julian Allen, my mother's brother, was
then a colonel in the U.S. Air Force. During the 1914–1918 war, he
signed up with the French army—at fourteen—and served two years
as an enlisted soldier. American, but French at heart, we got along
marvelously. He took me to dinner, but the evening ended badly.
Adjutant P. penalized me for two days for going out with an officer.
(I was still an enlisted woman.) 'Your uncle, my foot. Don't kid me!'
Meanwhile, like the other women candidates in our mixed group, I

---

*Later she learned that the FFL woman who carried her to the infirmary was Ève
Curie, daughter of Marie Curie.

studied assiduously in order to succeed, memorizing all kinds of military details. We stuffed our heads with figures, acronyms, and abbreviations. But my efforts paid off. I scored fifth out of our class of forty-two (and second on the military section). What a relief! Now I was a second lieutenant."

During February 1944, Vagliano-Eloy endured the renewed blitz and discovered that London nightlife continued under bombardment. A month later, the second part of their program started:

"The practical sessions were varied and sometimes surprising. We worked in kindergartens, maternity clinics, and rehabilitation hospitals for children traumatized by the bombings; in soup kitchens and factories; and in a laundry. We had courses in child care, first aid, and nutrition. We visited a hospital that outfitted amputees. Finally, we spent ten days at a large Ford factory, where we learned how cars ran; how to care for them; and how to repair them. Each day when we returned to London, we had gym sessions."

Of particular use in her future assignments were visits to the Citizens' Advice Bureaus in Wales—information offices set up to inform the public, furnish aid, evacuate areas, and staff canteens. The women's section of the French liaison mission was now a coherent unit, thanks to the efforts of the new head, Captain Claude de Rothschild, an energetic woman who knew how to command obedience and gain respect. Vagliano-Eloy was among the first group of French officers to attend the Civil Affairs Staff College in Wimbledon, which trained British officers to work with local French civil authorities. The setting and routine were luxurious, comparable to life on a country estate. Classwork alternated with practical exercises. Men and women followed the same program, with a few exceptions: Only the women were taught how to build outdoor kitchens and prepare meals for an entire school.

"The BBC announced that women military would not be sent to France until two months after D day. We resigned ourselves for the wait. Then, to the amazement of all—and the consternation of our male colleagues—we women were ordered to prepare to leave for France. They needed us to help with the many civilians in refugee camps. On June 28, 1944, sixty of us left for France under Captain

Rothschild. For security reasons, we changed trucks and trains several times. When we got to Newhaven, the activity was unbelievable—ships of all sorts and sizes. Two by two, we proceeded to the quay. On seeing us, the Tommies whistled and waved. One shouted, 'The war's over, boys; they're sending the girls.'

"I stayed out on deck and took over the wheel of the LCI [landing craft] while the pilot napped. I wished that extraordinary night would never end. Anguish gripped me as I made out the coast of France. That moment dreamed of for so long did not produce the strong emotion it should have. Instead, I was seized with panic. The beautiful French coast was now just an unattractive beach covered with military matériel and swarming with people. I was paralyzed by thoughts of the perils that awaited me. But my thoughts were quickly interrupted by the thundering voice of an angry Captain Rothschild: 'Where were you during the crossing? Why didn't you come down and make tea for your ill comrades?' "

Now back in their native land, the French women reported to a British officer, who was furious. The sixty liaison officers they sent him turned out to be sixty women! The British High Command and de Gaulle obviously had gone mad. Captain Rothschild calmed him down, and he finished by welcoming them. Nearby soldiers who approached soon left, disappointed, when they learned the women were neither canteen nor USO personnel.

In short order, the group started work in the town of Bayeux. To their amazement, the outdoor oven they constructed—according to the Staff College method—worked very well. Invited to dine with Colonel Chandon and other male officers one evening, Vagliano-Eloy managed to look presentable thanks to her colleagues. The beach landing had ruined their uniforms, so she washed hers in the only water available—holy water. The duty officer she passed several hours earlier did not recognize her—reassurance that she looked all right. When she entered the restaurant, the officers raised their champagne glasses to wish her Happy Birthday!

"After organizing things at Bayeux, we were divided up and sent to different villages. When our mud-covered vehicle finally made it to our new destination, we once again found an officer angry that he had been sent some women—and young ones at that. He already had eight hundred refugees on his hands 'who didn't even speak English.' We set about organizing life in the camp. Yvonne—our specialist in feeding crowds—set up the kitchen. I was assigned to information and 'leisure' activities. Each morning, I made my way across the muddy fields to an artillery post and listened to the news on field radios. When I returned, I prepared and posted new bulletins in French and English. The bulletin board also listed practical information about camp services.

"Afternoons I helped Louise take the children to the fields and organize games for them. This was my favorite assignment. Elsewhere, I made daily rounds, often settling disputes. In one tent were two groups of women who did not get along. The peasant women made a chalk line to separate themselves from the other group, a joyous twenty-some band I decided must have come from the city, hence the antagonism. The leader of that group was Mme H., who had very large breasts—like an advance guard. She acted like a duchess. Finally I realized what everyone knew—they were prostitutes. That explained their good health and their good spirits. They had not suffered from food privations, and they were looking forward to renewed business with the Allied soldiers."

One day, when Vagliano-Eloy was absent, her charges resumed their "business" in fields near an American contingent. When Vagliano-Eloy returned that evening, Mme H. asked her if she could continue some "work" she had started that afternoon. She agreed, not realizing what the work was. Catastrophe arrived that night. A sentry informed his superiors that there was a line of GIs in front of tent number three. Word had spread like wildfire. Summoned, Vagliano-Eloy was asked if she had given permission for the tent to be used as a brothel: "Not on your life!"

The captain was enraged: "I can't understand how the army could send us such idiots, such innocents. You'd be better off taking care of the women of your parish. This isn't a Scout camp." The whole army soon knew about this ridiculous affair.

The refugees protested. A delegation of "fathers of families" came to demand the expulsion of the prostitutes, who, for their part, were so upset they stayed in their tent. Vagliano-Eloy went to comfort them and take them food. She and a companion were ordered to drive the women to the neighboring village, where there was a camp for suspected collaborators. The two had the impression they were taking the women to the guillotine. When they arrived at the *maquis* camp, the women began to cry as the men brutally ejected them from the truck. The two lieutenants asked the men not to mistreat the poor women. Laughing mockingly, a tall, bearded man overseeing the operation said derisively, "One can see, *ma petite,* that you [*tu*] weren't here when the Fritz [Germans] were." As they drove off, they saw two men seize one of the women while a third shaved her head. The engine noise did not cover her cries.

Other assignments to organize refugee camps followed. At Cavigny, near Saint-Lô, reporting for a new assignment, a brusque American officer was amazed to discover that the young French woman officer spoke English—or, rather, American—so well. He questioned her further.

"I told him I was nearly twenty-five—which was somewhat exaggerated. When he asked me why I joined the army, I told him that I was in France when the armistice was signed and the Germans marched in. I was revolted and heartsick to see German soldiers walking the streets of Paris as conquerors, as if Paris belonged to them: seeing their black-and-yellow posters everywhere, hearing them singing as they marched—in short, all that. I couldn't really explain it; it would take too much time. It was a reflex. They were there, *chez nous,* and that was unbearable. I wanted to do something, to serve. That was all.

" 'You must be very arrogant and sure of yourself! How do you think a young girl like you could do something useful in this immense, mechanized war? This is a man's war, a war between brutes,' he answered.

"I felt my cheeks getting hot. The major's sneering tone and words really upset me. In spite of that, I answered as calmly as possible: 'That is indeed my pretension. Allow me to inform you, major, that what my comrades and I have done since the debarkation only confirms my views. Your officers and your detachments of GIs may well be here, but they are incapable of running a refugee camp filled mainly with women and children, old people and the sick. Furthermore, they don't speak French, and they consider such work an insult to their masculine, military dignity.'

"He told me to calm down and said that they ran camps without women's help. 'They must really be a mess,' I couldn't help muttering. He smiled and said he was forced pretty much to agree with me, the 'little lieutenant.' What really bothered him was that we were women—and young women at that—in the middle of an army of men. He was certain that my group was going to get involved with his men. He didn't want any 'monkey business.' He made me responsible for the conduct of my team. Then we settled down to talk about plans to organize camps in the area. He warned that it would be difficult, even dangerous. Since that was what I wanted, he wouldn't spare me. I agreed and promised to try to avoid too much attention. My arrival at the camp had caused a sensation. The men hooted and whistled as I was driven to headquarters. They seldom saw women."

The major was not exaggerating. Vagliano-Eloy found herself in dangerous situations. Once, while returning from transporting several refugees, she became lost and was about to enter a village when a young man named Paul—who turned out to be a *résistant*—signaled her urgently and directed her hurriedly into a barn. They hid the truck and made their way through a series of cellars to a hidden room with an opening looking out across the town square. Paul let her see the Germans—just a few feet away. Finally, the Germans left the village. After what seemed a very long wait, American troops arrived. She continued to her destination. And, wherever she drove, there was always the danger of land mines.

As the Allies advanced, the women liaison officers set up relief centers in the newly freed territories. Meeting a young *résistante* one day, Vagliano-Eloy came to understand some of the distance and differences between the Resistance of the Interior and the Resistance of the Exterior—a subject frequently discussed when she was in London. For Yvonne L., those who stayed in France waged *real* war; she personally had no interest in caring for refugees. She accused Vagliano-Eloy of being a tool of "Anglo-Saxon Jewish capitalists."

When Paris was liberated, there was a large family reunion. Sonia Vagliano-Eloy had returned after almost four years away. Her father was now a member of the Resistance Committee. The joy of the Liberation was short-lived, however. What she describes as a "hangover" ensued. Communist and non-Communist *résistants* were opposed over how the country should be governed. When she returned to Paris from Belgium on a brief supply mission, Vagliano-Eloy was pained to observe that Parisians considered the war over now that the capital was free, even though it went on for many difficult months elsewhere. The Parisians were absorbed in their personal affairs. Vagliano-Eloy and

the other women liaison members headed for Germany to continue
setting up camps. She received orders to report to the city of Weimar.

"Colonel Lewis called and asked me to meet him in the hotel bar.
He ordered two scotch-and-sodas for us. I was amazed, because I had
never seen him drink, and there he was, swallowing his in one gulp.
Later he told me it was his first drink in thirty years. He needed
courage: He had a very difficult assignment to propose, and I could
honorably refuse. The assignment was Buchenwald. 'Of course, my
girls and I will go,' I answered. I knew virtually nothing about the
camps, except that people were mistreated there and dozens died.
'Thousands,' he interrupted. 'There are about fifteen to twenty thousand prisoners still in the camp. The Germans kept very good records.' We made plans to visit the camp the next day. When he left,
I remembered that he didn't tell me about Buchenwald, as he said
he would. Later I observed that those who had been to the camps
did not talk about it.

"Our guide was so thin that his striped garments hung on him,
like a scarecrow. Like all the others, his head was shaved, his face
pale, his eyes red; he had few teeth. He was particularly proud to
have been chosen as guide by the Americans because he had been
an inmate there for five years and spoke as many languages. He
spared no details.

"In each barracks we tried to distinguish the living from the
dead. We learned how far the imagination can go in finding the
means and instruments to inflict the cruelest tortures. With diaboli-
cal sadism, those men and women took pleasure in assisting at the
worst scenes imaginable, in the shrieks of pain of the tortured."

This inspection tour gave Vagliano-Eloy the "distinction" of being
the first woman officer to enter Buchenwald. Installed in the comfortable, gemütlich, homey villas of the camp's former administrators—
after removing all the cozy furniture and installing military fittings—
she and her team set about trying to organize the camp. Their primary
concern was to save lives—a heroic task.

She devoted particular attention to the children, from babies—
presumably born in the camp—to the older ones, up to about eight
years of age. Taken from their mothers at birth, these children lived
like savages. They were all boys; they had never seen a woman.
Vagliano-Eloy and her team had to tame them like animals. The chil-

dren had to be taught the most elementary skills, beginning with standing upright rather than going about on all fours. They even had to be taught how to play. No one in the camp knew of their existence. Undoubtedly, they were held for use in medical experiments. As the days passed, the children responded slowly to the women's loving care. When the war ended and the Russians took over the area, Vagliano-Eloy and her team prepared to return to France.

"Paradoxically, the months I spent in Germany after hostilities ended were the most difficult from a morale standpoint. The enthusiasm that spurred us on evaporated when the guns stopped. Victory, so ardently sought, seemed to bring nothing but confusion and chaos. I could no longer bear the sight of those camps crowded with stateless refugees. The world had changed. The first atomic bomb was dropped, killing eighty thousand people.

"My war ended with the last fine days of summer. I left Germany for Paris and demobilization and serious things. I was only twenty-three years old, yet I felt very 'old' and very 'wise.' My two years of military life coincided with the brief passage from youth to adulthood. Those two years taught me many things—above all, to recognize what is important and what is not. I'm glad people are starting to become interested in what women did during that war. General de Gaulle grudgingly acknowledged that women helped 'a little'!"[8]

The women's section of the FFL was organized along traditional military lines. Members were assigned "women's work," befitting their sex. To participate in missions and maneuvers ran counter to traditional, patriarchal wisdom about the role of women in the military. Even when they were assigned to run refugee camps—assignments the men found "beneath their masculine dignity" and did not carry out as well—women were not welcome in such close proximity to the troops. In one respect, the men were partially right. Some of the FFL women had led rather sheltered lives—as the incident with the prostitutes reveals. But they were quick learners. And, if they did not become "brutes" who wage war, they undertook difficult assignments—such as parachuting into enemy-held territory and saving the lives of concentration-camp survivors. In January 1944, de Gaulle created a separate women's auxiliary, the Auxiliaire Féminin de l'Armée de Terre

(AFAT), thus institutionalizing women's presence in the French army. Their role? To free men for combat.

In contrast to the situation in France, there were a considerable number of Italian women partisans. Of the 35,000 women so recognized, 5,000 were imprisoned, 650 were executed or died in combat, and approximately 3,000 were deported to Germany. The first detachment was formed in the mountainous Piedmont region. Ninety-nine women partisans died there. "For the first time in Italian history, large numbers of women were partners with men, fighting together as equals for a common cause," according to Maria de Blasio Wilhelm.[9]

Among the narratives Eleni Fourtouni translated into English for her book on women in the Greek Resistance was that of Levendo-katerini, from the island of Crete. The Germans captured Crete in May 1941, a few weeks after occupying Athens. She was a twenty-one-year-old war widow with two children, yet she left them to join the partisans, taking the gun of a seventy-five-year-old man. The widow promised to be "worthy of it." She was, and she helped free her native land, but she and other members of the Cretan Resistance were executed during the civil war that followed the defeat of the Germans.[10]

The Resistance exploits of women in Italy and Greece, then, as throughout occupied Europe, were similar in certain respects to those of French women—the major difference being the smaller number of French women partisans. One cannot attribute this exclusively to the Latin temperament, for both Italy and Greece are Mediterranean cultures. This difference may be partially explained by the fact that both these countries attained their present form as nations only in the preceding century, and only after considerable nontraditional warfare. France, on the other hand, has a much longer past as a nation, and the military there has a long-established tradition.

8

+>==--=<+

Support Services:
Women's Eternal Vocation

Incensed by the Resistance . . . the Germans are committing acts
of unimaginable ferocity and instigating a veritable reign of terror
in our country. Dealing with so much misery and so much pain
has become an overwhelming task for the social services. Our
social workers—whose devotion, self-sacrifice, and courage have
faced every trial—deal with every crisis under extremely difficult
circumstances; pursued, facing numerous difficulties, unfortunately too often without funds. Above all, their task is thankless,
difficult, and dangerous.
  —*Bernadette Ratier, regional head of the social services of MUR,
  in an August 15, 1944, report forwarded Charles to de Gaulle
  via Switzerland*

WHEN ONE MENTIONS *RESISTANCE*, ONE THINKS OF INTELLIGENCE NET-
works, the *maquis*, and so forth—but not of support services. Resistance support services developed in response to arrests by Vichy and
the Germans for acts of resistance. The work of the clandestine social
assistants was not very visible. Those recruited for this work were
devoted young women who did little else. They took many risks, yet
their work is viewed as somewhat peripheral. Little has been written
about the subject because of the marginalization of women's contributions. Yet support services also were the only area of Resistance work
where positions of authority generally were held by women.

171

With rare exceptions, women served as clandestine social workers in occupied France. Social services sought to help prisoners and their families and to ensure the security and survival of *résistants* who had gone underground. Those in prison were poorly nourished and often poorly treated. They needed food packages to supplement their meager rations. Prisons were dirty and infested. The exchange of laundry was used to pass on news when correspondence was forbidden. Messages written on extremely thin paper were rolled and inserted into hems. Some enterprising women typed messages on silk, sewn to paper so that it would pass through the typewriter. The fine cloth was easily concealed. Newspapers used to wrap parcels for prisoners could convey news and information; partially completed crossword puzzles contained short messages. Brief conversations with guards and chaplains often provided important information. Clandestine social workers—working at times with their duly accredited colleagues—secured plans of prisons and helped prepare escapes.

Early on, when the Resistance was primarily an individual affair or the work of small groups, there was no pressing need for such help. Starting in 1941, however, the need arose for formal, organized Resistance support services.

Prior to the war, social services were set up for internees in French detention centers opened under the Third Republic for foreigners judged undesirable: refugees from the Spanish Civil War; political refugees from Germany; Jews and gypsies from other countries. Jewish and other organizations set up "underground railroads" to try to spirit Jewish children out of the country when Vichy and German anti-Jewish policies became evident. While some succeeded in living hidden in France throughout the war, it was preferable to send them to Switzerland, even though the Swiss did not always welcome them. Members of the Jewish scouting group (Éclaireurs Israélites Français) often served as guides for the children. A number of members of their movement were killed or deported, such as Marianne Cohn. The young woman led twenty-eight children to the Spanish border without difficulty. Two-thirds eventually were able to cross, but the rest were taken into custody by the Germans. Cohn was offered a chance to escape, but she refused to leave the children. On D day, her grave was discovered. She had been so badly beaten with clubs or shovels that only her shoes enabled her brother to identify her.[1]

By November 1940, an umbrella organization known as the Nîmes Committee was formed by various humanitarian groups trying to help detainees in French camps, two-thirds of whom were Jewish. Prominent among the groups on this committee was CIMADE (Intermovement Committee for Evacuees), under the direction of dynamic young Madeleine Barot. CIMADE had been set up by Protestant organizations in September 1939 to help those evacuated from Alsace and Lorraine. A small group of committed Christians—composed largely of young women, since their male colleagues had been mobilized—donated their time during the "phony war" to help refugees. CIMADE concentrated on helping foreign Jews when Vichy's anti-Semitic laws made them extremely vulnerable. Protestants and Jews shared links as minority groups that had suffered persecution in earlier centuries in Catholic France. Under Pétain, France again was more militantly Catholic. Barot and a colleague, Jeanne Merle d'Aubigné, a nurse, installed themselves in the French camp at Gurs, near the Spanish border. (See chapter 2 for more details on these camps.) Little by little, other groups—Quaker, Swiss, and Jewish organizations—managed to send representatives to the camp. As more internment camps were set up inside France, other teams were sent to help.

CIMADE undertook a new phase of refugee work when a small number of detainees were allowed to live outside the overcrowded camp as residents under surveillance, provided housing could be found for them. The group's last major project was to try to halt the deportation of Jews to Eastern Europe for extermination, a process that began in August 1942. Madeleine Barot and her colleagues directed "God's Underground." They hid many Jews, mainly children; some were in France for the duration, others were secreted out of the country. Even after having made arrangements with Swiss Protestant families to receive them, the volunteers who accompanied children to the border were at peril. They risked prison or death camps, not to mention dogs and fusillades, or possible execution in France, as was the case with Marianne Cohn. After the war, CIMADE continued its mission of helping prisoners. In spite of criticism, the organization helped imprisoned collaborators, even as it formerly had helped their victims.[2]

Polish-born Sabine Zlatin served with the French Red Cross as a nurse during the fighting of 1939–1940. Early in 1941, when she learned of the shocking conditions in the camp at Agde, in south-central France, Zlatin volunteered to work with those detained in French camps. Her husband moved to nearby Montpellier. Appointed social assistant for the internees at Agde, she set out to try to improve their living conditions. Zlatin was shocked that the forty Red Cross workers at Agde spent their days doing little. Further, she testified later, some of these nurses realized handsome profits by buying the internees' jewelry for a pittance. Others accused the Red Cross nurses of being little more than sexual partners for the guards.

Zlatin worked with a group of clergy who succeeded in having the twelve thousand internees at Agde transferred to the Rivesaltes camp, in the Pyrénées region, where conditions were marginally better. Their group was in contact with Admiral William Leahy (United States ambassador to Vichy), who arranged for foreign relief groups to set up an office inside the camp. Zlatin was particularly concerned about the many children among the twenty-five thousand detainees at Rivesaltes. Given the unsanitary conditions, there were many deaths; disease was widespread. She secured permission to free a hundred children under the age of twelve each month—usually more, because passes were reused. Once released, the children were taken to a vacant sanatorium nearby. Sabine Zlatin had rented the facility so the children could be treated before being placed with families. At times she resorted to dangerous tactics to save children. Once Zlatin camouflaged in her bike basket the two-year-old son of a Jewish woman scheduled for deportation. Zlatin gave him some chocolate to keep him quiet and walked her bike by the guards, saying she had to run a short errand. Her ample nurse's cape covered the boy. Outside the camp, she entrusted him to someone in the village.

When the Germans occupied all of France in November 1942, Zlatin continued to care for the children in the Rivesaltes camp, where German sentries now joined the French guards watching them. In the spring of 1943, local authorities asked her to take seventeen Jewish children, "forgotten" by officials, to the Alps region. With the help of an assistant prefect, they found what seemed like a safe home in the mountainous region of Izieu, east of Lyon. They were joined there in the spring of 1943 by Zlatin's husband, a woman doctor, several helpers, and other children—at times up to eighty. Sabine Zlatin and her husband sold personal effects—jewelry and paintings—to help finance operating expenses for the children's home. For a while, all went well. Then a *maquis* was set up in the region during the winter of 1943–1944. Zlatin feared it would attract German attention, so she decided to look for another place for the children, although her husband and

German troops marching down the Champs-Élysées under the Arc de Triomphe after Paris was declared an Open City on June 14, 1940, and surrendered without a struggle.

A Vichy propaganda poster urges French women to encourage their loved ones to go to work in Germany. Under the June 1942 *Relève* program, one POW would be returned in exchange for three skilled French workers willing to work for the Reich war machine. (Photos reprinted by permission of the Musée d'Histoire Contemporaine—BDIC)

Unless otherwise noted, photos are reprinted by permission of the Ministère des Anciens Combattants et Victimes de Guerre, Paris.

French women spent many hours in lines waiting to purchase food for their families during the Occupation years. Because of ever-increasing shortages, even the required ration tickets were no longer assurance they would find the most basic staples.

A German propaganda poster portrays the German soldier as the protector of the "abandoned population," part of a campaign to dispose the French more favorably to the occupying forces. On the left, someone has written, "Replacing the father he killed."

POPULATIONS
abandonnées,

faites confiance
AU SOLDAT ALLEMAND!

Permits were required to cross the demarcation line between the occupied zone in the north and the so-called free zone in the south. At German checkpoints along the line, officials examined all parcels and baggage.

In the absence of fuel, bicycles became *the* means of transportation throughout France during the war years. Here is one of the parking spots for the numerous bikes used in Paris.

The last known photo of Resistance heroine and martyr Berty Albrecht, who presumably committed suicide after her third arrest. The photograph was taken by her teenaged daughter, Mireille, whose shadow is visible at the lower right.

One of the many stickers, or "butterflies," that were posted in public locations. This one urges the "Women of France" to organize and protest the shortages of bread, milk, butter—and gas to cook the family soup. (Courtesy of Lucie Aubrac)

Femmes de France !...

Groupez-vous dans les Comités Populaires pour obtenir

DU PAIN !
DU LAIT !
DU BEURRE !

Et du gaz pour faire cuire la soupe !
Les ménagères en ont assez de priver leurs familles pour engraisser les boches.

L'Union
des Comités Populaires
Féminins

Lucie Aubrac, shown here in 1943 in front of the *lycée* where she taught, arranged three times for her husband's rescue from French and German prisons.

Ethnographer Germaine Tillion joined one of the earliest Resistance movements. Betrayed by a French informer, she was arrested, tried, and sent to Ravensbrück prison camp.

All French were required to carry identification cards like this one. Resistance members successfully counterfeited these and other documents for clandestine members, Jews, refugees, and others pursued by the Germans.

This unidentified woman is one of the few allowed to join the clandestine *maquis* fighting groups. Even fewer were allowed to bear arms; custom dictated that "war is a man's affair."

Produced by the Communist-sponsored Comités Féminins, these are short messages addressed to French women urging them to go to town halls to protest food shortages, high prices, and their husbands' low salaries. (Courtesy of Lucie Aubrac)

Combat and *Libération* were two prominent clandestine newspapers. The earthy headline in the issue of *Libération* shown here urges French youth to sabotage the conscription of workers who were to become "slaves in Hitler's service." (Courtesy of Lucie Aubrac)

The account in the *Progrès* of Lyon describes the Militia raid on the hidden Combat printing shop in which Lucienne Guezennec was the only survivor. (Courtesy of Lucienne Guezennec)

DAILY EXPRESS TUESDAY AUGUST 29 1944

GOLDEN-HAIRED FRENCHWOMAN WAS MAQUIS LEADER

'Madame X' shot a German from colonel's jeep

'WE HARRIED THE GERMANS ALL THE TIME'

GESTAPO PUT PRICE ON HER HEAD

From MONTAGUE LACEY: With the Maquis, Monday

HER name is "Madame X." And this golden-haired young Frenchwoman with a price on her head, who rode with an American tank column into Plouigneau is one of the most daring leaders of the Maquis in Brittany.

For many weeks until the Americans arrived she had roamed the countryside with armed bands of Patriots, sleeping and camping in the woods.

They have attacked German troops, guarded vital communication points, and taken many prisoners.

Madame X is spoken of as a kind of Joan of Arc in these parts, and everyone talks about how, on another occasion, she rode in the leading jeep with an American colonel into one Breton town and shot a German soldier with her pistol.

I have just spent several days with the Maquis, and have been into the isolated parts of the country where guerrilla warfare still goes on. In some of these places the people had yet had no chance of welcoming an American or a Briton who had arrived with the liberating forces.

MADAME MARIE LOUISE X

Like film star

Madame Marie Louise X is the wife of a doctor. She is tall and slender, with blue eyes, and her golden hair falls over her shoulders.

"I joined the Maquis the day the Germans first came into Brittany," she said. "My sister went to England by one of the escape boats to London.

"Our job in those early days was to map all German positions, keep a watch on their troops, send some of our men to England, and hide the Allied pilots who were shot down in these parts.

"Three times I was arrested by the Gestapo. The first time was in 1941. I saw the Germans come to my home. I asked them to answer the door, and that just gave me time to burn all the incriminating papers I had.

"It was a cold January morning, and only eight o'clock, and they took me away and questioned me for hours.

Arrested

"The Gestapo stayed in my house a week. They put my husband in prison. They could get no evidence about me, so they made an order that I was to report every day to their headquarters for several months.

"In October 1943 I was arrested again, and taken to the Gestapo headquarters at Brest for questioning. I was accused of sheltering British and American pilots, but I denied it.

"They let me go again.

"The third time I was arrested was on June 1, a few days before the Allies came. My husband was beaten with a steel rod, and put on a train to be taken to Germany.

"I have since heard that he managed to escape.

"The Germans just stripped and looted our house. They took every bit of clothing, and broke up the furniture.

"I was taken again to a German headquarters by the soldiers, but while they were still waiting for the Gestapo to arrive I feigned illness, and after a lot of persuasion my guard let me go to a wash-room.

"I managed to escape, and after walking and running nearly 20 miles that day joined up with an underground camp in a forest.

Harried Nazis

"There I met a young Frenchman, Lieutenant Robert, who had come from England. I posed as his sister as we roamed the countryside, making war on the Germans.

"We heard the Gestapo had circulated a picture of me, and offered a reward for my capture. But there were many trusted friends in these parts, although there were a few French people who would have been willing to give me away.

"All through June and July I slept in camps in the woods or in farmhouses. We harried the Germans all the time. Once we ran into a village where there were 400. Our car was shot up and burned out, but we got away across the fields.

"The Germans seemed terrified of the Maquis, and they had reason to be.

"Then came the day when we saw the American tanks coming down the road to Plouigneau. I jumped on the leading one and showed them the way in."

Madame X, who is 30, has three sons, who were cared for by friends while she was away with the Maquis. American officers are full of praise for her.

"Madame X.," Marie-Louise Le Duc, was a leader with the *maquis* in Brittany. Prior to the Liberation, she sheltered Allied aviators and others and helped them reach remote beaches, where they were picked up by British corvettes. (Courtesy of Yvonne Pétrement)

Wherever Simone Martin-Chauffier lived, her home was a Resistance center. She fed and housed leaders from various groups but had difficulty finding food for her many "guests."

France Pejot and her sister Raymonde were very active in the Franc-Tireur movement, all the while managing the family's lingerie store in Lyon. Although France's acting skills would serve her well during each of her three arrests, she was ultimately deported to Ravensbrück. (Courtesy of France Pejot-Jarre)

Marie-Madeleine Fourcade was the only woman to head a major Resistance network, which the Germans dubbed "Noah's Ark" because its 3,000 or so agents adopted the names of birds and animals. (Photo by Inge Reethof, reprinted by permission of the Polaroid Company)

The niece of General Charles de Gaulle, Geneviève de Gaulle, was involved in the Resistance from the first days of the Occupation, as was the entire de Gaulle family. She was captured and eventually deported to Ravensbrück, where she almost lost her sight. (Photo by Inge Reethof, reprinted by permission of the Polaroid Company)

When Evelyne Sullerot, today a well-known historian and sociologist, was arrested for anti-Vichy activities, she took and passed her *bac* examinations in prison. (Photo by Inge Reethof, reprinted by permission of the Polaroid Company)

Gabrielle Ferrières helped her husband and her brother, philosopher Jean Cavaillès—both Resistance leaders—in setting up their operations. All three were captured, and she spent five months in French prisons. (Photo by Margaret Collins Weitz)

Annie Kriegel ended up with the Communist Resistance through chance; her precocious "education" with the Resistance helped her later in her very successful academic career. (Photo by Inge Reethof, reprinted by permission of the Polaroid Company) the other adults were against the idea. On Holy Thursday 1944, while she was away searching for possible locations, the Germans arrived and captured everyone but a male helper, who escaped. None of the forty-four children returned; presumably they went directly to the crematoriums. The group had been denounced by a refugee from the annexed province of Lorraine. The fate of these children of Izieu, as mentioned in chapter 1, led to the 1984 extradition, then prosecution and condemnation, of the infamous Klaus Barbie. His telegram stating that he had "cleaned out" the Jewish children's home was a major piece of evidence at his trial.

Although all the children she thought saved were lost, and her husband was missing, Zlatin continued Resistance work in Paris and the surrounding region, as well as in Rouen, where she was wounded slightly in an unsuccessful attack on a prison.

Later, in Montpellier, Sabine Zlatin was arrested and taken to Gestapo headquarters, where she was brutally beaten: All her teeth were broken, and she bled copiously. A high-ranking officer came in and violently reproached his subalterns for beating her in his office. "I don't want any blood here," he shouted. "Do it in the cells. Clean up this place at once." In the panic that followed the general's departure, the officers told Zlatin to go and wash herself. Since she understood German, she was aware of their situation. Taking advantage of the distraction, she spoke German to the guard outside: "I was brought here as a witness but have a bad nosebleed. It happens from time to time. I need a shot of brandy from that café across the street." The guard helped her across the yard and instructed the guards at the entrance to let her back in. She went to the café—and out a back door. The café owners, it turned out, also were members of the Resistance.[3]

The Oeuvre de Sainte-Foy was set up in July 1942 by Yvonne Baratte and Marie-Hélène Lefaucheux. The organization's goal was to assist prisoners. (Sainte-Foy was their patron saint.) Baratte had a Red Cross nurse's diploma and had worked in the military service centers in the early days of the war. The group set up libraries in French prisons and, subsequently, in prison camps in Germany. Through solicitation, they acquired more than forty thousand books for the prisoners. By 1944, in spite of all the logistical difficulties, Sainte-Foy was sending more than a thousand anonymous packages a month to Parisian prisons and helping families send others. At Fresnes, prisoners helped unload the parcels delivered by students and young people. Since it took some time to transfer the packages, there were opportunities to exchange valuable information. The work of the Oeuvre increased steadily. Many people involved with the group did more than simply prepare and send parcels. For example, they found clothing and arranged for false documents for prisoners and escapees. Because this went beyond their permitted activities, they risked prosecution. Yvonne Baratte was arrested in the summer of 1944 and deported to Ravensbrück, where she perished.[4]

Under clandestine conditions, this traditional "women's work"—support services—was difficult and dangerous. Funds were essential, most supplies were rationed, and everything had to be done in secret. Even locating those who had been arrested was no easy matter. Women posing as fiancées helped gather information. Next, someone had to communicate with the prisoners to try to help them escape. By October 1943, Combat had a significant number of clandestine social workers taking care of more than a thousand prisoners and their families. Children whose mothers were arrested had to be cared for. Yvette Farnoux covered many miles on an old bicycle seeing people and seeking funds and supplies. Agents who had gone underground no longer had paid jobs. Resistance movements tried to provide a minimum income for clandestine agents and their families who were without independent means. Initially, funds came from contributors. With time, London helped provide funds and air-dropped food, but there never was enough. Ration cards of all sorts were needed. To supplement counterfeit cards, some were obtained from obliging employees, others by raids on municipal offices. Women were sent in first to survey the scene and see what action was indicated.

Madeleine Baudoin, in her memoirs, pays tribute to the help of the clandestine social services. Baudoin recounts how she and another Resistance comrade forced a mayor and his colleagues to open a safe and hand over all the ration tickets and other papers—enough to fill two suitcases. Her colleague came into the office brandishing a gun. Baudoin had come in earlier, on the pretext of doing business in the town hall. Baudoin was "held up" by the "terrorist," along with the other good citizens. When he escaped, she gave the police a very *inexact* description of her comrade. This scenario was repeated in other government offices. At times, women employees agreed to be tied up to make their story more convincing. Baudoin notes: "The social services [of the Resistance] were in constant need of food coupons to be distributed among the families of the imprisoned, the deported, the wounded, and those shot."[5]

To find tobacco for packages destined for prisoners, women at times walked into tobacco shops and demanded it. In general, they found the shopkeepers less than pleased to "contribute" to the Resistance, as it hurt their black-market business.

+⟫━⟪+

Berty Albrecht was the animating force in Combat, set up by her companion, Henri Frenay. It was Berty (as she was known to all) who conceived of and organized formal social services for Combat—a major contribution to the Resistance that was copied by other movements. As agents went underground, or were captured or deported, support—both material and moral—was needed for their wives and families. Such was the case when the Parisian section of Combat was decimated in February 1942, betrayed by a double agent. In addition, several dozen members in the unoccupied zone were arrested and imprisoned during this period, after a courier was arrested carrying a list, contrary to orders.

Who was this exceptional woman? Berthe Wild was born in Marseilles in 1893, the only child of a bourgeois Swiss couple of strong Protestant faith. The Bible was a constant reference in her upbringing. At eighteen, Berty started nursing studies, receiving her diploma in 1913. She went to London to improve her English (one of seven languages she learned) and there became engaged to Frederic Albrecht, a family friend she had met when she was ten. Frederic's family were Dutch Catholics settled in Germany—a country he could not abide—so he moved to England. Albrecht, a pacifist, was sent to the Isle of Wight for the duration of World War I.

Their projected marriage thus deferred, Berty worked long hours in Marseilles hospitals doing her patriotic and evangelical duty. The couple married in Rotterdam a few weeks after the armistice. Son Freddie was born in 1921 and daughter Mireille in 1924. The family settled in London, where her husband's affairs prospered. Bored by her worldly life, Berty joined Sylvia Pankhurst and the British Birth Control Movement. She met intellectuals such as Bertrand Russell, George Bernard Shaw, and H. G. Wells. As her son put it: "One could say my mother was at the front starting in 1930."[6] When her husband lost most of his fortune during the depression, Berty convinced him she could live more modestly in Paris, where she and the children moved in 1932. The following year, she founded a review devoted to sexual problems, *Le Problème sexuel*, very much in advance of its time but short-lived because of funding problems. With Madeleine Braun, she helped set up the World Women's Commission. When Mussolini attacked Ethiopia, she organized an ambulance service for the wounded populace. And she founded an organization to help German Jews fleeing Nazism. For this she was blacklisted by Hitler in his *White Book*. Always independent, Albrecht never joined a political party. In 1935, Berty met Catholic career army officer Henri Frenay, who describes himself in his memoirs as belonging to the French Right—"traditional, poor, patriotic, and paternalist." The two became close, although Frenay was twelve years younger than Berty. She introduced him to her friends—intellectuals and leftists, a milieu new to Frenay. Anxious to do more to help the less fortunate, she decided to attend the École des Surintendantes d'Usine (School of Women Factory Supervisors) in Paris.

When Berty applied for admission to the school in 1936, she was forty-three, well beyond the usual entry age, but the directress recognized her exceptional qualities and accepted her. Berty and her two teenaged children were now students at the same time. Her training included a month-long internship in the Galeries Lafayette department store, ticketing merchandise. Appalled by the regimented conditions there, Berty wrote an excellent report with suggestions for improving working conditions for women factory workers.* In October 1938, Berty started as a social worker in an optical factory. (Recently passed Popular Front legislation required social services in factories.) Her husband, unable to comprehend his wife's new projects, cut off her allowance, obliging her to sell her only ring as well as some furniture.

After several short assignments, Berty was appointed to a factory outside Paris. When the Germans invaded, she set up cots in her apartment for those fleeing and packed most of her belongings for storage, before sending sixteen-year-old Mireille to stay with a friend in Nevers. Son Freddie was away at boarding school. Berty helped transfer the factory to a town near the demarcation line. Finally, she heard from Frenay, then setting up Combat in the unoccupied zone.

---

*The text was published by Annie Fourcaut in *Femmes à l'usine dans l'entre-deux-guerres*, 1982.

She volunteered her services. With Mireille's approval, she sent her daughter to live with a strict maiden aunt in Marseilles.

Berty joined Frenay in Vichy. She proposed an information bulletin for their fledgling movement and typed up what was to become the newspaper *Combat*. Claude Bourdet holds that "the movement—and, by extension, the entire French Resistance—owed a great deal to this militant woman of the Left who was without prejudices. Without her, many things would have been different."[7] Not surprisingly, Mireille Albrecht is upset when she finds her mother referred to as Frenay's secretary in Resistance accounts.

When Berty obtained a posting as head of the Unemployment Commission in Lyon, Mireille returned to live with her mother in a small rented apartment in that city. Her memories of that period are vivid:

> A lot of visitors—agents responsible for the organization of the movement in various regions—came to our place. They reported their situation to Berty and received orders. Some crossed the line with false papers, frequently poorly made. They were afraid of checks, so they did not want to stay in a hotel. Mother and I slept together—which freed the sofa (where I usually slept) for one person at least—although often enough there was someone else sleeping on the floor in our room. In this case, we put a large screen next to our bed.[8]

The elderly concierge watched all this activity from her lodge and drew her own conclusions. Here were two women who received a steady stream of mostly male visitors. Some spent the night. Obviously they were prostitutes, so she reported them to the police. When the police arrived at the apartment, Mireille played the innocent young girl, claiming that she used the wall map with pinpoints for homework assignments, and that the cigarette butts were those of her absent mother. Before the police could return, mother and daughter moved to a new apartment, where they limited their visitors. Mireille attended *lycée* classes and led a double life. The police visited frequently, so it was important not to raise questions by repeated absences from school: "It was essential for our security to do nothing that would attract attention to us."

With characteristic energy, Berty reconciled her clandestine work with that for her regular job. For the commission, she organized workshops to make costumes for the theater—one of her passions—as well as workshops to prepare infant layettes using flour sacks sent from the

United States, among other materials. She worked with social and charitable organizations, including Catholic Relief and the Salvation Army, until she was arrested in May 1942 and imprisoned in Vals-les-Bains, in the Ardèche. While Berty was in prison, Mireille served as liaison between the movement and her mother. Combat social services provided a modest monthly allotment to the young girl, now on her own, and made arrangements for her to eat at the Salvation Army canteen. Weeks passed without any sign of a trial, so Berty decided to force the issue and went on a hunger strike, along with fellow prisoner Emmanuel Mounier, editor of the Catholic review *Esprit* and affiliate of the Uriage center Vichy founded to train the future—male—leaders of France. Eventually they were hospitalized (Berty lost almost thirty pounds), but Vichy was forced to bring them to trial. On one of her visits to the hospital, Mireille arrived wearing large white earrings then fashionable. Berty, ever the concerned mother, greeted her:

> "But what are those? You're crazy, my daughter. Can't you see what you resemble—a barmaid! And the young lady thinks she looks attractive. Take those off at once!" [Berty's messages to Frenay reveal her deep doubts about leaving her teenage daughter alone in Lyon.] "Did I do the right thing? I sacrificed my daughter to the Resistance. I failed in my maternal duties."[9]

Instead of being released while awaiting trial, Berty was transferred to St. Joseph prison in Lyon and incarcerated with common criminals—the price she paid in order to be tried. But, as a movement comrade recounts:

> She adapted well to her new life in prison. She even found it an interesting experience. She was appalled by prison conditions: the lack of cleanliness, air, and elementary hygiene. [As she had during her department-store work, Berty decided to draw up a program of suggested prison reforms.] She secured paper and pencil and drew up a report on prison conditions that she succeeded in secreting outside the prison. She was convinced that something would be done eventually. Just a few days after her arrival, she had us cleaning the toilets, an epic undertaking. At one point, we were doubled up with laughter. Berty could not resist recalling the time she lived in London and had the same dressmaker as the queen.[10]

Mireille now took private lessons to prepare for the *bac* school-finishing exam—between weekly visits to her mother—because her school had expelled her. Finally, Berty was tried with the other members of Combat. Sentenced to six months, she had, in theory, less than two months left to serve. She arranged for Mireille to go to a school at Chambon-sur-Lignon (southwest of Lyon).* Every letter encouraged her daughter to study. When Berty learned that she was being transferred to a prison in the southwest Tarn region for the rest of her sentence, she decided to simulate madness: Escape from an asylum, she figured, would be easier to arrange. Mother and daughter embraced for the first time in six months when Berty was sent to a nearby psychiatric clinic. But as the weeks passed, this strong woman worried that she might really become insane if she were not rescued soon. Mireille, her mother's only contact with the outside world, witnessed all this during her daily visits: "I passed some very difficult moments with her. She became increasingly depressed, convinced she had been forgotten."

Finally, thanks in part to a doctor who lent his keys to Mireille for duplication, Berty escaped on Christmas Eve. Mireille joined her in a small town nearby. Both de Gaulle and the Resistance leadership urged Berty to go to England for her safety, but she refused. "I can't wage war from a leather armchair in London," she insisted, "[but] I can fight here." So she sent her daughter to stay with friends and resumed her work for the movement. In early April 1943, Mireille heard from her mother. Berty was staying nearby with the Gouze family. During visits to her mother, Mireille had become a good friend of their daughter Danielle (later Mitterrand). The idyll was short-lived. Berty was captured May 28, 1943, at a rendezvous in Mâcon. She was last seen being taken from the Hôtel Terminus in Lyon to a car, her face bruised and swollen. The circumstances of her death shortly thereafter are unclear; presumably she committed suicide rather than face more torture. As a key figure in Combat, she knew too much about the movement. In her last letter, sent to her husband in England two weeks before her death, she wrote, "To die is not that serious. What matters is living according to the ideal one has formed."[11]

+>==<+

Renée (Mely) Bédarida worked with Témoignage Chrétien (Christian Witness). After the war, she wrote a history of the movement and a biography of its founder, Father Pierre Chaillet. Bédarida, a member of the women's branch of Jeunesse Étudiante Chrétienne Française (JECF, Young French Christian Students), was studying at the Uni-

---

*Protestants in this town sheltered many Jewish children; see Philip Hallie's *Lest Innocent Blood Be Shed*, and the film *The Weapons of the Spirit*.

versity of Lyon when war broke out. With classmates, she began distributing handbills and took up collections for the refugees from Alsace-Lorraine. In 1942, she lived in a student center for girls run by
the sisters of Notre Dame of Zion, while working on degrees in both
English and law.

"The mission of the Order of Notre Dame of Zion was to improve
relations between Christian and Jews, with the hope of converting
Jews to Catholicism. The order was founded in the nineteenth century by two brothers who were themselves converted Jews. Throughout the war, the sisters aided persecuted French and foreign Jews;
that was part of their mission. With Germaine Ribière, I helped the
sisters hide many people. They were given false baptismal certificates and false papers. Today I still occasionally meet Jews who were
hidden in our foyer in Lyon. I also joined an interdenominational
group, Amitié Chrétienne (Christian Friendship). Our tasks were to
find homes for 'illegal' families or children and to help with escapes
to Switzerland. I worked with the false-paper service and did liaison
for the Secret Army in the Rhône-Alpes region.

"One assignment I remember well was to accompany about
twelve young Jewish girls from Grenoble to Sainte-Baume [in the
south, near Aix-en-Provence], where Dominican nuns ran a hotel
school reserved for young girls evacuated from Alsace-Lorraine.
Since the girls were from Central Europe, they spoke not a word of
French. All had false papers. After rounding them up from the
homes where they had been staying, I put them in two compart-
ments of a night train bound for Marseilles. Each time conductors or
German soldiers passed, the girls paled and became upset. At long
last, we arrived safely at Sainte-Baume—after a bus trip from Marseilles. That is a night I have never forgotten.

"Holy Thursday 1944 [date of the raid on Izieu], I made a stupid
mistake that forced me to leave Lyon. I went into a church to pray
and left my purse in the pew. I missed it almost at once and went
back to get it, but it had disappeared already. The purse contained
my real identity card with my family's address and compromising papers. [The person who found them in the church turned everything
over to the authorities rather than discreetly contacting her.] The
Gestapo went to my parents' home in Bourg. Fortunately, they were
not bothered. Father Chaillet insisted that I now move to Paris.
There I was given a new assignment. The comrade in charge of the
distribution of our paper, *Témoignage Chrétien*, in eastern France had

been arrested and the sections were rather disorganized. So I went there to take his place and renew the links with Paris. From then on, I traveled throughout the region by train. When train service was disrupted [by the bombings and fighting following the Allied landings], I went about by bicycle. On the eve of the liberation of Dijon [November 9, 1944], I managed to print the last clandestine *Courrier du Témoignage Chrétien*. Three young women teachers responsible for our newspaper (*Témoignage Chrétien*) in Dijon and I distributed the paper to French soldiers and the inhabitants of the city, who were all celebrating.

"Some years ago, while working on a biography of Father Chaillet, I realized that this was the sole sector of the Resistance where only women were involved. It is always women who direct and animate support services. It was the women who managed Resistance social services—a woman's job. In each movement, it was the women who supervised and undertook the social work."

Renée Bédarida agrees that women's roles in the French Resistance have been largely overlooked. Apart from the problem of documenting their work, much of what they did has been considered secondary.

"In their personal accounts, there are a few heads, like Claude Bourdet of Combat, who mention the work of women in the social services. Others—including Marie-Madeleine Fourcade of Noah's Ark—never refer to it. Resistance group budgets allotted considerable sums to help families and prisoners. By examining these figures, one realizes the full scope of the Resistance social services run mostly by women.

"I joined the Resistance because I am Christian and deeply convinced of the dignity of each human being. I had to prove to myself that I was faithful to my convictions. Because I knew that Nazism was anti-Christian and antihuman, I simply had to do something to oppose this ideology. Besides, for me, a Jew was like any other human being. Because the Jews were mistreated, because they were pursued, I had to intervene and help as best I could. I could not simply remain idle. Obviously, I would not have become a historian of that period if I had not been in the Resistance. I never would have thought of working on that period if I just had quietly continued my studies and been a better student. Actually I did not have much time to study in those days. I never thought of writing my

memoirs; I never had major responsibilities. It would be interesting
if the 'small fry' (*piétaille*) of the Resistance wrote their memoirs
some day—anonymous testimony, so to speak—because they ended
up in the prisons and camps, as did the leaders. For example, I have
a great deal of remorse about what happened to a classmate at the
university, where, unfortunately, my involvement in the Resistance
was known. She begged me to help her join the Resistance. Finally I
agreed. Three weeks later, she was arrested and then deported. Fortunately, she came back from the camps, but that was terrible for
me. That young woman spent less than a month working for the
Resistance, but she spent two years in Ravensbrück. She represents
the 'small fry' of the Resistance, yet her work and that of others like
her could cost dearly.

"Our group was composed principally of young people, mostly
students. There were very few girls in the central team of Témoignage Chrétien. The Jesuit fathers were more comfortable dealing
with laymen. Remember, it is more difficult among Catholics to
participate when you are a woman or a girl—or at least such was
the case at that time. The situation is different now, but in those
days, if you were a girl, you had to really win the confidence of
Jesuits or priests in order for them to confer responsibilities on
you."[12]

Clandestine support services were set up all over occupied France.
In Paris, local aid committees in each district helped youths avoid
forced labor in Germany. In 1947, Céline L'Hotte, writing about the
impact of social work, spoke from personal involvement. A trained
professional, she worked throughout the war and the Occupation with
other groups, such as the Red Cross and teachers. All had to respect
the limits that Vichy—which "tolerated" them—permitted. Before
the Liberation, they never were allowed to enter a camp or a prison
in the Paris region.

I have virtually no documentation or accurate recollection about
dates. Nevertheless, the essential facts remain very precise. Secours
National/Entr'aide Française was an epic undertaking. It served as
the basis for the future French social services, the fortunate impetus
of truly new initiatives.[13]*

---

*Secours National (National Help), an umbrella organization that coordinated
various private relief agencies, and the Unemployment Commission were run by the
Vichy government.

Clandestine medical services were linked to social services. Initially, medical services for the fighting forces of World War II resembled those in earlier conflicts. British and French forces had their respective medical corps, and, as in World War I, women served in these corps. Women ambulance drivers, like Odette Fabius, evacuated the wounded.

During World War I, Fabius's mother volunteered to help with the wounded returning from the front; an entire floor of their spacious Paris townhouse was turned into a temporary hospital. When World War II broke out, Fabius volunteered her services (as did her mother). She joined a group of other upper-middle-class and aristocratic women to form the Section Sanitaire Automobile (SSA, Mobile Health Units). With ambulances purchased thanks to their connections and resources, the SSA aided refugees heading south and sent supplies to prisoner-of-war camps. One of Fabius's first assignments was to transport the Red Cross's treasury in her ambulance to Bordeaux, where the government had been transferred in the wake of the German invasion. After the armistice, she joined her family—including her young daughter—in the southwest Basque region and helped arrange for the reception of trains carrying the wounded.

With the Occupation, Fabius unhesitatingly joined a network even though she was doubly vulnerable because she was Jewish. "The biggest shock of the war for me was the discovery of anti-Semitism," she acknowledges. Odette Fabius had a sheltered upbringing in a prominent, assimilated Jewish family. As it turned out, her "education" was further extended when she was captured and sent to Ravensbrück. Even in the camp, she found discrimination.

"I was always amazed—proof, no doubt, of my naïveté—when I observed that the suffering that we underwent together was not enough to end prejudice. There were continual instances of contempt that were not only revolting, but, given that we were all threatened by death, absurd as well. One morning, after roll call, our German guards asked for volunteers for the BDA (army brothels). A long murmur of indignation greeted this request. The SS then designated four deportees whose record indicated they were prostitutes. They left at once. That evening, two of them returned sheepishly. They had been rejected for health reasons. Chantal, one of them, asked me what I thought of her. I answered her reassuringly and told her, 'I said to myself that you were lucky to have had that profession, for it would help you, through close contacts with offi-

cers, to find a way of escape that the rest of us could not even
dream of. . . .' Perhaps she believed me, but she was not completely
reassured. 'Your profession is your affair. Up until now, you have behaved well with all our comrades. Their attitude toward you is not
going to change.' "

However, one of their group wanted to put the two "lost" women
in quarantine, adding total isolation to all the infamous treatment
that women prisoners already received from the guards. It certainly
would have demoralized the two women. The implacable "judge" who
wanted to mete out this punishment was a very pretentious woman
who continually boasted of her palatial estate in France. For this reason, her comrades referred to her as "Madame Two Castles and Six
Towers."

"Since this woman was religious, I pointed out to her that the condemnation of the two unfortunates did not conform to the Bible, to
which she referred frequently. She scornfully answered, 'By what
right do you refer to the Bible when you don't even belong to our
religion?' How could anyone answer such stupidity? Fortunately, Tatiana de Fleurieu was present. 'Be quiet,' she told the would-be
judge; 'Odette Fabius is certainly more Christian than you are.' All
our comrades backed Tatiana and me, so the two brothel rejects
were not ostracized."

While at Ravensbrück, Fabius achieved the dubious distinction of
being the only known escapee of that notorious women's camp. Her
dearly acquired freedom lasted only four days. When captured, she was
treated brutally: fifty lashes of the *Schlag* (whip), followed by ten days
nude and isolated in a bunker. When the German officer compli-
mented her for not crying out during the terrible beating, she answered: "I am French, commandant." She fainted under the blows that
followed that remark.[14]

As the French Resistance evolved, clandestine medical services
(*services sanitaires*) were needed. Following the pattern found in other
areas of Resistance work, services developed to address specific needs.
Practicing medical personnel—doctors, nurses, and technicians—
worked for the Resistance under cover of their regular functions.
When the compulsory labor decrees (STOs) were issued, medical
workers altered or substituted X rays so that young men appeared to
be tubercular or suffering from serious illnesses. This freed them from

being sent to work for the Reich war machine. False diagnoses of allegedly contagious diseases spared others. There were even instances in which the Germans redeployed troops because medical personnel produced false reports of an "epidemic" in a particular region. They were obsessed with health concerns—an obsession the Resistance sometimes could use to its advantage.

When the Germans retreated across France in front of the Allied advance in 1944, there were battles and many skirmishes. Medical services became a pressing necessity for Resistance combatants. Anyone with serious wounds or in need of surgery had to be evacuated. Clinics willing to operate and treat the wounded were sought, as were homes where they could recuperate. Resistance health services—now run largely from Paris—worked closely with Resistance social services. On occasion, they were impeded by Red Cross directors unsympathetic to the Resistance; the Red Cross was regarded as officially linked to the Vichy government. But by and large, medical services were unstintingly provided by nurses from all stations in life.

+──►─◄+

Sister Edwige Dumas worked in a Calais hospital run by Franciscan missionaries of Notre Dame. Her background was international: Her mother was Argentinian and her maternal grandfather was British. Her French father often would tell Dumas and her sister of their grandfather (his father), who died on the battlefield during the Franco-Prussian War. Sister Dumas experienced war firsthand when German troops blitzkrieged across northern France in the spring 1940 offensive; shellings and bombings were heavy, and hospital personnel could go out only at night. The hospital was filled with an unending stream of wounded military, along with civilians who had been machine-gunned by German aviators as they tried to join the mass exodus fleeing the conflict. To satisfy her curiosity, she once went up to the attic to observe an RAF bombing raid. The hospital was struck in one such raid: The directress and several women employees were killed, and the basement was flooded.

"Little by little, we adapted to the situation. We sisters slept in a little dormitory set up in the basement and ate our scanty meals rapidly. Our concern was not to leave the wounded and ill without care. Eventually, everyone ended up living in the basement— patients and staff alike. The Nazis forced French youths to help build concrete blockhouses along the Channel coast, where they

were exposed to RAF bombings and to illness (some volunteered
for the assignment because of high pay and other benefits). When
they were brought in for treatment, we kept them in the hospital
as long as possible. One Resistance fighter was brought in with a
jaw fractured under torture. When the Gestapo returned for him, I
was able to arrange to have him sent to another hospital—not to
prison.

"German authorities ordered that all radios be turned in. I hid
mine in a coal bin, so I heard de Gaulle's 1940 appeal from London.
I understood my duty as a French woman. In spite of my weakness
as a woman, and being a nun, I really wanted to do something for
France. I decided to join the Resistance as soon as the opportunity
presented itself. In addition to all my hospital work, I cared for an
abandoned infant. After a few months, I gave the baby to a deserving couple. I was very upset by the loss. Mother Superior reminded
me that life is composed of sacrifices. After that, I took over the
care of the infants born at our hospital and subsequently abandoned.
Privately, I confided in a doctor with whom I had worked for some
years and explained that I wanted to work for the Resistance. Dr.
Drujon encouraged me. The problem was the vow of obedience I
had taken; I could not engage myself freely. This was a difficult decision that I discussed with Mother Superior. After listening, and reflecting momentarily, she told me I had complete freedom to join.
But I was to be careful!"

Throughout the Calais region of Normandy, small groups were
forming to fight the oppressor. In June 1941, Sister Dumas joined the
Alibi Jean de Vienne network. Dr. Drujon continued his work at the
hospital—although under house arrest because of Resistance work. He
had a secret radio and sent information to London. When he was
forced to go underground, Sister Dumas concealed him and later
helped him flee—as she had helped dockworkers and others escape.
Among her patients was a badly burned German soldier she nursed
carefully. She also helped Robert X., head of a Communist *maquis* in
the Calais region, her patient at the beginning of the war. In the
summer of 1944, the Germans were after him. He simulated illness to
seek her out and confide in her.

"Robert X. had orders to sabotage the Brampton factory, which
manufactured parts for the German war machine. Before he could
undertake his mission, he was arrested, tortured, and condemned to

death. Someone had denounced him. The night before his execution, he was able to escape by cutting through his chains and handcuffs with an iron file hidden in the toilets. I helped arrange his escape. The Germans who came to see me accused me of hiding a terrorist. They searched my cell and checked all the patients. I told Mother Superior about it and then returned to my work as usual. Still, I was quite upset. I knew they would return.

"At midnight, a German soldier came and asked for me. He questioned me—in excellent French—about Robert X. In spite of my fear, I refused to sign a paper saying I would denounce someone who in my view was a true patriot. I reminded him of Christ's message: 'Love one another.' I also had a visit from a French man who asked many questions. However, I was on my guard and said nothing. Meanwhile, Robert was hiding in a friend's home. While the Germans searched, he hid in the flooded basement. After their departure, he had to move. I explained his situation to the other sisters. They proposed hiding him in the morgue, but finally, that didn't seem acceptable. There were posters everywhere offering a reward for his arrest. Several women in town sheltered him. With the aid of the central commissioner—also in the Resistance—we got him a false ID."

While Robert was in hiding, Sister Dumas went out once or twice a week during the afternoon period, the only time when area residents could circulate. Dressed in her habit and a long black cape, she went out with her medical kit and a small parcel of food. Robert was now staying in a little shed at the end of the garden linked to the hospital by an electric buzzer—which alerted him in case of danger. When the Allies approached, the hospital was evacuated. Robert left with the patients, his face swathed in bandages. In the suburbs, he was reunited with his mother and sister, who thought the Germans had killed him.

While still at the hospital, Sister Dumas attended a young foreign woman, a slight blonde who had been captured by a tall SS man—with skulls on the lapels of his black uniform, Sister noted. The woman parachutist turned out just to be frightened, not wounded. Dumas took her water with a little Cognac to drink—and regretted she could not help more.

"As the Allies approached, a twenty-four-hour truce was declared to permit the population to leave Calais. I stayed and helped a German doctor with his German patients. In appreciation, he gave me

his surgical kit. After the city was liberated, the other sisters and I
returned to our badly damaged hospital. It had been pillaged as well.
Once more we set up our dormitory in the basement. In anticipa-
tion of the Allied landings, the Germans had mined the beaches.
Two young women driving Red Cross ambulances were not aware of
that when they drove out to rescue several wounded soldiers. Both
were killed, along with an FFI man who tried to save them. German
prisoners were put to work clearing the mines. I nursed those
wounded. As I changed the dressings of one, he observed, 'You care
for me, Sister, yet I am an enemy of France. I bombed the city of
Calais.' I explained that he was wounded, and suffering, and it was
my duty to help him—as Christ told us. In the network, they called
me the sister-soldier. Do I deserve that name? I don't know. I belong
to the peaceful army of St. Francis of Assisi. I only obeyed."[15]

One could say of all the women who served in the medical and
social organizations of the Resistance that they, too, obeyed an inner
voice as they offered aid to the injured and needy.

Historian Hélène Eck notes that during the Occupation, there
was also sharply increased state intervention in social and health fields.
"Workers in this field became more professionalized, and their activities were supervised by a new government department in charge of
family and health services." She also observes: "In one sense the war
marked the end of an era: Never again would the social-service profession be quite so apolitical, autonomous, or exclusively female." This
was partly because social workers were not always neutral or innocent.
Combat, as we have seen, was helped by women from the École des
Surintendantes d'Usine, such as Berty Albrecht and Yvette Farnoux,
as well as Jeanne Sivadon.[16]

At the other extreme, there were social assistants who encouraged
French workers to accept work in Germany. There were assistants who
returned from Germany in 1943 and broadcast reassuring reports over
German-controlled Radio Paris of conditions there and some members
of the Mouvement Populaire des Familles (MPF) who took "bitter
note" in 1945 of their failure to help the Resistance. Other social
workers who supported Vichy found themselves in a "delicate" position when Liberation came.[17]

9

Dangerous Liaisons

> She [Joan of Arc] is the model young Frenchwoman. Feminine enough to be flirtatious and like nice clothes, human enough to weep and tremble over her unfortunate lot when her condemnation is announced. . . . Remember also, that this virgin, although continually surrounded by rough soldiers, was always respected by them. Young Men of a renewed France, you must respect Young Girls, who are France's new spring. Leave to the sad and ugly past, leave to our former debased society, the filthy promiscuity that defiled our young people. From henceforth, may an honest and joyful camaraderie reign between Young Men and Young Girls of our France. May it be without prudery and without ambiguity, excluding all promiscuous familiarities, allowing only the love that faithfully unites spouses.
>
> —*Message of Education Minister Abel Bonnard, to be read to classes on Joan of Arc's feast day, May 1942.*[1]

ALTHOUGH ROMANTIC LIAISONS WERE DISCOURAGED, SINCE THEY could lead to capture, couples did meet in the Resistance. There were, after all, many young people involved—this age group was freer to participate. In his 1994 biography of François Mitterrand, Pierre Péan notes that with the intense pressure building around the future president and his Resistance entourage, the group appears to have decided to live a passionate life. Members in the Resistance often shared a sense of adventure and *joie de vivre*. They fell in love and some had children, even those who had gone underground. Marriage was virtually out of the question for clandestines, for they had changed identities and had no legal status. A few did marry, but most couples waited until after the war, when there were many marriages among those who had met during the Resistance.

For those in the Resistance, life went on—often more intensely, as many were experiencing what was to be the high point in their lives. Needless to say, the presence of children complicated the decision to work for the Resistance: Children were potential hostages. For security, Henri Frenay and his companion, Chilena Ciosi, a doctor who had gone underground and was also a Corsican—a further administrative handicap—declared their son born in October 1943 "of unknown mother and father." They placed him in an orphanage. At the end of hostilities, the couple married and recognized Henri junior.[2] PCF leader Charles Tillon and his wife, Colette, wrestled with the problem of giving a name and legal father to the child they were expecting. A prison guard—who locked up his colleagues and freed all Resistance prisoners—took his wife and young child to a new location after that escapade. The couple acquired false identity papers. When the wife became pregnant again, they "married" under their false names and declared the baby, when it was born, the child of that "marriage." After the war, there were often complications when clandestine Resistance members tried to acquire legal recognition of children born under false identities.[3]

Young *résistante* Brigitte Friang became romantically involved with her leader. Spending sixteen hours a day together in an atmosphere of survival brought forth powerful feelings. Working side by side, sharing common ideals, running the same risks—all contributed to the growth of strong passions. When she joined the BOA (Bureau of Aerial Operations) in 1943, she was a medical student. From the outset of the war, she had tried to protest and harass the Germans, but, she says, without much effect. Once in the Resistance, the situation changed: "Our lives were filled with tension, the permanent fear of being followed or arrested at any moment. During this time, I slept little. Sometimes I stayed up all night coding and decoding."[4]

Marie Granet lists many postwar marriages among the young people in the movements about which she wrote. Although she does not mention it, some of these marriages were between partners of differing backgrounds, religions, and regions—not such a common occurrence in French society. But for the Resistance, they never would have met. One such example is that of the Chambruns. Noëlle de Chambrun's parents were poor, and her grandparents had themselves been illegitimate. In the Resistance, she met aristocrat and *maquis* head Count Gilbert de Chambrun. One might say that Noëlle, a doctor, established her "legitimacy" through her exceptional work in the Resistance, for which she was awarded the Legion of Honor. The war brought together this couple with very different social backgrounds.[5]

In addition to serious relationships, there were, to be sure, short-lived liaisons due to chance encounters. Often they were interrupted by outside circumstances, or they had never been considered long-term. Simone Colin had an affair for some time with her leader, but eventually she broke it off on moral grounds: He was married. She also became more aware of the implications of her situation when her lover asked her if she were "of age." She had, in fact, just turned twenty-one, but she had been living with him for some time before that.[6] The Resistance was not composed of saints. As noted, there were obvious security dangers in these brief encounters. It is difficult not to reveal names or secrets, not to compromise one's anonymity in intimate settings. The Communists tolerated liaisons among urban members because being involved with someone from your own group was viewed as the lesser of two evils.

In seeking to explore sexual activity in the Resistance, one is handicapped by the reticence, modesty, and discretion of many of the women participants. They were brought up in an era when such matters were not discussed. There is a generation gap. A countess in the Resistance who was married at nineteen states that she went to the altar not knowing how children were conceived. Even today, most of these women—now in their late sixties and older—are not comfortable speaking about this topic. Several interviewees referred to lovers as husbands. The same difficulties occur with sexual harassment, a problem being addressed today in France with limited success. Accounts reveal that women in the Resistance did on occasion have to deal with the problem—by wearing wedding bands, inventing fiancés, and using other ruses.

Parachutist Jeanne Bohec found that while being a young woman never posed any problems for her among Resistance comrades, the opposite was true with the military. She tried to forget all the sexist remarks and sexual innuendo to which she was subjected. Resistance

activist Simone Debout participated with Jean-Paul Sartre and Simone de Beauvoir in the Socialisme et Liberté discussion group, which
met during the Occupation. Debout describes male Communist Party
members she worked with as being very "macho." In her view, they
used women. Later she left the Party. (Debout, incidentally, faults
Sartre for barely touching on the issue of the Resistance in their discussion group, and then only in the most vague, abstract terms—even
though the philosopher was to claim otherwise after the war.) Male
operatives were separated from their families. In spite of an ascetic
side to their lives, available women at times served as mistresses, even
though only "pure" friendships are claimed in some PCF accounts.[7]

Trying to marry was difficult, especially for clandestine résistants.
Such was the case with Paris-born Françoise de Boissieu. Her father
was a university history professor in Paris; other relatives were professors and intellectuals. As she explains, the family had been in France
for centuries.

"We [the Cahen family] were Jews who had been in France for a
very long time. One of my ancestors participated in the Convention
during the French Revolution. He obtained cemeteries for the Jews,
who had just been made citizens. Earlier, Louis XVI made him a no-
bleman. It is just chance, of course, that our family has been established in France for centuries. That is not the case with many
French Jews.

"I was brought up in a completely open-minded milieu, without
constraints or orientation, without any religious instruction. Because
I had an inquiring mind, I was allowed to attend services at Protestant and Catholic churches, as well as at Jewish temples. At sixteen,
I almost converted to Catholicism. My husband, Michel de Boissieu,
is from an old, established Catholic family. When we met, I found
he was without prejudice of any sort—completely open. He had
done graduate studies in the humanities. This was the tradition in
my family as well—a commitment to the humanities. We became
engaged in 1939. At the time, Michel was convinced that France
would win the war, while I never for a moment imagined that possibility. I did not believe France could win. I had read quite a few
books about Hitler, so I had few illusions—unlike a lot of other people, including members of my own family.

"Michel was called up for military service and went to war, so I
resumed my studies in Montpellier. My father had been sent to the

University of Montpellier for the duration of the war because there was a shortage of teachers for the advanced courses. I was doing a degree in philosophy, although studies didn't seem so important to me at that point. Then the armistice was signed—one of the most painful periods I can recall. It was the first time I saw my father cry.

"All the refugees came fleeing southward—Belgians and Luxembourgeois as well as French. We had people sleeping everywhere in the house we were renting—even in the bathtub! I considered going to England to continue the fight and did look into some possibilities. But, through a chain of unfortunate circumstances, I was an only child, and I did not feel I could leave my parents alone. Moreover, my fiancé was somewhere in France. So I stayed, but I was determined to do something. The distinguished professors who were my father's colleagues were certain Pétain was going to save us. With considerable boldness, I would argue that this was not the case. In my view, the Germans would occupy all of France. Those of us in the southern zone would lose our freedom. My pessimistic views were not well received—although they proved accurate.

"Finally, Michel managed to get back to Montpellier, where we had a civil wedding on October 18, 1940, the very day the statute on the Jews was declared. He insisted we get married because he was concerned that the decrees—which were being discussed, although the details were not known—would prevent us from getting married because I was Jewish. Even though it was difficult for him, we married under an arrangement that keeps couples' property separate, in case something happened to me. We had a civil ceremony for security purposes but did not really consider ourselves married. Our situation was the opposite of many couples today, who marry to 'regularize' their situation. We had promised Michel's parents that we would have the religious ceremony when they could get permission to leave the occupied zone and come south. For this reason, we had asked the newspapers not to mention the event. Unfortunately, a local paper ignored our request and published a notice of the civil ceremony. This caused some difficult moments in the following days.

"Resistance leader Pierre-Henri Teitgen had escaped south with his family. He was introduced to Michel just that week and congratulated him on his marriage, about which he had read. Michel, embarrassed, insisted he was not married. Teitgen said to his wife, 'Either that fellow is a real bastard who has married a wealthy Jewish woman [to take advantage of her situation] or a great guy because she does not have a penny.' He invited us to dinner. I was so timid I could hardly speak. Teitgen soon realized I was not wealthy and that Michel was indeed a 'great guy.' He asked us to come again a day or so later, and that is how I became involved in the Resistance just a few days after my marriage.

"In the fall of 1940, Teitgen was involved with some other Montpellier university professors in organizing a Resistance group. The group was called Libertés, after their paper. The following fall, Libertés joined with several similar groups to form the Combat movement. During the day, Michel and I did liaison: contacting people in the occupied zone, ensuring the distribution of clandestine tracts, instructions, and newspapers. Our main mission was to contact professors and students in the southern zone to enlist their help: We were from that milieu and could talk with them. We went to Marseilles often. Once some relatives told us about a daring escapade about which people were talking. Someone, they said, had managed to bring back the latest *Combat* issues by train from Marseilles, even though the Montpellier station was closed. Obviously, we never said a word about our difficulties with that adventure. In spite of all this activity, we managed to spend evenings with exceptional people. Those were extraordinary times.

"Late in the fall of 1941, we were ordered to Vichy. Our main assignment was to establish a liaison between the American Embassy there and the Resistance. Thanks to one of my cousins, my husband obtained a cover job in the Ministry of Food and Supplies. Georges Bidault was among the Combat agents then staying in Vichy. We knew him because he was a historian, like my father. He was extremely bright and cultivated. We ate with him several times a week. Bidault was always charming with my husband, but he was a misogynist. Working with someone like that was not very easy for women agents like me. For example, one day I was sent to meet an American official. By then our clothes were old and worn, but I made an effort to appear presentable. I tried to fix my hair, to look a little less dowdy. On my way to the appointment, who should I bump into but Bidault; Vichy is not a very big place. I still remember what he said to me, with his icy humor: 'There you are, being truly frivolous.' As easygoing as he was with men, he was quite the opposite with women agents: He was always very cold and distant. You got the impression that he thought we were a bunch of imbeciles—which probably was true, but not very nice for him to imply. We women agents gave so much and took so many risks.

"Then came Pearl Harbor. I was still trying to establish contact with the American Embassy. I decided to write Mme L., who lived in a townhouse across from the hotel where we were staying. I composed a letter carefully, mentioning some of our relatives who knew members of [President Franklin] Roosevelt's entourage (to establish my credentials), and asked her to see me. To my amazement, I received an appointment to meet with her a week later. At the meeting, I was very nervous; two policemen were there. Of course, this was normal because, while they had had time to check my references, she really knew nothing about me. That first visit was very difficult, but things became much better afterward. She put us in touch with Tyler Thompson and Doug MacArthur [the general's nephew] at the American Embassy. Finally I had established the contact.

"Initially, it was somewhat difficult to deal with the Americans. They still had confidence in Pétain and assumed that most French people also did. The Americans also thought the Resistance in France involved only a small group of intellectuals. Thanks to our friends in the region, we arranged for them to meet with members of the Resistance who were from very, very different backgrounds— shopkeepers and peasants, among others. We showed them aspects of France they did not know. Because this connection was so important—too important for my husband and me to use alone—we brought Teitgen, Bidault, François de Menthon, and others into contact with the American Embassy.

"Life was not easy. We lived in one small hotel room with very, very thin walls. One day, the woman manager warned me, 'Watch out. You have Bidault to dinner all the time. People know. What you are doing is very risky.'

"To cook potatoes on a little heater—which did not want to heat—I had to start at 2 P.M. so they would be ready at 8 P.M. On top of it all, I was pregnant. Undoubtedly, this was not the ideal time to have a baby, but in those days, you didn't ask whether it was an intelligent thing to do or not. We rented a tiny apartment on the outskirts of Vichy so we could continue our liaison work. We had to be very careful, as my husband had been 'exposed' by someone who worked for him, someone who became a very high official in the postwar government. Probably Darnand [head of the Militia] and all his police knew what the two of us were doing anyhow. After the war, my husband shook the hand of the man who had betrayed him. I never could, no matter where we met.

"The night before the Germans came down and occupied the southern zone, Ruth Thompson, wife of one of the American diplomats [Tyler Thompson], came by bike to tell us we had to leave at once. If not, she warned us, we would be among the first arrested. It was a difficult moment: The baby was due within three or four weeks. First I went to the embassy to see our friends for the last time. I quickly realized that the Germans were there already, for I was introduced as 'Mme Hervé,' one of my two assumed names. I left at once. That evening, we went by bus to the home of friends who lived in the vicinity of Roanne. They were Jewish, which obviously did not make their house an ideal hiding place. Furthermore, the town was small—a village, really. And then there was the problem of the baby about to arrive. The doctor of the clinic in Roanne, an Alsatian refugee, suggested we stay in his clinic. So we arrived at the clinic eight days before the baby arrived. This proved most fortunate, because the Germans came looking for us at the home of the friends we had just left.

"There we were with Muriel on our hands. I called my daughter Muriel because it was an English name. It was stupid, perhaps, but it was one way of showing our loyalties. We accepted an invitation from friends to stay with them in Cannes. At least we did not have to deal with the cold down there, and things generally were better in the Italian zone—that is, with the exception of finding food. Poor Muriel almost died of starvation. I did not have much to eat, either. But then there are worse things in life. I took care of the baby while Michel continued his underground activities.

"In 1943, we moved to Lyon because the National Council of the Resistance (CNR) met there and Michel was a member of the council; he was with de Gaulle's delegation. In Lyon, I had the impression I was living in a trap. Agents were arrested continually; it was frightening. Then the CNR moved to Paris. I decided to leave my daughter with her two grandmothers in the Loire region. I figured that if the Jewish one were arrested, the other would take care of her.

My decision to join our Resistance group in October 1940 entailed my decision to work for de Gaulle. At the same time, it's curious. I realize also that I could not have stayed in the Loire region

and worried about my husband all the time. It was not courage that
kept me in the movement with him; it was selfishness. I just could
not have dealt with the uncertainty about my husband. From the
very first days until the Liberation, there was not a single morning
when we did not wonder whether it was the milkman we heard—or
someone coming to arrest us.

"At least being in Paris was easier. It was bigger, so you could
hide more easily. Absent friends lent us their handsome townhouse;
that was wonderful. We were on our own there. Leaders from Combat and other groups stayed from time to time, and all of them had
to be fed. In addition, I organized a dinner for different members
who met in our place every Tuesday. Then we were involved in the
Liberation of Paris. When the new government was put in place,
Teitgen asked me to join his cabinet. My husband (who already had
accepted a position) told him, 'No, one family member in the government is enough. She has been running around a good deal. Now
it is time for her to stay home and take care of the baby. She's going
to cook potatoes.' My initial reaction was, No, I could not possibly
spend all my time at home, cooking potatoes. But then I had already made that choice in marrying him."[8]

+>=<+

A rare rendezvous with her husband led to arrest for journalist Hélène
Renal, born in 1923 to a middle-class Parisian family. When war was
declared, she was studying to become a doctor. Joining the Resistance,
she had to stop her studies and never was able to resume them again.

"While still quite young, I had rather clear views on what was happening in the world—on politics. In the 1930s, my father frequently
took me to lectures devoted to events in Germany. I remember one
speaker describing how the Germans burst into a nursery for Jewish
infants and threw all the children out of the window. That horrified
me. I was very frightened of the Germans—after all, I am Jewish.
Like my father, I paid close attention to what was going on. My
mother, on the other hand, was easily frightened. She did not want
to hear about all that. Then the Germans invaded France. I tried, I
really wanted to do something. Eventually, I was able to join the
Resistance, but that was quite some time later. Initially, I did small
things like carrying red, white, and blue flowers on July 14 [Bastille
Day] and distributing under doors some photos of de Gaulle a friend

had obtained from London. This was in Savoy, where I spent my summers. Most of the year I live in Paris. I am a true Parisian, and proud of it. My friend, a Socialist in hiding, worked as a tax collector—which seemed very funny, given his political orientation. He became a major political figure after the war. While working with him in Thonon-les-Bains [on Lake Geneva], I produced my first false identity cards. I liked to copy other people's handwriting, so I had great fun as a counterfeiter and made many false cards. I dirtied them so they looked authentic. I could imitate the prefect's signature perfectly. So I made all those false cards and felt I was doing something—but not enough.

"Finally, I was able to enter the Resistance—what I call the real Resistance—when I joined a network in 1943. I met a man in Paris (I did not know his name then or the fact that he was a doctor) who asked me to go to Lyon and work for a network. I dropped everything and left like that; I went to Lyon. And so I became the secretary of the Transmission-Action network. It was a sort of central post office for all the action groups (the 'terrorists,' as the Germans called them) and all the maquis—all those who fought, really fought. The network had two divisions: intelligence, which collected information and reported on what was happening; and action, the hit squads that blew up trains, placed bombs, killed the Germans. I worked for a very large network, although I did not know that until after the war. Our main job was to train radio operators to receive and send messages. We set up a school, for many operators were needed, and we furnished them to small networks that requested them. It was a major undertaking, although I did not realize it at the time, because my boss was extremely prudent and said very little. Nevertheless, I was involved in an amazing operation.

"While in Lyon, I moved thirty-two times. That gives you an idea of how careful we were, what kind of precautions we took. So I was in thirty-two places I remember well. Each time, I was surrounded by cases of arms, machine guns, revolvers—everything you can imagine. I almost died from fright in the middle of all that. My work consisted in receiving the telegrams destined for my chief. You could say I was his private secretary. I did not know how to type, but that did not matter. I learned on a machine with an English keyboard—not even a French keyboard—but I managed, pecking away with two fingers at a time. The telegrams I received were coded, so I also learned to decode. It was extremely complicated work. I had my own personal code, which even my boss did not know; only I knew it. I also had a code for the telegrams my boss wanted to send. These telegrams were not all that interesting, just technical details. For example: 'We received this document or that information.' It may not have been very exciting, but it was *very* important work. Only after the war did I learn the full importance and extent of our work. We sent many requests for equipment and received transmitters of all sorts: large, small, average; all of them were designed to send and receive telegrams and messages."

Another thing Renal did often—because, as a young woman, she was the only one capable of doing it—was to supply the radio operators. She took them the parts they needed. Sometimes she delivered small elements for fixed wavelengths called "sugars"—because they were the size of a sugar cube. Everything was technically perfected. In addition to parts, Renal also delivered food (because the "poor" radio operators had little to eat) and tobacco (because they had nothing to smoke). Since she was enterprising, her boss also asked her to get such treats as chocolate from the black market to make life a little easier for the operators. Consequently, Renal traveled about a good deal with baskets filled with vegetables, replacement parts, and other things hidden in the bottoms. Sometimes she also carried documents when the liaison was interrupted, replacing those agents when needed. As she explains, that was normal in a network.

"My duties as network secretary included taking care of my boss's mail. Sometimes I had to take it to him in Paris when he was not scheduled to return for a while. There were some amusing incidents. Once I was in a wagon-lit [sleeping car], above a German officer. There were not many trains, and few wagon-lit berths. In a wagon-lit, you typically are perceived as someone of means, hence generally not bothered. In the network, we were required to travel in safe, regular conditions for many reasons—above all, for security. So there I was, in a berth above a German officer, decoding the telegrams I was taking to my boss. Another time, it was awful. Because I needed to take a lot of documents to my boss in Paris, I sewed them into the shoulder pads of a jacket. The paper made a lot of noise; it was horrible. I had the impression that everyone on the train heard the noise, but nothing happened. I could not always get a place in a wagon-lit, but I was always the one chosen to go to Paris, because I was Parisian and knew how to use the Métro. Once I noticed someone changing at the same stations I did. I did not like his looks—you had to be so careful. Being a young woman complicated things, because you never knew whether they were just following you for that. As it turned out, this man was another agent, and we both had a meeting with the boss.

"If people say they were not afraid during the Resistance, so much the better, but I can assure you I was frightened from morning to night. I was never calm. To begin with, I lived in some strange places. You should have seen some of them! Most had been lent to us. There were mice and freezing temperatures. Lyon is a dirty city, so I was always cleaning up, because I can't stand dirt. Once someone rang the doorbell at the place where I was staying. I went into the bathroom and stood on the toilet. Looking through the garret window, I saw a policeman. This is it, I said to myself; I am going to be arrested. The policeman rang and rang, but I did not answer. Finally, he went away. When my boss arrived shortly thereafter, I was stiff with fright. He explained that I was in the policeman's own apartment and that he probably had come to pick up something!

"Frequently I had to type at night, so I tried to stifle the noise. I put blankets on the table, and then the typewriter, and I surrounded it with all kinds of things. I typed as quietly as possible so no one would hear me. I lived in places where you froze because there was no heat. Sometimes the boys brought me some coal, but how cold it was! I made mittens with holes for several fingers so I could type telegrams and reports—which I did not understand. I had to type them because I was the only one who could type—even though badly.

"It was surprising and miraculous, a true miracle, each time we succeeded in sending material to England. Our operation functioned; there were liaisons; telegrams were dispatched and received, as were radio messages. The system worked because it was carefully organized. It amused me to fill in messages that were not quite clear, a bit like doing crossword puzzles. I was very well protected by my network head and by all the young men in the network. I was the apple of their eye. They seldom came to my place except to get arms.

"Once I was stopped [she says *arrested*] while supplying the radio operators. I was riding my bicycle. The suitcase on my baggage rack contained documents I had picked up from a *maquis* where I had delivered supplies. This was very dangerous, but I was in a great hurry and had not taken time to conceal the documents. They had 'Radio Alger' on them in big letters. Thank heavens, a dumb German from the Wehrmacht stopped me, not one from the Gestapo. 'What's this?' he asked. 'Radio Alguerr?' 'I don't know,' I replied, 'perhaps a movie.' He returned my suitcase and I took off. How I managed to ride more or less straight after that, I really don't know. I was very, very fortunate not to be arrested.

"Another time, I was also lucky, escaping arrest during a security check on a train. I had fixed a bag with a double bottom. Documents went in the bottom, and then I carefully reglued the lining and filled the bag with vegetables. There was little food, and everyone was heading for the countryside looking for food. So I went about like a dumb girl carrying a bag filled with carrots, turnips, and leeks.

"For my work, London sent some marvelous gadgets for hiding documents. One was a large bar of soap carefully cut in two, with a hiding place in the middle for documents. I also had an umbrella with a removable handle camouflaging a hiding place. And, marvel of marvels, there was a tube of toothpaste that opened at the bottom. Something extraordinary, which I still have, is a wallet with a hidden compartment for my codes. Codes were in miniature on tiny cards. They were only used once. I burned them afterward. The day I was arrested with my husband, I managed to swallow a compromising paper when they let me go to the toilet. But they never found the code hidden in the wallet. It was normal for me to have it. I was to keep it on me at all times.

"When I was arrested the first time, it had nothing to do with our network. I was with my husband, who headed another network—an important intelligence network. We were seldom together, but by bad luck I was with him when he was arrested, so I was arrested, too. I played the complete imbecile who knew nothing, who did not understand what it was all about, who had never heard of the Resistance. That worked more or less. What helped me above all was that I spoke and understood German. During the interrogations—which were very, very rough; I had fourteen, quite a number—the Germans spoke among themselves. When they asked me about myself, what languages I spoke, I told them I knew English. I never mentioned knowing German, and that was extremely

helpful because I followed their conversations and could orient my
answers somewhat according to their remarks. I have no idea why I
did not tell them I knew German. There are some things that just
fall out of the heavens, so to speak."

The couple was arrested on May 18, 1944. Tragically, the entire
network was dismantled just as it was apparent that the end was coming. There was a double agent in their network—an Alsatian who
really believed the Germans would win. He betrayed them all. Thirty-
two were arrested. Renal's husband escaped from a hospital in Lyon,
where he had been sent after having been tortured horribly. Only three
members of the network returned from deportation.

"Fortunately, I knew virtually nothing about that network. I knew
some locations, which changed constantly, so that information was
useless. In any event, I said nothing, absolutely nothing. They questioned me repeatedly about my husband's network. I kept repeating
that I did not know what the Resistance was. I played the complete
idiot, an imbecile who knew nothing. I felt they would eventually
release me because they had said they would. Nevertheless, all this
time I was questioned by Klaus Barbie's assistant—the infamous Barbie who tortured my husband. I was not tortured. I was beaten, continually beaten, but that is not the same thing. It is not as serious.
But I was forced to watch others undergo torture. Blows are nothing
in comparison to the torture I saw inflicted on others. The man who
questioned me, Barbie's assistant, is now living comfortably in Stutt-
gart, where he has a prosperous carpet business. Afterward, he
worked for the Americans as a double agent, you see, so he was
completely exonerated after the war.
    "After those close encounters—and my release after the first ar-
rest—I resumed my activities. That first arrest had been a shock.
Nevertheless, I continued as valiantly and as lightheartedly as I
could, even though I nearly died of fright. There were very few of us
in the Resistance. I tried to recruit members among the people I
knew, but it was always: 'I would love to do it, but, but. . . .' Those
of us in the Resistance used to say among ourselves, 'If all those who
didn't have an elderly father, sick mother, fiancé, children, illness, or
this or that, had joined, then everyone in France would be in the
Resistance.' You just could not find anyone. The result was that
once you were in the Resistance, you had to continue because you

realized how serious it was and how few we were. You had to continue. And then there were the arrests. That happened all the time.
You had to improvise, replace. There were astonishing people in my
network. My boss was a doctor of Hungarian origin who left his wife
and children to join the Resistance. He was a marvelous man who
resumed his practice as a country doctor after the war."

What complicated Renal's life, she maintains, was that she was
always very frightened, more frightened than she had ever been in her
life. She was constantly in anguish, convinced she was going to be
arrested. Hence, it was almost a relief at last to be arrested. It was
over. Something else was about to begin, but at least the young woman
no longer had that terrible fear tying her up inside. After interrogations, Renal was sent on the long deportation route to Ravensbrück,
like so many other women in the French Resistance.

"I was very, very sick when I returned from deportation. The first
time they weighed me, I was only fifty-five pounds. I was in very bad
shape. It took me a long time to recover, little by little. Initially,
although I weighed little, I looked better on return than most of my
comrades. That was because when the factory no longer functioned,
they took us out into the woods to pick up brush and wood chips—
for twelve hours a day! We picked up the brush so that sparks from
the trains would not start forest fires. This was in April, and the sun
was out. I got a suntan!

"Then I did something crazy. I said I wanted to work for the Allied occupying forces in order to avenge myself and others, poor
creature that I was. As it turned out, I did make a contribution. I
was sent to Germany with a friend of my husband, also a former
network head. His assignment was to seek out the Nazis who had
been involved in unusual activities. In particular, we found those
who had built the V-1s and V-2s [rockets]. I was charged with questioning them. It was neither tiring nor terrifying. On the contrary, it
was very interesting. Interviewing the Nazis, we discovered a hidden
wind tunnel, an enormous hangar built into subterranean grottoes in
the Tyrol where they studied the effects of wind. I was charged with
bringing all this information to the Air Ministry in Paris. The discovery caused a sensation. I had—and still have—problems with
speaking German. Our assignment in Germany, seeking out hidden

Nazis, was a continuation of the Resistance. I was happy to do something in memory of all those I saw disappear.

"When I returned from Ravensbrück, I spent fifteen years without talking about that experience. I did not want to hear anything about it, or participate in associations or whatever. Above all, I never wanted to talk about it with my family. But my comrades from the camp persisted and sought me out. Eventually, I joined them and we decided to write a book about our experiences. I was asked to coordinate the responses to our questionnaire. More than two thousand women deportees responded. I was working on this when I fell ill. I had terrible nightmares. Others completed the book [*Les Françaises à Ravensbrück*, 1965].

"It took me a great deal of time to adjust to life in France with 'normal' people. I did not understand their language or have the same interests. And my marriage had broken up. I had a lot of problems, particularly with my mother, who could not bear to see me tired. I was terribly, terribly tired. She was upset because I was not like everybody else. But I could not tell her what I had been through. I had seen such terrible things. At Ravensbrück, I was with a group of seven hundred women who worked in a munitions factory where conditions were terrible. We worked directly under the Germans. I still cannot talk about it, not even today. It is impossible even to think about what took place. Working on that book did help. And I was in analysis for almost eight years.

"My family probably should have encouraged me to resume medical studies, but I was convinced it would be too hard. In any event, I had to work, because even though my parents had not been arrested—which was the exception—they had lost everything. The family did not have a penny. The same thing happened in my husband's family. I felt I had to go to work. I was paid for my job in occupied Germany. When the French military took over, I decided I had to leave; I could not work with them. They were all like the French general who took over command of Austria. He was a career officer who had done nothing throughout the war. He came to enjoy the good life with a chauffeur, car, and all that. So I returned and sought work. An uncle got me a job with *Elle* [one of the mass-market women's magazines founded just before the war]."[9]

Petite, blonde Yvette (Barnard) Farnoux received unwelcome attention from German soldiers. But she found an excellent way to discourage them: She told them—in German—that she was tubercular. But at times her appearance served her well. Several "gallant" men assisted her when she carried out a task that she did not realize was a trial assignment for Resistance work. Later, carrying out other Resistance errands, the young woman was to pose often as someone's fiancée. Then she met her own fiancé. She recounts their tragic love story:

"I was born in 1919 into a French Alsatian family of Jewish origin. They left Alsace rather than become German when the province was annexed after the Franco–Prussian War. The maternal branch moved to San Francisco; the paternal side settled in Paris. I wanted to pursue a medical education, but by the time I would have been starting at the university, war had broken out and very few Jewish students were admitted. [Vichy instituted a *numerus clausus*.] So I decided to attend a private school that trained social assistants, and completed the degree.

When the German army invaded Paris, I did what all my friends did: put up stickers, gave wrong directions to Germans, changed road signs. On November 11, 1940 [Armistice Day], I joined friends to walk up and down the Champs-Élysées—one dressed in red, another in white, another in blue. More than a thousand girls who had the same idea joined us. Beyond that, I thought about really getting into the struggle against the Germans. German soldiers used to approach young girls in the street. When one spoke to me, I would tell him I was tubercular—in German! At that, he would quickly cross the street and not bother me anymore.

"Little by little, people became organized. Obviously, you could not approach just anyone in the street to find out if they were involved in Resistance work. It was not evident at that time *who* was in a Resistance group; it was difficult to find out *where* the Resistance was. My family was now on the other side of the demarcation line in the unoccupied part of France. I was completely opposed to working in the occupied zone, so I went south and stayed in different student lodgings. When I received my diploma, our director, Jeanne Sivadon, an early *résistante*, gave me the Lyon address of the Unemployment Commission.[10] I went to the commission and found myself in Berty Albrecht's arms.

"Berty had been appointed director of the Unemployment Commission in Lyon (see chapter 8), and she wanted me to work for her.

I was very nervous; this was my first job, and I did not know that she was spending nearly all her time working for the Resistance. She could undress you with her eyes. The first assignment she gave me was to contact prisoners in Clermont-Ferrand. One day, Berty gave me a list with the names of eighteen young people held in a Clermont-Ferrand prison: 'You have to bring them food and news from the outside and bring back news of them. How you manage it is your affair.' Fortunately, I remembered a friend who was doing social work in Lyon for Secours National. Secours National was responsible for finding work for the unemployed, running soup kitchens for the needy, and similar projects. I told my friend about my assignment and asked her if she had any ideas about how I could get some food, since I had neither money nor ration coupons. 'Come to my office tonight,' she said. So I went to her office and we took eighteen one-kilo [2.2 pounds] jars of apricot jam. They really weighed down the flimsy suitcase I had purchased to transport them.

"The next day, I went to the station to board the train for Clermont-Ferrand. When I put the suitcase down on the quay, it broke open. Everyone was staring at me. People assumed I was in the black market. This was 1941, and the black market flourished. The jam jars rolled around everywhere. It was awful. Two gallant men helped me collect them and tie up my suitcase.

"Once I finally got on the train with my precious jars, I looked at the list of names of those I was to contact and saw that one was the son of family friends. The problem was that I hadn't seen him since I was twelve or thirteen. I decided to ask for the prison chaplain and tell him I wanted to see my 'fiancé.' Once in town, I had to drag the suitcase a long, long way. At the prison, I asked for the chaplain and told him I wanted to see my fiancé, Marcel Peck. When Peck saw me, he was furious. He told me to leave at once and to tell those who sent me to keep me out of this affair: 'You're just a kid.' He treated me as if I were still twelve or thirteen. All the same, he gave me information to convey to Berty Albrecht. I delivered the rest of my jam jars and brought back the prisoners' dirty laundry and a lot of messages. But I should have been given some idea of what I was doing.

"When I returned, I told Berty she should have let me know that I was not visiting 'ordinary' war prisoners. It was a test, she explained, and she asked me if I would be willing to do social work for these people. That is how I started. I got into Resistance work very easily. I was young and unattached. Married women were not always as free. It is true that they had to get their husband's permission. [Married women were still legally bound to obey their husbands.] And there were women with children, like my sister, who could not join as readily. Frankly, I do not know if I would have joined if I had had children then. Fortunately, our parents were living safely on a farm, so I did not have to worry about them. Besides, everything in my home life and my education reinforced my beliefs and readiness to join.

"I broke off contact with my family and went underground. My name now was 'Claude.' I was under the orders of Berty Albrecht. My assignment was to help her care for the prisoners and develop what became the social services for Combat. This entailed talking with the chaplains, the prisoners, the families. When people were arrested, their families often were without any resources. The Resistance gave them a little, but that was all they had. Family or friends who might have helped were frequently elsewhere. Our contacts with these families sometimes were very difficult, since they did not always know that the father or son was in the Resistance [another instance where secrecy had a negative impact]. Other families knew and approved. But to be effective in the Resistance, you had to be secretive and not tell even loved ones what you were doing. We dealt with the lawyers, who also were members of the Resistance.*

"By and large, the chaplains were fabulous. I remember a priest who did everything he could to help me. He even gave me keys to one of the prisons. He passed all sorts of papers and documents in and out of the prison and helped us arrange escapes. We had to hide the escapees while waiting for a plane to pick them up and take them to London. We had to find hospital beds for some, and medical supplies. Women were better suited to do this work. They were more secure, less suspect. They knew how to solve these problems. After all, they were not that different from the problems women take care of all the time."

One day, Yvette noticed a handsome young man going into the office of Jacqueline Bernard, another assistant to Berty Albrecht

---

*The prisoners' lawyers aided greatly. They advised them on what to say and how to defend themselves. They brought family news. The lawyers also obtained information that was very valuable in assessing what the enemy knew and in preparing escapes.

(Combat's "one woman band"). "Too bad," she thought, "it must be her fiancé." No, it was not Jacqueline's fiancé, but her brother Jean-Guy Bernard, Henri Frenay's assistant:

"He was good-looking and seductive—tender, in spite of having a strong temper. It was love at first sight. We started to live to-gether—that is, when we could manage it. Those were happy days. At the time, I did not think beyond the moment. Our common goal was to rid France of the Germans.

"When Berty was arrested [May 1942], I was asked to head our social services. Then, after the major Resistance movements joined to form MUR (United Movements of the Resistance), I became na-tional head of the Resistance social services in April 1943. We di-vided the unoccupied zone into six zones; each zone had a head. Martine Peck, Marcel's sister, headed one zone. And there were de-partmental heads. Our biggest job was with the prisoners. They needed food above all.

"Supplying prisoners could be extremely dangerous. To give but one example, once a biscuitmaker gave us a substantial supply of bis-cuits to distribute. The Germans noticed that this particular biscuit was being sent to many prisoners, so we had to take great care to diversify our food parcels. The supplies at our disposal varied greatly. At times, I spent entire weeks scouring the countryside just trying to get food. We Resistance members needed it, too. We had nothing, absolutely nothing. Stores often were closed, and besides, there was no time to stand in line. From time to time, we had to use the black market.

"We had no training for this kind of work. At first, we did not know what we were dealing with, and what we should be doing. Luck played an important part. We tried one thing and then an-other. We were truly amateurs, but we learned. I started in 1941 and was arrested in 1944. When you consider all that was happening, three years was a long time. Little by little, we built up the support services until they met our needs. Then the work becomes habit and you are not as careful. That is generally when arrests occur.

"Those of us who worked with the Resistance support organiza-tions undertook an enormous task. At first, not too many needed help. Then young men took to the *maquis* to avoid being shipped to Germany to work in factories or on farms. That meant a lot of peo-ple to take care of. When the Allies landed in the south, I was overwhelmed with work. The Germans were entrenched in the mountains. There were skirmishes, which meant casualties.

"In the summer of 1943, I discovered I was pregnant. Since both of us had gone underground, this was a real problem. Getting an abortion in those days was very difficult. [The Vichy government had made it a crime against the state, punishable by death.] And in any event, we were opposed to the idea. I think there was the notion of perpetuating oneself—in spite of everything—when you are living so dangerously. At least that is what I think now, although I am not quite certain about how I viewed it at the time. Fortunately, Jean-Guy's family was wealthy, so they could hire a nanny and care for the child. I could continue my Resistance work. They could support the child if something happened to us. That was important. We knew they would welcome the baby.

"We got married in a small village when my pregnancy was quite advanced. In those days, you did not consider having a child without being married. That was more than fifty years ago. That was part of our way of life then. We had to find a village where we could get married without having the banns published. In France, the names—the full names of the couple—are posted in front of the mayor's office. Obviously, that was out of the question. Pierre de Bénouville found a Resistance comrade mayor willing to marry us without publishing the banns. We were married in Margency in Seine-et-Oise. Six of us took the train to this little village, which none of us knew—except Pierre. The ceremony lasted thirty seconds, the time it took to sign the papers. The entire wedding party was clandestine."

In the fall of 1943, the Germans stepped up their pursuit of Resistance members. Yvette Barnard-Farnoux continued her clandestine activities, using her maternity girdle to conceal documents, funds, even pistols. Jean-Guy was now in charge of both NAP/Fer, the railway sabotage program, and NAP/PTT, the sabotage plan for the mail and telecommunications of the Lyon region. His picture appeared on wanted posters. Early in January 1944, his secretary was arrested. Instead of taking time off from their clandestine work and hiding, Yvette and Jean-Guy looked for a place to stay in occupied Paris (a major problem), where they could continue their work. After three weeks without incident, the couple assumed the secretary had not "talked" (if captured, you were to remain silent for at least twenty-four hours), and felt out of danger. They moved into an apartment that had been made available to the group. As it turned out, after holding out for three weeks, the secretary gave the Germans that address, thinking it was now safe to do so. Yvette and Jean-Guy were arrested on a Sunday they had decided to "give to themselves." When the doorbell rang, they could have fled by back windows, but no one had been arrested on a Sunday evening—before. From her experience, Yvette holds that the worst thing imaginable is being arrested with someone you love, and then being forced to watch that person be tortured or killed.

"I was told that unless I talked, they would kill my baby as soon as it was born—unless, of course, they decided to give it to a German family to raise. That evening, I decided to commit suicide with a razor blade I had hidden in my coat hem. I was not afraid of torture or death, but I could not bear the idea of the Germans taking my child. I was seven and a half months pregnant. In the dark, I cut my left wrist deeply. The next morning, I was bathed in blood—but still conscious. They dragged Jean-Guy into my cell, thinking that the sight of me would make him talk. He did not. Before taking him out, they beat him in front of me. That was the last time I saw him. A German nurse stitched my wrist. There was no anesthesia, but I was in such a state that I didn't even feel it. On February 17, three weeks after my arrest and alone in my cell, I gave birth to a stillborn daughter. You simply cannot imagine what that was like.

"My sister-in-law, Jacqueline Bernard, managed to arrange my escape from prison five days later. However, since the house of the woman who had agreed to shelter me was under surveillance, we went to another place. Jacqueline was convinced that this place was being watched as well, so she went to find an ambulance. I was still very weak. When the Germans arrived the next morning, I was not there. Suspicious myself about this latest 'safe' house, I decided to leave at dawn. How I managed to walk about five miles, I do not quite know. A car stopped and offered me a lift. It was the adopted daughter of the woman whose house I had just left. Having met the young woman the previous evening, I was relieved. She gave me a lift—to the police station. I was put in prison, in Vendôme, after eight days of freedom. It turned out that this girl was the mistress of the notorious, so-called Rudi von Mérode, a Frenchman working for the Gestapo. She betrayed both her adopted mother and me.

"In the prison cell, no one wanted to make room for me except a prostitute, who insisted I be given the best place on the straw; she also cleaned my infected wounds. Then I was taken to Gestapo headquarters in Paris for more interrogations. After one month in a cleaner French prison, I was shipped in a convoy of Jews to Auschwitz, where they put me with a group of eastern Jews who spoke Yiddish—which I did not understand. I decided that the only way to survive that nightmare was to be an observer. I spent ten months there and then was sent with other prisoners to Ravensbrück—on foot. After the war, I learned that Jean-Guy was put on the second-to-last train to leave for Auschwitz. That was July 13, 1944, just a few weeks before Paris was liberated. He was already in bad condition because of the tortures he had undergone. [Catherine Roux encountered him in prison and did not recognize him. See chapter 6.] He must have been gassed shortly after arrival—on August 3, 1944."

After her return from the camps, Yvette resumed social work. She founded Revivre (Back to Life) to take care of orphans of the Resistance—the children of those who had been executed, killed in *maquis* encounters, or died in the camps. She also remarried and had three children. When liberated by the Russians in Germany, she met the man who was to become her husband. He, too, was a freed deportee. Now they are grandparents. But Yvette cannot shake off the anguish caused by what she endured. Like Hélène Renal and others, she cannot stand the German language. While acknowledging that her reaction is childish, she leaves if she finds herself in the company of Germans. Once, when in New York, someone noticed the number tattooed on her arm and asked her if she had been in a concentration camp because she was Jewish. Yes, she replied, she was indeed Jewish, but she had been deported because she was in the Resistance. This, she emphasizes, is a very important point: Jews who might have lived out the war in hiding took a double risk when they joined the Resistance, but in another way they could understand why they had been arrested.[11]

Women and men in the Resistance involved in relationships—however brief—were very vulnerable. Both Renal and Farnoux were arrested with their husbands. Françoise de Boissieu barely escaped arrest when she and her husband fled Vichy just a few weeks before her first baby was due. Children were one of the complications in the lives of clandestine couples. Modern methods of contraception were not available then. In Farnoux's case, her German captors threatened her unborn infant's future. Children, like parents, were hostages in the vicious efforts of the Occupation forces to destroy the French Resistance. However, human relationships are unpredictable and not always subject to control, particularly for those living under such intense pressure. Resistance agents fell in love, like their noninvolved compatriots. Here, as with everything else that touched their lives, they did so at great peril.

10

Room and Board:
Critical Concerns

WHEN SHELTER HAD TO BE FOUND FOR THOSE TRYING TO HIDE FROM German—and in some instances, French—authorities, it generally was women who offered this "hospitality." Women who harbored political refugees, Jews, escaped prisoners, downed Allied aviators, and clandestine Resistance members took on a particularly difficult role. For those with families, it meant the entire family had to accept the "guest" and share possible retribution under the Nazi policy of collective responsibility.

Women who hid the wanted and persecuted do not figure prominently in the traditional histories of the French Resistance, yet this work was very dangerous: If caught, these women risked deportation or death. Those found sheltering refugees from the provinces of Alsace and Lorraine—which the Germans annexed when the armistice was signed—could be shot for treason. Some escapees were easily identifiable—such as Paul Irion, who had tattoos on his hands and fingers—which complicated hiding them. In his account of British Wing Commander Forest Yeo-Thomas's setting up safe houses (see *The White Rabbit*, 1952), Bruce Marshall details the process whereby women volunteered for liaison and shelter and brought family and friends into the group:

Madame Peyronnet's daughter, Poucette, aged sixteen, was engaged
to carry messages on her bicycle. . . . Madame Denise Martin, the wife
of a solicitor, and her sister Nicole Bauer also volunteered to help
them. Nicole Bauer, nicknamed Maud, became another cyclist mes-
senger and she in turn brought in the plump little Jacqueline Devaux
and her flat in the rue Leverrier.[1]

Among the first looking for refuge after the 1940 armistice were
the youths and men trying to flee France and reach England, where
they hoped to continue the fight. They were sheltered and hidden by
women such as "Madame X."

+———+

"Who is Madame X?" asked an article in the London *Daily Express* of
Tuesday, August 29, 1944. The accompanying photograph showed a
woman who resembled Marlene Dietrich. According to the paper, the
Gestapo had put a price on her head. She was "one of the most daring
leaders of the *maquis* in Brittany." The article went on to explain that
she shot a German soldier while riding in the Jeep of an American
colonel during the battles to liberate France. The American press
subsequently dubbed her "the Joan of Arc of Brittany." Some twenty-
five years later, British naval commander David Birkin, father of actress Jane Birkin, also tried to locate "Madame X.," the French woman
he had met in a remote area of Brittany in mid-August 1943. During
the Occupation, this woman sheltered Allied aviators in her home in
a Breton port and helped find boats so that they could return to England. "Madame X.," the intrepid young woman who worked for the
Resistance, was Marie-Louise Le Duc.

"I came from a military family. Father was an officer in the engineering corps. Even before the war, I had an adventurous side. I learned
how to fly as well as to shoot. There were not many women in prewar France who knew how to fly. To perfect my English, I was sent
to a convent school in England, where a relative was mother superior. When still quite young, I married a doctor. We had three sons.
It was for our children that I joined the Resistance early on, as did
my husband. I felt I had to fight to ensure their future in the world
we believed in.

"Our hometown of Morlaix [in the Finistère district of Brittany]
faced England directly—right across the Channel—so it was only

natural that many of those who wanted to join de Gaulle and the
Free French in England escaped in boats from there. Fortunately, I
was able to find a place for my sister, diplomat Yvonne Pétrement,
in one of these boats. She, too, wanted to join de Gaulle in London. In 1941, Yvonne managed to escape to Algeria, where she
hoped to join the Free French Forces, but she was obliged to return
to France. Eventually, though, she did sail to England on a fishing
vessel from a shipyard in Carantec. Twelve young men traveled with
her aboard the *Meteor*. Twenty-five hours later, the group reached
Plymouth Harbor. My sister was one of five women assigned to high-
level positions in the French Foreign Service after the war because
of their Resistance records. She held diplomatic postings around the
world. After her retirement, she represented the International Wom-
en's Council at UNESCO, in Paris, for some years.

"The main problem for those trying to get to England—other
than crossing the Channel—was that they needed to be sheltered
and fed for weeks, sometimes months, before their passage could be
arranged. Hiding them was a difficult undertaking. Apart from the
danger of discovery or denunciation, extra food and supplies were
hard to come by, since so much was rationed. As the war progressed,
we also hid Allied aviators who had been shot down and were trying to return to their bases in England. Like most women in the Resistance, I did liaison work and intelligence. Our group was asked to
locate all the German positions in the area. Toward the end, as I
became more and more active, my parents and friends assumed the
care of the children. I wanted to protect them.

"The first of my three arrests occurred when the Germans came
to the house in January 1941. We had been denounced. At that
time, there were papers hidden in a kitchen drawer. Most of the secret papers were in the barn, however. They were mainly documents
to be sent to the Free French in London with the next boat. I managed to tell the maid to burn the papers in the drawer and hide
what was in the barn attic in the bottom of a basket of potatoes.
One of the Germans who had been searching the house came into
the kitchen. He knew at once what had happened when he saw the
smoke and ashes in the kitchen fireplace. But I was lucky. He could
not report me without incriminating himself. He was guilty of leaving me alone. Nevertheless, they took me to headquarters and questioned me for hours. Several German soldiers stayed in the house for
a week.

"My husband was not so fortunate. He was arrested and put in prison with others from our group. I managed to send someone to visit him there and inform him that the documents had not been discovered. This message was delivered—actually shouted—in front of the Germans themselves! It was in Breton, which of course they could not understand. He was released two weeks later, but we both were kept under surveillance after that, even though they had not found any incriminating evidence. Each day, I had to go to the German police headquarters and sign a register. Eventually, they got tired of seeing me. They told me they were letting me off because I had young children.

"As the war progressed, I joined the *maquis*. My expertise with arms was very useful. I showed the young men how to use weapons. One day, I was stopped with other travelers at one of the roadblocks the Germans set up from time to time. As they got closer to me, I decided I had to risk getting away. I slipped through a hedge opening and ran as fast as I could. I stopped at several farms, but no one would help me. Finally, I found a peasant couple who were willing to let me hide in their barn with the cows. I felt safe enough, as I was certain the Germans had not noticed me. And if they had, it seemed unlikely they would look for me there.

"Our town was badly bombed in January 1943, so we moved to our summer home in Carantec, a few miles away, also on the Channel coast. The following month, I heard someone calling for me at the window one night. A fishing boat, the *Yvonne*, was preparing to leave for England with ten people. For the first time, the group included two American aviators who had been rescued. Because I knew English, I was asked to explain to the men that members of the Resistance would lodge them in safe homes until the time came for the boat to leave. I also had to make contact with a British Intelligence Service mission directed from London.

"I was arrested again in October 1943. Again someone had denounced me. This time, I was taken to Gestapo headquarters in Brest, where they accused me of sheltering British and American aviators. But since they had no proof, they had to let me go once more. I continued to help on other missions. I joined a group meeting a Royal Navy ship that landed secret agents and materiel on a remote area of the coast. That was during the night of August 12/13, 1944. Two weeks later, there was another landing, followed by others. Each time, the MGB 318 stayed off the coast to avoid mines. A corvette made the trip to shore. David Birkin was a navigator on thirty-one of these landings.* At this time, I was also responsible for our group's liaison with Paris, and I went there frequently, because we needed to coordinate parachute drops.

"I was arrested for a third time on June 1, 1944, just a few days before the Allied landings. This time, I was taken to Gestapo headquarters by German parachutists. I had a false identity card. While they waited for their superiors, I feigned illness. Finally, I persuaded my guard to let me go to the toilet. I was determined to escape; death was preferable to torture. So I climbed out the window and escaped. I covered almost twenty miles that day. Then I hid four days in a stable. Eventually, I found one of our *maquis* units. Unbeknownst to me, my husband was arrested on June 3 while returning from a parachute drop. He was severely beaten but was able to escape. The Germans ransacked and looted our house; the place was devastated.

"I was lucky, having managed to escape prison. I continued my Resistance work and helped liberate Brittany when the Allied troops landed. Brittany, by the way, was the one part of France that was mostly freed by its own Resistance forces. At the *maquis* camp, I met a French lieutenant who had been parachuted back into France. I posed as his sister. Together we harassed the Germans. We spent nights in camps hidden in the woods or in farmhouses. Once we encountered more than four hundred Germans in a village. They ,hot up our car, but we managed to escape. When the American tank units arrived, I jumped onto the lead tank and directed them into the town of Plouigneau. I wanted to make certain they avoided the mines the Germans had planted. During this period, the Germans circulated 'wanted' posters with my picture. They even offered a reward for my capture. Fortunately, most of the people in that area were friends—with a few exceptions.

"These wartime experiences had a major impact upon my life. It was difficult to return to my prewar role of bourgeois housewife in a provincial town. I moved to Paris, where the boys were educated. I remained there. My husband remained at Morlaix, where he had his practice and was mayor and later a deputy. I tried various things and set up an art gallery. I wanted financial independence. I took up ce-

---

*Former president François Mitterrand was among those picked up by Birkin's corvette.

ramic work. This is not perhaps so surprising, as there have been well-known artists in our family. My main work, however, focused on helping veterans reintegrate into society, find work, and so on. After the war, there were so many who returned from the prisoner-of-war camps. Much needed to be done for them. I set up a pilot program to help implement and expand these vital and necessary services even before the war ended. I spent twenty-five years working with that program."

Marie-Louise Le Duc's granddaughter, a medical student, was present during the 1986 interview. She looked at the newspaper clippings and "thank you" notes from the many "guests" her grandmother had sheltered during the war. There were also medals that Le Duc and her sister had received from grateful governments. The young woman was astonished to learn the details of her grandmother's fascinating past.[2]

After the armistice, escape networks were improvised to rescue the many French and British troops still stranded in France. These underground railroads helped all those who wanted to continue fighting the Nazis. As the war progressed, Allied aviators who had been shot down and agents on missions landed in France in increasing numbers. More and more hiding places were needed for them. Among the least-suspected places—for those fleeing the Nazis—were convents. From the beginning of the war, convents in various parts of France took in men, for they were not suspected of harboring fugitives, especially men—at least early on. Presumably—like Sister Edwige Dumas—the nuns felt that Christian charity and patriotism were higher rules than those imposed by their order.

An important escape route led to the shrine of Lourdes. The convents in that area hid the fugitives until *passeurs*, or guides (often smugglers), could take them across the Pyrénées mountains to nearby Spain. The mother of Dr. Robert Debré, one of the heads of the Medical Resistance, spent the war in a convent near Montauban, safe from persecution as a Jew. Her son was able to visit her there several times. Debré, in turn, and Dexia, his companion and future wife (Countess Elisabeth de la Bourdonnaye), who helped publish *Le Silence de la mer*, later hid in a mental asylum with others threatened by French and German police.[3]

For those trying to hide during the Occupation, the choice of lodgings was limited; hotels were not recommended. Apart from financial considerations—some clandestine agents worked full time for movements, with minimal salaries, if any—one had to fill out a hotel register for the police. In addition to possible police checks, there was the uncertainty of the political views and possible complicity of the hotelkeeper. Some were very generous. Victor Hammel, leader of a Jewish Resistance group, describes his stays at the Hotel Victoria in Lyon. Sometimes he slept in bathtubs or on ironing boards. Madame Gay managed the Hotel Victoria during the day; her husband worked the night shift. She was aware of Hammel's underground work. Each time his welcome was more generous. There were baskets of lovely fruit.

> The more difficult things became, the more she spoiled me. Toward the end [of the war], she served me complete meals with white bread, butter, and cheese, yet she never asked me to pay for those feasts. So, even though the hotel was close to the train station, I kept returning, for I knew I was secure there. [Stations were closely guarded.] And Mme Gay never asked me to fill out the required registration form.[4]

When the Vichy government's repressive racial policy became more evident—starting with anti-Jewish legislation passed in the fall of 1940—Jews were sheltered by French citizens of all backgrounds. As mentioned in chapter 8, the Protestant group CIMADE, one of the first organizations to try to help Jews held in detention camps in southwestern France, set up a series of safe homes to receive Jews trying to escape to Switzerland. Two devout Catholics, Marinette Guy and Juliette Vidal, working at the dispensary Mother's Aid, were among those who sheltered Jewish children being shepherded to Switzerland. For their work, the state of Israel recognized them as "Just Gentiles."

Large cities in the unoccupied zone, such as Lyon, were overcrowded with all those who had fled the Germans at the outbreak of the war. As German repression increased, more and more *résistants* went underground. On occasion, sympathetic proprietors rented rooms or apartments to the clandestine and the pursued. Still, caution was necessary, even when using a pseudonym. Consequently, several movements—notably Combat and Ceux de la Résistance—created virtual housing bureaus in 1943. These bureaus were run by women who sought out and rented empty lodgings or found families willing to harbor agents in their homes. Thus, there was housing available immediately when someone had to go underground or change residences.

The Parisian lodging service for Ceux de la Résistance was entrusted to two actresses: Lise Delamare (who played in Jean Giraudoux's play *Sodome et Gomorrhe* during the 1943–1944 season) and her sister, Rosine. Between them, the actress sisters had many acquaintances and were able to secure a fair number of vacant places. Running their "housing bureau" entailed many hours, but it was very important. For example, they were able to offer Jean de Vogüé, head of Ceux de la Résistance, six Paris apartments during his days in hiding. All were poorly heated, from the most luxurious to the simple maid's accommodation where a washing machine served as a bathtub. But thanks to these different lodgings, de Vogüé was able to escape active pursuit by the Gestapo.[5] One "guest" even suggested a tourist-style guide about accommodations for future Resistance agents, awarding stars for hospitality.

In Paris, members of Libération-Nord and the Cohors intelligence network met in the rue Vaugirard apartment of Mme Elisabeth Roserot de Meslin ("Rosine"). Many were fed and put up there. One day, Rosine asked Libération-Sud leader Suzanne Tony Robert if she could spare a few potatoes (a precious commodity at that time) and a pair of clean sheets for a *résistant* who was spending several nights in her apartment. The *résistant* in question was General Audibert, head of the Secret Army in southern Brittany. Mme Roserot de Meslin had lodged so many clandestines in the preceding weeks that she had no clean sheets. And, she added timidly, she had not eaten all day. A fervent royalist, Rosine had a library filled with books devoted to the French royal family. Some of the secret agents meeting there decided that if caught, they would say they were working to restore the Bourbon monarchy. That was less dangerous than to acknowledge working for the liberation of France.[6]

Obviously, when a Resistance member had only a minimally furnished room, meals had to be taken in restaurants. This increased the risks, because decent, adequate meals generally were served only in black-market restaurants where ration tickets were not required. The most secure and most agreeable arrangement was to stay with friends or those working for the movement, preferably in homes. In apartment buildings, one sometimes had to deal with curious concierges.

Evelyne Sullerot mentions an English aviator found hanging with his parachute caught in a tree. The Allied parachutists posed special problems. Apart from the fact that most did not know French, they often had to be sheltered and fed in France for long periods—until specialized escape networks could arrange their return passage either via Spain or, as Marie-Louise Le Duc recounted, through Breton ports. During these lengthy waiting periods, generous rations were required. Also, to escape, they needed civilian clothing, yet clothing was rationed and stores were empty. Besides, many Allied servicemen were taller than most Frenchmen. Women's sewing and tailoring skills were brought into play.

Countess d'Hespel, daughter of Dr. Debré's companion, Dexia, was among those who sheltered Allied military. Her husband had been killed in action in 1940, so his young widow, a medical student, carried on the fight—in spite of the objections of her in-laws, who protested about the "impropriety" of her sheltering men. All in all, she harbored some twenty Allied parachutists—British, Australian, and American. Some stayed only a few days; others stayed several weeks. With the help of friends, the countess managed to clothe and feed them. The greatest difficulty, however, was keeping them occupied and getting them to accept their "captivity." An excellent solution to the problem of hiding Allied military was to contact a wealthy family, for there one might find companions with spare time who spoke English. These women often had to use their entire repertoire of card games. Allied aviators sometimes were taken on walks to secluded Parisian parks. Although none were known to have been caught, this was very dangerous. As one former *résistant* observed, had they encountered Germans, their pale skin (from staying indoors) might have given them away.[7]

Sheltering those in hiding was a major responsibility. Women who accepted this task had to feed extra people who often did not have ration coupons, real or false. As noted, food scarcity was *the* major problem during the war years. The French "Système D" (for *débrouillardise*—that is, improvisation) was used extensively.

"All of us in the Resistance were sheltered by women and by families while we were underground," testifies Anne-Marie Soucelier, Catherine Roux's courier friend:

"Consider the Humblot family, a typical bourgeois family in Lyon. There were six children. In spite of the dangers that represented, they received everyone at their home at 20, rue Vauban. I was never afraid when I stayed with them. Besides, their concierge was 'in' on things; she kept her eye on everything. The police came several times to ask questions. She would say to them, 'Don't talk to me about this family. There are six children. They have friends over. There are comings and goings all the time.' That is what saved them. When the Gestapo came in the summer of 1943, the family was at their vacation home.

"When I arrived shortly thereafter, the concierge warned me that the Gestapo had come, and she advised me to get rid of compromising papers. This, by the way, gives you an idea of the role a concierge could play. On the one hand, she fooled the police, and on the other, she warned me. So I gathered up incriminating papers and took them with me. That was when I was arrested. But at least the family got away. There were people from every milieu in the Resistance."[8]

"Annette," who joined the exodus with her mother, also acknowledged the help of concierges:

"Certain concierges were exemplary. They helped without hesitation. They told the police or the Gestapo they did not know the whereabouts of those being sought—when in fact they did. At times, concierges warned those about to return to an apartment or room where capture awaited them. Take the case of an escaped French soldier staying with our family. When he learned he was about to be captured, he jumped out of a second-floor window but broke his leg in the fall. There was only one chance. He rang the concierge in the nearest building and explained his situation. It could have meant capture, but in this case the concierge called some patriotic friends and helped get him transported to safety. Unfortunately, not all concierges acted this courageously. This I learned from personal experience. Once I was almost arrested when the Germans set a trap for me at the place where I was to meet another young woman agent. The two of us worked together. As it turned out, my friend was arrested before I arrived. She asked the concierge to warn me the moment I came to the building. The concierge did nothing of the sort. When I arrived, I sensed something was wrong. It is a feeling that is difficult to explain. In the Resistance, we were taught to act on those feelings, so I left quickly.

"The soldier who got away was one of a number of those in danger we sheltered. Our family apartment in Paris was quite large. A Jewish woman stayed with us for almost a year. Technically, she had 'sold' her apartment to a French couple with the understanding that she could have it back after the war. [Owning property was one of a number of civil rights the Germans had forbidden to Jews.] Although she spent nights with us, she went to her own apartment during the day. It must have been very difficult for her to be turned out of her own home. But at the same time, it was extremely dangerous to go back there. Luckily, our part-time 'guest' was never bothered.

"When I joined a Resistance group in 1941, I did a lot of liaison work and helped with the social services. We frequently had to hide relatives of those who were arrested or had gone underground, as well as those on the run. Family members were potential hostages. As you can imagine, all this required a major support system. Besides the concierges, and the peasants who helped when we were in the countryside, there was another group I want to mention who did much for the Resistance. These were the *cheminots*, the railway workers. Since I did a lot of traveling by train, I had ample opportunity to observe this. Once, while staying in a room above a station café, I heard a loud explosion during the night. Rolling stock and switches were blown up. [Others have faulted the railway workers. Not a single train or coach—usually cattle cars—deporting those to the camps was sabotaged.]

"One morning, the Gestapo rang the doorbell of the apartment in Paris at five in the morning. Someone had given out my name under torture. No, I am not bitter about that. Quite honestly, how do you know how you will hold up under torture? My mother answered the door and told the officers that I had gone out early to look for food, as I often did. She asked for time to get dressed. This was just enough time for me to flush documents down an old toilet and escape. I left the apartment by another door, still in my nightgown. Friends hid me until the war's end."[9]

When "Annette" was forced to flee, the young woman faced a number of dangers—some perhaps not readily apparent. Not only was she going out into the streets dressed in scanty attire, but the curfew was still in effect, and she risked being caught and questioned.

After the war, "Annette" resumed legal studies as well as her job.

In her view, it was essential to focus on law, for during the Occupation, French laws were violated in every way. The times were very ambiguous. Resistance members violated laws in their efforts to combat a regime they viewed as illegal. Collaborators took advantage of the times and committed many crimes. "Average" French citizens resorted to deceit in order to survive. Restoring morality and order after the war was not an easy feat. Even in the 1990s, France is still dealing with the troubled heritage of the Occupation.

In some instances, women whose husbands were important figures in movements or networks could not work with their spouses because of family obligations. Yet, by assuming full responsibility for the children while their husbands worked full-time for the Resistance—in most cases, clandestinely—these women assuredly served. Nevertheless, little has been written about them in Resistance accounts. These women themselves often had difficulties securing shelter.

Ida Bourdet's husband, Claude, was a Combat leader. Born in Moscow, she lived in Russia during the Revolution. This, she maintains, was excellent training for dealing with the Occupation. The Bourdets lived in Paris with their three young children. Before the war, Claude Bourdet was managing director of Radiodiffusion Française, the main French broadcasting station.

Early on in the war, he joined Henri Frenay and Combat. Bourdet's biggest contribution was setting up the NAP (Noyautage de l'Administration Publique) system. Members of the Resistance were to infiltrate French public-administration offices—such as the railways, the police, and the post office—to conduct espionage and, when the time came, sabotage. These infiltrators at times were able to tip off those about to be arrested. According to historian David Schoenbrun, author of Soldiers of the Night (1980), Bourdet's project was copied by other movements and became one of the mainstays of the Resistance. Bourdet eventually became Frenay's second in command, replacing him when he was in London.

"Claude accepted a job in the south of France. In early 1941, he was designated head of the Mouvement de Libération Nationale [later named Combat] for the Alpes-Maritimes region. We lived in Vence, trying to have as few contacts as possible with people. In spite of

these precautions, the Vichy government became increasingly interested in his and other movement members' activities. They had to
assume false names, which changed frequently. Early Resistance
members had no experience in an undertaking where so much
needed to be done and everything had to be invented. In 1942,
Claude was named to the administrative committee of Combat.
This entailed frequent trips to Lyon. To facilitate his work there, he
stayed with the Brossets, who lived in the suburbs of Lyon. They
were like a family to him. I went to visit Claude from time to time,
for he could now visit Vence only on rare occasions.

"I told the children that their father was a prisoner—as were so
many in those days. I did not send them to school but taught them
myself. My mother and an *au pair* girl helped me. We had to move
about frequently. That was very, very difficult. There were few
movement leaders who were married and had young children."

When Claude went underground and returned to Paris, Ida remained in Vence with her mother and the three children. But occasionally she went to see her husband and relay messages. On one visit,
she told him that his former boss, Jean Couitéas de Faucamberge—
who wanted to see Claude—was viewed by most in the Resistance as
a strange figure, someone who collaborated with the Germans. Ida, on
the other hand, believed in him, for she had once been on a train
with a group of Jews from the occupied zone for whom Couitéas had
arranged passage to the southern zone, away from the immediate men-
ace of the Germans. Ida also knew of an incident when this former
French tennis champion deliberately lost a match with the Gestapo
head of Nice in order to save a Jew from deportation. Couitéas wanted
to sound out Claude on the possible response of Resistance heads if
there were a coup against Hitler. Claude seriously doubted that he
could have intelligence of such an event. Events were to prove otherwise. During captivity in Germany, Claude saw thousands of smartly
dressed German military figures captured after the abortive coup attempt; their faces were covered with black paint.

When Claude was arrested, Ida was informed of the event by Father Bruckberger, a chaplain with the FFI who accompanied her to
Paris and back to see what could be done to help him. Claude's assistant was sent south to help her spirit the children away. The Gestapo
arrived shortly after he did so. Ida greeted them with total ease, even

though they came in looking furious, ready to ransack the place. She politely asked them to sit down.

"Their first question was, 'You are Jewish, naturally?' I responded in excellent German by asking, 'And what is he?', referring to the interpreter. My family was Russian Armenian, but I knew from his accent that the interpreter was a Russian Jew. That disconcerted the Germans somewhat. Then, in their search, they found a firecracker left by one of the children. 'What is that?' 'As you can plainly see, it is a bomb.' They told me I had no right to make fun of them. I answered that since they did not believe what I said, I was justified in saying anything. Then came a comical interlude amid the questions and threats. One of the agents pointed to the orange trees in the garden: 'What are those?' 'As you can see, they are orange trees.' 'Naturally, they are bitter oranges; the French don't have sweet oranges.' 'They are sweet oranges.' 'You are lying.' 'Go see for yourself.' And this agent, who presumably was there to arrest me and take me away, tiptoed into the orange grove to taste an orange and verify that it was indeed sweet. 'You see,' I said, 'I always tell the truth.'

"Since the questioning was not finished and it was getting late (who knows *what* their plans were for the evening), they forbade me to leave the house under threat of severe punishment, saying they would return the following morning. Needless to say, shortly after they left, I contacted several friends to help me leave. Transportation was a major problem, so we put the three children on bike luggage racks and cycled off to take the night train north. I left the three of them at Saint-Pierre-de-Chartreuse with the parents of Claude's assistant. They stayed there until the Liberation. I was very pleased about outwitting the Gestapo and wanted to remain, but my mother and our friends insisted that I leave.

"How did I succeed? Claude thinks my polite yet arrogant attitude put the agents in an inferior position. There was an element of social class that I exploited by playing the 'lady' in front of these individuals who respected established order. It does not always work, but one should not pass up the possibility of trapping Germans with their stereotyped views of French society. Being well dressed always impressed the Gestapo and others. For example, once several Jews who had been antiques dealers in Paris were stopped. The Germans wanted them to take their pants down [to see if they were circumcised], but they could not do it because I was there—they would not do it before this 'lady.' It would have been otherwise were I a peasant woman."

In May 1944, Ida was on her way to Saint-Pierre-de-Chartreuse to visit her children in hiding. By chance, she stopped in the town of Voiron on the very day the Militia was exacting revenge for the killing of their local leader. The execution of a man like Jourdan was normal in those times, Claude Bourdet holds. He had condemned and executed many. Unfortunately, evidently panicking when they realized there were witnesses to their initial killing, six Resistance members who carried out the execution—teachers and students of the professional school in Voiron—then assassinated Jourdan's wife, elderly mother, and two young children. As Bourdet explains in his memoirs, there is no excuse for such acts. Still, he adds, one must remember the climate of the period and the rage of men driven to the point of madness by the crimes of the Militia.

Three of the *résistants* were captured, tortured, and shot in front of twenty pupils and teachers of the school as an "example." When Ida Bourdet arrived that day, the town was in a state of siege. The Militia members were taking their revenge and shooting in all directions, even killing pregnant women in the street. A passerby alerted Ida Bourdet and led her into a café, which undoubtedly saved her. She was doubly lucky: The Militia overlooked her during an identity check in the café. With her Russian maiden name, Adamoff, listed on her identity card, she surely would have been killed with the others.

"It was very difficult to move about with three young children. No one wanted them when it was a question of finding a place to stay— not even Claude's family, because he had been arrested. So his arrest in March 1944 was a catastrophe. We could not stay in the street. Obviously, I could not move with them by myself. Another major problem was identity papers. I was born in Moscow. Another catastrophe. That really complicated things.

"Even when I managed to get to Paris after the children were safely hidden elsewhere, I still faced lodging problems because the Gestapo was looking for me. I had to go underground. Finding housing was really a nightmare. Combat wanted me to go to Switzerland, as others in my situation had done, but I preferred staying in Paris, hoping to see my husband. At the very least, I felt I could try to help him, wherever he was. One of the few courageous friends who offered housing was the actress Arletty. She was in love with a German officer, but she was not a collaborator, in spite of what people say. Friends in Neuilly [a Paris suburb] put me up, but it was dangerous there. They had young children. The wife was a Jew who had not declared herself. They took risks putting me up, so I did not stay long. I also stayed with a distant aunt. It was truly a gypsy life. I looked like a gypsy, too. I was virtually without funds. The movement helped with limited funds. Friends got together enough money for me to buy a dress so I could be a true *Parisienne*. Appearance was very important.

"Finally, I found a place in an apartment with four exits. Three other clandestines were staying there as well. Each evening, we would decide which exit to take should the Germans arrive. Figuring out how to pass all the free time on our hands was another problem. We carried messages and joked among ourselves. You could not go to the cafés because the Gestapo watched them. Meetings took place while walking along the street.

"I could tell you many amusing stories about life during the Occupation. You adjust and accept the fact that you may be arrested. We did some ridiculous—and dangerous—things, like go out to elegant restaurants from time to time, even though the Germans were looking for us. We needed to eat. We needed to get out. Life continued. It is difficult now to generalize about those times. The atmosphere changed constantly, particularly after the Germans invaded the whole country.

"From the first days of Claude's captivity, his father or my cousin, Marianne Doresse, took parcels I prepared to the prison where we thought he was incarcerated. For some time, they were refused. Finally, two were accepted. Claude later told me that something in the way the packages were put together led him to believe that I had assembled them. This he found very reassuring. At the same time, when those two parcels were accepted, we were virtually certain he was there.*

"The wife of Claude's distant cousin, Maurice Bourdet, had succeeded in corrupting an SS guard, and from her I learned that Claude had been transferred to the Compiègne camp. She paid this SS guard a lot of money to keep her husband there rather than be-

---

*While at Buchenwald, Claude learned the details of his family's escape from the Gestapo.

ing deported to Germany. She urged me to do the same thing. I managed to procure the funds needed. Then something—perhaps my Russian temperament—made me fearful of trying to change destiny. As it turned out, Maurice stayed at Compiègne until almost the end, thanks to his wife's payments. When the Germans retreated, he was transferred to Dachau, where he died shortly before the camp was liberated."

In February 1944, Claude was in the Sachsenhausen camp, near Berlin. One day he returned to his barracks to find a package of warm clothing that had been brought in by an SS guard. After the war, he learned how this astonishing delivery had occurred. Through Combat's liaison with Switzerland, the prodigious parcel arrived at the home of a woman friend in Geneva who worked for the International Red Cross. (Claude Bourdet studied in Switzerland before the war.) For months, she was unable to do anything about sending the parcel until a Swiss officer was sent on a Red Cross mission near Berlin. He acceded to her request to take the package, and a young Norwegian colleague got the SS officer to deliver the package. So it was that this completely irregular and unexpected package was carried through the main gate by an SS guard, who carefully checked it to ascertain which block Bourdet was in, and deposited it on the barracks table before Claude's amazed comrades.

Ida sent parcels in unorthodox fashion, rationalizing that they would help someone even if they never reached Claude. With black-market prices, assembling these packages was very expensive. Her Russian relatives helped, even though they were as short of funds as she was. Claude's French family, on the other hand, criticized this "extravagance" and refused to contribute, insisting those boxes would "surely be lost." As Claude observes, it was a question of differences of nationality and temperament.[10]

Simone Martin-Chauffier offered hospitality to many in their home, an active Resistance center. Her husband, Louis, a journalist with *Paris-Soir* before the war, became a prominent figure in the Libération movement, assuming the editorship of their newspaper, *Libération*. Son Jean was an assistant to Emmanuel d'Astier de la Vigerie of Libération. Teenaged daughters Claudie and Hélène helped in many ways and shared their parents' anti-Nazi stance. When asked to dance by a German she met at a skating rink, Claudie replied, "No, thank you. I am in mourning, mourning for France." The family subsequently was joined by their ward, Luce, the young daughter of deceased cinéaste Jean Vigo, whom they were raising, as her mother requested before she died. Claude Aveline—author and longtime friend who was working with Combat—joined the family when the persecutions of Jews increased. Another important family member was Mouni, the cat. And there was a continual stream of "guests" when the Martin-Chauffiers moved to Lyon.

Before the war, Simone Martin-Chauffier worked at the Rockefeller-supported Center for the Study of Foreign Politics in Paris. The foundation closed shortly after the Occupation, so she turned to translation in hopes of contributing to the family budget; the Martin-Chauffier family had to work to survive. All around her in Paris, Simone saw people stocking up on anything that was not rationed.

"Besides hoarding food, people with means amassed stocks of another sort. A woman friend of mine made a small fortune in precious stones. I, on the other hand, had to sell the only piece of jewelry I owned, my engagement ring from Cartier. Two thousand francs would keep the family going for a month. I was also pained to observe that, in spite of my illusions, anti-Semitism was now acceptable in France. *Les Dernières Nouvelles de Paris* 'respectfully' requested Marshal Pétain—whom the paper generally covered with mud—to annul the Crémieux decree, which gave French citizenship to Algerian Jews. We were struck by frightened reactions to the anti-Jewish regulations that only added to the poisonous atmosphere. For example, the optical firm Lissac Brothers assured the public that they were not Jewish: 'Lissac is not Isaac.' "

Once a week, their circle of friends (later referred to as the Musée de l'Homme Resistance group) met in Louis Martin-Chauffier's Paris office. (One of the earliest Resistance groups, it was betrayed by a priest who volunteered to serve as informer for the Germans. He was executed after the war; see chapter 4.) Agnès Humbert was secretary and typist for the group. Simone's role was to keep others away and to prepare tea and snacks for the group. The first edition of the group's clandestine newspaper, *Résistance*—two modest mimeographed sheets—appeared in mid-December 1940. The editorial (quoted in chapter 4) urged the French to resist.

"Mid-February [1941], most of our group was arrested. With much difficulty, the next edition of *Résistance* appeared. It was crucial to try to show the Germans that those they had arrested were *not* involved in its publication. I had a meeting with Boris Vildé, the group's head, on March 26, 1940. He was to give me his photo and the name and address he had chosen for his false identity card. I arrived ahead of time—slightly before three—and settled in a café with a book. I watched as the hands of the clock facing me slowly moved. At four, 'Didier,' another of our members, entered. Urging me to keep smiling and not to move my head, he told me that Vildé had left him just before three to meet me. Undoubtedly, he had been arrested. His arrest affected me personally. I felt guilty that I escaped his fate so narrowly—the mere crossing of a square."

Simone Martin-Chauffier agreed to shelter some Belgian youths trying to get to England to enlist. The youths and her daughters got along very well together. She had the girls invite classmates to dance so that the Belgians could have some fun. Shortly thereafter, she asked the girls to arrange another party. This time, Simone wanted to cover the noise of her packing: The family planned to slip out of their flat unnoticed and head south. She packed to the rhythm of fox-trots and tangos. Once in the south, they rented space in a large home in Collonges, on the outskirts of Lyon. The whole family suffered from privations.

"Physically, I was not in much better shape than the others, but I was not as hungry. This 'privilege' added to my feeling of failure about my inability to provide enough for my family. A few friends were stoic enough to spend a night or two in our 'icebox.' In those early months of 1942, we anguished over the fate of our friends in the Musée de l'Homme group. All ten arrested were sentenced to death; the seven men were shot almost immediately. The three women—Agnès Humbert, Yvonne Oddon, and Sylvette Leleu—had their sentences commuted to hard labor for life. All three came back from deportation after the war—God alone knows by what miracle of heroism and interior strength. For myself, I felt guilty to be living and free."

234 Sisters in the Resistance

In her ongoing efforts to feed her family and friends, Martin-Chauffier pondered the contradictory messages the population received. The church declared black-market dealing no longer forbidden. Cardinal Suhard decided that "modest extralegal operations" were justified, given their insignificance and people's daily needs. The Vichy government reversed its stance and now approved infringements to satisfy "personal or family needs." In the black market, buying was acceptable; selling was not.

"Our house became an active Resistance center. The heads of the three major movements met there once a week. Our discretion was exemplary, our prudence less so. My daughter Hélène developed a taste for the British cigarettes d'Astier brought back from a mission to England. He also brought back a battery-operated radio for Claudie—a spectacular invention, obviously American. I blamed myself for letting the girls take needless risks by accepting these gifts. Yet, at the same time, I didn't have the courage to deny them. The girls were so helpful. Hélène agreed to take d'Astier's place in the train from Lyon to Villefranche. The Gestapo was looking for him, so he couldn't take a train from Lyon. If things looked clear, he would board at Villefranche. It was a major undertaking for a girl of seventeen. Our ward, Luce, going on twelve, marvelously played the role of not knowing what was going on in our household. Then Claudie developed tuberculosis."

To pay the bills for Claudie's treatments and sanatorium stays, as well as to keep the family going, Martin-Chauffier was obliged to sell family furniture. Toward the end of September 1943, she went to Paris and called her son to arrange a celebration for his twenty-first birthday: "You are now of age. I bring you your freedom," she said. Jean never made it to his party; instead of being free, he became a prisoner of the Germans. Besides helping to alert members of their group of the arrest, his mother spent days going through every book in the family apartment, trying to find the false identity cards Jean had hidden there.

To help her son continue his medical studies in prison, Simone contacted his teacher, Claude Hertz—who became their son-in-law several years later. When Jean's personal effects were returned, there was much anguish. Was he dead? His mother carefully examined all the pages of his anatomy manuals, hoping to find a message. As it turned out, there had been a mistake in the system. Jean was alive

and en route to Weimar; he was sent later to Buchenwald. Her husband was arrested and deported too, but both father and son returned.
To deal with all her anxieties, Martin-Chauffier threw herself into
housework and fixing up her home. Rule number one was: "Life continued, as normal as possible," a motto other Resistance families also
followed.[11]

+>=—=<+

In his memoirs, Claude Bourdet stresses the importance of rest and
relaxation in a "normal" family for a clandestine agent:

> You can't imagine what it meant in terms of rest and relaxation for
> a clandestine agent to find oneself each evening in a friendly setting.
> Here were friends who thought as you did, who approved of what you
> were doing, and who were living the ordinary private life of French
> families. For those who had gone underground, that life was but a
> memory.[12]

In interviews, Lucie Aubrac also observed how a home environment helped the morale of movement members on the run. With the
Aubracs and their young son, "guests" were reminded that their struggle was to make France once again an environment suitable for families.

In addition to these women, there were those who took over someone else's child or children, as friends and relatives did for Marie-
Louise Le Duc, for Lucie Aubrac, and for others. Assuredly, those
women made a significant contribution to the Resistance, although
they seem destined to remain among the many "unknown" who stayed
at home and helped. Evelyne Sullerot points out:

"The last war was a war with civilians. In the 1914–18 war, the men
were at the front and the women were in the rear. It was not easy to
be in the rearguard, but being at the front was atrocious. But that
was not true in 1940–45. Who were the members of the Resistance?
Civilians, not the army. Consequently, I think women naturally
found their place in that combat because they were threatened like
everyone else.

"Think of the women who hid someone. In those cases, maternal feelings were often brought into play. Some elderly women were
absolutely extraordinary. There were many women whose husbands
asked them to hide someone. They came home saying, 'Fix a bed for

so-and-so. And remember, you didn't see him.' But there were also many women who took that upon themselves and helped for long periods. You can't imagine what that entailed and how exhausting it was."[13]

When World War II broke out, barely twenty years after World War I, older French people found themselves once again involved in a major conflict. For them, memories of World War I were all too present. Most had lost family members among the almost million and a half French war dead. They were only too aware of what hostilities with Germany meant. Yet some wanted to "do something" to rid French soil again of the German presence—even though they no longer were young. So they did what they could. This included welcoming strangers into their homes.

+═══+

Simone Lefranc-Lemoine was born the year before the twentieth century began. As an adolescent, she had experienced what proved to be the ironically designated "war to end all wars." After that war, she married and raised a family. Her son, Pierre Lefranc, joined the FFL. (For some years, he directed the Charles de Gaulle Institute in Paris, which was established in 1971.) However, Pierre was not the only family member active in French Resistance. His mother was involved as well. During the Occupation, she went out into her garden every day. This surprised her neighbors, because Mme Lemoine had never gardened before. But food was extremely scarce, so people raised food wherever they could. City dwellers used window boxes and crates— and, if they were lucky, designated plots in parks. What those around her did not know was that the real purpose of Mme Lemoine's daily excursions to the garden was to take food to the man she was sheltering there in a small shed. It seemed the least she could do to help, she decided.[14]

The elderly Buisson sisters also housed those seeking shelter in Lyon, capital of the Resistance in the southern zone; and they stored supplies. Described by those who knew them as "characters," or "originals," the two spinsters ran an antiques shop. Their names were Marie and Renée, but they always were referred to as the Buisson sisters. Once they were arrested briefly, but the police did not keep them, as *résistante* Anne-Marie Soucelier recounts:

"Because they were so eccentric, they got away with a lot. For example, if they passed a German officer on the street [on occasion, German officers would force French pedestrians off a sidewalk], one of them would brusquely open the parasol they always carried—right in the German's face—and walk on. They were typical of Lyon, in a sense. And they did much for the Resistance. Below their antiques store was a sloping basement used to store supplies for the movement's social services. One of the regular clients of their shop was a police commissioner named Gussonac [a notorious collaborator executed in the purge following the liberation of France]. Now Gussonac knew the Buisson sisters well. They were longtime friends. Moreover, he was not stupid; he had some idea of what they were up to. But he never turned them in. When he entered their shop, he often would remark how unusual it was for an antiques shop to smell of cheese and sausage, or whatever. Unperturbed, they would say, 'What do you expect, dear friend? In these times, you have to manage as best you can.' They implied they were in the black market. Even though he did not denounce them, he was not duped.

"The Buisson sisters lodged everyone. In their apartment on rue Dandin, they sheltered all the heads of the Resistance: Father Chaillet [founder of Témoignage Chrétien], Henri Frenay [founder of Combat]—all the heads. They also had Jacques Renouvin of Combat. He had once been an active member of Action Française, the ultraconservative monarchist group. They also took in Jean Gay [known as Jacqueline]. Gay was a committed Communist who joined Combat early on, because he wanted to serve. He was the dynamic director of Action Ouvrière [Worker Action] in the unoccupied zone. This gives you some idea of the varied backgrounds of those involved in the Resistance. But then we all were committed to the same cause, the same ideal. We were united then. Sometimes, however, there were epic discussions in their place because the Buisson sisters were ardent republicans. They had a bust of Marianne [symbol of the republic] in their living room. Renouvin would tease them because he had been with Action Française. Yet all of us would have given our lives for each other."[15]

Jeanne Chaton was among those who had to deal with the German invaders—once again. Chaton was born in Lorraine at the turn of the twentieth century in a small village just a few hundred yards from the German border. When Chaton was four, her mother died.

She was brought up by her maternal grandparents in her natal village. Her father, a teacher at the prestigious Lycée Louis-le-Grand in Paris, spent all his vacation periods with Jeanne. He was there when World War I broke out and the Germans took over the area. French forces bombarded the region heavily. Her grandfather was suspected of providing information to the French gunners: The Germans knew he had been a colonel in the 1870 war. In retaliation, Chaton and her father were arrested as hostages, along with a dozen other villagers. The Germans told the group they were going to be shot. In the end, however, the hostages were sent to different camps in Germany. Her father—then fifty—was sent to work as a woodcutter. With the other women, young Jeanne was condemned to forced labor.

"Initially, I was sent to a German factory that bleached linens. They used chlorine vapors to bleach covers. This was in late 1914; I was fourteen at the time. My health suffered, and after two and a half months of this work, I became sick, spitting up blood and so on. Eventually, I was sent to a military hospital where there were wounded French soldiers. I was fortunate and recovered fairly quickly. Now it was a question of what work I could realistically undertake. I suggested farm work. The one thing I knew was that I did not want to return to factory work. With a single German guard, I was sent to a farm on the island of Rügen, in the Baltic Sea.

"I was placed with a peasant family, very poor people. They asked me to milk the cows. I understood what they wanted, because I knew a little German, but this was something I had never done. Well, I went and looked at the cows. Imagine, they just didn't give milk like that! The farmer came and swore at me, then he locked me in a shed. Two days later, the pastor of that small village came and found me. He wanted to know why I wasn't willing to milk the cows. I began to cry, telling him that I did not know how to milk cows. He explained this to the farmer, who then showed me how to do it. From that time on, I took care of—and milked—eight cows. I slept in the barn above them. And I drank as much milk as I could, which was good for my health. I spent six months there, and it was not that bad. At fifteen, you are so determined to survive.

"But there was a rule that prisoners doing agricultural work could stay for only six months in any one place. So a German soldier once again came to get me. This time, I was taken to Saxony, where I was placed in a factory that soldered cans. By now, my German was quite good, so I was put in charge of seventy-five women prisoners. Some were French women convicts; others were from Poland—quite a few Polish women. The rest came from different places. My job was to organize our daily departure from and return to the prison. We were supposed to solder a certain number of cans each day. I had trouble meeting my quota. I had learned how to milk cows, but I did not know how to solder well. Besides that, my health was in very bad shape again. One day, some Swedish doctors working for the Red Cross visited our camp. Before they came, we hurriedly had to plant flowers around our barracks and brick over the dirt floor. During the inspection, one of the doctors asked me my number [you were not tattooed then]. I represented our group during the inspection. Six months after their visit, I learned I was to be returned to France. In 1917, I was repatriated via Switzerland.

"Throughout my stay in Germany (1914–1917), I had been without news of my father or my family—no news at all. Eventually, I made my way to Paris, where my father had an apartment, part of his appointment to the Lycée Louis-le-Grand. When his colleagues saw me, they could not do enough to help me. As you can imagine, I had a lot of lost time to catch up with: I was behind in my schooling. A little later, I finally heard from my father and went to join him in Switzerland, where he had been interned.

"In the early postwar period, my father and I lived together again. It was not easy. We both had a lot of recuperating to do. We had been through very trying times. He was not well, and I had become independent—very independent for a girl my age at that time. We returned to Paris, where I began graduate work. Before the war, I had successfully passed a competitive exam to prepare for a teaching career in secondary education, so I resumed my studies. My father wanted me to take advantage of the special dispensations for former prisoners of war. He thought it would be too difficult for me to be accepted at the Sèvres Normal School, which I wanted to enter. I told him I would be accepted in three years without special advantages, and I was. Actually, I was accepted by both Fontenay and Sèvres, schools that train women to teach in higher education. I chose Sèvres. In three years, I completed the *agrégation* in history, a graduate degree.

"After this, something quite extraordinary happened. The Peugeot company announced that they would give prizes to those who ranked first in their subject in the national examinations: a bicycle for the elementary level, a motorbike to the boys who were first in their *licence* class. And, they said, if there was a first prize for the *agrégation*, they would award a car. Now I knew that there were no firsts among the young men who received the *agrégation*. At that time, I was spending my vacation with friends in the south of France. They had a car, which I used a good deal. Few people had cars then. Obviously, my teacher's salary would not be enough for me even to consider buying a car. So I told my friends that perhaps I would ask the Peugeot company for one. I went to the Peugeot firm and said, 'Look, I saw your announcement about the prizes you are giving. As it turns out, I am the only woman to come in with a first in the *agrégation*. What prize are you giving me?' Toward the end of October, a Peugeot representative came and presented me with a little five-horsepower Peugeot.

"And so I had a Peugeot car, which I used a great deal in the Jura region, where I had my first teaching post in 1925. The authorities may have given me this post because they realized I had been very affected by all that I had been through. (My classmates were younger than I was.) Initially, though, I was offered a position in Algeria, because I had been first in the *agrégation*. But I am an anticolonialist, so I refused. This shocked the administration. Instead, I was given a job in the smallest *lycée* in France, at Lons-le-Saunier in the Jura region. In retrospect, I regret not having gone to teach in Algeria. Over the years, I have met Algerian women and become involved in African issues. These women told me how much they would have liked to have had teachers like me. However, had I found myself under colonial domination, I would have spoken up and intervened in various matters. If I had gone to Algeria, I certainly would have been sent back by the governor-general himself!"

"With my car, I went to Geneva frequently; it was not far away, and my teaching load was not heavy. Because I had had an excellent philosophy teacher at Sèvres, I was considering switching subjects and becoming a philosophy rather than a history teacher. Twice a week, I went to Lyon to prepare the *licence* in philosophy, planning to do the *agrégation* later. My father did not approve of this idea; he thought one *agrégation* degree was quite enough. But I persisted. A friend of mine was the director of the museum in Lyon. He had been an art-history professor at Sèvres while I was a student there. His appointment included a very handsome apartment in the town hall of Lyon. Every Wednesday, he invited me to supper. My friend had been a classmate of Édouard Herriot, who was then a delegate to the League of Nations. Herriot often came to visit my friend and dined with us. Knowing of my interest in contemporary history, he asked me if I wanted to work for him and the League of Nations. Of course I accepted, even though he could not offer me a salary. I served as his secretary and attended a number of sessions of the League. I observed that milieu at close range. For example, I was there when the leader of Abyssinia quit the League—when the Italians invaded Abyssinia. There are things that happen in your life—exceptional opportunities. I have always taken advantage of whatever opportunities came my way."

After several years teaching in the Jura, Chaton was assigned to Besançon, where she prepared students for graduate degrees. In 1935, one of her supervisors recommended that she teach in Paris. Since her father had just died, she accepted the chance and returned to Paris after ten years of teaching in the provinces.

"I returned to Paris in 1936 and taught first at the Lycée Lamartine, then at the Lycée Claude Monet, a new school, where I stayed until I retired. My pupils were girls; the sexes were still separated then. We had some outstanding principals. They were mainly Protestant, as most Catholic teachers went to parochial schools. While I was at Claude Monet, the war broke out and the Germans arrived. One of my former pupils was staying with me then. I was helping her prepare for the *agrégation* in English while she taught in Orléans. In the exodus, we went south to the Corrèze region with several other colleagues. It was then that I had to learn how to ride a bike! Finally, in October, the schools were reopened and we resumed teaching. Between the two wars, I had been very pacifist—extremely pacifist. But there was the question of liberty. How can you remain pacifist when your country is occupied? Several teachers, former *normaliens*—such as Jean Cavaillès, who helped us prepare our students for the competitive exams—asked me to help out, to distribute tracts. I accepted. This was in the first days of the Occupation. That is how it began.

"I began by distributing tracts. First I worked with Défense de la France and then, for a time, with Libération-Nord. A little later, I was asked to hide British parachutists. I was also in contact with a Belgian network that helped prisoners escape. I had a large apart-

ment then. There were only three of us—my friend [her former pu-
pil], the maid, and me. We had room to hide people. When the
compulsory labor laws were enacted, friends from a Resistance group
in the south asked me to help out. With great difficulty, I managed
to go down and assist them. For some time, I worked with young
men who went underground rather than be sent to Germany. Many
joined the *maquis*."

Jeanne Chaton did not always have an easy time with those she
hid in her Paris apartment. Once she sheltered a group of six Belgians.
The first thing they had to be told was to take off their shoes so they
would not make noise. Feeding them was a major undertaking. Then
there was the problem of three English parachutists with big feet.
(Allied aviators generally were bigger than their French equivalents.
Additionally, Germany requisitioned all of France's leather stock.)
Chaton's colleagues from the *lycée* contributed their husbands' clothes.
But those Englishmen had such big feet! Finding shoes to fit them was
a difficult task. When taken on outings, the airmen had to be reminded constantly not to speak, particularly not in the Métro. They
were to make a designated sign if they suspected danger. Naïvely, they
assumed everyone was on the side of the Allies. Unfortunately, that
was not always the case. The British understood, but Chaton felt that
the Americans were not always serious. Women whom Chaton knew
were captured—one never returned from deportation—because American servicemen they hid did not realize the gravity of their situation.
They were told not to smoke, not to make noise, and so forth, but
they did not fully cooperate. This, for Chaton, was one of the worst
aspects of clandestine work.

"The closer it came to the Allied invasion of France, the more difficult things became. Many members of the Resistance had been captured and sent to Germany. Those of us who remained did things we
would not have done earlier. For example, toward the end we received some supplies by parachute. Women collected them because
the Germans never imagined that French women could or would do
things like that, even toward the end of the war. The situation in
Paris was different. The German presence was very evident elsewhere in the country, but it was virtually impossible for them to totally occupy Paris. Assuredly, there were Germans in the Métro and
on the Champs-Élysées, but you saw few Germans elsewhere in the

capital. But in the provinces—such as Touraine, where I spent my vacations with friends—it was very different. In Tours [the major city of Touraine], there were Germans everywhere. I know, because I traveled a good deal transporting parachuted materiel.

"French youths who wanted to serve had to be taught to use weapons. Most were clandestines who had gone into hiding to escape being sent to work in Germany. That was something about which my Resistance comrades had taught me a good deal. As things turned out, I never had to use a weapon—not even during the Liberation of Paris. But I can assure you that if I had had to, I would have. I would have fired.

"Toward the end of the war, I was in contact with several Parisian academics at Troyes [south of Paris]—such as famed physicist Paul Langevin, who put me in contact with his colleague Frédéric Joliot-Curie, another noted physicist. Joliot-Curie was one of a group of Communists in our Resistance group, the Front National Universitaire (FNU). The FNU had members from all the ministries and members from the academic world; there were also lawyers and writers. That is how I became acquainted with such writers as Louis Aragon, Georges Duhamel, and François Mauriac. I worked with them. We all worked hard, very hard. Only at the end of the war did I learn the identities of those I worked with in the FNU. By then, I was FNU vice president. One day, I was reproached for not attending a meeting about which I knew nothing. So I resigned. Perhaps I am too proud, too headstrong. I don't know. All that was ugly, quite ugly. FNU meetings were becoming more like reunions of the Communist Party than reunions of a Resistance group. Mauriac left the FNU at the same time I did.

"While working with the FNU, I was almost captured by the Germans. One of my colleagues came and warned me not to go to a rendezvous we had arranged. For reasons I never fully understood, he went—and was captured. But he saved me. Another near-escape occurred when I was asked to hide a young Jewish girl who had just fled from Holland. When she arrived, she asked me to go and get her suitcase at an apartment in Neuilly [a Paris suburb] that she had just left. It was not safe for her to take it with her when she left. I went, and so did the French police. They took me to police headquarters and questioned me for a long time. Then I was taken to Gestapo headquarters. 'What were you doing there?' they asked. I invented a plausible excuse, but they still gave me a difficult time.

They asked me about my dissertation, about the books I owned. Evidently, they had searched my apartment. 'Why have you so many books?' 'Why are you working on a dissertation on a religious movement?' 'Because that interests me,' I replied. 'And who is your professor?' I did not tell them; I gave them the name of another history professor to protect my adviser, who was Jewish. They took all my index cards—which represented years of research—saying they were going to verify my alibi. I was told to come back later and get them—which explains why I never finished my dissertation. When the Germans finally released me, they told me I could collect my research material later. I left and never returned. Sometimes it is best not to get back into something.

"All this was frightening, very frightening, and yet—I do not know quite why—I was not frightened. Throughout this war, I said to myself, 'During World War I, I was sent to prison even though I did nothing; my father and I had done nothing against the Germans. This time, if they take me, at least it will be because I did something.' "

When asked why she had never written her memoirs—even though she was a trained historian—Jeanne Chaton explained that she was not really involved in World War I and had not really done anything in World War II either. For "doing nothing," Chaton received the Legion of Honor and the Medal of the Resistance. For her "nonactivities" (she does admit to helping a few comrades) in World War I, she was decorated by President Raymond Poincaré with the Medal of French Recognition (Reconnaissance Française). The Polish government also honored her for helping Polish women in the World War I work camps. Perhaps she did not write about her Resistance experience because her postwar activities kept her so busy. Various foreign countries invited her to visit, so she traveled extensively. She became president of the International Association of University Women.

"There were three of us French women who were heads of international women's organizations: Mme Irene de Wilkovski with the Women's International Alliance; Marie-Hélène Lefaucheux, with the International Council; and me. [All three had served in the Resistance.] To be president of an international organization involved a great deal of work and responsibility. I was concerned about the postwar situation of Germany. It was a terrible mistake to isolate Germany after World War I—to cut it off from everyone else, from the world. Cutting off the Germans from others sowed the seeds for revenge among the German people.

"Recently, the Lebanese government awarded me the Cedars of Lebanon medal because I helped colleagues while teaching in Lebanon. Then things got worse there. It was my idea to have a Lebanese student dormitory similar to those of other countries at the Cité Universitaire in Paris. I tried to help the Lebanese. If you want to conserve your authority, your personal worth, and have some impact in what you do, you cannot harbor hatred."[16]

Chaton's situation was unusual in that she had been a prisoner of the Germans during World War I. Her narrative provides details about the education of girls in interwar France and illustrates the difficulties women had in trying to pursue educational goals and careers. She shares the values of French women of all ages who worked to restore freedom to their native land.

11

+>===<+

Choosing Roles

A STRIKING FEATURE OF THE *RÉSISTANTES'* NARRATIVES IS THE RE-peated use of the expression *playing a role*. In fact, these women often had the opportunity to try out unsuspected acting skills. Changing identities meant changing roles. To escape capture and difficult situations—or just to carry out missions—women assumed different personalities and different appearances. Hélène Renal played the imbecile when arrested; Mireille Albrecht played the innocent schoolgirl when police came to their apartment; her mother, Berty, who loved theater, played an insane woman in order to be brought to trial; Madeleine Baudoin organized a "scene" in a mayor's office to steal ration tickets. Lucie Aubrac played the part of a seduced young woman from a conservative upper-class family. Her performance convinced the German officer, who arranged for a "marriage" to her husband. According to Resistance colleague Emmanuel d'Astier de la Vigerie, Aubrac excelled in using charm and candor—and lies.

Acting usually entails changing appearance, something that also helped *résistantes* in some situations. Women experiment with different styles and makeup. On occasion, they helped disguise male colleagues, as did Suzanne Tony Robert when she secured bleach to help men in her network treat their hair and mustaches and thus escape the ban on men under sixty circulating freely. For Célia Bertin and

others, changing hair color and style helped them elude capture. Another factor that helped was the stereotyped view of *la Française* held
by the enemy—at least in the early days of the war. Attractive young
women seldom were suspected of working in the underground, sometimes even after being caught *en flagrant délit*. Jennie (Rousseau) de
Clarens worked in a French company dealing with German firms
building the V-1 rockets. With her braid and innocent appearance,
no one suspected the nineteen-year-old of gathering intelligence.

The accepted view of women's presumed vanity provided cover
for those undertaking decidedly nontraditional feminine roles. As secret agents, women reproduced the male stereotypes of what women
are presumed to be—when it served their ends. When two German
officers came to her Parisian home, Geneviève Fontaine arranged to
have her young son accidentally spill his tea on compromising papers—which the maid carried out. Then she faked an attack of nerves.[1]

Among French women who discovered they could act—and lie
well—was France Pejot. France's Resistance name was "Marianne,"
the woman who symbolizes the French Republic. Her family owned
"La Lingerie Pratique," one of Lyon's best-known stores for laces and
luxury trimmings. The family supported the Resistance from the beginning and helped with the means at their disposal. In addition to
the parents, the family included older sister Raymonde and France,
born in 1914. The girls' mother died in 1933; their father died in
January 1942, after a long illness. Since her sister had married, France
now was on her own. Thus, it is perhaps not surprising that family
friends asked her to join the Resistance. In so doing, she acquired a
new "family."

"Our family followed politics passionately. We were very interested
in events, especially the war. We read Resistance tracts and papers.
And we heard de Gaulle's call of June 18 [1940] on our radio. That
was an emotional moment for all of us. My father had tears in his
eyes. We asked ourselves, Who was this man and what did he want
us to do? We did not know what the Resistance would become.
Barely a week after my father's death in January 1942, people we
knew—who had already brought us copies of their newspaper, *Franc-
Tireur*—asked my sister and me if we would meet with friends who
lived on our street. These were the Ferstenbergs, who changed their
name because they were Jewish.[2] It was in their home that we met
Jean-Pierre Lévy [one of the founders of the Franc-Tireur movement]

and joined the Resistance. They used our store to hide clandestine records and newspapers. Our family apartment—4, place des Jacobins—served as a meeting place. [It was located in the center of the city, hence ideal for all the comings and goings.] Lévy met there with the heads of Libération and Combat. Jean Moulin came to the store frequently. At that time, I did not know how important he was. We just knew that he came from London to contact all the Resistance movements. He was a modest man with a piercing look. He always wore a hat and a scarf to hide the scar from his attempted suicide.[3]

"So we helped as we could. We stored papers, did liaison, and helped make false identity cards. Sometimes we took the train to distribute papers and mail. In short, we did everything that had to be done to run a Resistance movement. Soon the apartment became the movement's office. I lived alone in the large family apartment after my father's death. Raymonde was married and lived above our store, not too far away. The two of us did all the secretarial work [for Franc-Tireur] until it became too much. Remember, we also were running the shop. Then Micheline Eude [a young law student] volunteered to become full-time secretary.

"One morning, after an arrest in our group, police came to the family apartment. They had been given my name. Micheline was already there looking over the movement's mail. When the bell rang at nine, I thought it was one of our members. I was holding my lipstick and finishing dressing before going to open the store. Two men in civilian clothes were at the door—Vichy police. I made a sign to Micheline and escorted them into the living room. Micheline took the typewriter—no, not the typewriter, compromising papers—into the back room, where she hid them. The apartment was very big. It had a separate servants' entrance and quarters in the back where we stored things. Unfortunately, they found the typewriter and some compromising carbon papers. But they did not find our major documents. My sister had had an excellent idea: She typed clandestine information—such as the names and addresses of our agents elsewhere—on tissue paper. We sewed these papers into the linings of our clothes, which hung in the closet. These papers were never found. That would have meant taking the garments apart.

"My mind was working rapidly. Lévy would be arriving soon. What could be done to save him? As soon as he rang, I rushed to meet him and embraced him. I was very timid then, and he intimidated me. He was very reserved himself and was about to become engaged. But this was the normal thing to do, under the circumstances. So there I was embracing him and kissing him with my newly painted lips. There is always an amusing side to situations like that. 'Darling,' I said, and he understood right away. He wasn't stupid. 'Look what has happened. The police are here. Forgive me. I didn't tell you—I was wrong—but I have been helping the Resistance.' 'What?' he answered. 'You did that when you know I am Jewish?' Officially, he was a salesman for a Strasbourg firm, although he spent most of his time with the movement. He entered into the game and scolded, 'You should never have done it.' I spent the entire interrogation seated on his lap, although I was *very* intimidated by having to do this.

"Then I remembered that Noël Clavier—another of our leaders—also was scheduled to come. Clavier's business was metal security doors. My mind worked feverishly to find some plausible reason for his visit. Then I remembered that a building on our street with a glass front recently had been bombed—by our group. Everything blew up. It was the headquarters of a collaborationist group. So I decided to say that we had a glass storefront and needed protection. We needed a metal door—his business. Once again, I rushed to the door when the bell rang. I said I was glad to see him so we could discuss the door. Stupidly, he answered, 'I brought you the soap you wanted.' He had some business sidelines. For him to say he was bringing me soap, however, he should have had some soap with him—but he didn't. So I said, 'Yes, I know you are going to bring me some soap, but today I want to discuss the security door with you.' At last he understood. I stuck to my story. I insisted that Lévy didn't know anything and Clavier was there for the security door. Micheline said the same thing. We were all arrested anyhow. The police searched the men's lodgings but found nothing, so they were obliged to release them.

"They kept Micheline and me. I stayed in prison. Here, I have the dates. I made this agenda in prison so that I could remember the dates. 'Friday . . . a charming dinner.' Yes, it was my birthday: October 17, 1942. I celebrated it with Lévy, his mother, and two friends. They brought me perfume and roses. It was very, very lovely. Saturday, the next day, I was arrested. It's marked 'Arrest.' And the following day, 'Arrived at the temporary prison.' I stayed there three days. 'Arrived at Saint-Joseph' [the common-law prison]. And the next day I noted, 'Micheline's first louse.' You amuse yourself as you can. Micheline made quite a fuss over that first louse. Then: 'Micheline's departure.' She left November 12. They were able to arrange her release. She was young, barely nineteen. We in the Resistance were put in prisons with common criminals. The other prisoners called us 'diplomats.' They were really kind to us—all those thieves, prostitutes, petty criminals. And we were very, very good to them.

"Among other Resistance members in that prison was someone special—I am trying to remember her name—that white-haired woman who was decapitated [Berty Albrecht, who presumably committed suicide; see chapter 8]. She was the one who got Micheline freed. She had a daughter who looked like Micheline. She wrote a letter to the authorities, pointing out how dangerous it was to expose a young girl to the company of hardened criminals and pleading with them to free the nineteen-year-old from such sordid surroundings. She won. I was kept there three months. Now I'm not going to give you all the details; they really aren't that important.

"We were very bored in prison. However, instead of releasing me on the date they should have—everyone was waiting at the apartment for me; they were all there and had filled the place with roses—the authorities took me back to the temporary jail. The government had decided that those arrested for resistance were to be sent to special camps. I had been sentenced to three months in jail and had served my sentence. But the government decided to send Resistance members, and all the madames and johns—all those spoilsports—to a camp in the Midi. I spent three weeks in the temporary jail. They couldn't make up their minds about sending me to the camp. Normally, you spent a short time in a holding cell; it was temporary. They put everyone there—street people, prostitutes, and the like. And there were lice. I have never seen such big ones—body lice. But they didn't stick to me. They just went over me. I washed myself well—at least as well as I could. There were a few streetwalkers with me. It was an extraordinary experience to be with women like that.

"Some of these women were touching; some were of high moral character, so to speak. I remember there was one woman of the street—unbelievably filthy—who told obscene stories. Another woman told her to shut up: 'Don't you see that that young woman isn't like us? You must respect her.' She was about to hit the woman telling the stories, but I stopped her. There is a certain standard of behavior among these women. The place was filthy, horrible. I spent three weeks there, yet my memories are not all that bad.

"One day, I was in the courtyard. It was like a medieval fair; the filth was indescribable. To keep busy, I swept the courtyard. I like to keep things clean. Also, down below there were male agents and many British and Americans. We could communicate somewhat through the bars. I could help a little. One day, a young Frenchman came into the courtyard when I was sweeping and asked me what I was doing there. I didn't look like the other women. I explained, and he said he was going to look into the matter. I never saw him again. The next day, I was released, without being told why. It was certainly his doing. The moment the order was received, they didn't want me anymore. They pushed me outside with my suitcase and shoes—without laces. I left dragging my feet, and that is how I was freed in January 1943.

"I resumed my Resistance work. I was arrested a second time in 1943, but this time it was by the Militia. Again, this was after someone in our group had been arrested. I don't remember the exact dates. I was deported on June 30, 1944, so it must have been toward the end of 1943. In any event, the dates aren't important. They came to get me at the store. I was just going to open it. My sister wasn't there because she was on a mission. This was the Militia— the French equivalent of the SS, which was serious. They were much worse than the Vichy police. There were a lot of unsavory characters in the Militia. They took me to their headquarters and kept me there for the day. It was awful. You could hear the screams from the basement where they were questioning people, torturing them. For my part, I always played the idiot—the dumb, naïve young woman."

The Militia told Pejot that they were looking for her sister as well. Some time earlier, France had decided to bleach her hair and wear it in a chignon. This altered her appearance completely. When arrested, her hair was natural brown again, and hanging down her back. When asked for a picture of Raymonde, she gave them one of her own with the earlier coiffure, pointing out that her sister was blonde, and much shorter—even though she wasn't. So they posted people at all the train stations looking for someone completely different from Raymonde. France's ability to improvise and play different roles served her well.

"A big Militiaman—a sort of gorilla covered with medals—appeared. At that time I had a tendency to—well it's not modest to say it, but I had a good figure and I used to take advantage of it somewhat. My concern was to get them to release me. I didn't want to be tortured because it's pointless to play Joan of Arc, to play the martyr. So I did all I could so they would release me. I played the unhappy young thing. I looked at him with pleading eyes. 'What's the matter with you, little one?' he asked. 'I don't know what's going on, but I have been here all day. They are looking for my sister, but I don't know what for.' 'Wait, I'm going to look into this.' 'If only you could do something for me.'

"Shortly thereafter, I was called to his office. 'If only you could keep me from having to spend the night here!' I pleaded. What I was thinking of was that our apartment had two exits. Perhaps I could do something there—warn someone who could warn my sister. 'We're going to take you home,' he said. So they gave me two *malfrats*—that's slang; two hooligans—to accompany me home. It's funny, but one was a real thug and the other was a thug who wanted to play the dandy. He had a white turtleneck top and tried to look distinguished. Now I was wearing shoes with high wooden heels [as did most French women, since the Germans had commandeered all leather]. Going down a bumpy street, I took his arm—the arm of the dandy—and asked him to help me. 'Since we are going to be spending the night in my place,' I said, 'I'm going to make you some coffee, real coffee.' 'Don't think you can win us over with coffee.' 'I wouldn't even think of it.'

"So we arrived at my parents' large, handsome apartment. I settled them into comfortable chairs and turned on the radio. 'Look, I'm locking the front door while I fix coffee.' They were somewhat intimidated in that setting. I played the gracious hostess to the hilt. They didn't even ask to go to the toilet. What they should have done was check to see if there was another exit. They were really stupid. I told them we were going to be spending the night together. They could assume all was possible. So I went back and forth, putting clothes and things—only what was absolutely necessary—into a box that didn't look like a suitcase. I put it on the back doorstep, beyond the kitchen. All the while, I fussed about making the coffee.

They were seated on the edges of their chairs. They couldn't be arrogant. I was very gracious with them. I brought them two cups on
one trip, then two saucers, and so forth. 'Now,' I said, 'you will have
to wait a few minutes while the coffee drips.'

"They waited a long time, because I piled up many obstacles between us. Off the kitchen were two servants' rooms and the back
service stairway. I propped up stools, copper pans, all kinds of
things. A minute is always a minute gained in such cases. I went
down the back stairs in total darkness. The automatic light system
(*minuterie*) wasn't working, and we lived on the fifth floor. My
throat was dry. It felt like I had a million pins in my mouth. I can
still feel it. So I went out into the street with my box and over to
the place des Jacobins, where there was one of the *traboules* [pas-
sages] for which Lyon is famous. They go under houses and come
out at a different level, on another street. I went into one right
away. If they looked out the window, they couldn't see me. And
they were waiting for their coffee, anyhow. I found refuge with
friends."

Later, Pejot learned from the concierge that there had been quite
a fuss when the two men from the Militia discovered what had happened. The whole building was awakened. The men returned with
machine guns and put one against the concierge's chest, accusing her
of being in on the escape. They were frightened because they had let
Pejot escape while she was in their custody. France was able to arrange
for someone to go to the station and warn her sister not to go home.
The mission was not too dangerous because they were looking for a
petite blonde. So Pejot was arrested—and had escaped—for a second
time.

"I left for Paris. I won't tell you all the ups and downs of that trip. I
had to get to Paris because Lyon now was too dangerous. They were
really looking for me. Nevertheless, I did manage to return to the
apartment to get a few things. I was disguised as an elderly woman.
It's quite easy to dress like one of those women who live in convents—they wear long coats and enormous old hats. We had our
moments of fun, fortunately, for there were tragic times as well. I
walked into the building under the noses of the guards they had
posted. This was with the concierge's help. I went into the apartment with a flashlight, because the shutters were closed. They had

turned the place upside down, emptied the mattresses, and all that. Well, I managed to take some lingerie, which was very scarce—a few things. And so I left for Paris.

"There I continued my work with Franc-Tireur. I was also involved with NAP/Police [infiltration of the police administration]. Our mail drop was on rue Saint-Honoré, not far from the Comédie-Française. The tea salon there was our 'mailbox.' Every day, I went there to collect the mail and take it to a café on the rue du Renard, near Châtelet. One day, I arrived at the tea salon shortly before noon. It was rather poorly lit. Then a woman appeared who everyone knew had been arrested a week earlier. 'Bonjour, Marianne!' 'What a surprise to see you, Solange! We thought you were arrested.' 'Not at all, not at all. I was in bed with a liver attack.' Then two men appeared—two 'iceboxes.' They were Frenchmen—gangsters working for the Gestapo. She said to me, 'I brought two friends from the provinces who want to meet Boucher, one of our leaders. They have some important things to tell him.' At once I understood, but I didn't let on that I realized who they were. 'Of course, but the problem is you will have to wait until six tonight.' Fortunately—it is something you never know beforehand—I realized that I hadn't lost my nerve. I kept my *sangfroid*. That really helped me, because I started to tell them things. I have a wild imagination. I can come up with a story right away. I can lie very well and yet—at the same time—there is always something plausible in my tales. Of course, I avoided mentioning my other rendezvous. Instead, I told them I had a meeting with Boucher at six that evening. That was when we met daily, I said. 'Fine, fine,' they responded, and then we went out. Out on the sidewalk, they surrounded me and grabbed me by the arms. I was expecting it, but I jumped all the same. 'Follow us. German police.' So we were all driven to rue de la Pompe, where I underwent a long interrogation. I always followed the same line of conduct. I wasn't indignant; I did *not* play the brave Resistance agent—ever.

"When they captured me, I was carrying our mail. There were the plans for the Paris uprising, with a list of all the police and firemen—all who were going to join in the uprising. It wasn't coded. There were just little points marking the various stations. I told them, 'You know, I don't even know what I am carrying. No, I'm not going to deny it. I am a courier for the Resistance and these are Franc-Tireur newspapers.' And then I continued with a story I made up. I told my interrogator that I had been arrested in Lyon and had fled. When asked why I was a courier for the movement, I told him I didn't have a work card. Without one, I couldn't work. They were looking for me in Lyon. 'And why were you in the Resistance?' 'I was never in the Resistance.' So what I told him was partially true. There was always an element of truth in the stories I made up. They were not idiots. 'There are all kinds of denunciations and jealousies,' I continued. And God knows there were many, many denunciations [a tactic all too prevalent during the Occupation, as in earlier centuries when there had been denunciations of witchcraft out of vengeance or to settle vendettas]. 'My sister and I were denounced as members of the Resistance because of the success of our store. I had to leave, but I never did anything. Jealous women denounced us, so I had to leave. And here, in Paris, a Resistance movement contacted me and offered me a job. You have to eat.'

" 'That's why I do it. They pay me.' '*Ma pauvre petite,*' he answered, 'you don't know what you are doing. It's espionage.' 'And I thought all I was doing was carrying newspapers. Well, I'm going to do all I can to help you catch them. I'm going to take you to their six o'clock meeting place. If we don't go today, you won't be able to catch them. They change meeting places every day.' Fortunately, I thought of that. 'Each evening, they decide where to meet the following day, which means I don't know where they will meet tomorrow.' That seemed plausible, quite plausible. My only concern was that one of our members might recognize me on the way and not realize I was in the company of the police. They placed me at the supposed meeting place and stayed a little farther off.

" 'I'm going to do everything I can to help you,' I insisted, 'because they deceived me so. It's unbelievable!' I lie very well. Of course, no one came. In all this, I gained time. The rule was that if you were arrested, you had to hold out and say nothing for twenty-four hours. After that, they knew you had been arrested. You could talk then. There are times when you can't ask people *not* to talk. So I had been arrested at noon, and here it was the evening already. I just had to hold on until noon the next day. While we were waiting, they threatened me with torture, such as the *baignoire* [bathtub]. All kinds of threats. The only one who didn't threaten me was the German leader. He was much more effective, though, more subtle. He questioned me. The atmosphere between us became so relaxed that he confided in me that he had been a conductor at the Leipzig

Opera before the war. But he asked me—since I told him I had been arrested in Lyon—why I fled if I were innocent. So I told him, 'But you must know what the men of the Militia are like; they aren't like you.' It was a stroke of genius to say that. You know, there is nothing like treating someone like a gentleman to make him behave like a gentleman. So he was extremely courteous with me. Then I asked him, 'Are you going to arrest me after all?' 'Ah, *ma petite*, I am forced to. You will be sent to Fresnes prison. But I can offer you an alternative. Come and live with me. We will go out a lot. Each time you see someone you recognize, you will point them out.' I didn't react with indignation, but instead seemed to consider the proposition seriously. 'Yes,' I said, 'I could do that.' Then, after a pause, I said, 'No, I really couldn't do that after all, because they would kill me. I'm not courageous enough to do that.' 'Very well, we will go to your place tomorrow.'

"He asked me where I lived, but I couldn't tell him, because I lived in a hotel on rue d'Assas with all the Franc-Tireur archives: newspapers, addresses, everything. That was the only address I had. It was the room of an elderly spinster. She was a social worker and wasn't there often. I had to hold out twenty-four hours. But I knew he wanted an address, so I made up one. I didn't want to be beaten.

"The next day, around eleven-thirty, when we were in the car en route to the false address I had given him, I told him I had something to confess. I was really frightened—really afraid. He was seated in the front, next to the chauffeur. I told him I hadn't given him the right address the day before. I really lived on rue d'Assas. He turned around and gave me such a look! I learned afterward that he could be really ferocious; he tortured a lot of people. He gave me a fierce look. I assumed my wounded-dog air. I explained to him that it was because of the woman I stayed with that I hadn't wanted to give him my real address. 'She's a fine woman. She doesn't have the slightest idea of what I'm doing. She knows nothing, absolutely *nothing* about what I'm doing. You must not arrest her. I gave you a false address yesterday because I did not want anything to happen to her.' Again, my story was plausible. Then he turned—I remember it still—and gave me a flick on the nose. '*Ma petite* Marianne (my Resistance name), you better not be fooling me.' 'No, no, I'm telling you the truth.' He seemed to believe me.

"When we got to the apartment—what a relief! I wanted to laugh. The place was so clean. Everything had been polished, waxed—and cleaned out. When I didn't go to the rendezvous or didn't telephone, they understood what had happened. They went to the apartment at once and emptied it. I told them after the war that they went a little too far. They didn't leave me anything—not even lingerie. All they left me was a kilo of sugar and a pair of underpants. 'Well, *ma petite,* you don't have many things,' the officer said. 'No. As I told you, I came from Lyon with nothing.' I did manage to take an old cape belonging to Mlle Joseph, the social worker, from the apartment, for all I had on was a light summer dress. He thought it was my own coat. Men just don't notice things like that.

"I spent two and a half months at Fresnes prison before I was deported to Ravensbrück. After a few weeks there, I was sent to Torgau [near Leipzig]. First I harvested potatoes, then I worked in a factory. By sheer chance, I was not selected when half of our group was sent to the salt mines in Silesia. I've always been lucky in misfortune, but never lucky in my life. My marriage failed. Perhaps I had to endure misfortune in order to see that I was lucky in some things. Anyhow, I went with a group on an infernal train ride that lasted two weeks. We had next to nothing to eat. Two teenaged SS brutes were in charge. When it rained, I wanted to put a can out of an opening to catch the water—I was dying of thirst—but my companions wouldn't let me; I risked death. It was February and raining heavily.

"So we arrived at the camp. When I saw all my companions with their heads shaved, I couldn't help laughing. There were so many different shapes. I tried not to cry when they shaved mine. I had beautiful long hair. Now they put us to work leveling the earth—the work of ants! We suffered from hunger, from brutalities. It was a nightmare. That's how it was. Then the Americans approached. The Germans marched us from the camp in columns. It was cold, raining. It was February, I think . . . or March. I've forgotten the dates, but it doesn't matter. With a companion, I escaped to the woods. We threw ourselves flat out on the side of the road on a black, moonless night. My head was in a puddle, but it didn't matter. When we heard the column marching off, my heart beat so. The sense of deliverance—of being saved—was the strongest emotion I have ever experienced."

Pejot finally located American soldiers, but her troubles did not end there. She and her friend were nearly raped by drunken American soldiers who invited them to celebrate the Allied victory. Because they were French, they were presumed to be women of loose virtue. When asked why she resumed Resistance work after having been arrested and released twice, she explained that it was normal; you were with other members of your "family."

"Fear didn't exist. Besides, the Resistance was stronger than we were. Our comrades were there. You found them again. You could not do otherwise. I didn't wake up one morning and say, 'I'm going to join the Resistance.' No, you were caught up in it gradually. All our group thought alike. The Germans were there; something had to be done. I didn't decide to save France just like that. You got caught up in it. My sister was arrested somewhat later, in Toulouse. She spent a few weeks in prison, but a French prison. She wasn't deported."

France Pejot was young, attractive, and *bien élevée* (well brought up). During each arrest, she played the role that would be expected of a young woman of her background. Although very frightened, she found that she could assume disguises and improvise plausible explanations. Pejot also discovered the ability to keep calm and respond appropriately during harrowing and dangerous encounters—and even to help keep the family store going until she was obliged to go underground. She was more intimidated by having to assume a role of intimacy with Jean-Pierre Lévy when the police came to her apartment to arrest her. Her irrepressible humor stayed with her in the darkest moments.

After the war, Pejot married, then divorced Maurice Jarre, a movie score composer. Their son, Jean-Michel Jarre, has had a very successful career as a composer and music producer of international renown. He married actress Charlotte Rampling. The state of Texas engaged him to organize a concert-spectacle on the Houston skyline to mark the state's 150th anniversary. Jean-Michel has also been named a UNESCO goodwill ambassador. With her talent, his mother might well have had an acting career of her own. Instead, she still plays down her Resistance roles.[4]

Lucie Aubrac does not like to speak of the many roles she has played. In truth, she does not need to, for she has written an account of her

Resistance exploits—which excels most dramas: *Outwitting the Gestapo* (1984; English edition 1993).

"My parents, the Bernards, were vine-growers from the Mâcon re-gion of Burgundy. I was born into this modest, Catholic milieu in 1912. A committed pacifist at an early age, I was strongly influenced by the serious wounds my father received in World War I. While attending the Sorbonne [the University of Paris], where I received the *agrégation* in history, I worked to support myself. [Few French young women of the time attained that degree, and even fewer did so while working.]

"In 1938, I was appointed teacher in a girls' *lycée* in Strasbourg. In the course of that year, I went to consult Raymond Samuel, a young Jewish engineer doing his military service in Strasbourg. I had been awarded a scholarship to the United States to work on my dis-sertation; Samuel had just returned from a year of study at MIT. It was the proverbial *coup de foudre* [lightning bolt]. We decided to marry upon my return from the States. As things turned out, we married shortly after World War II broke out. Both of us had visas and positions to go to in the United States, but we couldn't leave families, friends, and occupied France. That decision meant staying in France. In August 1940 I helped Raymond—who had been mo-bilized—escape from a German POW camp. We settled in Lyon, where we helped create and develop a Resistance movement. At the same time, our 'everyday' life continued. Jean-Pierre was born in 1941."

But the couple had other names and other addresses. To her com-rades, Lucie was "Catherine"; on her false identity card, she was once again Lucie Bernard. Raymond was "Valmont," then "Aubrac" (the surname they kept after the war). In 1940, the Aubracs helped organ-ize Libération-Sud—one of the first movements to fight Vichy as well as the Germans—with journalist Emmanuel d'Astier de la Vigerie and philosopher Jean Cavaillès. For the next three years, Lucie was wife, mother, teacher, and active participant in the Resistance. She helped publish and distribute the clandestine journal *Libération* and other underground publications, and she did liaison work. In 1943, she joined a hit squad that rescued *résistants* from Vichy and German pris-ons. When one of their captured agents "talked" in mid-March, close to thirty Resistance agents and Secret Army members were captured in the following days. Among them was Raymond, by this time one of the directors of the Secret Army in the Lyon area. Lucie succeeded in freeing Raymond from his French prison in mid-May by going directly to the prosecutor's home and threatening him with reprisals from London. While Raymond was in prison, their son, "Boubou," stayed with friends. Then, for safety, she decided to place him in a children's home in the Vercors, because—barely a month later—her beloved husband was in prison once again. But this time the prison was German, and more torture by Klaus Barbie and certain death awaited him.

After careful reflection, Lucie decided upon a daring and dangerous plan to get Raymond out of Barbie's clutches by staging an armed attack while he was being transported somewhere. Lucie went to Gestapo headquarters and met a sympathetic German officer particularly appreciative of her gifts—Cognac, Champagne, silks, and stockings. Posing as the aristocratic "Guillaine de Barbentane" seduced by "Claude Ermelin," Lucie, who was indeed pregnant, begged an SS lieutenant introduced to her by the officer to arrange a marriage before "Ermelin" (Aubrac) was executed. She claimed not to care for him—all the more so now that he had been "exposed" as a "terrorist"—but she was adamant that her unborn child be legal. French law permits marriage *in extremis* to regularize such situations. She came from a conservative, Catholic, military family, and, she insisted, honor was at stake.

"During this time, while I was meeting with the SS lieutenant, I planned and executed a raid that rescued several of our wounded comrades from the hospital in Saint-Étienne [southwest of Lyon], where they were being treated under police guard. For a number of days I made the lengthy trip from Lyon to St. Étienne, circulating about the hospital in a doctor's smock with a stethoscope. This allowed me to contact the wounded agents, memorize their medical charts, and make arrangements to free them. Our rescue operation was successful, but I almost had a miscarriage.

"I also visited the Lyon morgue regularly to see if Raymond had already been executed. And I pursued plans for his escape. A doctor friend injected a dozen candies with a typhus culture from contaminated meat he had been asked to examine. [When Raymond ate them, he would become very ill and presumably be hospitalized. As Lucienne Guezennec, Berty Albrecht, and others found, it was much easier to arrange an escape from a hospital or clinic.] At my request, *résistante* friend Simone Martin-Chauffier reserved a room in the clinic of a trustworthy doctor. Everything was in place to free Raymond on the evening of September 21. The Gestapo lieutenant arranged for me to confront him that day. A hit squad was to attack the armored car returning him to prison. But there was no attack. The timing was off, so the operation was deferred.

"Because of chemical problems, the candies did not work. Now I confronted another problem: how to kill the German driver and guard in front of the van without alerting the two guards inside in back with the prisoners? Then I remembered reading somewhere about silencers, which were new at the time. With Raymond's cousin Maurice, I arranged to go to Switzerland to procure silencers. I crossed the border but stayed only twenty minutes in a country where I could have remained—free."

Another meeting with Raymond was arranged by the obliging German lieutenant for October 21. On this occasion, "Guillaine de Barbentane" and her future "husband" were to sign the marital property arrangement Lucie had drawn up—another ruse for getting Raymond out of prison. The hit squad practiced trial runs with the silencers. Including Lucie, there were fourteen in the group, using two cars and a pickup truck. The hit squad comprised youths of unassuming background—workers, railroad employees—modest folk, as she puts it. According to Aubrac, these young men would have followed her anywhere. The night before the attack, they held a last reunion to finalize their plans and enjoy an improvised feast. On October 21, Lucie once again met Raymond; they signed the contract. On his return to prison that evening, the hit squad attacked the police van and escort. Thirteen prisoners were released with Raymond, who was wounded. Three German guards were killed.

Lucie and Raymond were reunited and whisked away to a clinic in the countryside where Raymond could be treated. He described the beatings Barbie had inflicted and recounted what he knew of the last days of Jean Moulin. Colleagues brought news of events after his escape, but the news was not good. The Gestapo now was looking for Lucie as well as Raymond. Then the Aubracs learned that the Germans had discovered the location of their son: The head of the children's home had written them for permission for a vaccination Jean-Pierre needed. Resistance members managed to rescue the child just an hour before the Germans arrived. When Lucie first saw her son again, he was playing with a live grenade the agents inadvertently had left in the truck. Lucie managed to get him to put down the lethal

"toy." Then she fainted. The couple decided it was essential to go
elsewhere in order to relieve the doctor who had risked his life by
sheltering them. The movement wanted Raymond in London, but
there was the problem of Lucie. She had been in the movement since
1940, she knew too much, and she was six months pregnant.

"The Resistance leaders decided that the three of us had to go to
London. We went into hiding in central France to await the low-
flying British plane that was to take us to England and safety. All
the peasants and villagers in the area were aware of our situation.
They were extraordinary and took us from one home to another. Because of unfavorable atmospheric conditions, two full moons passed.
We were transferred to the Jura area. The farmers—who had little
enough themselves—treated us (and a downed British aviator now
with us) royally. I think of the peasant woman who cut up one of
her precious blankets to make diapers for the baby I was expecting.
We learned then that some of our family—including Raymond's
parents—had been betrayed and captured. In preparation for the
next landing, we were taken to stay with three elderly sisters—
fiercely patriotic. Finally, on the evening of February 8, 1944, a
plane managed to land—only to become stuck in the mud. Villagers
in the area came with their oxen and horses to help pull out the
plane. Three hours later, the plane finally took off for London. Two
days later, Catherine Aubrac was born in a London clinic."

While still in the maternity clinic, young Catherine's mother—
who gave her daughter her Resistance name—was decorated. In July
of that same year, Lucie Aubrac was designated by London to set up
departmental liberation committees in the liberated areas of France
in order to ensure the interim government. She was also chosen by
the Resistance of the Interior to serve on the Provisional Constituent
Assembly in Algeria, thus becoming the first French woman parlia-
mentarian.[5]

Agents who went underground, as we have seen, were obliged to
change roles and appearance often. They tried to eradicate any dis-
tinctive characteristics that would make them easily recognizable.
Gisèle Joannès (see chapter 4) used her dressmaking talents to make

chic outfits from old clothes that people had given her: "I was dying of hunger, but I looked like a woman of the bourgeoisie. In addition, I changed my hair color and style all the time—as often as I changed my identity card."

For Jeanette, Joannès's coworker in a textile factory, playing roles had a long-term effect. According to her husband, when they were reunited after their respective deportations, his wife was no longer the timid, reserved young woman had who acted in his shadow. She now had a strong personality and sought autonomy. She no longer wanted a supporting role.[6]

Being taken for someone of a different class was somewhat easier to arrange in those days. Before mass production and international favorites like jeans, clothes were social indicators. Hence the concern of women such as Françoise de Boissieu, who was anxious to make a favorable impression on a contact and appear a little less "frumpy." Nor were all attempts at disguise approved. One Communist leader objected when members wanted to dress one of their agents as a woman of the bourgeoisie. He told her: "It isn't wise to try to pretend that you are a bourgeoise when you don't have the gestures and manners. You are more secure in your housing-project milieu."[7] Conversely, elegantly attired Odette Fabius spent three days walking around the port of Marseilles before she was able to contact the dockworkers' head, who was vital to her group's operation. The appearance of a smartly dressed woman attracted less than reassuring attention in the dock area.

France Pejot recounts how she broke into laughter when she saw her fellow camp inmates with their heads shaved. This hysterical laughter, notes journalist Ania Francos, sounded like a death sentence for some. How else, she asks, can one explain that some of these women died within a few days of their arrival, even though they were not yet sick or weakened from camp conditions. Shorn and naked, they were reduced to numbers, to "nothing."[8]

Throughout the war years, French women assumed many roles—without prior practice. In the absence of the men, many became heads of households and breadwinners. They played center stage. To carry out missions, those in the Resistance chose different roles—often that of the wide-eyed innocent. They gave many successful performances.

12

+>=+=<+

Collaboration

WOMEN WHO HELPED IN THE FRENCH RESISTANCE DISPLAYED MANY remarkable characteristics—strength, courage, daring, adaptability, among others. However, to really understand how exceptional their conduct was, it needs to be placed within the context of collaboration. *Résistants* and collaborators were but a minority of the French population during the Occupation years of 1940–1944, but the collaborators were a dangerous minority. According to historian Philippe Burrin, the total circulation of collaborationist newspapers suggests that perhaps one to two million people were inclined that way. In his authoritative study, he notes that about 15 percent of the notorious Militia members were women, a particularly surprising figure given the fact that women had no political status at the time. Most were relatives or companions of male collaborators. On the whole, Burrin found that women collaborators were few in number, more visible in the Collaboration and Francisme group. Here, too, they were largely the wives, companions, or daughters of militants.[1]

The many women who used the black-market traffic have—with a few exceptions—been excluded from this category. Black-market trading was pervasive in France, and, in some instances, it was absolutely necessary. Resistance members were forced at times to resort to the black market. For many women, it was the only way they could

adequately feed their families.[2] This was a difficult decision, further
complicated by the fact that both the Vichy regime and the Catholic
Church initially condemned and later condoned black-market purchases for the hard-pressed public. There were those who insisted that
the black market should never be utilized because it furthered German
goals of weakening French morals and encouraging dependency. For
instance, a woman who advertised in the German Ministry of Propaganda weekly, *Pariser Zeitung*, that she had fabric (normally rationed)
for sale obviously was involved in a clandestine commercial undertaking. She was using the services of the enemy, a form of collaboration.
If material on women in the Resistance is limited, women's collaboration with the enemy is even more difficult to document. The term
collaboration—like *resistance*—does not lend itself to ready definition.[3]

The 1939 French Penal Code addressed serious crimes of collaboration with the enemy—that is, treason—but did not envision the
circumstances of the Occupation and the range of offenses that took
place under varying circumstances. Retroactive legislation had to be
introduced to cope with the summary justice that occurred in the wake
of the Allied landings. Yet even these laws failed to fully define *collaboration*. Historian Henry Rousso stresses that the term meant different things to different people, at different times. It could designate
a choice or constraint, a means of social promotion, or an ideological
commitment. In most cases, it was a state of mind. The term *collaborator* was applied indiscriminately to followers of Marshal Pétain as
well as to hard-core collaborationists who were guilty of treason.
While it is true that some of the marshal's followers accepted his invitation to *collaborate* with the enemy, most of the French restricted
their activities to support for his government—during the first two
years, in any event. Attitudes evolved as the situation changed. Historians sometimes use the term *collaborationist* for French Fascists to
distinguish them from Vichy supporters. However, one cannot ignore
Vichy's extensive links with Fascist collaborators.[4]

Throughout the Occupation, the German police presence in
France was very limited. The Germans could not have rounded up
and deported so many—several hundred thousand—without French
collusion. This was part of Hitler's strategy. By allowing the Vichy
government with its pretensions to autonomy and legitimacy to function and carry out his directives, he could govern France with a minimal German presence and save his forces for use elsewhere. Paxton
observes that the Vichy regime provided Hitler with French neutral-

ity—which the regime vigorously defended against the Allies—along with a massive contribution to the German war effort, and, at least until the beginning of 1944, comparative security. All of this the Führer obtained with few men and without spending a single Deutschmark.[5] Gerhard Hirschfeld's study of Franco-German collaboration shows how the Germans relied on the extensive help of the French police and civil administration, particularly in the roundup of French as well as non-French Jews. He holds: "There was no other occupied country during the Second World War which contributed more to the initial efficiency of Nazi rule in Europe than France."[6] French police staffed French camps. French authorities carried out German directives for the control of information in the press and on the radio.

British author David Pryce-Jones, another who has written on this topic, believes that perhaps as many as nine million Frenchmen worked directly for the Germans—building the Atlantic defenses, producing aircraft and armaments in factories, or growing food for the Reich's needs. Philippe Burrin puts the figure at four million.[7] The problem with figures—however approximate—is that not all who worked for the Germans did so willingly. Many were coerced, although this was less true of many in the industrial Right and the upper bourgeoisie, who collaborated more extensively with the enemy than did the rank and file. High-level administrators saw the opportunity to settle scores with the workers who had frightened them in 1936. In a more general way, executives and administrators saw in the defeat untold opportunities for unlimited power and profit on an international scale.[8] As the war progressed, the Occupation proved a propitious setting for all manner of secret activity, including unexplained disappearances and the settling of scores both personal and professional. The situation was further complicated by competing German organizations—fighting for better positions and political advantage—that favored different collaborationist groups and organizations.

Rousso maintains that the "Vichy syndrome" has hindered France in dealing with the memory of 1940–1944. Since the early 1970s, France has been obsessed by the memory of the *années noires* (the black years)—the title of a two-volume collection of essays published in late 1993.[9] Henri Amouroux has written a best-selling eight-volume study of the Occupation years that includes volumes on *Les Beaux Jours des collabos* (*The Great Days of the Collaborators*) and *Les Passions et les haines* (*Passions and Hatreds*), assuredly eloquent titles.

The problems inherent in dealing with such a sensitive topic are compounded by the problem of archival access discussed in chapter 1. There is some documentation on women collaborators in the testimony of Resistance members, in French and German archives, and in some recently available proceedings of postwar purge trials. Several self-serving autobiographies were written by women accused of collaboration. While not historical records per se, fictional accounts such as Jean Dutourd's satirical novel *The Best Butter* provide all-too-credible accounts of those who sided with the enemy—only to switch allegiance when events favored the other side—as well as of the general climate of the Occupation.

+>==<+

Lise Lesèvre mentions an example of one who hedged her bets:

"After ten long days waiting for my death sentence to be carried out, I was taken from my cell to a room where I met a Resistance colleague, Lucienne B. . . . She had been arrested for placing a bomb in the Carlton Hotel in Lyon. Condemned to death, B. was now collaborating with the Gestapo in order to save her life. At ease, elegantly dressed, she met me alone in a Gestapo office. She offered to help me. She assured me that what she was doing she did for the French. Disappointed that I would not work with her, she asked me to testify in her favor after the war. The young woman was aware that she might have 'difficulties.' Consulting the dossiers, she recognized that I belonged to a 'solid, well-organized' group, as she put it. Although she could do nothing for me—given all the evidence— she offered to free my husband and son, since there were 'no charges against them' (an outright lie). My silence was the problem. If only I could 'name' someone. No, I could not, but if she released my husband and son, I promised to help her 'afterward.' 'No,' she insisted, 'you must name someone, a low-level liaison agent who doesn't know too much. That is all the Germans want.' 'If I knew someone, you would already have the name,' I maintained."

On her way back to her cell, as described in chapter 5, Lesèvre passed her husband and her son Jean-Pierre. Her son had grown so; now he was a young man of sixteen. She managed to pass them some chocolate and bread she had saved. Suddenly she realized the terrible truth: Lucienne B. was but a tool of Klaus Barbie, who would wreak vengeance by torturing her husband and son. Jean-Pierre had come to the same conclusion. Before they were separated, he tried to joke. "Remember, Mother, I'm ticklish."

Trying to escape the fleeing Nazis and find their way back to France at the end of the war, Lise and several of her companions in captivity met a group of "volunteer" workers (those who went to work in Germany of their own accord for promises—largely unkept—of higher salaries and better living conditions). They refused to help the camp escapees—not even to tell them where they could find water or shelter on a cold, dark night. These collaborators appeared to realize that hard times awaited them with the Allied victory. Lise and her friends earnestly hoped that that would be true.[10]

⌖

The role of gender in assessments of collaboration merits attention. Tony Judt notes that the association of collaboration with women was a widespread myth in the late war and early postwar years. To cite but one example, Claude Morgan's novel *La Marque de l'homme* (1944) portrays a would-be female collaborator who is

> ... tempted to yield to the charms of [German] seduction, illustrating a view of collaboration as an activity essentially restricted to and indulged in by women influenced by the strong masculine appeal of the dominant occupier.[11]

Sartre treats collaboration as feminine in nature and describes the "typical" collaborator as marked by "his femininity" [sic]. The philosopher viewed the masses as essentially feminine: "They agree to submit, they wait to be forced, to be taken." Because the Occupation blurred the boundaries between private and public life, a significant number of women were brought up on charges of collaboration for having affairs with the enemy. Hélène Eck notes that almost 40 percent of those tried in the Orléans region, where enemy troops were stationed, were women.

Apart from a small group of hard-core Germanophiles and collaborators who subscribed wholeheartedly to Nazi doctrines—a group that included few women—many collaborators were opportunists who used the *années noires* to settle personal or professional rivalries. One major index of this practice is the large volume of letters of denunciation—signed and anonymous—sent to prefects and the police. This is an area that has not yet been studied seriously; no credible figure has been advanced thus far for the number of these missives. André Halimi published a collection of documents relating to denunciations, including sample letters. A 1993 book by Antoine Lefébure portrays the war years from the censored telephone conversations and correspondence, but it touches only briefly on letters of denunciation.[12] Vichy overheard many telephone calls and opened an extraordinary amount of mail. According to some accounts, the Germans themselves were amazed by the number of French informing on one another. But wartime occupation does not necessarily bring out the best in people. One can better appreciate the French nation's inclination to forget this period. A 1943 film, Le Corbeau (The Crow, slang for stool pigeon), shows the impact of anonymous poison-pen letters on a small village.

Monetary awards for denunciations made Jews particularly vulnerable to this reprehensible practice. Witness a sample letter addressed to German authorities from a woman denouncing her husband's mistress:

> Since you are concerned with Jews, and assuming your [anti-Semitic] campaign is not just a pretense, consider the activities of the "prostitute" M . . . A . . ., a former dancer, now living in a hotel at 31 Strasbourg boulevard. This individual, not satisfied with being Jewish[!], corrupts the husbands of true Frenchwomen. Protect women from these Jewish women. This will serve as the best example of your campaign. And you will return a French husband to his wife.[13]

Journalist and editor Françoise Verny writes of her family's situation during the Occupation. Initially, her parents reacted to the defeat in the same way as most of the French—they put their confidence in Marshal Pétain. But this did not last long, for her mother was Jewish. When denounced—presumably by their concierge—her parents were taken to police headquarters in Paris, where a German officer showed them a large cupboard full of filed papers: "Those represent only a small part of the letters Parisians have sent us denouncing Jews. Most are anonymous." After Resistance liaison work (which she downplays as *petites missions*—insignificant errands), Verny, like others, joined the Communist Party in early 1945, "imbued with the spirit of the Resistance":

> I felt it was my duty to join. The illusion was very widespread in the post-Resistance generation that we would build a better world where

justice would prevail. Obviously, confusion reigned in our minds, but then that period favored intellectual ferment.[14]

Hélène Parmelin, author and friend of Pablo Picasso, also joined the PCF:

"This was the period when the Communists wore a sort of halo of glory because of their Resistance record. Everything was oriented in that sense. There were many intellectuals in the Party then. Like many, I signed up with my eyes more or less closed. Politics and writing were to become the dominant passions in my life; they were intermingled."[15]

The question of silence—not speaking on German-censored radio or publishing in German-approved journals or presses, discussed in chapter 4—was to trouble Simone de Beauvoir after the war. While some colleagues chose to publish *only* with clandestine presses or not at all, de Beauvoir worked briefly as writer-producer for the official state radio station. Like many Parisians, de Beauvoir believed that her main responsibility was to keep a low profile and survive. Sartre's biographer, John Gerassi, views Sartre (and, by extension, de Beauvoir) as being involved in a "kind of moral collaboration. . . . [T]hey were into survival." On the other hand, de Beauvoir's biographer, Deirdre Bair, sees the famed couple as having no better or worse a record than most of the population, although she does note that de Beauvoir did not mention this work in her memoirs and became upset whenever journalists tried to question her about it in later years.[16]

The *épuration* (purification or purge) in France after the Liberation was short-lived but brutal. The country imprisoned and executed fewer collaborators than did any of its neighbors. Some presumed collaborators were summarily executed without judicial proceedings. The Occupation had given rise to resentments, rivalries, and hatreds that could not always be contained; violence erupted at times. Moreover, criminal elements sometimes infiltrated the FFI or posed as members of the Resistance to camouflage crimes of looting and murder. Approximately half of the close to ten thousand people executed in France for collaboration without legal trials were killed just before or shortly after the Allied landings. The arrival of General de Gaulle and the installation of his government in Paris in late August 1944 did not necessarily ensure his immediate authority throughout France. In his memoirs, the general contends that the PCF took political advantage of the opportunities offered by the disorders and fears following the Liberation.

Critic Jean Paulhan holds that the majority of those in charge of *épuration* trials were Communists. They were there to follow Party instructions and condemn. Viewing themselves as "pure" Resistance figures, they sometimes acted worse than those whom they condemned.[17] Ted Morgan stresses the irony of the evolution of the situation in France. Formerly pro-German following the Nazi–Soviet pact, the Communists turned against the occupier when Hitler attacked the Soviet Union on June 22, 1941. During the period when they were ostensibly pro-German, Communists picked up by French police were released on German orders. As a classic example of hypocrisy, Morgan cites the July 4, 1940, clandestine issue of the Communist newspaper *L'Humanité*:

> It is particularly comforting, in these times of misfortune, to see many Parisian workers engaged in friendly conversations with German soldiers, either in the street or in the corner café. Bravo, comrades, continue, even if this displeases certain bourgeois, as stupid as they are malicious.[18]

Dominique Ory notes that since French collaborators were unable to exercise political power extensively, they turned to the power of words.

Official trials of collaborators continued into the early 1950s. More than half of the almost seven thousand sentenced to death in these trials were tried in absentia. Fewer than eight hundred ultimately were executed. Some of the judges in purge trials were former Vichy judges—including, ironically, a few who had presided earlier at trials of *résistants*.* To this day, hard-core Vichy supporters tend to exaggerate the "crimes" committed in the *épuration* process. In reality, because of de Gaulle's concern over avoiding a national bloodbath in the climate of potential civil war then prevailing, sanctions for collaboration were comparatively mild.[19]

In the early years of the Occupation, teachers were singled out by vigilantes who sought to undermine the state school system. Accord-

---

*A special French court was set up in November 1942 to handle Resistance "crimes."

ing to Roger Austin, a 1944 inquiry into those accused of collaboration revealed a significant number of cases of priests charged with denouncing state school teachers in order to close their schools. Charges brought against state teachers included defying official directives to hang Pétain's portrait in their classrooms. In some instances, women teachers were accused of having affairs.[20] This called into question their moral qualifications for instructing French youth.

The Resistance did what it could to counteract collaboration. Early in 1943, the clandestine journal *Défense de la France* denounced the directress of a girls' *lycée* who expelled a student found carrying Resistance leaflets. Furthermore, on her own initiative, she sent her dossier to Minister of Education Abel Bonnard, who had the young woman arrested.[21] *Défense* published an account of these events and informed the directress that her activities now would be known to the paper's 100,000 readers. Other clandestine papers also spotlighted women collaborators. *La Voix du Nord* denounced twenty-three-year-old Mme D.:

> A very elegant woman who favors mannish attire and wears pants in the winter. She travels a good deal [at a time when it was very difficult for the average French person to do so]. While her husband, a captain, is a prisoner in Germany, she has a German officer for a lover.[22]

Some French women who slept with German soldiers did so for sentimental reasons. Thousands of babies were born of German fathers, just as French men fathered children when they occupied Germany after World War I. Allegiance to such abstract ideals as patriotism is not always possible. The situation was compounded by the absence of more than a million and a half French men who were either German POWs or had been sent abroad to do forced labor. Their wives and sweethearts faced years of solitude. While some of these women rejoined their families, others found themselves alone in large cities. After studying the lives of the wives of prisoners, Jacqueline Deroy became more tolerant of those who had affairs with the occupiers: "I don't think they should be stoned. Certainly what they did was very serious. But those who shaved their heads did not understand. It was an extreme reaction responding to the times."[23]

Geneviève de Gaulle described the invading German soldiers as smartly uniformed "young war gods." Evelyne Sullerot commented on the extraordinary appearance of those tall, blond "angels of death." The German soldiers were different and seductive to some—and the victors. Assuredly, some French women who had affairs with Germans did so for material advantage. Their lovers could provide them with scarce commodities that their compatriots lacked. Those involved with officers enjoyed a much more luxurious lifestyle.

Additionally, there were ambiguous situations. Dr. Robert Debré of the Medical Resistance recounts the curious story of a Belgian baroness who secured the release of an arrested medical student—on the grounds that he was needed to help fight epidemics, a German obsession. The baroness had been living in Paris for several years. Profession: presumably spy, probably a double agent. As the result of an injury received in a bombing raid in her own country, she had lost a leg. With her wooden leg, she tirelessly maneuvered around Paris. She furnished Debré and his Resistance group with information and important help, for her links to the German authorities made her extremely useful. She helped the Resistance—at least in part—because she was a morphine addict and Debré could get her the drug. His hospital agreed to provide him with morphine for a good cause. The baroness arranged to have Debré's telephone line kept open (when those of other Jews were cut off), arguing that he needed to be available to care for Parisian children. Once Debré went to her place because she had not responded to an urgent request. He found her in an opium trance in a disheveled room on an unbelievably filthy bed—with her daughter.[24]

The testimony and appointment books of German officials reveal how renowned Parisian hostesses—particularly aristocrats—competed for the elite among the occupiers. Accounts detail their elegant cocktail parties welcoming the occupiers. Ferdinand de Brinon, who had the dubious distinction of being "ambassador" in his own country—that is, Vichy delegate to the Germans in Paris—writes in his memoirs of the large number of French who volunteered to do the dirty work of the Germans. He had firsthand knowledge of this because they sought access to the Germans through him.*

On rue Lauriston, at the headquarters of the notorious Bonny-Lafont gang (French Gestapo assistants), tortures took place in the basement while extravagant feasts were held in the salons. On the upper floors, prostitutes and beautiful women consorted with the gang and their guests. Former petty criminal Henri Lafont—now in charge

---

*Pétain had German authorities designate de Brinon's Jewish wife and the Jewish wives of several prominent French figures as "honorary Aryans."

of the gang's operations—loved to entertain, to offer sumptuous gifts. With the seduction of power and money, women flocked to Lafont's soirées. Among them were cabaret dancers, part-time call girls, titled aristocrats, and a Russian princess. A marquis involved in the gang's extensive financial dealings (selling what they expropriated illegally) obligingly offered Lafont his wife, a former model with many lovers. But even gangster Lafont was appalled by this woman who denounced people simply for the pleasure. The leaders and some members of this group were tried and executed after the war.[25] Yvette Farnoux, whose prison saga was described in chapter 9, was betrayed by the mistress of a French criminal working for the Gestapo. Presumably the mistress received a handsome reward for her treachery.

Corinne Luchaire was the film-star daughter of collaborationist journalist Jean Luchaire, head of the national French press corporation during the Occupation. After the war, he was executed, while she was sentenced to several years of "national indignity," which included loss of civil rights.* *Résistante* Simone Martin-Chauffier expressed her own indignation—and satisfaction—when she read in the January 3, 1941, edition of *Le Matin* that Mlle Corinne Luchaire had had the imprudence to forget her case filled with very expensive jewels in the car that drove her home one evening. The case disappeared. While her compatriots were beginning to feel the privations of the Occupation, Luchaire's autobiography reveals she was enjoying *la belle vie* for which Paris is famous:

> It was the first official party in Paris. The [German] embassy on the rue de Lille shone with all the light, contrasting with the total black-out that cloaked Paris in obscurity and uncertainty. There was an elaborate buffet. The period of restrictions had not yet arrived. However that may be, even before the war it would have been impossible to find such a variety of gastronomic products. Delicacies from across the Rhine mingled with British biscuits and French *petits fours*. Champagne flowed. The German officers—particularly the aviators in their dress uniforms—flitted and circulated. Not a single one used the German language. It was truly the 'French soirée' the ambassador's wife [a French woman, the former secretary of Luchaire *père*] wanted. Speaking German was forbidden. . . . And around those officers and diplomats were what is referred to as the *Tout-Paris* in literature, art, politics, theater.

*This new sanction was promulgated after the war to punish those whose conduct, while blameworthy, was not really considered treason.

To be charitable, Luchaire decided not to name names in her postwar account (1949). After the war, many people who appeared thrilled to be there at the time chose not to remember their presence—and meeting her then:

> There was no dancing because of orders, but people spoke in small groups. You went from one group to another, flaunting and showing off. Paris had only been occupied for a few months, but this was the period when all agreed that the Germans were very "correct." New fortunes were being made. The Gestapo had not yet grasped the capital in its iron fist. One assumed that all things could be arranged and prepared for the best of tomorrows.[26]

For most prostitutes, it was business as usual during the Occupation. French brothels were closed in 1946 because they had been seriously compromised by collaboration with the Nazi occupiers.[27] Because of differing standards of behavior, sexual indulgence for men was tolerated during the war. Prostitution was still legal, even as Vichy preached family values and made adultery with the wife of a war prisoner a serious crime. The madam of Paris's best-known brothel writes in her autobiography that she was never so happy as during the Occupation. There were many clients from among the black-market profiteers, the underworld, and so forth.[28]

The Germans set up tightly regulated brothels and houses of prostitution for the occupying forces. Since there were not enough French women to supply the sexual needs of German soldiers, coercive ways were found to recruit women. This taboo subject remains largely undocumented.[29] Some prostitutes actually helped the Resistance, obtaining useful information from their German clients. Male Resistance agents on occasion were hidden in brothels; anonymity prevailed there. One prostitute protested at her trial that she was a patriot, not a collaborator. Had she not infected twenty-eight German soldiers, thus contributing to the war effort?[30]

One account of a young girl having an affair with a German soldier comes from Resistance member Anne-Marguerite Dumilieu. Mlle X., Dumilieu recounts, secured work at the local German headquarters and became—without "complexes," but also without much thought on the matter—the mistress of a Bavarian officer. Her widowed mother appeared indifferent, not revealing to her daughter that she was a member of the Resistance. The mother learned much from her talkative daughter. Often the officer invited himself to supper, always arriving with a generous supply of provisions and Armagnac from the wine cellars of the region. On those occasions when he had had too much to drink, he stayed in the guest room. Mlle X.'s mother warned Dumilieu (then staying in their home clandestinely) with a signal. Thus, a young woman in the Resistance was able to live for more than a year in a home where an Oberleutnant (first lieutenant) often stayed. The widow referred to her daughter as "the damned one." Dumilieu, on the other hand, learned from "the damned one"—through Mlle X.'s mother—that the Gestapo was looking for her, so she was able to escape capture.[31]

What is striking in all accounts of the "cleansing" is the intensity of the vengeance unleashed against women who consorted with the enemy. Marguerite Duras's famed film Hiroshima, Mon Amour depicts women who collaborated with the enemy paraded through provincial Nevers with heads shaved, subject to the insults and sometimes the blows of the crowd. In some towns, they were stripped naked as well. Having one's head shorn is a sign of humiliation and a symbol of loss of power that can be traced back to Samson in the Bible. Former résistant Jacques-Augustin Bailly notes that while some men were shorn at the beginning of the Occupation, the punishment became more physical with the Liberation. Men were beaten and shot. Toward the end of August 1944, head shaving became a widespread practice for women thought to have collaborated. Given the importance accorded a woman's appearance, shaving her head brings social exorcism in addition to being a major punishment.[32] Virtually all women so treated were of modest background; few upper-class women who consorted with the enemy—such as couturière Coco Chanel or well-known actresses—were persecuted. Major industrialists and businessmen also got off lightly. As noted in chapter 3, the prestigious Réveillon fur firm was not seriously bothered after the war, even though it had manufactured fur vests for German soldiers on the Russian front. If women were treated more harshly, it was because French womanhood symbolized the nation. Having physical relations with the enemy was the defilement of France. When the camp survivors returned in 1945, their shorn heads were seen as badges of honor to be contrasted with those of the collaborators.

As *Behind the Lines* observes:

> In postwar rituals of commemoration, women were generally ignored; when they were singled out for attention, it was often for their role in events that emphasize their sexual status. Women who had been victimized through rape, imprisonment, or execution were contrasted with those who had consorted with the enemy or been unfaithful to husbands and sweethearts. In both cases, their identities were encoded in a complex system of nationalist and gender politics. . . .[33]

Young Marie Gatard, whose beloved *résistant* father was executed by the Germans, was appalled by the spectacle of "cleansing":

> The war was not finished, but in Paris it assumed another form—more perverse, more degrading. At least that is how I viewed it. This was the *épuration*. The "shorn woman" of rue Petit-Musc was a large young woman with a nacreous, rosy complexion. She walked along with her wedge-soled shoes tied around her neck, stiff like those undergoing a major initiation. Her face was frozen like a Buddha, her carriage tense and superb in the midst of a shouting, screeching mob of faces contorted by hatred, groping and opportunistic hands, eyes congested by excitement; festivity, sexuality, sadism.[34]

The spectacle of shorn women (*les tondues*) is discussed and illustrated by Alain Brossat in *Les Tondues: Un Carnaval moche* (1992). The pictures he reproduces include one of a woman who has been stripped nude and others of women holding the "German" babies born of these affairs with the enemy. The women frequently are elevated on platforms, reinforcing the carnival aspect Gatard noted. Most of these degrading spectacles took place in rural areas where neighbors were aware of the conduct of others and feelings ran deep. There were similarities between the treatment of these women and that meted out to those accused of witchcraft in earlier centuries. It seems clear also that some were denounced by jealous rivals. Peter Novick holds: "It is more than likely that many girls who were shorn were, unbeknown to themselves or their barbers, the instrument of salvation for *miliciens* and collaborators who might otherwise have died to appease their fellow citizens." The shearings of "horizontal collaborators," as they sometimes were called, responded to a deeply felt need for emotional release. Novick cites FFI chaplain Father Bruckberger entering a café full of German soldiers and their French girlfriends. In his diary, the priest noted: "Those girls could be dipped in tar and burned in the public square and it would affect me no more than a fire in the fireplace of a neighbor's house." During the purge, however, the Dominican cleric was one of the chief proponents of forgiveness and reconciliation.[35]

During interviews, former *résistante* Evelyne Sullerot was very outspoken in her criticism of the women collaborators she observed. They betrayed others and provided names while some women were dying from hunger. These women slept with the enemy and enjoyed all the luxuries of life while others suffered deprivation. Why, she asks, was there so much sympathy for them? These women collaborators generally are portrayed sympathetically—viewed as victims of the conformism of the Resistance. Célia Bertin holds that the betrayal by women collaborators was very serious because it had not necessarily been programmed by masculine minds:

> And it was worse because it was aimed specifically at innocent civilians who were not of the right religion, or at clandestine agents labeled "terrorists" in order to send them all to their deaths. Had propaganda truly blinded these women? Were they convinced that the Nazis held the truth? What hatred motivated them? Or what aberration? What revenge did they hope to take?[36]

The Bluet Files at the French National Archives (AN)—stenographic accounts of postwar trials—provide considerable data on women collaborators. One dossier details the 1949 trial of fifty-year-old Victorine Lefaucheur. She and a male colleague took over a confiscated Jewish firm that they obtained for a pittance and renamed the European Textile Firm. They used their profits to expand into other businesses. At her trial, Lefaucheur's lawyer took umbrage with the fact that, although she was an extremely qualified secretary—not the "little typist who comes from Quimper or Cahors with just a certificate"—she was being judged as a "mere" secretary. (French snobbery is evident here.) While freed of the most serious charges, Mlle Lefaucheur was convicted of economic dealings with the enemy. This was but one of a sizable number of instances where the forced aryanization of Jewish firms and property increased the fortunes of some French citizens.

Another postwar trial in the spring of 1949 was the "Affaire Marcheret." It revealed that women who sheltered Allied aviators were betrayed by other women in league with Guy Marcheret, a journalist with links to the German army. Marcheret used Yvonne Lallier and Jeanne Lemaire-Billiez as spies. These two women helped infiltrate a network of *résistants* who sheltered Allied aviators. When the Germans rounded up the group, forty Allied aviators were captured, along with those helping them—mainly women. The prosecutor at the trial paid tribute to all those women in the Resistance who "displayed such devotion, self-sacrifice, heroism, and generosity." Lallier was sentenced to death (later commuted), along with Macheret (AN 334 AP 29).

Violette Moriss's collaboration was so notorious that Resistance forces executed her before the Liberation. An invaluable assistant of the Gestapo, she participated in numerous operations against the Resistance, according to court records. Moriss denounced a colonel, his wife, and a captain—all members of a French military group specializing in parachute drops and sabotage. Their arrest exposed the group's "letter box." She accompanied the Germans, who simply waited and arrested all those who came for their "mail." Six more were taken, then tortured and executed. On Easter Sunday 1944, Moriss accompanied the Germans for a second time to the scene of an important parachute drop near Montlhéry, south of Paris. It was she who reported these drops. And it was Moriss who directed the expedition during which the Germans encircled Resistance members guarding the arms. In the ensuing battle, seven *résistants* were killed outright; ten others were captured, badly treated, and presumably executed. Immediately afterward, Moriss helped the Germans reenact the same scenario at Meaux (AN 334 AP 25).

And then there was the 1944 "Affair of Montgeron Château," named for the home of General Pierre Lelong, who joined de Gaulle in London in 1941. The general's wife and daughter stayed on in the château, located in the Seine-et-Oise departement. There the two women sheltered members of two French military groups. In May 1944, Mme Lelong was arrested and sent to Fresnes prison. There, she told her cellmates about her husband—who was with the FFL—and about her daughter's continuation of their Resistance work. Among those who listened with much interest was Fernande Gallet, there on a minor charge. Freed shortly afterward, Gallet went to the château and sought shelter from Mlle Lelong. Without suspicion, the young woman accepted and hid Gallet—with her lover—for three weeks.

Then the couple left, ostensibly for a trip; in reality, they left to denounce Mlle Lelong. All those staying in the château were arrested in a Gestapo raid. Mlle Lelong was brutally beaten by the French police. She then was tortured and deported to Ravensbrück, where she was reunited with her mother. Both survived (AN 334 AP 25).

There were six women among the "Neuilly Gestapo" group tried in November 1945. Under cover of commercial enterprises, thirty satellite offices of the "Otto Services" pillaged France and furnished an enormous quantity of merchandise—from leather stock and goods to Impressionist paintings—to the Germans, thus hindering the Allied war effort.* The Neuilly band acted with impunity under Gestapo protection. Trial transcripts relate how gang member Pierre La Haye used the Gestapo to threaten his ex-wife with deportation unless she relinquished their children to him.

Twice-divorced Éliane Derquenne, in her thirties, became secretary to the Neuilly Gestapo gang and soon thereafter one of the mistresses of Bernard, a leader of the group. Bernard enriched himself on their operations and enjoyed a luxurious lifestyle. Derquenne denounced him to the Gestapo because she coveted the fortune in gold bars he had buried at a farm. Bernard managed to escape to Switzerland. At her trial, Derquenne acknowledged knowing her "office" worked for the Germans but insisted: "It was not possible to undertake operations of that extent unless you were working for the Germans." For her part, she explained, she chose to ignore what went on, all the while accepting a generous salary, much jewelry, fine clothes and furs, as well as a country estate and a requisitioned Paris apartment building. To protect her property, she married again in November 1944 and put the property in her husband's name.** "And this woman," the prosecutor pointed out, "pretends to be patriotic, having arranged to acquire a certificate of Resistance participation. She claims she stayed with Bernard even after learning of his Gestapo connection because she was sentimentally attached to him." These "sentiments," however, did not prevail when she denounced him for the gold.

---

*These and other German "offices" confiscated approximately 30 percent of the French national revenue during the war years. On the seized art, see Lynn H. Nichols, *The Rape of Europa* (1994).

**War profiteers formed an association to secure their claims should the dispossessed Jewish owners return. A new profession was created, employing more than forty thousand: administrators of Jewish property. As German archives reveal, many profited handsomely.

Another woman of the Neuilly group—also interested in buried treasure—was Lucie Onstein van Houten, a former hostess in a Montmartre nightclub who married and was the mother of three. Onstein was only too aware that her husband worked for the Germans. She was richly maintained. Pictures were introduced at the trial as evidence of the couple's many feasts in the company of German officers, while their compatriots starved. They, too, buried gold bars in their garden. When her husband was arrested, Onstein became the mistress of a colleague and arranged to retrieve her husband's fortune (AN 334 AP 16).

The name of Mata Hari is well known; she was executed for her espionage activities during World War I. Although perhaps less widely known, World War II also produced a famed woman spy (a double agent, she claimed): Mathilde-Lily Carré, known as *la chatte* (the cat). She wrote *I Was the Cat* (first published in French in 1959) to justify her complicated double-dealings. The English edition is subtitled "The Truth about the Most Remarkable Woman Spy since Mata-Hari, by Herself." Gordon Young's biography designates her as *The Cat with Two Faces* (1957) and leaves no doubt about the sinister woman's lack of moral scruples.

> In April 1942, while I was still a free woman in London, the British asked me to write the "Memoirs of a Cat." The story was almost complete at the time of my arrest on July first of that year, but I refused to finish it in prison. The manuscript was confiscated. I heard no more about these memoirs until my trial, where they played an important role. By chance, these memoirs were returned to me in 1957. Here they are. I have shortened them but retained all the actual facts.[37]

Mathilde-Lily Carré was born in 1908. Her beloved father served in World War I. As a schoolgirl, Carré feigned accidents and illness to avoid assignments she disliked. To please her parents, she began studying law, but then she married a schoolteacher of whom they disapproved. The couple secured teaching posts in North Africa, which meant a chance to escape from bourgeois life. Several years of teaching, writing, and travel followed. When the war broke out, Carré returned to her family in Paris and enrolled in nursing studies at the French Women's Union to help her country. Her husband was mobilized. During the exodus, she helped escort wounded soldiers southward under Luftwaffe attacks: "I found a strange thrill in realizing that

I was in danger, and that any moment could be my last. This sensation was purely subconscious and cannot be analyzed. The body lives, lives intensively. Life escapes through all the pores; the vital fluid is in a whirl."

Carré had a short affair with a soldier. Then, when France surrendered, she looked for something to do: "The Resistance was starting to organize, and the Allied High Command needed information about everything that was going on in France. I realized that this was an area I should explore, to find out what I could do."

Carré met a Polish fighter pilot, Roman/Armand, and helped him set up the Interallié (Inter-Allied) network. "I was now totally involved in this service, and launched into my new life. . . . I—who had never read a spy story in my life, or seen a spy film—had to learn the profession." Because of his difficulties with French and his nationality, Armand decided that Carré, a French citizen, should give the agents their assignments.

> In addition to the recruiting, I had to explain to the agents the kind
> of information they were expected to furnish. I had to train them,
> give them examples of the reports they had to send in, study those
> they compiled, and then compose the military reports destined for
> Marseilles, London, and Vichy. . . . The agents in the ports had to
> report the ships seen in harbor on such and such a day . . . , the
> camouflage, the flak, work in progress in the port, etc. . . . We also
> had to review the entire French and German press every day.

She and Armand lived and worked together as cousins, she maintains, rejecting the claims of reporters at her trial who blamed the collapse of the network on the rivalry between Carré and one of Armand's mistresses. The radio in their apartment played dance music all day long. They never tuned to the forbidden BBC for uncensored news; that task was given to Carré's mother. A year after its founding, the Inter-Allied group in Paris was captured by the Gestapo. Carré was among those arrested.

"Night fell and it was terribly cold and damp in the cell. . . . I had lain down in all my clothes, including my fur coat, because I was so cold. At last I began to take in the situation: It was the end. All my work had been destroyed. . . . Where were all the others?" The next morning, after an excellent breakfast, she met Abwehr agent Bleicher, who vowed "never to leave" her.* Bleicher advised her to save her

---

*The Abwehr was the special intelligence service of the German military.

own skin, and get it into her head that England was doomed. He offered her work with the Germans at 6,000 francs a month—much more than the Allied contribution:

> I felt chilled to the bone. He took me by the arm and I found myself in a private French car driven by a man in plain clothes, seated beside Bleicher—who was also in civilian dress. He told me a host of stories, but I did not listen. I felt as though I had been hit with a sledge-hammer.

And so former Resistance agent Mathilde-Lily Carré accompanied the Germans to all the rendezvous listed in the agenda they found on her when she was captured. Bleicher listened as she called others in the Interallié group—including her own mother—at his direction. At a pâté and Champagne feast that the jubilant Bleicher held to celebrate his success in rounding up network members (with her assistance), Carré again claimed to feel as if she had been hit with a sledgehammer—one that affects the mind. That night, she became Bleicher's mistress—a fact that weighed heavily against her in the postwar trial.

> Now [the following morning] I was fully cognizant of the greatest act of cowardice in my life, committed on November 19 [1941] with Bleicher. It was purely animal cowardice, the reaction of a body that had survived a night in prison [one!]; had suffered cold; had felt the icy breath of death and suddenly found warmth once more in a pair of arms, . . . even if they were the arms of the enemy. I hated myself for my weakness, and, as a result of my abasement, I hated the Germans even more.

Bleicher invited himself to Carré's parents' home for lunch. Her father was livid and remained silent. Her mother contradicted everything Bleicher said and proclaimed her love for England. For his part, Bleicher warned Carré's parents to continue forwarding the messages they received in their role as a "mail drop" for the network. While the roundups and arrests continued, Carré cringed under her captured Resistance comrades' gazes of implacable hatred. She was installed in a villa with Bleicher and some of his colleagues, where she lived a life of luxury. Then, she claims, she outwitted the Germans. Somehow managing to meet other Resistance contacts, she encountered Lucas, an agent about to return to England, and convinced Bleicher to let her go along with him so that the Germans could install a spy in

London. How this could happen when her betrayal and new address surely must have been known to her former Resistance colleagues is not fully explained. But Carré was back in her element.

> I felt that I was living once more. My responsibility was enormous. I had to play the German game with ultimate cunning and camouflage Lucas's organization. There would be not the slightest mistake or distrust. That could bring about a major catastrophe. . . . The atmosphere in Paris that winter was very cold and terribly gloomy. People were to reproach me later for not having suffered from either cold or hunger—for having lacked nothing. That was true. But I would have them know that I would often have preferred to exchange my spiritual sufferings for physical ones.

After several unsuccessful attempts, Carré and Lucas reached London (with German collusion). The two made separate reports to the British services about the situation in France. Carré describes herself as physically and mentally exhausted in the days that followed.

> I was aware of my state, but in my pride, and in order not to weaken, I drank far too much. I admit, believe it or not, that I was almost happy. The nightmare was behind me. I felt that a great weight, a great anxiety, had been lifted from my mind. I had the impression of being among friends [the British]. It was probably this impression that made me avoid any contact with the Free French.[38]

One can presume that there were other reasons for avoiding contact with her fellow countrymen, given her recent activities in France. Carré describes the French as cheating, stealing, and forging ration coupons while the British accepted their rationing system. After several relaxing months in England, Carré was arrested at the request of the French on July 1, 1942. In prison, she began to feel guilty about her husband, who had been killed fighting the Germans. Returned to France a few weeks after the war's end, Carré was taken before a military tribunal. Several of her former Resistance colleagues supported her; others denounced her. Her real role in all this never will be fully known. She blamed her trial on vengeance, maintaining that the Resistance wanted her head: "The people who judged me, the journalists who dragged my name in the mud, never knew me. They had based their opinion on hearsay. Others vilified me because they had a guilty conscience." Condemned to death, Carré's sentence was commuted to hard labor for life. During her imprisonment, Carré—who had never been baptized—embraced Catholicism. After twelve years in prison, she was released in the summer of 1954. But, as her British biographer observes, unlike many of the other former members of the Inter-Allied network, she was free—and still alive.

⊹⊱⊰⊹

During the Occupation, as throughout French history, views on women tended to polarize; the "saint" who resisted was contrasted to the "sinner" who collaborated. The Communists, in particular, compared women PCF members to Joan of Arc. In effect, they canonized militant Danielle Casanova.[39]

Collaboration with the enemy during wartime Occupation remains a complex, controversial, and disturbing topic. As Philippe Burrin puts it in his authoritative study (*La France à l'heure allemande 1940–1944*), France was on German time—and in more than just changing the clocks. German policy was to divide the French in order to rule more easily. Their policy favored collaboration. Partisan books still appear defending or condemning both acts of collaboration and the ensuing purge. A 1991 book in the latter spirit (*Épuration sauvage*, by Philippe Bourdrel) details the "savage 'cleansing.' " Nevertheless, no study of women in the French Resistance would be complete without data on the less-than-heroic wartime activities of some French women that project a broader light on the record of wartime France. Rather than pass judgment, one should perhaps heed the admonition of Stanley Hoffmann, who, as a partly Jewish teenaged alien, lived in France during the Occupation:

> For Americans—who have never experienced sudden, total defeat and the almost overnight disappearance of their accustomed political elites; who have never lived under foreign occupation; who do not know what Nazi pressure meant; who have never had an apparently legal government, headed by a national hero and claiming total obedience, sinking deeper and deeper into a morass of impotence, absurdity, and crime; who have never had to worry first and last about food and physical survival—the wise and gentle warning of Anthony Eden must be heeded: do not judge too harshly.[40]

13

━━━━

Conclusion: Women and the Legacy of the Resistance

Those women represent faith, virtue, reason, equity, modesty, pride, justice.

—*Victor Hugo*

HUGO'S CHARACTERIZATION OF THE WOMEN OF PARIS WHO MARCHED to Versailles and forced Louis XVI to return to the capital was cited in a clandestine French journal asking Parisian women to remember October 5, 1943, the 154th anniversary of their ancestors' march.[1] Like the approximately five thousand women who assembled and marched to Versailles to beg for bread for their families, French women demonstrated for bread—and other food—during the Occupation. Historians consider the 1789 women's march to be one of the most significant events of the French Revolution. Similarly, women's protests during the Occupation were among the first forms of Resistance and arguably among the most important. In addition to food, women sought the return of the POWs and the right to send them packages. From the small groups that demonstrated in Paris and the surrounding municipalities in 1940, the numbers steadily increased as the situation deteriorated under restrictive laws and social injustice. Historically, French women always have helped defend their country and participated in revolutions—from Saint Geneviève holding off Attila and his hordes in the fifth century to Louise Michel fighting in the 1871 Paris Commune uprising. The best-known French woman who fought for her country is Joan of Arc. A cult developed around her in the nineteenth century, starting with the romantic image of the Maid of Orléans as savior of France—portrayed by Jules Michelet in the second volume of his monumental *Histoire de France* (1833–1867). Throughout the nationalistic nineteenth century, her popularity grew. In the early twentieth century, the "maid" was canonized. During the Occupation, partisans on all sides laid claim to the fifteenth-century peasant-girl-turned-soldier. To this day, politicians invoke her name. As recently as the early 1990s, controversial ultraright leader Jean-Marie Le Pen "enlisted" Joan of Arc for his National Front party.

Joan of Arc's feast day (May 8) was celebrated by three groups seeking French women's allegiance during the Occupation. From 1940 to 1944, she was invoked continually; her picture was everywhere; she was the subject of books and plays, as well as Honegger's extremely popular oratorio with text by Paul Claudel (*Jeanne d'Arc au bûcher*). The Germans emphasized her defeat of the British. Vichy held her up as the symbol of all that was best in French womanhood, a martyr to national unity. Resistance papers stressed Joan's struggles against those who occupied the country. There is, then, considerable ambiguity inherent in the use of the warrior saint as a symbol of women in the French Resistance, even though the comparison is made frequently.

From all walks of life, French women rendered indispensable services to their country during the Occupation, as they had in the past. There was no sphere of Resistance work where women were not involved—although the military and the *maquis* did not welcome them readily, and few held leadership positions. These volunteers had no weapons, no defense, no training—just their enthusiasm and their commitment. There were no precedents for what they did. Once involved, women proved to be extremely flexible and adaptable. They played many roles and they organized as they went along; each agent frequently served in different capacities. The problems they faced were comparable in many instances to what some women face in their daily lives—a factor that made their interventions particularly efficacious.

Cécile Rol-Tanguy, wife of a famed PCF Resistance figure, is among those who maintain that women adapted more readily and more quickly to illegality and clandestine life than did men, who tend to be less flexible.[2] Society has codified male conduct more. Women displayed an astonishing spirit of initiative and imagination. Additionally, women appear to have been more sensitive, vigilant, and alert. They were quick to sense when something was "not quite right." Traditionally, young women study languages. Knowledge of German proved very valuable to those who understood it and did not acknowledge it to the Germans. Several interviewees claimed that women's tendency to be on time and to be precise also helped them in clandestine work.

Women in the Resistance had obstacles to overcome. They had to prove themselves continually—to the military, the Jesuits and others, to male comrades. As some have noted, France is a Latin nation, and gender difference was invoked to dictate the forms of girls' behavior. Female stereotypes did not allow women to undertake nontraditional activity—above all, fighting the enemy. Yvette Farnoux was told she was "just a kid," even though she had graduated from professional school. Jacqueline Bernard chose not to assume the title of editor, although that in fact was her position. She felt that a man with that title would command more respect. The same held for *maquis* leader Claude Gérard, who pretended she represented a male leader. Once accepted, women did not necessarily find some of the men's groups to their liking. Marie-Madeleine Fourcade was upset by the infighting and bickering she found among the French groups that de Gaulle brought together, but she agreed to join them because she was a committed Gaullist. (Earlier, she had worked for the British.)[3] Because politics were involved, disagreements among *résistants* often went beyond the personality conflicts endemic to human endeavors. Not having the vote proved a negative advantage for women. With the possible exception of some enrolled in the PCF or committed Socialists, women seldom had a political agenda. From most accounts, it appears that women were more willing to sacrifice for the general good. Germaine Tillion holds that women in general are less given to dissension.

━━━

Shelter was a preoccupation for women agents. Women who went underground had more difficulty finding lodgings than did the men. As it was, well-brought-up young girls such as Denise Vernay and Catherine Roux slept in houses of ill repute on occasion. Wherever they were housed, cleanliness and appearance were concerns. Those who have studied the concentration camps find that housekeeping skills aided in survival. Hygiene helped prevent the epidemics that took the lives of many men. Women who "let themselves go" were perceived as doomed. At risk of death, women crushed bricks and used charcoal as substitutes for lipstick and eye makeup. It was a question of dignity for them, assuredly not coquetry. France Pejot was released from prison because she kept the prison courtyard clean; Hélène Renal was "forever doing housework." In some instances, women were assigned such tasks. Most presumably did them because that was what they "normally" did.

Women of all ages stayed at home and sheltered the pursued—at risk of imprisonment, torture, deportation, even death. Liaison agents generally were young, since students and young women were freer to become clandestine. However, the presence of young people in networks and movements was not without drawbacks. Their lack of experience and their eagerness sometimes created problems. In underground work, small errors could be fatal. The Défense de la France movement had a few "scatterbrains" as well as several agents who joined for the salary. At times, liaison agents were entrusted with very large sums of money sent from London. The equivalent of about two months' worth of their budget—a great deal of money—disappeared from Ceux de la Résistance, along with those who carried it.[4] In most cases, however, members of the Resistance made many sacrifices. Women sold rings and prized family possessions to help the cause. Funds were always scarce.* In the early days, support came from generous contributors (a few loans were repaid after the war). Later, the Allies supplied capital, but there were problems with deliveries—in a few instances, because of theft; in others, through interception, bombings, fires, and the like.

Given the many young people involved, it is not surprising that, as several women acknowledge, "we had our moments of fun." Living on the edge did not necessarily mean that *résistants* were grim and determined all the time. On the contrary, they needed the release that humor brings. Liaison agent Janine Lévy holds excellent memories of that period:

"I even have the impression that I often had a good time. It is true that when young you find it amusing to throw off someone who is

---

*There is not enough information to examine the question of equal pay. When funds were available, agents were paid according to presumed need; in any event, salaries were minimal.

following you, or cross a Paris bridge under fire, on the pretext of an urgent mission to complete—even if you obviously know nothing about the mission. I'm sorry that I have nothing really heroic or glorious to recount. I can't sound the heroic trumpet. [Here is yet another example of a woman downplaying dangerous assignments.]"[5]

Henri Frenay notes in his memoirs that because they were young, they were not only happy, but even joyous. He faults the stereotype of *résistants* continually suspecting traps, hugging the walls. After prolonged meetings discussing military matters, their group often ended up joking and having pillow fights.

Résistantes often compared joining an underground group to finding a new family. The members of Brigitte Friang's small group were so committed to one another that it was like a family. They did everything they could to protect each other. They were united as a small group standing alone against the world. Anne-Marie Soucelier stresses the willingness of her Resistance "family" to give up their lives for one another, as did France Pejot. Many similar remarks could be cited. Several women—Lise Lesèvre, Gabrielle Ferrières, Mme Hartmann—got their husbands involved in the Resistance. One interviewee chose anonymity because her in-laws have never forgiven her for involving her husband in a movement. Although he returned from deportation, his health was seriously compromised, and he died shortly after his return.

A camaraderie comparable to camping and Scout life prevailed among the *maquis*. Rita Thalmann recounts how girls as young as thirteen and fourteen supplied *maquis* units. When they had to stay overnight, they slept on the straw with the men—sometimes as the the only female there. In the instances she mentioned, the young girls were not "bothered."[6] While liaisons were discouraged in the movements and networks—they seriously compromised activities and sometimes led to betrayals—human emotions could not be repressed completely.

Unlike most men, these women are not reluctant to admit to fear. Men seldom do because it is not viewed as acceptable. Hélène Renal was consumed with fear, but that did not deter her from returning twice to assignments after her release from arrest. This was also the case with France Pejot and others. Their group and its mission were more important than the individual.

Living in permanent fear and anxiety required a new kind of courage—a daily heroism. Liaison agents faced possible arrest many times each day, while their chiefs were more protected. Lucie Aubrac feels that farm women who hid arms had a much more dangerous assignment than she did as leader of a hit squad (and, by implication, more than the men who generally formed and led these squads). Attacks were rapid and soon over, while the farm women spent months not knowing when the enemy might discover their arms caches. They had to live daily with that fear.

Women had varied reactions to using weapons. Some became crack shots and experts in explosives, while others, such as Hélène Renal and Danielle Mitterrand, discovered they were "allergic" to weapons. Few women undertook sabotage. It has been suggested that this is a psychological response: Women do not like to destroy. Yet women volunteered to blow up bridges and factories. If few did, it was partly because they seldom were given the opportunity. Weapons and explosives were in short supply. Then there was the problem of training. Jeanne Bohec's background in explosives was unusual.

Another apparent distinction between the sexes was their response to torture. According to network head Marie-Madeleine Fourcade and others, women held up better under torture. None of her women agents broke under torture, while some men did. She believes that menstruation and childbirth condition women to deal with pain and blood. Germaine Tillion also states that women talked less when tortured.[7] Women interviewed did not condemn those who talked under torture. Geneviève de Gaulle wondered what she would have done if her child or grandchild were tortured in front of her. Yvette Farnoux saw her husband tortured, and she considers it the worst thing that can happen to anyone. When Lise Lesèvre glimpsed her husband and youngest son in prison, she knew from her own ordeal what they were enduring. Evelyne Sullerot mentions a woman who remained silent even as the Germans smashed her baby's head against a wall.

+==+==+

Participation in the French Resistance led to a series of major discoveries for the women involved. First, they discovered their country and its people. Denise Vernay and Claude Gérard were among the many young women who moved to areas and cities they had never before visited. Parisian Hélène Renal left Paris to do Resistance work in Lyon for a man she had just met. Violette Morin, a young girl from a relatively isolated region of the country, found herself traveling in un-

known parts of France to deliver messages and search for out-of-the-
way places suitable for hiding men and materiel. In a June 1983
interview, Anne-Marie Bauer recounted that even though she was the
one who scoured the countryside looking for suitable landing sites for
parachute drops, she was not allowed to be present when the actual
drops occurred. Liaison agents were constantly on the move. Those
imprisoned met women from different regions and very different backgrounds. They met prostitutes for the first time and came to understand these women better. Catherine Roux found a group of honorary
grandmothers and learned from them about a France she knew only
through history books.

But not all the discoveries were pleasant. For Jewish women such
as Odette Fabius, who had led relatively sheltered lives in an assimilated milieu, the war brought a painful discovery—that of endemic
French anti-Semitism.

Young women involved in the Resistance had to deal with France's
paternalistic view of women. Prior to the war, most girls were supervised and chaperoned by their families. As Annie Kriegel points out,
they seldom were allowed out on their own. To be certain, there were
families and regions—such as the eastern part of France, according to
Simone Colin—where young women had more independence. The
situation of French women in the interwar years requires more in-
depth study. Hélène Eck holds that in the 1930s, a generation of young
girls "discovered the world through group activities, dances, trips to
the movies, and working side-by-side with men in white collar jobs."[8]
On the other hand, in the many interviews I conducted, as well as in
available testimony, young women from all social backgrounds note
how circumscribed their lives were prior to the war: from Catherine
Roux (who worked in factories and factory offices) to Brigitte Friang
(from a conservative Catholic home) to Annie Kriegel (whose family
was nonobservant Jewish). One can assume that young women who
chose to undertake risky work for clandestine groups were somewhat
more enterprising than their peers.

Whatever their situation prior to the war, résistantes often experienced unheard-of freedom during the Occupation. On assignments,
they traveled the country day and night without knowing where they
were or, often, whom they would meet. Being on one's own had its
negative side, too. Liaison agents led very lonely lives. One seventeen-
year-old ate her meals in front of a mirror in order to feel less isolated.
When the opportunity arose, they undertook other jobs—such as Hu-

guette (see chapter 4)—even if that work was more dangerous than typing in a hidden location. While the latter task offered comparative security, it was a solitary occupation requiring long periods indoors.

A major discovery was that of self. Pursuing assignments, *résistantes* found unexpected resources and aptitudes. During their wandering, gypsylike existence, liaison agents undertook activities and savored a freedom of movement not always possible previously. They enjoyed independence from their families and assumed new identities and occupations as they led new lives—lives that went against tradition. They helped disprove the contention of Vichy and the Church that French women were spoiled. Young women in the Resistance confronted problems their male colleagues did not have to face. A serious one was trying to ascertain whether the German soldier, policeman, or man eyeing or following them was displaying male interest or perhaps tracking them. Obviously, this was not easy to discern.

By and large, girls in prewar France accepted the norms of a male-dominated society and its role assignments. But young women who chose to work for the Resistance did many things that were out of character for their milieu. Those who remained home behaved according to standards of the time—not telling their parents of their Resistance activities, leaving home when it became too dangerous to remain there. Brigitte Friang stored her radio equipment beneath her bed in the home of her strict, Catholic family until November 1943. Her parents accepted the vicissitudes of the period and let her stay out all night at times, on the pretext of the blackouts. Nevertheless, the suspicious concierge noted her late returns: "I was a young girl and in those days young girls did not go out every night." After leaving her family, Friang lived "everywhere." She had a cyanide capsule and learned to take apart a gun while blindfolded. The war proved to be the collective failure of her parents, Friang holds: "It put a number of their cherished principles into question. They could no longer set themselves up as an absolute standard."[9]

Cutting ties with immediate families was a deliberate rupture in some cases—not just a move required for clandestine work—for not all families shared their daughters' views.

All the women who participated in the Resistance acknowledge that their lives were changed by that experience, although changes differ from one individual to another. For many, the intense experience of the Resistance was the high point of their lives, a period of exultation. "I was being useful; I was truly living," one woman remembers. For some, coming-to-consciousness carried over into the postwar period. At the very least, it reinforced character traits. According to young militant "Mounette":

> Yes, the return was very difficult. Many women committed suicide [she exaggerates]. We idealized liberated France. And we, the women, had changed so, while the rest of society had not changed. Those who married too young discovered another world in the Resistance— and other men. We learned to manage on our own. We were both tougher and more indulgent. For me, a Communist, the Resistance was the sequel of my commitment.

While joining the Communist Party was the major event in Mounette's life, the Resistance revealed unsuspected capabilities: "The Resistance showed me what I could do. Now I am not afraid of anything; not sickness or death—or the cops."[10]

Resistance involvement changed French women's thinking, in some cases profoundly. For some, this was the logical outcome of their pre–1940 development; for many others, it was a discovery that disposed them to act in ways that they would have considered illegal, even unthinkable, before the war. Conventional morality was overturned during the Occupation in the face of the suppression of traditional liberties. Carrying out Resistance assignments, respectable citizens became counterfeiters and thieves, even killers.

These women learned many things about themselves they would not have learned in peacetime. Because of the Resistance interlude in their lives, a fair number later chose professions other than those they might have selected under normal circumstances. One characteristic of many of the young women who joined the Resistance on a full-time basis was the interruption of schooling. As Annie Kriegel puts it, her studies left her. Danielle Mitterrand chose to go clandestine just before she was scheduled to take the final exams for the *bac*. Renée Bédarida left her university studies to concentrate on Resistance work. Both Yvette Farnoux and Hélène Renal wanted to become doctors but were excluded from medical school under Vichy legislation because they were Jewish. After their return from deportation, they were not up to undertaking medical studies. Not all could overcome the gap created by their dedication to their country rather than to themselves. Jeanne Chaton and Germaine Tillion lost irreplaceable research materials. On the other hand, one might say that the Resistance offered a very special education. While in many instances it extended their horizons, some learned lessons that complicated their lives. Lise Lesèvre was taught hate; Annie Kriegel was exposed to brutality. It took a long time and much effort to overcome this negative instruction.

+⊨━⊨+

Were there role models for these rebels? In their testimony, fathers or stepfathers are mentioned over and over again: fathers who served in World War I, fathers who had been wounded. War records recounted by fathers to their children seem to have influenced many women. (Several narrators mentioned seeing their fathers cry for the first time upon hearing Marshal Pétain announce that he was seeking an armistice.) French women were painfully aware of the dark heritage of a million and a half men lost in that bloody encounter. The interwar birthrate campaign continually stressed that loss. With "total" war, women could serve their country, emulating their fathers—as well as their brothers and other male relatives. Little mention is made of mothers in the narratives—unless the mother differed from the traditional *mère de famille* through profession or strongly held convictions.

After the war, most women wanted to resume their past lives. As Lucie Aubrac explains:

"When the war ended, I had a husband, a young son born during the war, and a little girl born in London. I wanted a home. I had been married five years, but I had never had a domestic life. Foolishly, I wanted to have a spare pair of sheets and more than two plates in the china cupboard. I had nothing. Those were our feelings then. So I resumed my teaching. During the Occupation, one of our goals was to help reform secondary schooling in France, to make secondary schooling more democratic so that university studies would be open to all. Anticolonialism was on the agenda of the National Council of the Resistance. Those were the sorts of noble sentiments we believed in then."[11]

Adjusting to "normal" life after the war proved difficult. These women had changed, but society had not. For France Pejot, there was a brief marriage and the birth of a son. She plays down her Resistance role just as she tends to denigrate her life as a woman, because of a failed marriage. Violette Morin's commitment continued after the war.

With her first husband, sociologist Edgar Morin, she organized an international exhibition on war crimes. The war and her Resistance involvement helped sharpen her reflexes. It revealed her basic convictions: rejection of injustice and racism in every form. Prior to the war, anthropologist Germaine Tillion had lived among North African tribes whose women had never seen a foreigner. Her denunciations of the French military's use of torture during the Algerian struggle for independence was a direct result of her Resistance experience and deportation. She, too, felt obliged to protest injustice wherever it exists.

Françoise de Boissieu's observations hold for many:

"We had four children in all. I tried working, but it was too difficult. It cost more to work than to stay at home. My husband was a civil servant. We didn't have much money. Moreover, we had my ailing mother and my in-laws with us. That was a lot of responsibility. So I had to stay home. Taking care of children is wonderful, but it is also very tiring and confining. I kept up my professional qualifications by replacing guidance counselors when they were ill or on vacation. When my youngest reached seventeen, I resumed work—in spite of my husband's objections. For two years, I taught in a school for special educators. Then I was president of an organization concerned with pedagogical issues. This was in 1968, just after the 'events.' When the law permitting abortion was passed [in 1975], Simone Veil, then minister of the family, asked me to become secretary general of the Sexual Information Council. Because I am convinced that abortion is *not* what women really want, I accepted the position.

"Our goal was to make contraception available to all so that there would be less need for abortions. Even if we did not succeed entirely, what we did was exceptional for that time. Here my Resistance background helped me. The Resistance experience brought people together from the extreme right to the far left who agreed to work on our projects. When the government changed, I resigned. I had given my word to the unions and various associations when we worked on some important projects together. I could not continue to promote projects that probably would never be realized.

"From my own experience, I know that women who were in the Resistance became more enterprising. They were less timid, more willing to take risks. What surprised me was that there were so many people from our background who refused to help in the Resistance. All in all, there were not that many of us—men or women—who served. I guess you could say I have a complex because I was never arrested or deported. But then it is really a matter of chance.

"Things in postwar France did not always turn out for the best. Take anti-Semitism. Teitgen* was right when he said France would be more anti-Semitic after the war. In the 1980s, I was interviewed about my postwar work with Monique Pelletier on Antenne 2 [French television]. This was shortly after a bomb exploded in a Jewish restaurant in Paris, killing four people. In the course of the interview, I was asked what I thought about the incident. I replied that I was very affected by the incident because I am Jewish. Obviously, a name like de Boissieu does not sound Jewish. Moreover, a distant cousin of my husband married de Gaulle's daughter. In the little village where we have a vacation home, where my husband is mayor, everyone—including the parish priest—was astonished. They asked me how I could have declared that I was Jewish before eight million spectators. I told them it was something I felt I had to say."[12]

There were other deceptions. Lucienne Guezennec joined the crowds celebrating in the streets when Lyon was liberated. Suddenly she saw two naked girls trying to protect themselves from a group of shouting women, who were spitting on the girls and trying to hit them. Further along were other unfortunates with shorn heads, weeping while the crowd insulted them. Lucienne cried out in protest (even though her voice was still weak from the bullet that had punctured her lung). A youth yelled at her for trying to help the "sluts." Then he grabbed her and shoved her into an open truck filled with silent, visibly terrorized men and women, and the procession continued, surrounded by the menacing crowds. Fortunately, just down the street, someone she had made false papers for recognized her. Lucienne was taken under guard to an FTP commandant, who released her. The assault on the Combat printing shop was well known. As some sort of "reward" for her heroic actions, she was offered a whip to use on Militia men who had been rounded up. She fled outside and burst into tears. Was it for this, she asked herself, that so many comrades—

---

*Progressive Catholic Pierre-Henri Teitgen became minister of justice after the Liberation.

including Vélin—died? Could this have been the reason for their struggles and sacrifices?

Those who made the return trip from the camps had the most difficulty trying to reintegrate into society after that nightmare universe. Few in France realized what that experience was like. One anticipated the worst—but not the unthinkable. The first deportees did not come back until the late spring of 1945, after Germany surrendered. Returning when France was in full reconstruction, the deportees were greeted with incomprehension. The survivors were a small group, possibly an embarrassment to those who had done nothing to help their country during the war. The women made valiant efforts to assume their prewar activities in spite of being in frail physical condition. Lise Lesèvre, for example, held out for a year and a half before collapsing.

The camp survivors were in bad shape; all had health problems of one sort or another. Some were sent away to sanatoriums to gain strength and learn to live again. Nonrecognition of their service had a major impact on the disability pensions that deportees received after the war. Women deportees able to prove they belonged to a movement were entitled to more than twice the amount of those who could provide no such proof. The witnesses who might have vouched for the latter group died in the camps. Consequently, in a fair number of cases, women deportees returned to a difficult readjustment, handicapped by insufficient pensions yet physically unable to undertake full-time paying positions.

When they reentered society, they were silent. As Lucie Aubrac observes, they did not talk about their experience. There was a sort of reticence in speaking about the atrocious things they had seen and undergone. Moreover, they had been humiliated. It was impossible for them to speak about the misfortunes they had undergone, the tortures inflicted, the people they had seen die. No effort was made to urge them to speak out. Perhaps they would not have been listened to or believed had they done so. People were interested in other matters—such as heroism. Misfortunes and other less appealing aspects of the war years were forgotten, she holds.

Hélène Renal could not talk about her experience with anyone, not even her family. The difficulty in discussing torture and camp life, until fairly recently, has been yet another factor in women's absence from Resistance history. Former camp inmates had to deal with the "survivor syndrome." They saw cherished comrades perish. Why were they spared? To a lesser degree, those who were never captured also experienced a form of survivor syndrome. Like Simone Martin-Chauffier, they felt guilty. Germaine Tillion returned from Ravensbrück alive and termed it bad luck.

Brigitte Friang recounted a telling personal experience to André Malraux, who incorporated it into his *Antimémoires:*

> She was the only deportee on the train returning from Germany. At the reception center they did not believe what she told them of conditions in the camps. The paymaster ruled she could only receive her accumulated base pay "because she had been housed, clothed and fed by the Germans"! In a bank line Friang suddenly felt ill. A charitable woman supported her and arranged for her to go to the head of the line upon learning that Friang had just returned from deportation. A distinguished man in his fifties protested. "She should have stayed in her camp!"[13]

Perhaps this incident partially explains Friang's contention that some of their early exploits—such as taking guns from German officers in the Métro—were stupid and not worth the risk. Upon her return, liaison agent Anne-Marie Bauer was designated a social assistant—for the record—a title to which she had no claim and one hardly descriptive of her dangerous assignments.

Anne-Marie Soucelier's experience upon returning to her position in France's highly structured national education system makes for painful reading:

"I was sent to Ravensbrück on the first major convoy of French women, convoy number 27,000. I returned June 5, 1945, because I caught typhus at Bergen-Belsen. I returned, but most of my companions did not. I was lucky to find my family again. Miraculously, my sister returned as well, but she died a few years later. What was terrible was to return and find only a few Resistance comrades. Most had been shot, or died under torture or during deportation. That was one of the worst aspects of my return. I resumed my work, but, like others who had been deported, I met with total incomprehension. No one understood what deportation had been like. We returned exhausted and physically weak. Typhus had affected my memory.

"We were reintegrated into a society that had no idea of what we had been through. I asked the academic administration if I didn't have the right to a leave of absence. You needed a minimum

of a year to rest, especially if you did intellectual work. They passed
the sponge over my two years of captivity. 'But you've had a long
vacation' I was told! So I returned to teaching under very difficult
conditions. For the rest of my career, I was behind. I worked very
hard, but it took me three times as long as my colleagues to do the
work. Correcting exams and papers is difficult work. But no one understood what I had been through.

"When I returned from the camps, they gave me a graduating
class in philosophy for fall 1945 [a few months after her return].
This was a difficult class no one wanted. But since I was the last to
arrive, I had to take it. Fortunately, the directress of the *lycée* understood my situation. The next academic year, she gave me a class of
beginning Greek so that I could have Saturdays off, two days free. I
was thrilled. That would have been the only time in my teaching
career that I had Saturdays free. Two days later, I got a telegram
stating that the offer had been withdrawn and I was assigned to a
new school. I went to see the principal. She was very upset at what
her supervisor had done. I asked her if the teacher taking my place
had a more advanced degree than mine. 'Not at all,' she said. 'The
only difference is that unlike you, she wasn't in the Resistance.' I
could have done something, because the whole thing was revolting.
I could have pointed out the inequity. It disgusted me. But I went to
the new school because my replacement was someone I knew and I
would not have wanted to be in her place."[14]

Here we see the full measure of the sacrifices made by some.
Thanks to the heroic contributions of the Resistance and the Free
French Forces, France was able to take its place with the Allies in
postwar Europe. But these sacrifices were not always recognized, let
alone appreciated. Catherine Roux and Lise Lesèvre were among those
who noted the general indifference of the population during the Occupation. People appeared to exert all their efforts toward trying to
lead the same daily lives that they had prior to the war. More tragically,
deportees such as Lesèvre, Soucelier, and Gabrielle Ferrières were deceived by postwar France. They had given so much, only to see the
ideals of the Resistance give way to the realities of cold-war politics
in a *révolution manquée*, a failed revolution. For poet Charles Péguy,
the Resistance tended to go from *mystique* to *politique*.

During the Occupation, there were major changes in French society. The war provided women in the Resistance with the chance to play different roles, as they had in World War I, but those roles were of limited length and often gender-bound. In war—as in peace—women were assigned traditional supporting roles, ones vital to the success of the undertakings to be sure, but supporting roles nevertheless. Admittedly, there were women who undertook military operations and "men's tasks," but only for the war's duration. French women who had been in charge of families for five years or more, had worked in field or factory, or had enjoyed considerable independence during the Occupation were expected again to become vestals of the hearth and give up their jobs to the returning men—as Rosie the Riveter had done in the United States. The ideology of domesticity with its imperative *femme au foyer* still prevailed. The postwar social policies of de Gaulle's government did not differ significantly from those of Vichy: The general subscribed to the values of Vichy's triptych—*Travail, Famille, Patrie*. In a postwar radio broadcast, de Gaulle called for twelve million babies. Women were presumed to be in the service of their country—once more.

The Resistance experience did not radically alter the situation of French women. What did, ironically—given the emphasis on child-bearing—was the Pill. Germaine Tillion observes:

"The war transformed women temporarily into heads of families. But if they did not go to work, everything returned to the traditional pattern. It was the Pill that changed the condition of French women. Women have been objects since paleolithic times. The care of children is women's responsibility. It is their greatest joy, but at the same time, it confines them. Women are 'attached,' in every sense of the word. They are restrained. Men are freer, more apt to be active."[15]

Many *résistantes* resumed traditional feminine roles after the war. This is not surprising when one considers that for many of the French, the war had been fought for a return to prewar life—although a better life, assuredly, with more social justice. While women had been active in attempting to liberate their country, there were no real role reversals. The situation was comparable in the Reich. In *Mothers in the Fatherland* (1987), Claudia Koonz maintains that German women who rebelled did so mainly because of a personal ethic, not in the name of women's rights.

ADIR, the organization of women survivors, made one of its first postwar concerns the care of the children of those who did not return from the camps. Sonia Vagliano-Eloy worked with the children found abandoned in Buchenwald, as she had in the refugee camps. Although Yvette Farnoux and Lise Lesèvre were both in poor physical condition when they returned from deportation, Farnoux formed Revivre to help the orphaned children of *résistantes* and Lesèvre helped with the orphans in her movement. Women retained the friendships they had made in the Resistance, of whatever political affiliation. That experience was a lifelong bond. This was less true of male comrades, who often were divided once again by political affiliations.

Two major preoccupations of *résistantes* were set forth at the first UFF congress, held in June 1945. One was natality: "Let us give life to avenge our dead." The other focused on pressing social concerns—health, children, housing, diet, and so forth.* Sarah Fishman (*We Will Wait*, 1991) found an identical return to traditional feminine concerns among the wives of POWs, a large group. They did not use their situations as heads of families during the war to seek additional rights, to seek *liberation*, as the term is used today.

Nevertheless, women's horizons were extended and their consciousness raised through working in the French underground. Like Françoise de Boissieu, most found self-assurance. Marie-Louise Le Duc eventually moved to Paris, took up art, and spent several decades helping returned prisoners integrate into society. Writing of her war record in the late 1970s, Paulette Descomps noted the disparity between her husband's situation and her own, even though she served with a Francs-Tireurs-Partisans combat unit. She also approved of the French women's liberation movement (Mouvement de Libération des Femmes, MLF).

> I've served my husband all my life, and with pleasure. But all the same, he is the one who drives the car, even though I know how to drive. He became a famous scientist, while I gave up my career to take care of the children. Then that was another era.[16]

Several former *résistantes* claimed that if they were young women today, they would join the women's movement. (Once used by all French

---

*Commitment to social causes was codified in the implementation of France's comprehensive social-service program in 1945.

feminists, the MLF name has been copyrighted by a small, single group.)

On March 23, 1944, the provisional government, the Consultative Assembly at Algiers, voted, 51 to 16, for women's suffrage. (Two-thirds of the members represented the Resistance, including, for the first time in French parliamentary history, twelve women, from the Resistance.) Those who voted against the measure objected that with so many men still POWs, along with those lost in battle, women were more numerous: The women's vote would "distort' the balance. One speaker cautioned against France's throwing itself into the "adventure" of women's suffrage, given the troubled times that surely would follow. The following year, women voted for the first time in municipal elections. Women's right to vote was formally inscribed in the Constitution of 1946—the year in which women first voted in national elections.

It has become a commonplace to hold that French women were "awarded" the vote by General de Gaulle for their valiant contributions to the war. Yet, although the general first mentioned the vote for women in June 1942, the program of his CNR, the unified National Council of the Resistance, drawn up just a year later, contained no mention of votes for women. There was simply a call for universal suffrage—almost a hundred years after France voted "universal" suffrage for men. The discourse of the Free French radio was ambiguous; equality was confused with difference. Moreover, the Vichy government also addressed the question in 1942, when its National Council considered granting women the right to vote under a revised constitution.[17]

Prewar concerns about women's vote do not appear to have been significantly modified by French women's contribution during the Occupation years. The paternalistic concerns of the prewar period had not been forgotten. Then the Right was fearful that enfranchised women would become militant leftists, or at least influenced by the Left. The Left, for its part, was apprehensive lest the clergy ultimately control the women's vote. As it turned out, the Right's assessment was accurate. Since the 1970s, French women have been shifting from the Right to the Left in their vote, although in the 1995 presidential elections they moved more to the center. They have also become less observant in religious practices.

Virtually the only Resistance movement that advocated the vote for women was Défense de la France, composed principally of young people. Their January 1944 *Cahier* (*Notebook*) stated:

> Women's absence from the ballot box prevents suffrage from being truly universal. One cannot reasonably maintain that voting once a year would keep women away from their household duties [one of the charges made by those who tried to keep French women from voting].

On April 2, 1944, *Combat* published a "Revolutionary Charter of Free Men," setting forth the group's views on the structure of postwar France that called, in general terms, for the "will of the nation to be expressed by the universal suffrage of men and women." What remains striking in the editorials and statements in the clandestine press is that there is no mention of what the role of women might be in a reborn France.

Annie Kriegel holds that French women's efforts in World War II did not really benefit women:

"As for the war, I don't think it advanced the cause of women. Women have always been present in the wars to free their country. Look at Algeria, for example. The important contribution of Algerian women in the war to free their country did not bring any major change in their lives. No, it is not because there were women in the French Resistance that French women were given the vote. French women finally received the right to vote because the time had come. The vote for women had already been a major concern before the war, a part of what democracy implies. I personally do not believe their role in the war brought women the vote."[18]

When women finally ran for office in 1946, in the first national postwar elections, Resistance organizations and parties—particularly the Communist Party—drew upon their women members for candidates. Thirty-two women were elected in that first election (about 7 percent of the total); seventeen were PCF members. In subsequent years, even that modest number declined. Deception set in as *résistantes* found themselves relegated to the wings after a brief moment in the center of the political scene. Only recently, when the Socialists were in power—thanks in large measure to the women's vote—has the proportion of women in Parliament come close to that of the first postwar elections. And France still lags behind most of its partners in the Council of Europe in this respect—even behind Switzerland,

which did not grant women suffrage until 1971. Over the years, demands have been made for a mandatory percentage of women candidates, an affirmative-action program that would produce "Liberty,
Equality, Parity."

Ultimately, participation in the Resistance was not the major factor in French women's enfranchisement.[19] The "award" of the vote fit
in with the Gaullist myth created at the end of the war: to try to
ensure France's prominence as a world power and to ensure harmony
in the country as the unity of the Resistance gave way to party diver-
gences. Everyone had been a Resistance member or supported the
Resistance, and everyone was now working together to reconstruct
France; France was united. Or so the myth went. Vichy's record was
ignored in an effort to portray a France massively present in the Resistance. The Gaullist government presumably saw women's representation in the French political arena as a necessary step toward reconstruction. Another consideration was reducing Communist influence.

Additionally, one can presume that France wanted to be on a par
with her wartime allies. Here, as in other areas, circumstances appear
to have obliged the traditional, authoritarian de Gaulle to break with
older French institutions and attitudes to favor change—sometimes
revolutionary changes.[20] Women's franchise served de Gaulle's vision
of a France largely active in the Resistance, although, as noted in
chapter 1, he named but six women as Companions of the Liberation.
By equating French women's Resistance record with the granting of
the vote to all French women, as commentators did, the number of
women presumed to have served in the Resistance was increased. In
reality, *résistantes* were not that numerous and do not figure prominently in historical accounts. More seriously, attributing women's enfranchisement in France principally to their role in the Resistance
ignores the long history of efforts to obtain that vote that started in
the nineteenth century—efforts led primarily by women.

The MRP (Mouvement Républicain Populaire), a Christian Democratic party, was founded after the war by Catholics who served in
the Resistance. It offered an alternative to Communism and Gaullism.
The women's vote helped the MRP prosper in the early postwar years.
Led by Georges Bidault, the MRP received 28 percent of the vote in
the 1946 elections, followed by the Communists with 26 percent and
the Socialists with 21 percent. In spite of this early success, the MRP
group largely disbanded in 1958 when confirmed colonialist Bidault
opposed de Gaulle over the fate of Algeria. By that time, French

women were seeking other forums where they could challenge society's conventions. To find postwar progress for women, we must look to the social rather than the political realm, although that is not to deny the increased politicalization of women brought about by the Occupation years.

The new French women's movement of the 1970s grew out of student and worker demonstrations in May 1968. Feminist campaigns focused on passage of legislation aimed at helping French women obtain a full and equal place in French society. In 1974, French women finally won the right to receive family-planning information and access to birth-control devices. A year later, divorce became possible under less rigid and time-consuming conditions. Also in 1975, a law permitting abortion (with some reservations) was passed for a five-year trial period; in 1979, it was voted on again and inscribed permanently in the Constitution. First-trimester abortions currently are covered by France's extensive social-service system. Efforts continue to ensure equal rights in employment; women are often seen as competitors rather than colleagues.

Over the centuries, progress toward equal rights, equal opportunities, and equal participation in French society was episodic. Efforts to liberate women increased after World War I. However, major changes in the status of French women came about only after World War II. Women in the French Resistance helped implement those changes, even though many resumed their prewar roles when peace came. This paradox may be partially explained by the frequently quoted French saying that it is easier to change the laws than to change patterns of preconceived attitudes, *les mentalités*.

In some instances, Resistance commitment served as an initiation to activism on behalf of women that continued after the war. A number of former *résistantes* have focused on women's concerns. Marie-Jo Chombart de Laüwe (who, like others, kept her Resistance name after this new "birth") is a noted sociologist specializing in women and the family. Historian and sociologist Evelyne Sullerot is internationally known for her many studies and government reports on women and society. Françoise de Boissieu became secretary general of the Sexual Information Council. Jeanne Chaton was one of three *résistantes* who headed international women's organizations after the war. Other names could be mentioned. Nevertheless, it is probable that these women would have been active in humanitarian causes even without the war experience. Not all women, however, were "radicalized" by the Resistance experience; several became more conservative. And Raymonde Teyssier-Jore from New Caledonia came to regret her commitment to colonial France.

The brief period of the Resistance—which corresponded to France's capitulation and occupation—provided some women with the opportunity to work in clandestine networks and movements. An even larger number resisted as individuals in whatever manner they could. But women's wartime activism did not carry over to postwar political activism, at least not to traditional politics. This is revealed yet again in a 1994 collection of interviews of those who went from the Resistance to the exercise of power. There are no women among the fourteen politicians profiled.[21]

Only the largely Communist-dominated UFF provided a framework for the organization of women's activities. In various ways, former *résistantes* devoted themselves to women's issues, in some instances continuing prewar concerns. The major changes in postwar French society were facilitated, and to some extent accelerated, by the many and varied activities of French women during World War II. But one cannot claim that the war experience radically changed women's status. The changes in postwar society had been long in preparation, their roots traceable through the decades, as the history of French feminism reveals. The improved status of women in many other countries since 1945—as well as the strength of feminism in many different countries regardless of whether they had a wartime Resistance movement—also suggests this conclusion. However, to say that it was essentially a question of accepting the inevitable does not lessen the enduring value of what so many thousands of women did during the Resistance to liberate their country. France was France again, in measurable part because of what her daughters had done.

Appendix:
Brief Biographies of *Résistantes*

Berty Albrecht. An exceptional woman, Albrecht brought to the Resistance the same commitment that she had to her prewar undertakings: pacifism, better conditions for working women, and family planning. She joined Henri Frenay to help develop the movement Combat. It was her idea to publish a bulletin, which became the clandestine newspaper *Combat*, with a circulation of several hundred thousand. Captured a third time and tortured, she apparently committed suicide.

Lucie Aubrac. One of the founders of the movement Libération-Sud, Aubrac continued to teach in a Lyon *lycée* and care for her family in addition to doing Resistance work. Her account of her wartime experiences, *Outwitting the Gestapo*, published in 1993, covers nine months, the period of her second pregnancy, when she helped free her beloved husband, Raymond, from prison for the third time (the last two times, because of his Resistance work).

Renée Bédarida. Bédarida was a devoted Catholic in graduate school when the war broke out. She worked with several Resistance groups in Lyon, in particular with Témoignage Chrétien (Christian Witness), which published an important newspaper with that name. Bédarida wrote about the movement and its leader, Father Pierre Chaillet, in two books.

Célia Bertin. Studying literature, Bertin was recruited in the early days of the Occupation to help with hidden Allied aviators because she spoke English. When forced to flee Paris and hide in the eastern Jura region, Bertin wrote the first draft of her first novel. Among her many works is a study of this period, *Femmes sous l'Occupation*, published in 1993.

Jeanne Bohec. A chemistry major who worked in an arms factory, Bohec left for London when the armistice was announced. In spite of her technical expertise, she had great difficulty convincing the Free French to let her use it. But she succeeded. Ultimately, she was allowed to parachute back to her native Brittany to instruct young men in the use of arms. Bohec details her adventures in *La Plastiqueuse à bicyclette*.

Françoise de Boissieu. Married in the early days of the Occupation, de Boissieu and her husband devoted their time to working with the movement Combat in the south of France. Life became more complicated when daughter Muriel was born and they were sent to Lyon. Leaving the baby with her maternal grandparents, de Boissieu continued Resistance work in Paris.

Ida Bourdet. A mother with three young children, Ida Bourdet contributed to the Resistance by assuming care of the children when her husband, Claude, an early member and later leader of Combat, went underground. One of her biggest problems was finding shelter. When Claude was captured, Ida left the children with friends and went back to Paris to try and help him.

Jeanne Chaton. Chaton was arrested and sent to work in Germany during World War I. Upon her return, she resumed her education, received graduate degrees, and taught in the provinces and then Paris. When World War II broke out, Chaton worked with several Resistance groups, the last being the Front National Universitaire. Now, she reasoned, there would at least be justification for her arrest—which did not occur.

Sister Edwige Dumas. Sister Edwige—already a member of the "peaceful army of St. Francis"—joined the Resistance. She helped care for the wounded of both sides as well as the many civilians who were injured during the Allied bombings of Calais. Among others she sheltered—at risk of her life—was a Communist *résistant* sought by the Germans.

Geneviève de Gaulle-Anthonioz. Niece of the general, de Gaulle was an early *résistante*, following the family tradition. The last group she worked with was Défense de la France, a movement composed mainly of young people. With a team of young women, de Gaulle supervised distribution of their newspaper and did editorial work. Captured when their group was betrayed, she was deported to Ravensbrück.

Yvette Farnoux. A student, Parisian, and Jewish, she joined Combat and eventually went underground. Her major achievement was heading the movement's extensive clandestine social services. She met her husband, Jean-Guy Bernard, in the movement. Both were captured. Farnoux gave birth to a stillborn child in prison before being deported. Her husband never returned.

Gabrielle Ferrières. Ferrières joined the Resistance to be with her husband and her brother, famed philosopher Jean Cavaillès. Ferrières served as liaison for her brother and the groups he founded. All three family members were captured. She was released after five months in prison, and her husband returned from deportation. Her brother, however, was executed for treason.

Lucienne Guezennec. Guezennec joined Combat, eventually helping to print their newspaper. She almost lost her arm after it was caught in one of the automated presses. Because she was needed, she returned to work shortly thereafter. When the clandestine print shop was raided, she was the only survivor, although wounded. Members managed to rescue her from the hospital.

Annie Kriegel. Because she was only fifteen, Kriegel—from a close, nonobservant Jewish family—joined a Communist Resistance group, the only one that would accept such youthful members. Assuming major Resistance assignments, she worked on a Grenoble newspaper to help support her family. Eventually she had to sacrifice her studies—which she resumed, brilliantly, after the war.

Marie-Louise Le Duc. An active sportswoman, Le Duc and her husband joined the Breton Resistance to ensure their three sons' futures. She worked with a network that sheltered those wishing to flee Vichy France—including Allied airmen, who were picked up by British boats that landed secretly at night. "Madame X.," as the British designated her, was arrested three times but always managed to escape.

Lise Lesèvre. The mother of two adolescent sons who were in the Resistance—as was her husband—Lesèvre continued her maternal role by welcoming and working with young men who had joined the *maquis*. She was captured with clandestine documents and brutally tortured by Klaus Barbie before being deported with her husband and her sixteen-year-old. They did not return. Lesèvre's back was permanently injured.

Simone Martin-Chauffier. The entire Martin-Chauffier family was involved in the Resistance. Simone and her husband helped out in one of Paris's earliest groups, the Musée de l'Homme group, beginning in 1940. It was decimated by an informer. The Martin-Chauffiers then joined the movement Libération. The family moved to Lyon, where Simone hosted many clandestine meetings and housed Resistance "guests." Finding food for them and her family would prove to be a major, time-consuming activity.

Danielle Mitterrand. The wife of France's former president joined the Resistance when but a teenager. Her parents sheltered some of the leaders of Combat. She helped care for *maquis* fighters who had been wounded. During this time, she met her future husband, head of a Resistance movement composed of former POWs.

France Pejot. Pejot and her sister joined the movement Franc-Tireur early on, all the while managing the family store in Lyon. She hid movement documents in the family apartment. Pejot used her unsuspected skills as an actress to escape capture and save male leaders. After a third arrest, she was deported to work camps and Ravensbrück.

Hélène Renal. Parisian and Jewish, Renal went to Lyon to work with unknown figures in order to fight the Nazi Occupation. Secrecy obliged her to move constantly as she became a typist and code operator for the clandestine central Resistance "post office," Action. Although fear followed her, she resumed work upon release after arrest. Eventually she was arrested again and deported.

Catherine Roux. The young woman was asked by a boss in the factory office where she worked to do "a few things." Part-time commitment turned into full-time clandestine Resistance activities when she was directed to leave

Lyon for Paris. Roux—who had never been to Paris—went about the capital on liaison assignments until she was captured and deported.

Evelyne Sullerot. The Occupation found her Protestant family on vacation in southwestern France. After several moves, seventeen-year-old Sullerot returned to their home in Compiègne, where she did Resistance work—along with caring for two younger siblings. She then assisted her father at his psychiatric clinic, where Jews and the pursued were hidden. As the war ended, she helped a *maquis* in the Orléans region.

Suzanne Vallon. When they had to leave France because their Resistance work was discovered, ophthalmologist Vallon and her husband went to London. It was not easy, but she finally managed to be sent on active duty, as a doctor, to North Africa. She accompanied Allied troops making their way northward from Toulon as France was freed from the Germans.

Sonia Vagliano-Eloy. Because her mother was American, Vagliano-Eloy managed to leave occupied France. In the United States, the young woman tried to join de Gaulle's Free French. Finally successful, she trained in London. Barely two weeks after D day, she and her women colleagues were sent to France to oversee the refugee camps. Her final assignment was working with the survivors of Buchenwald.

Denise Vernay. Vernay left her family in Nice to join Franc-Tireur in Lyon, thanks to scouting connections. As a liaison agent, she had to memorize many messages and addresses—in a city she had not known. Like other couriers, she was ordered to have no contact with friends. It was a lonely life. Caught by the Gestapo, she was deported.

Notes

Preface

1. Agnès Humbert, *Notre guerre* (Paris: Émile-Paul Editors, 1946), 136. Their group met at the offices of Émile-Paul. The men were executed, while the women had their sentence commuted to life imprisonment. When initially captured, Humbert was told that her seventy-three-year-old, almost-blind mother would be arrested as well if she did not name names. She did not, so she found herself in the same prison (la Santé) where she had visited her father, Senator Charles Humbert, when he was imprisoned during World War I.

2. Max Hastings uses this term in criticizing Studs Terkel's *The Good War: An Oral History of World War Two*. Hastings maintains that most readers find it more rewarding to deal with books in which views are digested and analyzed into a coherent thesis rather than offered to the reader as "the rawest of raw lumber" (*Times Literary Supplement*, March 29, 1985).

3. "La Lutte avec l'ange," in *Le Monument*, 220–221; quoted by Helena Lewis in "Elsa Triolet: *Engagé* Writer and Heroine of the Resistance," *Contemporary French Civilization*, vol. 18, no. 1, Winter/Spring 1994, 52; her translation.

4. Robert Scanlan, "Another Go at *Godot*," ART News, vol. xvi, no. 2, January 1995, 10.

5. Paul Fussell, *The Great War and Modern Memory* (New York and London: Oxford University Press, 1975), 173, 310.

6. Cobb, Richard. *French and Germans, Germans and French: A Personal Interpretation of France under Two Occupations, 1914–1918/1940–1944* (Hanover, N.H.: University Press of New England, 1983), xxi.

7. Laure Moulin, *Jean Moulin* (Paris: Presses de la Cité, 1969), 240.

1. Women and the War-within-a-War

1. Interviews with Claude Bourdet, starting July 7, 1983. For a full account of the history of this major clandestine newspaper, which continued after the war, see Yves-Marc Ajchenbaum, *A la vie/à la mort: Histoire du journal "Combat" 1941–1974* (Paris: Le Monde–Éditions, 1994).

2. Interview with Lucienne Guezennec, April 9, 1986; *Le Progrès*, October 12, 1944. (She formerly spelled her last name with an é: Guézennec).

3. See Henri Noguères, *La vie quotidienne des résistants: De l'armistice à la libération* (Paris: Hachette, 1984). Noguères is the author, with Marcel De-

gliame-Fouché, of an authoritative five-volume history of the Resistance: *Histoire de la Résistance en France* (Paris: Laffont, 1967–1981).

4. Ted Morgan, *An Uncertain Hour: The French, the Germans, the Jews, the Barbie Trial and the City of Lyon, 1940–45* (London: Bodley Head, 1990; New York: Arbor House/Wm. Morrow, 1990), 4–5.

5. Henri Michel, *Bibliographie critique de la Résistance* (Paris: Institut Pédagogique National, 1964), 9. For Resistance writer Jean Paulhan, the French Resistance was a mystique, almost a religion, while for colleague Jean Cassou, it was a community of risks more fraternal than others in that it lasted four intense years.

6. Testimony of Lucie Aubrac in interviews and correspondence starting in June 1985, and subsequent interviews.

7. Interviews with Marie Granet, March 5, 1983, and May 20, 1986, plus correspondence. Also, Marie Granet, *Cohors-Asturies: Histoire d'un réseau de Résistance* (Bordeaux: Cahiers de la Résistance, 1974). See the preface by Jacques Debû-Bridel. Alban Vistel, among others, has spoken out against the large numbers who joined what had been a lengthy campaign—only at the end. He holds that the early volunteers who obeyed the virile voice of conscience (Vistel frequently refers to the Resistance as "virile") affirmed the values they deemed essential. Alban Vistel, *Héritage spirituel de la Résistance* (Lyon: Lug, 1955), 42.

8. Testimony of Odette Sabaté in Marie-Louise Coudert, with Paul Hélène, *Elles: La Résistance* (Paris: Messidor Temps Actuel, 1983), 146.

9. Robert Frankenstein, "Les Français et la Seconde Guerre Mondiale depuis 1945: Lectures et Interprétations," in *Histoire et temps présent* (Paris: CNRS/IHTP, 1981), 26.

10. Because he volunteered in 1940 to serve on the Vichy court reassessing previously awarded French citizenship, Mornet's view may be seen as representative of those who had personal reasons for wishing to forget that period. André Mornet, *Quatre ans à rayer de notre histoire* (Paris: Self, 1949).

11. Henry Rousso, *The Vichy Syndrome* (Cambridge, MA: Harvard University Press, 1991); *Le Syndrome de Vichy: 1944–198 . . .* (Paris: Seuil, 1987; rev. ed., 1990).

12. In addition to Zlatin's testimony in depositions cited in this book, details of the children and their guardians are related in Serge Klarsfeld, *The Children of Izieu: A Human Tragedy* (New York: Harry N. Abrams, 1985). See also Antoine Spire, *Ces enfants qui nous manquent* (Paris: Maren Sell, 1990).

13. Alan Riding, "Frenchman Convicted of Crimes Against the Jews in '44," *The New York Times*, April 20, 1944.

14. Recent revelations of François Mitterrand's activities during the Occupation, and of his continued friendships with convicted collaborators, have renewed the debate in France on the issue of collaboration examined in chapter 12. See Pierre Péan, *Une jeunesse française: François Mitterrand 1934–1947* (Paris: Fayard, 1994).

15. Antoine Prost, in *Histoire et temps présent,* 86; Deirdre Bair, *Simone de Beauvoir* (New York: Summit, 1990), 293.

16. Pierre Vidal-Naquet, *Voix et Visages,* no. 218 (January–February 1990), 4. For insightful studies of French commemorations, see *Lieux de mémoire* (Paris: Gallimard, 1984–1993), edited by Pierre Nora.

17. Interviews with Germaine Tillion, July 1985; her book, *Ravensbrück* (Paris: Seuil, 1973), 273. Interview with Rita Thalmann, June 30, 1985.

18. H. Roderick Kedward, *In Search of the Maquis* (Oxford: Clarendon Press, 1993), vii.

19. Violette Rougier-Lecoq joined the Red Cross in September 1939 as a voluntary nurse. After the painful stages of withdrawal before advancing German forces in May 1940, she was imprisoned briefly. Released, she joined the hospital at Compiègne, aiding wounded prisoners. At the same time, she helped some escape. Subsequently, Rougier-Lecoq became an active member of a network and worked gathering intelligence for eighteen months until her arrest, after betrayal by another agent. Held for more than a year in solitary confinement, she was informed one day that she would be executed; instead, she was sent to Ravensbrück. Interview with Violette Rougier-Lecoq, July 1989.

20. Marilyn Yalom, *Blood Sisters: The French Revolution in Women's Memory* (New York: Basic Books, 1993), 6.

21. Robert Frank, "La Mémoire empoisonnée," *La France des années noires* (Paris: Seuil, 1993), 486.

22. Marie-Elisa Cohen's deposition (#4331-07-72) at the Ivry Archives is but one example of this problem.

23. Anne-Marguerite Dumilieu, *Moi, une cobaye* (Paris: SEFA, 1975), 46.

24. Lucie Aubrac remarks, "Women in the French Resistance" conference, October 15, 1992.

25. Handwritten document from Marie Granet's private archives.

2. France under German Occupation

1. Tony Judt, *London Times Supplement,* Sept. 28–Oct. 4, 1990, 1020. The French High Command assumed that any German invasion would take the same route as the one used in World War I. Since France did not wish to antagonize its neighbors, the Maginot Line was not extended northward to the sea along the Franco-Belgian border. Instead, the Belgians were charged with defending that area. This need for maneuverability was ignored again when *maquis* units were installed in mountain hideouts in the last years of the Occupation—with tragic results.

2. Interview with "Annette," May 20, 1986.

3. Interviews and correspondence with Evelyne Sullerot, starting June 1983.

4. Henri Frenay, *La Nuit Finira* (Paris: Robert Laffont, 1973), 36. (*Night Will End,* New York: McGraw-Hill, 1975.)

5. Marc Bloch, *L'Étrange défaite: Témoignage écrit en 1940* (Paris: Éditions Franc-Tireur, 1946), 215. (*Strange Defeat*, New York: W. W. Norton, 1968.)

6. Interview with Geneviève de Gaulle, May 24, 1983.

7. Interviews with Lucie Aubrac, previously cited, plus extended correspondence.

8. See Preface regarding the role of prefects.

9. Robert Paxton, *Vichy France: Old Guard and New Order 1940–44* (New York: Morningside ed. 1982), 46.

10. Judt, 1018.

11. Michael Marrus and Robert Paxton, *Vichy France and the Jews* (New York: Basic Books, 1981). References to the situation of the Jews are largely drawn from this authoritative work. The French edition, *Vichy et les Juifs*, contains the texts of all the anti-Jewish legislation. Data from Paxton lecture, "Vichy and the Jews," at the Harvard University Center for European Studies, November 14, 1980. Pétain's private secretary, Henri du Moulin de Labarè-the, states in his memoirs that Vichy's anti-Jewish legislation was spontaneous, or "native": *Le Temps des illusions: Souvenirs juillet 1940–avril 1942* (Geneva: Éditions du Cheval Ailé, 1946), 280. For a more recent study of France's role in the persecution of Jews, which includes personal testimony, see Susan Zuccotti, *The Holocaust, the French, and the Jews* (New York: Basic Books, 1993).

12. The reviewer of a French book on the Jews' dismissal from French universities observed that the speed with which these regulations were implemented is still amazing—in contrast to the more customary plodding administrative pace.

13. Interview with Violette Morin, June 15, 1983.

14. Henri Amouroux, *La Grande Histoire des Français sous l'occupation*, I, 392. Commissioner Xavier Vallat deplored the "error" of the French Revolution in granting citizenship to Jews. In his view, this wandering race endeavors to take over wherever it travels with its dream of universal domination.

15. Marrus and Paxton, 343. Social worker Céline L'Hotte recounts how a nurse returning from Belgium was laughed at when she spoke of "extermination camps." Only in 1944 were the rumors given some credence and efforts made to do something. *Et pendant six ans . . .* (Paris: Bloud and Gay, 1947), 59.

16. Zuccotti, *The Holocaust*, 288.

17. There were three rival German police groups. Their aims were different, even conflicting at times. The average French person knew mainly the hated SS, the Gestapo. Those interviewed tended to refer to *all* German police as the Gestapo, whatever their affiliation. That designation has been kept in narratives, even in situations where it appears interviewees were dealing with other German authorities. French historian Jacques Delarue has

written several books on the subject of the French police during the Occupation. According to German records, at the most there were five thousand SS men in France: *Die faschistische Okkupationspolitik in Frankreich (1940–1944)* (Berlin: Deutscher Verlag der Wissenschaften, 1990), 31–32, cited in Philippe Burrin, *La France à l'heure allemande 1940–1944* (Paris: Seuil, 1995), 97.

18. Interview with Annie Kriegel, June 21, 1983. See also her *Réflexions sur les questions juives* (Paris: Hachette, 1984). For a summary of the roundup of July 16, see Zuccotti, *The Holocaust.*

19. Annette Muller Bessmann, "Manuscrit-témoignage," 48 (*La Petite*, 101), quoted in Zuccotti, 112. For other testimony on the roundup, see Claude Lévy and Paul Tillard, *Betrayal at the Vel' d'Hiv* (New York: Hill and Wang, 1969).

20. Francine Duplessix Gray, "When Memory Goes," *Vanity Fair*, November 1983, 122. As indicated in chapter 1, the archives of the Paris Prefecture of Police remain closed.

21. In recent years, the two principal Vichy police chiefs, René Bousquet and Jean Leguay, were indicted—again. Bousquet was found guilty of collaboration in 1949, but after some years of "national indignity," he was given a suspended sentence. He went on to a very successful career in banking. Leguay, who was never tried, also had a very successful postwar career. The two were accused of rounding up and deporting more than forty thousand Jews. Leguay was indicted in 1979 and died a decade later without ever having his case tried. In the spring of 1993, while awaiting trial, Bousquet was killed by a man avid for celebrity. Not all accept this explanation, however, believing he was executed to protect others.

22. Jacques Duquesne, *Les Catholiques françaises sous l'occupation* (Paris: Grasset, 1986).

23. Duquesne, 43 (my emphasis).

24. Interview with Danielle Mitterrand, June 16, 1992.

25. Anatole de Monzie, *Ci-devant* (Paris: Flammarion, 1941), 253.

26. Burrin, 232; see also Duquesne, 56.

27. Cited by Pierre Giolitto, *Histoire de la jeunesse sous Vichy* (Paris: Perrin, 1991), 558–559.

28. An F/IC III, 1143, Bouches-du-Rhône, June 5, 1944.

29. Deirdre Bair, *Simone de Beauvoir* (New York: Summit, 1990), 263.

30. Jean-Louis Crémieux-Brilhac, *Les Français de l'an 40*, two volumes (Paris: Gallimard, 1990), I, 413–414, 430.

31. Alice B. Toklas, *The Alice B. Toklas Cook Book* (New York: Harper & Brothers, 1954), 206–207.

32. Ephraïm Grenadou, with Alain Prévost, *Grenadou, paysan français* (Paris: Seuil, 1966), 204. Grenadou describes the difficulties of a peasant trying to outsmart those who wanted to requisition his horses among other problems.

33. Simone Martin-Chauffier, *A bientôt quand même* (Paris: Calmann-Lévy, 1976), 210–211.

3. French Women under the Vichy Regime

1. Gustave Combes, *Lève-toi et marche: Les conditions du Français* (Toulouse: Privat, 1941), 63: an example of Vichy's view of the providential—and assuredly unrealistic, given the circumstances—mission of French womanhood.

2. Combes, 58–59.

3. Cited by Pierre Giolitto, *Histoire de la Jeunesse sous Vichy* (Paris: Perrin, 1991), 57.

4. Miranda Pollard, "Women and the National Revolution," in H. R. Kedward and Roger Austin, eds., *Vichy France and the Resistance* (London: Croom Helm, 1985), 38.

5. Ania Francos, *Il était des femmes dans la Resistance* (Paris: Stock, 1978), 122.

6. Francos, 123.

7. Hélène Eck, "French Women Under Vichy," in *A History of Women: Towards a Cultural Identity in the Twentieth Century*. Georges Duby and Michelle Perrot, gen. eds., Françoise Thébaud, ed. (Cambridge, MA: Belknap Press of Harvard University, 1994), vol. 5, 213–214.

8. Giolitto, 26.

9. Pollard in Kedward and Austin, 42.

10. Sarah Fishman, *We Will Wait: Wives of French Prisoners of War, 1940–1945* (New Haven: Yale University Press, 1991), 45.

11. Francos, 123.

12. Combes, 62.

13. Jacques Duquesne, *Les Catholiques françaises sous l'occupation* (Paris: Grasset, 1986), 313.

14. Eck, 211; Philippe Burrin, *La France à l'heure allemande 1940–1944* (Paris: Seuil, 1995), 291.

15. *Les Françaises à Ravensbrück* (Paris: Gallimard, 1965), 39.

16. Agnès Humbert, *Notre Guerre: Souvenirs de Résistance, Paris 1940–41* (Paris: Émile-Paul Frères, 1946), 102.

17. Fishman, 79.

18. Dominique Veillon, *La Mode sous l'occupation: Débrouillardise et coquetterie dans la France en guerre; (1939–1945)* (Paris: Payot, 1990). Quotes and material in this section are drawn from this excellent study.

19. Eck, 201, 215.

20. Hammel, Frédéric Chimon. *Souviens-toi d'Amalek: Témoignage sur la lutte des Juifs en France, 1938–1944* (Paris: CLKA, 1982), 51.

21. Veillon, 223.

22. Giolitto, 255.

23. *Les Françaises à Ravensbrück*, 38.

24. Karen Offen's review of Fishman, *American Historical Review*, April 1993, 512.

4. Organizing Resistance in France

1. Interview with Geneviève de Gaulle, May 24, 1983, and subsequent conversations and correspondence.

2. Unpaginated notes from Marie Granet archives.

3. Guylaine Guidez, *Femmes dans la guerre: 1939–1945* (Paris: Perrin, 1989), 262–263.

4. Conversation at the 1983 Sorbonne CNRS conference with Élisabeth de Miribel, de Gaulle's secretary, who typed the famed June 18, 1940, speech urging resistance (which was not recorded). See her autobiography, *La Liberté souffre violence* (Paris: Plon, 1981), 37.

5. Charles Tillon, *On chantait rouge* (Paris: Laffont, 1977), 324, 350.

6. Paxton, *Vichy France*, 293.

7. Stéphane Courtois, "Le Front National," in *La France des années noires*, vol. II, Jean-Pierre Azéma and François Bédarida, eds. (Paris: Seuil, 1993), 98.

8. Interview with Lise Lesèvre, June 8, 1983.

9. Recording of Simone Signoret at the Caen Memorial. See also her autobiography, *Nostalgia Isn't What It Used to Be* (New York: Harper and Row, 1978); French original, *La Nostalgie n'est plus ce qu'elle était* (Paris: Seuil, 1976). Signoret was a student of Lucie Aubrac.

10. Interview with Anise Postel-Vinay, July 1, 1983; Guidez, 201.

11. Marie-Louise Coudert, with Paul Hélène, *Elles: La Résistance* (Paris: Messidor, 1983), 134–139. Riffaud chose the pseudonym of Rainier, not only because it was a man's name but also because of the German poet, Rainer Maria Rilke. The eighteen-year-old midwifery student, "in love with life, boys, and poetry," wanted to show that she was fighting the Nazis, not the German people. She published her memoirs, *Madeleine Riffaud: On l'appelait Rainier* (Paris: Juillard, 1994) in conjunction with commemorations of the Liberation. She recounts "only what I saw; little things." Little things perhaps, but, as a reviewer noted, this is an exceptional document that portrays the psychology of Parisian youth who were not yet twenty when the Allies landed. Although at seventy she is almost blind, she sought to pay her debt of survival—once and for all. Captured and tortured for shooting a German officer, she was put on a train to be deported to the camps. Two women shoved her outside and saved her life: "Since they died and I did not, I always believed that they confided me with some sort of mission. I am not a veteran, essentially. This book is in some way an act of grace, of memory; an ex-voto." Florence Noiville, "La Femme-flamme," *Le Monde des Livres* (Friday, August 19, 1944).

12. "Le Dimanche pendant l'occupation," *Strasbourg Magazine* (no. 48, September 1994), 9. Women in Alsace and the other annexed zones helped

in the Resistance at great risk, for their region had been designated part of the greater Reich, not just occupied territory. The young men were forcibly conscripted into the German army, which created a tragic dilemma for these *malgré nous* (literally, in spite of ourselves).

13. Paul Berman, "The Other Side and the Almost the Same," *The New Yorker*, February 26, 1994, 62.

14. Henri Noguères, *La vie quotidienne des résistants: De l'armistice à la libération* (Paris: Hachette, 1984), 74.

15. Antoine Lefébure, *Les Conversations secrètes des Français sous l'Occupation* (Paris: Plon, 1993), 285.

16. Lefébure, 267–268.

17. Edwige de Saint-Wexel testimony from Marie Granet archives.

18. Interview with Janine Lévy, July 3, 1983.

19. Suzanne Bidault, *Souvenirs de guerre et d'occupation* (Paris: La Table Ronde, 1973), 238; Granet archives.

20. Granet, unpublished manuscript; also narrated in *Défense de la France* (Paris: PUF, 1960), chapter 3.

21. Lucie Aubrac, remarks at Suffolk University, October 14 and 15, 1992, and at Harvard University the following day.

22. Henri Michel, *Les Courants de pensée de la Résistance* (Paris: PUF, 1963), 162.

23. Granet, *Défense*, chapter 3.

24. Vercors interview, Radio France, 1989, no. 3. The so-called Otto List was set up in October 1940 and reedited several times. The thousand or so prewar titles included English translations—except for the classics—and books by Jewish authors, excluding scientific works. After April 1942, manuscripts had to be submitted for review prior to publication. *Liste Otto: The Official List of French Books Banned under the German Occupation, 1940.* Facsimile of the Harvard copy, with a preface by Natalie Zemon Davis. Cambridge, MA: Harvard College Library, 1992.

25. Robert Debré, *L'Honneur de vivre* (Paris: Stock, 1974), 236–237.

26. Marie Granet, unpublished manuscript; Lecture by Dorothy Kaufmann, Harvard Center for Literary Studies, May 9, 1991.

27. Helena Lewis, introduction to Elsa Triolet, *A Fine of Two Hundred Francs* (London: Virago Press, 1987), xii.

28. Interviews with Colette Audry, May 26, 1982, and March 7, 1984. See Lynn H. Nichols, *The Rape of Europa* (New York: Knopf, 1994), for an account of Louvre curator Rose Vallard, who kept careful records of German pillaging of French artworks—in spite of repeated efforts to stop her.

29. Interview with Anne-Marie Soucelier, June 17, 1983.

30. Elisabeth Terrenoire, *Combattantes sans uniforme: Les Françaises dans la Résistance* (Paris: Bloud and Gay, 1946), 71.

31. Dr. Geneviève Congy and Marie-Jo Chombart de Laüwe testimony, in the Marie Granet archives.

32. Nancy Wake, *The Autobiography of the Woman the Gestapo Called "The White Mouse"* (Melbourne: Macmillan of Australia, 1985), 191.

33. Madeleine Baudoin, *Histoire des Groupes Francs (MUR): Bouches du Rhône de septembre 1943 à la libération* (Paris: PUF, 1962), 71.

34. *A la Mémoire des Sévriennes: Mortes pour la France* (Sèvres, n.d.), 57–58; Institut Charles de Gaulle.

35. Henri Noguères, *La vie quotidienne*, 25. See also his summary in "Égalité et participation des femmes et des hommes dans la Résistance," *Les Femmes dans la Résistance: Actes du colloque tenu à l'initiative de l'Union des Femmes Françaises* (Monaco: Éditions du Rocher, 1977), 57.

36. Testimony of Huguette, at the Ivry Archives, n.p., n.d.

37. Gisèle Joannès, *Cahiers de l'Institut C.G.T. d'Histoire Sociale* "Le Mouvement syndical dans la Résistance," November 12, 1984, 31–33.

38. Laure Moulin, *Jean Moulin* (Paris: Presses de la Cité, 1969), 293–294.

39. Terrenoire, 11.

40. Despite two acquittals, Resistance colleagues believe him guilty, as the film *Hôtel Terminus* reveals. Hardy invited himself to a meeting on June 21, 1943, in a Lyon suburb—he had not been scheduled to attend—where Moulin and other Resistance leaders were arrested by Klaus Barbie and the Gestapo. The only one of the group not handcuffed, Hardy supposedly escaped under German fire.

41. Maria de Blasio Wilhelm, *The Other Italy: Italian Resistance in World War II* (New York: W.W. Norton, 1988), 119. Historian Marc Ferro notes that the Italian Resistance was one of the most effective and most violent. More Italians were killed fighting the Germans than fighting the Russians or the British. "A chaque pays ses maquis," *Voix et Visages*, no. 240, 1994. Those who read Italian should consult Claudio Pavone's lengthy and authoritative *Una guerra civile* (Turin: Boringhieri, 1992).

42. Wilhelm, 128–129. See the chapter on "Resistance" in Lucia Chiavola Birnbaum, *Liberazione della donna: Feminism in Italy* (Middletown, CT: Wesleyan University Press, 1986).

43. Interview with Hélène Ahrweiler, March 12, 1984.

44. Eleni Fourtouni, *Greek Women in Resistance* (New Haven, CT: Thelpini Press, 1986), 42. I am grateful to Barbara Kapp for calling this work to my attention.

45. Coudert, 18.

5. Resistance: A Family Affair

1. Interview with Lise Lesèvre, June 8, 1983.

2. Marie Granet, *Défense de la France: Histoire d'un mouvement de Résistance (1940–1941)* (Paris: PUF, 1960).

3. Marie Granet archives.

4. Interview with Geneviève de Gaulle, May 24, 1983.

5. Interviews with Gabrielle Ferrières, June 23, 1983, and April 6, 1986. For details on the Protestant Cévennes area that offered refuge to many Jews, see *Cévennes, terre de refuge*, texts and documents assembled by Philippe Joutard, Jacques Poujol, and Patrick Cabanel (Montpellier: Presses du Languedoc, 1987).

6. Interview with Lise Lesèvre.

6. *Young and Alone*

1. Célia Bertin, *Femmes sous l'Occupation* (Paris: Stock, 1993), 173.

2. Interviews with Denise Vernay, June 8, 1983, and April 16, 1986. See also *Les Femmes dans la Résistance* and Ania Francos, *Il était des femmes dans la Résistance* (Paris: Stock, 1978). Interview with Simone Veil, June 1978. See Veil's "Réflexions d'un témoin," *Annales*, May–June 1993. Veil notes that while Vernay, as a *résistante*, was frequently interviewed when she returned from deportation, Veil and her older sister were viewed as "victims." They were deported because they were Jewish. This distinction was brought up bluntly even in meetings of former *résistant* deportees. I am grateful to Stanley Hoffmann for calling her remarks to my attention.

3. Bertin, 341.

4. Testimony from an interview with Célia Bertin, April 13, 1987; subsequent correspondence, with additional details drawn from her book.

5. In her study, *Femmes dans la guerre: 1939–1945* (Paris: Perrin, 1989), Guylaine Guidez quotes Mireille Albrecht, who credits Danielle with surreptitiously snatching the first stencil of a clandestine newspaper, hiding it under her blouse, and taking it out to the chicken coop, where she destroyed it (p. 173). This is yet another instance where one finds discrepancies in testimony. The essential fact remains that a member of the Gouze family hid the stencil for a clandestine newspaper.

6. Interview with Danielle Mitterrand, June 16, 1992. See also Michel Picar and Julie Montagard, *Danielle Mitterrand: Portrait* (Paris: Éditions Ramsay, 1982).

7. Interviews with Annie Kriegel, June 21, 1983, and March 15, 1984. See also her autobiography, *Ce que j'ai cru comprendre* (Paris: Laffont, 1991).

8. Isabelle de Courtivron, *Clara Malraux, une femme dans le siècle* (Paris: Éditions de l'Olivier, 1992), chapter 12.

9. Interview with Evelyne Sullerot, June 14, 1983, and subsequent interviews and correspondence.

10. Interview with Catherine Roux, June 13, 1983.

7. *War Is a Man's Affair*

1. Paula L. Schwartz, "*Partisanes* and Gender Politics in Vichy France," *French Historical Studies* (16, no. 1, 1989), 126–150. Women wanting to bear arms were not the only ones who faced male prejudice. Anne-Marie Bauer

was sent to locate safe areas for arms drops in the Corrèze region of south-central France. She went on dangerous reconnaissance expeditions, bringing back detailed plans of suitable locations. Understandably, she looked forward to the first parachute drop of arms and munitions in the winter of 1943. Instead, she was told by her superior that women were forbidden at drop sites. Her brother, Étienne, went instead, carrying the flashlight she had purchased for her anticipated participation. Interview with Anne-Marie Bauer, June 6, 1983, and subsequent correspondence.

2. *Les Femmes dans la Résistance: Actes du colloque tenu à l'initiative de l'Union des Femmes Françaises* (Monaco: Éditions du Rocher, 1977), 245.

3. Testimony of Claude Gérard, January 31, 1950, from the personal archives of Marie Granet. Nicole Chatel, *Des femmes dans la Résistance* (Paris: Juilliard, 1972). Gérard kept her resistance name of Claude.

4. Raymonde Teyssier-Jore, *Le "Corps Féminin"* (Paris: France-Empire, 1975). Initially called the "Corps Féminin," the designation was changed to "Corps de Volontaires Français" in 1941. *Corps* means both a military unit and a body in French. The possible interpretation of "feminine body" provoked much humor.

5. Jeanne Bohec, *La Plastiqueuse à bicyclette* (Paris: Mercure de France, 1975). FFL women were domiciled in Moncorvo House in London. From these accounts, it appears that French women had difficulty adapting to community living. The large FFL contingent from Brittany formed its own group and gave public performances of Breton dances. Shelley Saywell, *Women in War* (Markham, Ont.: Penguin, 1985).

6. Bohec, "Une femme dans la guerre: Du 18 juin 1940 à la Libération," in *Les Femmes dans la Résistance*, 38.

7. Interview with Dr. Suzanne Vallon, April 12, 1986.

8. Interview with Sonia Vagliano-Eloy, July 2, 1985; see also her book, *Les Demoiselles de Gaulle, 1943–1945* (Paris: Plon, 1982).

9. Maria de Blasio Wilhelm, *The Other Italy: Italian Resistance in World War II* (New York: W. W. Norton, 1988), 130.

10. Fourtouni, 24–25.

8. Support Services: *Women's Eternal Vocation*

1. Isaac Pougatch, *Un Bâtisseur: Robert Gamzon* (Paris: FSJU, 1971), 77.

2. *Les Clandestins de Dieu: CIMADE 1939–1945* (Paris: Fayard, 1968), edited by Jeanne Merle d'Aubigné, Violette Mouchon, and Emile C. Fabre; André Jacques, *Madeleine Barot* (Paris: Éditions du Cerf, 1989); see also Zuccotti, 19: 309.

3. Unpublished testimony of Sabine Zlatin, February 4, 1947, from the Marie Granet archives. Zlatin has now published her memoirs, *Mémoires de la "Dame d'Izieu"* (Paris: Gallimard, 1992), focusing on Izieu. She does not recount the Resistance undertakings described in her 1947 deposition.

4. Testimony about Yvonne Baratte, Institut Charles de Gaulle, n.d.

Marie-Hélène Lefaucheux came from a family of industrialists. She also worked with the clandestine section of the French Red Cross and undertook liaison and secretarial work with OCM (Civil and Military Organization), the major movement in the occupied zone. When the social services of the Resistance were joined into a central organization, COSOR, Lefaucheux was named codirector with Father Chaillet. After the war, she became one of France's first women deputies. COSOR (Comité des Oeuvres Sociales de la Résistance; Committee for Resistance Social Work) was created in early 1944 by General de Gaulle's delegate, Alexander Parodi. Agnès Bidault, sister of CNR head Georges Bidault, was treasurer.

5. Madeleine Baudoin, *Histoire des Groupes Francs (MUR): Bouches-du-Rhône de septembre 1943 à la libération* (Paris: PUF, 1962), 98.

6. "Un pionnier: Berthie Albrecht," in *Les Femmes dans la Résistance: Actes du colloque tenu à l'initiative de l'Union des Femmes Françaises* (Monaco: Éditions du Rocher, 1977), 79.

7. Claude Bourdet, *L'Aventure incertaine* (Paris: Stock, 1975), 125.

8. Mireille Albrecht, *Berty* (Paris: Laffont, 1986), 187.

9. Henri Frenay, *La Nuit finira* (Paris: Laffont, 1973), 200.

10. Albrecht, *Berty*, 238.

11. This composite portrait is drawn from a number of sources, particularly her daughter's biography.

12. Renée Bédarida testimony, July 6, 1983. See also her books: *Les Armes de l'esprit: Témoignage Chrétien 1941–1944* (Paris: Éditions Ouvrières, 1977), and *Pierre Chaillet: Témoin de la résistance spirituelle* (Paris: Fayard, 1988).

13. Céline L'Hotte, *Et pendant six ans . . . .: Réalités du travail social* (Paris: Bloud and Gay, 1947), 9–10, 56.

14. Testimony of Odette Fabius, April 6, 1986. See also her autobiography, *Un Lever de soleil sur le Mecklembourg: Mémoires* (Paris: Albin Michel, 1986).

15. Adapted from Edwige Dumas, *Souvenirs de guerre: Calais 1940–45* (Paris: Apostolat des Éditions, 1978).

16. Jeanne Sivadon, director of the school, served as general secretary for Combat until she and others were betrayed by a double agent and arrested early in 1942. She spent two years in solitary confinement before being tried in Germany and sent to Ravensbrück. Sivadon was charged with "helping start a major Resistance movement that placed the army of Occupation in danger." Of her imprisonment, she said, "It was a great privilege, once in a lifetime, to be alone for such a long period of time, facing oneself. . . . It was a great joy not to know what was going on in France during those two years." Elisabeth Terrenoire, *Combattantes sans uniforme: Les Françaises dans la Résistance* (Paris: Bloud and Gay, 1946), 118–119.

17. Hélène Eck, "French Women Under Vichy," in *A History of Women: Towards a Cultural Identity in the Twentieth Century*. Georges Duby and Michelle Perrot, gen. eds., Françoise Thébaud, ed. (Cambridge, MA: Belknap Press of Harvard University, 1994), vol. 5, 205.

9. Dangerous Liaisons

1. Pierre Giolitto, *Histoire de la jeunesse sous Vichy* (Paris: Perrin, 1991), 294.

2. Henri Frenay, *La Nuit finira* (Paris: Robert Laffont, 1973), 287.

3. Henri Noguères, *La Vie quotidienne des résistants: De l'armistice à la libération* (Paris: Hachette, 1984), 24–25.

4. Brigitte Friang, *Regarde-toi qui meurs (1943–1945)* (Paris: Laffont, 1970; new ed., 1989), 202. Friang describes the BOA as a sort of Resistance travel agency. Agents met parachute drops from London as well as clandestine planes bringing weapons to be stored for D day or distributed to *maquis* units. Funds for full-time agents were dropped, as was mail.

5. Interview with Noëlle de Chambrun (their daughter), March 1991. Her mother *did* tell her children about her exceptional Resistance experience. This made life difficult for her daughter, to whom she gave her Resistance name of Noëlle. "My mother used to tell me about her work in the Resistance. Since she wanted to be taken seriously, she told me about everything. Descriptions of amputations had quite an impact on me. I said to myself, 'I'm not like that; I'm afraid; I would have talked if tortured. I wasn't up to that heroism.' "

6. Interview with Simone Colin Cahn, November 24, 1993.

7. Interview with Simone Debout, April 12, 1986.

8. Interview with Françoise de Boissieu, June 23, 1983.

9. Interview with Hélène Renal, July 8, 1983, and correspondence.

10. See chapter 8, note 17, for background on Sivadon.

11. Interview with Yvette Farnoux, April 15, 1986, and correspondence. Farnoux's successor in charge of social services in Lyon was Colette Henry-Amar, another of Marcel Peck's sisters. Colette Henry-Amar was helped in her work by many people, including a German police translator. He was introduced to her by the regular social worker at the prison. Although Henry-Amar was clandestine, the two worked together. This German officer agreed to find out whether Henry-Amar's "cousins" were in prison. When she gave him several names—on different occasions—he observed wryly that with so many "cousins" she must have come from a large family. He was anti-Nazi and showed her pictures of his family. The day he saw her under arrest, he paled. (Testimony of Colette Henry-Amar, April 26, 1986.)

10. Room and Board: Critical Concerns

1. Bruce Marshall, *The White Rabbit* (London: Pan Books, 1952), 59.

2. Interview with Marie-Louise Le Duc, April 13, 1986; *Télégramme de Brest et de l'Ouest*, October 5, 1944; correspondence with Yvonne Pétrement.

3. Robert Debré, *L'Honneur de vivre* (Paris: Stock, 1974).

4. Frédéric Chimon Hammel, *Souviens-toi d'Amalek: Témoignage sur la lutte des Juifs en France 1938–1944* (Paris: CLKA, 1982), 127.

5. Marie Granet manuscript, 19–20.

6. Granet, 25.

7. Granet, 22.

8. Interview with Anne-Marie Soucelier, June 23, 1983.

9. Interview with "Annette," May 20, 1986.

10. Interview with Ida Bourdet, July 9, 1983; interviews and correspondence with Claude Bourdet; see also his book, *L'Aventure incertaine* (Paris: Stock, 1975).

11. Simone Martin-Chauffier, *A bientôt quand même* (Paris: Calmann-Lévy, 1976).

12. Claude Bourdet, *L'Aventure incertaine*, 125.

13. Interview with Evelyne Sullerot, June 14, 1983.

14. Interview with Simone Lefranc-Lemoine, June 12, 1987; interview with Pierre Lefranc, June 27, 1985.

15. Interview with Anne-Marie Soucelier, previously cited.

16. Interview with Jeanne Chaton, April 15, 1986, and subsequent correspondence.

11. Choosing Roles

1. Marie Granet archives.

2. Mme Ferstenberg moved the supplies for the press in her son's baby carriage. Once, while she was pushing almost a hundred pounds of lead, the springs scraped the wheels, but the baby never woke. This and other details on the movement Franc-Tireur are included in Dominique Veillon's exemplary study, *Le Franc-Tireur* (Paris: Flammarion, 1977), 78.

3. As prefect at the beginning of the war, Moulin—even after German torture—refused to sign a false report accusing a contingent of French Senegalese troops of atrocities against the civilian population. In reality, it was the German troops who were guilty of the atrocities.

4. Interviews with France Pejot, June 1983 and June 1986.

5. Interviews with Lucie Aubrac and extensive correspondence. See also her book, *Ils partiront dans l'ivresse* (Paris: Seuil, 1984; my translations); English-language edition: *Outwitting the Gestapo* (Lincoln, NE: University of Nebraska Press, 1993).

6. Dominique Lacan, "Syndicalistes, résistantes: Des femmes contre le Nazisme," Ivry Archives, n.d., 28.

7. Ania Francos, *Il était des femmes dans la Résistance* (Paris: Stock, 1978), 40.

8. Francos, 239.

12. Collaboration

1. Philippe Burrin, *La France à l'heure allemande 1940–1944* (Paris: Seuil, 1995), 438.

2. As stressed in chapter 2, obtaining food was the major preoccupation of French women during the Occupation.

3. Incident recounted in the Marie Granet archives. An example of a woman who supported the Germans for ideological reasons is pianist Lucienne Delforge, who wrote for several collaborationist periodicals. "As a woman, as a mother, and as an artist," she spoke out in all the campaigns the collaborationist press mounted against Allied bombings (Ory, p. 204). Again, it is difficult to assess the number of collaborators—which tends to vary with the vantage point of the observer. Ted Morgan (An Uncertain Hour) holds that active collaborators—the men of Vichy, the cliques in Paris, and the business community (although there were anti-Germans in all these groups)—comprised about 10 percent of the population, while the Resistance represented a smaller number.

4. H. Roderick Kedward, Occupied France: Collaboration and Resistance 1940–1944 (London: Blackwell, 1985), 41–43.

5. In the fall of 1940, the Gestapo had only a hundred men in France. Even after the Germans occupied the entire country, Gestapo forces never exceeded several thousand. By extending their influence, and, above all, by bringing in French criminal elements and Nazi sympathizers, the Germans were able to greatly extend their reach. See Jacques Delarue, "Les Polices allemandes en France pendant l'occupation" (Voix et Visages, March–April 1991, no. 224).

6. Gerhard Hirschfeld and Patrick Marsh, eds., Collaboration in France: Politics and Culture During the Nazi Era 1940–1944 (New York: St. Martin's, 1989), 14.

7. David Pryce-Jones, Paris in the Third Reich (New York: Holt, Rinehart and Winston, 1981); Burrin, 438. Henri Michel, Paris allemand (Paris: Albin Michel, 1981), details the close daily cooperation of French and German technical services in the administrations. This cooperation allowed the capital to continue to function.

8. A. Philips, Renaissances (Algiers, nos. 3 and 4, 1944), quoted in Courants, 170. After the war, some firms, such as the Renault car company, were nationalized because of their record of collaboration. See also the chapter "Les Capitaines d'industrie," in Burrin.

9. Jean-Paul Azéma and François Bédarida, eds., Les Années noires (Paris: Seuil, 1993).

10. Lesèvre interview. See also her book, Face à Barbie (Paris: Nouvelles Éditions du Pavillon, 1987).

11. Tony Judt, Past Imperfect: French Intellectuals 1944–56 (Berkeley: University of California Press, 1992), 49–50. He quotes from Jean-Paul Sartre's "Qu'est-ce qu'un collaborateur?" Situations, vol. 3 (Paris: Gallimard, 1949).

12. André Halimi, La Délation sous l'occupation (Paris: Alain Moreau, 1983), and Antoine Lefébure, Les Conversations secrètes des Français sous

l'Occupation (Paris: Plon, 1993). I am grateful to Robert Paxton for calling my attention to the Halimi book.

13. David Rousset, *Le Pitre ne rit pas* (Paris: Éditions du Pavois, 1948), 39. Quoted in Peter Novick, *The Resistance versus Vichy: the Purge of Collaborators in Liberated France* (New York: Columbia University Press, 1968), 31.

14. Françoise Verny, *Le plus beau métier du monde* (Paris: Olivier Orban, 1990), 24–25.

15. Interview with Hélène Parmelin, March 11, 1984.

16. Deirdre Bair, *Simone de Beauvoir* (New York: Summit, 1990), 260.

17. Jean Paulhan, *Lettre aux directeurs de la Résistance* (Paris: Éditions de Minuit, 1951), 34 ff.

18. Ted Morgan, *An Uncertain Hour* (London: Bodley Head, 1990), 102 (my translation).

19. In Peter Novick's view, collaboration increased as the Germans were losing, a paradoxical situation: "Moralists have sometimes pictured the evolution of Vichy as a classic case of the spiral staircase leading to hell. Concessions led inevitably to greater concessions; the first compromise of principle was the thin edge of the wedge, which made the next much easier, and the next easier still. . . . The picture is not totally false." *The Resistance versus Vichy: The Purge of Collaborators in Liberated France* (London: Chatto & Windus, 1968), 12. Antony Beevor and Artemis Cooper hold that while the purge was initially ferocious, it did not go far enough: *After the Liberation: 1944–1949* (New York: Doubleday, 1994). See also Burrin, 467.

20. H. R. Kedward and Roger Austin, eds., *Vichy France and the Resistance: Culture and Ideology* (London: Croom Helm, 1985), 21; also discussed in the Marie Granet manuscript.

21. Bonnard was an Academician with a penchant for blond German soldiers who tried to use the schools for propaganda purposes; his appointment was widely criticized.

22. Amouroux, *Vie quotidienne*, 561–562; Granet, *Défense*, 45; and Marie Granet archives.

23. Guylaine Guidez, *Femmes dans la guerre: 1939–1945*, 48.

24. Debré, 124.

25. Jacques Delarue, "La Bande Bonny-Lafont," *L'Histoire*, no. 80, 1985.

26. Corinne Luchaire, *Ma drôle de vie* (Paris: SUN, 1949), 140–142. Luchaire's character is further revealed in her liaisons. She took much pleasure in the attention of Count Ciano, Italy's minister of foreign affairs and Mussolini's son-in-law—"the most powerful and popular man in Italy." This was in April 1940. She claims here, as in other circumstances, that while dating him she found herself involved in "things I did not understand." Simply because she dined with this or that political figure or was received in this or that home, she was later to be faulted. "No doubt it was my destiny to be involved in major international events without understanding them." So she simply let herself "be cradled in that pleasurable atmosphere" (p. 114).

27. Burrin, 211. Guylaine Guidez maintains that since there were not

enough French women to supply the sexual needs of German soldiers, coercive ways were found to recruit women. Ration cards were taken, families were threatened, and other reprehensible means were used to force women to become prostitutes for the Germans—as the Japanese forced captive women to cater to the sexual needs of their troops. However, her reference to "this taboo subject" appears to apply to Norway, Holland, Luxembourg, and Belgium, not France; *Femmes dans la guerre*, 49.

28. Fabienne Jamais called her book simply *One Two Two*, after her brothel's well-known address: 122, rue de Provence; quoted in David Pryce-Jones, 28.

29. According to German reports, there were eighty thousand to a hundred thousand unregistered prostitutes in Paris because of the hardships of the times. The authorities viewed them with alarm as the principal source of infection. Franz Seidler, *Prostitution, Homosexualität, Selberverstümmelung. Probleme der deutschen Sanitätsführung 1939–1945* (Neckargemünd: Vowinkel Verlag, 1977), 145, 171; quoted in Burrin, 211. A 1942 prefect's report from the Aisne department (northeast of Paris) noted that prostitutes were under surveillance in cafés and other public places. Prostitution was actively regulated by French authorities. Many prostitutes were summoned and subjected to medical exams. Some were released after medical treatment but required to report regularly for checkups (AN F IC III 1135).

30. Morgan, 112.

31. Anne-Marguerite Dumilieu, *Moi, une cobaye* (Paris: SEFA, 1975), 70–71.

32. Jacques-Augustin Bailly. *La Libération confisquée: Languedoc 1944–1945* (Paris: Albin Michel, 1993), 159.

33. Margaret Randolph Higonnet, Jane Jenson, Sonya Michel, and Margaret Collins Weitz, eds., *Behind the Lines: Gender and the Two World Wars* (New Haven, CT: Yale University Press, 1987), 11.

34. Marie Gatard, *La Guerre, mon père* (Paris: Seuil, 1978), 135.

35. Peter Novick, *The Resistance versus Vichy: The Purge of Collaborators in Liberated France* (London: Chatto & Windus, 1968), 68.

36. Bertin, 103.

37. "I enjoyed two pleasant weeks in Vichy. I usually spent part of the evening in the Hôtel des Ambassadeurs, my hair tousled, kicking off my shoes and rolling up in a ball in one of the big leather chairs." One evening, the barman told her that some American reporters living in the hotel had nicknamed her "the Cat" because of her behavior. A former lover also used to call her "*ma petite chatte.*" This was the origin of her pseudonym, "the Cat."

38. Quotations from Mathilde-Lily Carré's *I Was the Cat: The Truth about the Most Remarkable Woman Spy since Mata-Hari, by Herself* (London: Souvenir Press, 1960), 49, 62–65, 87, 89, 95, 114, 129. French edition: *J'étais la chatte* (Paris: Morgan, 1959). Additional details from Gordon Young, *The Cat with Two Faces* (New York: Coward-McCann, 1957).

39. An editorial in the PCF paper for the Grenoble region demanded:

"Suppress pictures of those abominable shrews with their heads shaved . . . and give us front-page pictures of women who fought for France; give us the beloved image of our comrade Danielle Casanova, president of the Union des Jeunes Filles de France, who died in the depths of Nazi Germany because she represented all that is pure, youthful, and vibrant in French women." Alain Brossat, *Les Tondues: Un Carnaval moche* (Paris: Manya, 1992), 86.

40. "In the Looking Glass: Sorrow and Pity?" in Stanley Hoffmann, *Decline or Renewal? France since the 1930s* (New York: Viking, 1974), 58.

13. Conclusion: Women and the Legacy of the Resistance

1. Published by "Le Front National pour la liberté et l'indépendance de la France" (private collection).

2. Marie-Louise Coudert, with Paul Hélène, *Elles: La Résistance* (Paris: Messidor, 1983), 119.

3. Margaret L. Rossiter, *Women in the Resistance* (New York: Praeger, 1986), 128; interviews with Marie-Madeleine Fourcade, previously cited.

4. Marie Granet, *Ceux de la Résistance*, 122. Thefts were not restricted to the young. Temptation sometimes proved too much for other supposed patriots. From a key censorship position within Vichy, Suzanne Bertillon organized and led a network for the American OSS. In the beginning, she had to do most of the courier work herself. Eventually, though, she engaged full-time paid agents, although she herself refused any pay. One courier removed money before forwarding materiel to her, even though he was well paid. Two agents in the chain that reached to Barcelona kept asking for more money. Another sold intelligence to other Allies. Rossiter, 134.

5. Letter from Janine Lévy, October 10, 1986.

6. Interview with Rita Thalmann, June 30, 1985.

7. Interviews with Marie-Madeleine Fourcade and Germaine Tillion, previously cited.

8. Hélène Eck, "French Women Under Vichy," 203. Marie Louise Roberts's insightful *Civilization Without Sexes: Reconstructing Gender in Postwar France, 1917–1927*, published in 1994 (University of Chicago Press), helps fill in this needed examination of the interwar years.

9. Brigitte Friang, *Regarde-toi qui meurs* (Paris: Laffont, 1970), 37–38.

10. Testimony of "Mounette" in Ania Francos, *Il était des femmes dans la Résistance* (Paris: Stock, 1978), 452.

11. Lucie Aubrac interviews cited earlier, and her remarks at the 1992 "Women in the French Resistance" conference.

12. Interview with Françoise de Boissieu, June 23, 1983.

13. André Malraux, *Antimémoires* (Paris: Gallimard, 1975), 592–593.

14. Anne-Marie Soucelier testimony, June 17, 1983.

15. Interview with Germaine Tillion; see also Francos, 459.

16. Paulette Descomps testimony, in Francos, 133.

17. Eck, 222, 206.

18. Interviews with Annie Kriegel, previously cited.

19. See Margaret Collins Weitz, "As I Was Then: Women in the French Resistance," *Contemporary French Civilization*, vol. 10, no. 1, 1985. Margaret Rossiter, on the other hand, holds that Resistance participation was a major factor in getting the vote: *Women in the Resistance*, 222.

20. Douglas Johnson, *France*, 73, quoted in Arthur Marwick, *War and Social Change in the Twentieth Century* (London: Macmillan, 1974). Marwick concurs, 196–203. For details on the Constituent Assemblies, see Gordon Wright, *The Reshaping of French Democracy* (Boston: Beacon Press, 1948), chapters 5 and 6. Election figures cited are from Marwick. See also Mariette Sineau, *Des Femmes en politique* (Paris: Economica, 1988). Janine Mossuz-Lavau, "La Vote des Françaises dans les années quatre-vingt-dix," in *French Politics and Society*, vol. 12, no. 4, fall 1994; Jane Jenson and Mariette Sineau, *François Mitterrand et les Françaises: Un rendez-vous manqué* (Paris: Presses de la FNSP, 1995); and Christine Bard, *Les Filles de Marianne* (Paris: Fayard, 1995).

21. Wieviorka, Olivier. *Nous entrerons dans la carrière: De la Résistance à l'exercise du pouvoir* (Paris: Seuil, 1994).

Bibliography

Archives

Archives Nationales (AN)
Bibliothèque de Documentation Internationale Contemporaine, Nanterre (BDIC)
Bibliothèque Marguerite Durand (MD)
Centre de Documentation Juive Contemporaine (CDJC)
Conseil d'État, Judicial Archives
L'Institut de l'Histoire du Temps Présent (IHTP)
L'Institut Charles de Gaulle
Le Mémorial, Caen
Archives for the Musée de la Résistance, Ivry (later Musée de la Résistance Nationale, Champigny)

Interviews/Discussions

Ahrweiler, Hélène
Altman, Micheline Eude
d'Astier (de la Vigerie)-Bennett, Mme
Aubrac, Lucie
Audry, Colette
Bauer, Anne-Marie
Bédarida, François
Bédarida, Renée
Bertin, Célia
Boissieu, Françoise de
Bonnavita, Andrée
Bourdet, Claude
Bourdet, Ida
Bruneau, Jean
Cahn, Simone Colin
Capitant, Mme René
Chambrun, Noëlle de
Chaton, Jeanne
Cobb, Richard
Collin, Jean-Loup
Courvoisier, André

Debout, Simone
de Gaulle, Geneviève Anthonioz
Desanti, Dominique
Fabius, Odette
Farnoux, Yvette (Barnard)
Ferrières, Gabrielle Cavaillès
Fourcade, Marie-Madeleine
Garnier, Evelyne
Granet, Marie
Guezennec, Lucienne
Henry-Amar, Colette
Hermann-Gonard, Cécile
Juresco, Pierre
Kaan, Marie
Kriegel, Annie
Le Duc, Marie-Louise
Lefranc, Pierre
Lefranc-Lemoine, Simone
Le Prévost, Georgette
Lesèvre, Lise
Lévy, Janine
L'Herminier, Jeanine

Lipkowski, Irene de
Malraux, Madeleine
Mayer, Jeanne
Mella, Jacqueline
Mitterrand, Danielle
Morin, Violette
Parmelin, Hélène
Pejot, France
Perrot, Michelle
Pétrement, Yvonne
Postel-Vinay, Anise
Rameil, Jacqueline
Renal, Hélène
Renty, Christiane de
Rossi-Brochay, Pierrette
Rougier-Lecoq, Violette

Roux, Catherine
Rovan, Joseph
Saint-Saëns, Madeleine
Saulnié, Yseult
Soucelier, Anne-Marie
Sullerot, Evelyne
Thalmann, Rita
Tillion, Germaine
Tollet, André
Trempé, Rolande
Vallon, Suzanne
Vagliano-Eloy, Sonia
Vernay, Denise
Vey, Marie-Emilie
Wormser-Migot, Olga

Unpublished Documents

"Le Rôle des femmes dans la Résistance," manuscript by Marie Granet on reserve at the Archives Nationales (copy sent by Marie Granet to the author)

Personal archives of Marie Granet, including many depositions (sent to the author)

Prefects' Reports and Bluet Files at the Archives Nationales

Depositions at:
Archives Nationales
Centre de Documentation Juive Contemporaine
Institut Charles de Gaulle
Institut de l'Histoire du Temps Présent
Archives of the Musée de la Résistance, Ivry

Audoul, France, "Ravensbrück: 150,000 femmes en enfer," thirty-two sketches and portraits done at the camp in 1944–1945, plus some texts, privately printed, n.p., n.d.

"Les Echos de la mémoire," papers from the 1990 conference at the Sorbonne organized by La Ligne and the Secretariat for Veterans and Victims of War

"La Résistance et la renaissance française," mimeograph report from the French Press and Information Service, New York City, 1944

Rioux, Elisabeth, *La Guerre sans armes*, privately printed, n.p., n.d., 64 pp.

Schwartz, Paula L. "Precedents for Politics: Prewar Action in Women of the French Resistance," Master's thesis, Columbia University, New York, 1981

Texts from the Médaillés de la Résistance (courtesy Violette Rougier-Lecoq)

SEPT (Société d'Éditions et Programmes de Télévision) and INA (Institut National de l'Audiovisuel), "Les Femmes et la Guerre." Five one-hour programs with the testimony of twenty-five French women and an equal number of European women
Radio-France series of five audio cassettes, "Les Premiers résistants," 1989

Books

France Under German Occupation 1940–1944, an annotated bibliography compiled by Donna Evleth (Westport, CT: Greenwood, 1991), is a useful working tool. As indicated in chapter 1, however, the number of books published on this period both in France and elsewhere continues to increase. It is difficult to keep current. At the time this work was published, it contained only about half the titles I had used.

Ajchenbaum, Yves-Marc. A la vie/à la mort: Histoire du journal "Combat" 1941–1974. Paris: Le Monde-Éditions 1994.

Albrecht, Mireille. Berty. Paris: Robert Laffont, 1986.

Amouroux, Henri. Quarante Millions de Pétainistes. Vol. II of La Grande Histoire des Français sous l'occupation. Paris: Laffont, 1977.

———. La Vie des Français sous l'occupation. Paris: Fayard, 1961.

Aron, Robert. Histoire de Vichy. Paris: Arthème Fayard, 1954. English edition: The Vichy Regime. London: Pantheon, 1958.

Atack, Margaret. Literature and the French Resistance—Cultural Politics and Narrative Forms, 1940–1950. Manchester, U.K.: University of Manchester Press, 1989.

d'Aubigné, Jeanne Merle and Violette Mouchon. CIMADE 1939–1945. Paris: Fayard, 1968.

Aubrac, Lucie. Ils partiront dans l'ivresse. Paris: Seuil, 1984. English edition: Outwitting the Gestapo. Lincoln, NE: University of Nebraska Press, 1993; Introduction by Margaret Collins Weitz.

Azéma, Jean-Pierre. 1940: L'Année terrible. Paris: Seuil, 1990.

———. La Collaboration (1940–1944). Paris: PUF, 1975.

———. De Munich à la Libération. Paris: Seuil, 1979. English edition: From Munich to the Liberation. New York: Cambridge University Press, 1984.

———, and François Bédarida, eds. La France des années noires, 2 vols. Paris: Seuil, 1993.

———, and François Bédarida, eds. Vichy et les Français. Paris: Fayard, 1992 (papers from the 1990 conference).

Bair, Deirdre. Simone de Beauvoir. New York: Summit, 1990.

Baudoin, Madeleine. Histoire des Groupes Francs (MUR): Bouches-du-Rhône de septembre 1943 à la libération. Paris: PUF, 1962.

Beauvoir, Simone de. La force de l'âge. Paris: Gallimard, 1960. English edition: The Prime of Life. New York: Harper and Row, 1976.

Bédarida, Renée. *Les Armes de l'esprit: Témoignage Chrétien 1941–1944*. Paris: Éditions Ouvrières, 1977.

———. *Pierre Chaillet: Témoin de la résistance spirituelle*. Paris: Fayard, 1988.

Bellanger, Claude. *Presse clandestine 1940–1944*. Paris: Armand Colin, 1961.

Bertin, Célia. *Femmes sous l'Occupation*. Paris: Stock, 1993.

Bertrand, Simone. *Mille Visages, un seul combat*. Paris: Les Éditeurs Français Réunis, 1965.

Bessière, André. *L'Engrenage*. Paris: Buchet/Chastel, 1991.

Bidault, Suzanne. *Souvenirs de guerre et d'occupation*. Paris: La Table Ronde, 1973.

Bloch, Marc. *L'Étrange Défaite: Témoignage écrit en 1940*. Paris: Éditions du Franc-Tireur, 1946. English edition: *Strange Defeat*. New York: W.W. Norton, 1968.

Bohec, Jeanne. *La Plastiqueuse à bicyclette*. Paris: Mercure de France, 1975.

Bood, Micheline. *Les années doubles: Journal d'une lycéenne sous l'occupation*. Paris: Laffont, 1974.

Bourdet, Claude. *L'Aventure incertaine*. Paris: Stock, 1975.

Bourdrel, Philippe. *Épuration sauvage*. Paris: Perrin, 1991.

Brossat, Alain. *Les Tondues: Un Carnaval moche*. Paris: Manya, 1992.

Burrin, Philippe. *La France à l'heure allemande 1940–1944*. Paris: Seuil, 1995.

Carré, Mathilde-Lily. *J'étais la chatte*. Paris: Morgan, 1959. English edition: *I Was the Cat: The Truth about the Most Remarkable Woman Spy since Mata-Hari, by Herself*. London: Souvenir Press, 1960.

Chamming's, Marie ("Marie-Claire"). *J'ai choisi la tempête*. Paris: Éditions France-Empire, 1965.

Chatel, Nicole. *Des femmes dans la Résistance*. Preface by Jean Cassou. Paris: Juilliard, 1972.

Chevrillon, Claire. *Code Name Christiane Clouet: A Woman in the French Resistance*. College Station: Texas A & M University Press, 1995.

Cobb, Richard. *French and Germans, Germans and French: A Personal Interpretation of France and Two Occupations, 1914–1918/1940–1944*. Hanover, NH: University Press of New England, 1983.

Combats dans l'ombre. Villeurbanne, France: Consortium d'Impression, n.d.

Combe, Sonia. *Archives interdites: Les Peurs françaises face à l'histoire contemporaine*. Paris: Albin Michel, 1994.

Combes, Gustave. *Lève-toi et marche: Les conditions du Français*. Toulouse: Privat, 1941.

Corbin, Alain. *Les Filles de noces: Misère sexuelle et prostitution aux 19e et 20e siècles*. Paris: Aubier, 1978; *Women for Hire: Prostitution and Sexuality in France after 1850*. Cambridge, MA: Harvard University Press.

Cormier, Manon. *Une Bordelaise martyre de la Résistance*. Bordeaux: Pechade, n.d.

Cotta, Michèle. *La collaboration, 1940–1944*. Paris: Armand Colin, 1964.

Coudert, Marie-Louise, with Paul Hélène. *Elles: La Résistance*. Paris: Messidor, 1983.

Courtivron, Isabelle de. *Clara Malraux, une femme dans le siècle*. Paris: Éditions de l'Olivier, 1992.

Crémieux-Brilhac, Jean-Louis, ed. *Les Voix de la liberté (1940–1944)*. 5 vols. Paris: Documentation Française, 1975.

——. *Les Français de l'an 40*. 2 vols. Paris: Gallimard, 1990.

Debré, Robert. *L'Honneur de vivre*. Paris: Stock, 1974.

Defrasne, Jean. *L'Occupation allemande en France*. Paris: PUF, 1985.

Delarue, Jacques. *Trafics et crimes sous l'Occupation*. Paris: Fayard, 1968.

——. *Histoire de la Gestapo*. Paris: Fayard, 1962. English edition: *The History of the Gestapo*. London: Macdonald, 1964.

Delbo, Charlotte. *Le convoi du 24 janvier*. Paris: Éditions de Minuit, 1965.

Deroy, Jacqueline. *Celles qui attendaient témoignent aujourd'hui*. Paris: Association Nationale pour les Rassemblements et Pèlerinages des Anciens Prisonniers de Guerre, 1985.

Diamant, David. *250 combattants de la Résistance témoignent*. Paris: L'Harmattan, 1991.

Duboscq, Geneviève. *Bye-bye Geneviève*. Paris: Laffont, 1978.

Dufournier, Denise. *Ravensbrück*. London: Allen & Unwin, 1948. French edition: *La Maison des mortes*. Paris: Hachette, 1945.

Dumas, Edwige. *Souvenirs de guerre: Calais 1940–45*. Paris: Apostolat des Éditions, 1978.

Dumilieu, Anne-Marguerite (pseud. Capitaine Simone). *Moi, une cobaye*. Paris: SEFA, 1975.

Duquesne, Jacques. *Les Catholiques françaises sous l'occupation*. Paris: Grasset, 1986.

Durand, Yves. *Vichy 40–44*. Paris: Bordas, 1972.

Duroselle, Jean-Baptiste. *L'Abîme 1939–1945*. Paris: Imprimerie Nationale, 1982 (2nd ed., 1986).

Les Enseignants: La lutte syndicale du front populaire à la libération. Paris: Éditions Sociales, 1973.

Fabius, Odette. *Un Lever de soleil sur le Mecklenbourg: Mémoires*. Paris: Albin Michel, 1986.

Fabre, Emile C. et al., eds. *Les Clandestins de Dieu: CIMADE 1939–1945*. Paris: Fayard, 1968.

Les Femmes dans la Résistance: Actes du colloque tenu à l'initiative de l'Union des Femmes Françaises. Monaco: Éditions du Rocher, 1977.

Fishman, Sarah. *We Will Wait: Wives of French Prisoners of War, 1940–1945*. New Haven, CT: Yale University Press, 1991.

Fontaine, Marguerite. *Journal de guerre*. Paris: La Manufacture, 1984.

Foot, M. R. D. *S. O. E. in France*. London: Her Majesty's Stationery Office, 1968.

Fourcade, Marie-Madeleine. *L'arche de Noé*. Paris: Fayard, 1968. English edition: *Noah's Ark*. London: Allen & Unwin, 1973.

Fourcaut, Annie. *Femmes à l'usine dans l'entre-deux-guerres*. Paris: François Maspero, 1982.

Fourtouni, Eleni. *Greek Women in Resistance*. New Haven, CT: Thelpini Press, 1986.

Les Françaises à Ravensbrück. Paris: Gallimard, 1965.

Francos, Ania. *Il était des femmes dans la Résistance*. Paris: Stock, 1978.

Frenay, Henri. *La Nuit finira*. Paris: Robert Laffont, 1973. English edition: *Night Will End*. New York: McGraw-Hill, 1975.

―――. *Volontaires de la Nuit*. Paris: Laffont/Opera Mundi, 1975.

Friang, Brigitte. *Regarde-toi qui meurs (1943–1945)*. Paris: Laffont, 1970 (new ed., 1989).

Friedlander, Saul. *Quand vient le souvenir. . . .* Paris: Seuil, 1978. English edition: *When Memory Comes*. New York: Farrar, Straus & Giroux, 1979.

Fussell, Paul. *The Great War and Modern Memory*. New York and London: Oxford University Press, 1975.

Gatard, Marie. *La Guerre, mon père*. Paris: Seuil, 1978.

Giolitto, Pierre. *Histoire de la jeunesse sous Vichy*. Paris: Perrin, 1991.

Gordon, Bertram. *Collaborationism in France during the Second World War*. Ithaca, NY: Cornell University Press, 1980.

Granet, Marie. *Ceux de la Résistance (1940–1944)*. Paris: Éditions de Minuit, 1964.

―――. *Cohors-Asturies: Histoire d'un réseau de Résistance*. Bordeaux: Cahiers de la Résistance, 1974.

―――. *Défense de la France: Histoire d'un mouvement de Résistance (1940–1941)*. Paris: PUF, 1960.

―――. *Les Jeunes dans la Résistance: 20 ans en 1940*. Paris: France-Empire, 1985.

Grynberg, Anne. *Camps de la honte: Les internés juifs français, 1939–1944*. La Découverte, 1991.

Guéhenno, Annie. *L'Épreuve*. Paris: Grasset, 1968.

Guidez, Guylaine. *Femmes dans la guerre: 1939–1945*. Paris: Perrin, 1989.

Halimi, André. *La Délation sous l'occupation*. Paris: Alain Moreau, 1983.

Hallie, Philippe. *Lest Innocent Blood Be Shed*. New York: Harper and Row, 1979.

Halls, W. D. *The Youth of Vichy France*. New York: Oxford University Press, 1981.

Hammel, Frédéric Chimon. *Souviens-toi d'Amalek: Témoignage sur la lutte des Juifs en France 1938–1944*. Paris: CLKA, 1982.

Hennequin, Gilles. *Résistance en Côte-d'Or*. Bretigny: Union Typographique de Domois, 1981.

Higonnet, Margaret Randolph, Jane Jenson, Sonya Michel, and Margaret Collins Weitz, eds. *Behind the Lines: Gender and the Two World Wars*. New Haven, CT: Yale University Press, 1987.

Hirschfeld, Gerhard, and Patrick Marsh, eds. *Collaboration in France: Politics and Culture during the Nazi Occupation, 1940–1944*. Oxford, U.K.: Oxford University Press, 1989.

Histoire orale et histoire des femmes. Paris: IHTP, 1982.

Histoire et temps présent: Journées d'études des correspondants départmentaux 28–29 novembre 1980. Comité d'Histoire de la Seconde Guerre Mondiale and Institut d'Histoire du Temps Présent. Paris: CNRS, 1981.

Hoffmann, Stanley. *Decline or Renewal? France since the 1930s*. New York: Viking, 1974.

————, et al., eds. *In Search of France*. Cambridge, MA: Harvard University Press, 1963.

Jacques, André. *Madeleine Barot*. Paris: Éditions du Cerf, 1989.

Jäckel, Eberhard. *La France dans l'Europe de Hitler*. Paris: Fayard, 1968.

Jeannin-Garreau, Éliane. *Ombre parmi les ombres: Chronique d'une Résistance 1941–1945*. Issy-les-Moulineaux: Muller, 1991.

Jenson, Jane and Mariette Sineau. *François Mitterrand et les Françaises: Un rendez-vous manqué*. Paris: Presses de la FNSP, 1995.

Josephs, Jeremy. *Swastika Over Paris*. New York: Arcade Publishing, 1989.

Judt, Tony. *Past Imperfect*. Berkeley, CA: U. of California Press, 1992.

Kedward, H. Roderick. *In Search of the Maquis*. Oxford: Clarendon Press, 1993.

————. *Occupied France: Collaboration and Resistance 1940–1944*. London: Blackwell, 1985.

————. *Resistance in Vichy France*. Oxford: Oxford University Press, 1978.

————, and Roger Austin, eds. *Vichy France and the Resistance: Culture and Ideology*. London: Croom Helm, 1985.

Knibiehler, Yvonne. *Nous, les assistantes sociales. Naissance d'une profession*. Paris: Aubier-Montaigne, 1980.

Knight, Frida. *The French Resistance, 1940–1944*. London: Lawrence Wishert, 1975.

Koonz, Claudia. *Mothers in the Fatherland*. New York: St. Martin's, 1987.

Kriegel, Annie. *Ce que j'ai cru comprendre*. Paris: Laffont, 1991.

————. *Réflexions sur les questions juives*. Paris: Hachette, 1984.

Labarèthe, Henri du Moulin de. *Le Temps des illusions: Souvenirs juillet 1940–avril 1942*. Geneva, Switzerland: Éditions du Cheval Ailé, 1946.

Laborie, Pierre. *L'Opinion française sous Vichy*. Paris: Seuil, 1990.

Laska, Vera, ed. *Women in the Resistance and in the Holocaust: The Voices of Eyewitnesses*. Westport, CT: Greenwood, 1983.

————, ed. *Resistance and Holocaust in World War II*. Metuchen, NJ: Scarecrow Press, 1985.

Latour, Annie. *La Résistance juive en France*. Paris: CDJC, 1947.

Lazard, Lucien. *La Résistance juive en France*. Paris: Stock, 1987. English edition: *The Jewish Resistance in France*. New York: Schocken, 1981.

Lefébure, Antoine. *Les Conversations secrètes des Français sous l'Occupation*. Paris: Plon, 1993.

Lesèvre, Lise. *Face à Barbie*. Paris: Nouvelles Éditions du Pavillon, 1987.

Lévy, Claude, and Paul Tillard. *Betrayal at the Vel' d'Hiv*. New York: Hill and Wang, 1969. French edition: *La grande rafle du Vel' d'Hiv*. Paris: Laffont, 1967.

L'Hotte, Céline. *Et pendant six ans . . . .: Réalités du travail social*. Paris: Bloud and Gay, 1947.

Lottman, Herbert. *The Left Bank*. London: Heinemann, 1982.

———. *The Purge*. New York: Wm. Morrow, 1986.

Luchaire, Corinne. *Ma drôle de vie*. Paris: SUN, 1949.

Luizard, Pierre. *La Guerre n'était pas leur métier*. Paris: Éditeurs Français Réunis, 1974.

McMillan, James F. *Housewife or Harlot: The Place of Women in French Society 1870–1940*. London: Edward Arnold, 1981.

Malraux, André. *Antimémoires*. Paris: Gallimard, 1967.

Marrus, Michael, and Robert Paxton. *Vichy France and the Jews*. New York: Basic Books, 1981. The French edition—*Vichy et les Juifs* (Paris: Calmann-Lévy, 1981)—has an appendix listing Vichy's anti-Semitic legislation.

Marshall, Bruce. *The White Rabbit*. London: Evans, 1952.

Martin-Chauffier, Simone. *A bientôt quand même*. Paris: Calmann-Lévy, 1976.

Marwick, Arthur. *War and Social Change in the Twentieth Century*. London: Macmillan, 1974.

Mayer, Daniel. *Les Socialistes dans la Résistance: Souvenirs et documents*. Paris: PUF, 1968.

Michel, Henri. *Les Courants de pensée de la Résistance*. Paris: PUF, 1962.

———. *La Guerre de l'ombre*. Paris: Grasset, 1970. English edition: *The Shadow War: European Resistance 1939–1945*. London: Deutsch, 1972.

———. *Histoire de la Résistance en France*. Paris: PUF, 1962.

———. *Paris allemand*. Paris: Albin Michel, 1981.

Miller, Annette. *La Petite Fille du Vel' d'Hiv': Récit*. Paris: Denoël, 1991.

Milward, Alan S. *The New Order and the French Economy*. New York: Oxford University Press, 1970.

Miribel, Élisabeth de. *La Liberté souffre violence*. Paris: Plon, 1981.

Monestier, Marianne. *Elles étaient cent et mille: Femmes dans la résistance*. Paris: Fayard, 1972.

Monzie, Anatole de. *Ci-devant*. Paris: Flammarion, 1941.

Moreau, Emilienne. *La guerre buissonière: Une famille française dans la Résistance*. Paris: Solar, 1970.

Morgan, Ted. *An Uncertain Hour: The French, the Germans, the Jews, the Barbie Trial and the City of Lyon, 1940–45*. London: Bodley Head, 1990; New York: Arbor House/Wm. Morrow.

Moulin, Laure. *Jean Moulin*. Paris: Presses de la Cité, 1969.

Nichols, Lynn H. *The Rape of Europa: The Fate of Europe's Treasures in the Third Reich and the Second World War*. New York: Knopf, 1994.

Noguères, Henri, with Marcel Degliame-Fouché. *Histoire de la Résistance en France*. 5 vols. Paris: Laffont, 1967–1981.

———. *La vie quotidienne des résistants: De l'armistice à la Libération*. Paris: Hachette, 1984.

Nora, Pierre, ed. *Lieux de mémoire*. Paris: Gallimard, 1984–1993.

Novick, Peter. *The Resistance versus Vichy: The Purge of Collaborators in Liberated France*. London: Chatto & Windus, 1968.

Ory, Pascal. *Les Collaborateurs, 1940–1945*. Paris: Seuil, 1976.

Ouzoulias-Romagon, Cécile. *J'étais agent de liaison FTPF*. Paris: Messidor, 1988.

Paulhan, Jean. *Lettre aux directeurs de la Résistance*. Paris: Éditions de Minuit, 1951.

Paxton, Robert. *Vichy France: Old Guard and New Order 1940–44*. New York: Knopf, 1972.

Péan, Pierre. *Une jeunesse française: François Mitterrand 1934–1947*. Paris: Fayard, 1994.

Pedersen, Susan. *Family, Dependency, and the Origins of the Welfare State: Britain and France, 1914–1945*. Cambridge, U.K.: Cambridge University Press, 1993.

Pestourie, Roger. *La Résistance, c'était cela aussi*. Paris: Éditions Sociales, 1969.

Picar, Michel, and Julie Montagard. *Danielle Mitterrand: Portrait*. Paris: Éditions Ramsay, 1982.

Pougatch, Isaac. *Un Bâtisseur: Robert Gamzon*. Paris: FSJU, 1971.

Pryce-Jones, David. *Paris in the Third Reich: A History of German Occupation 1940–44*. London: Collins, 1981.

De la Résistance à la révolution: Anthologie de la presse clandestine française. Neuchatel, Switzerland: Éditions de la Baconnière, 1945.

Roberts, Marie Louise. *Civilization Without Sexes: Reconstructing Gender in Postwar France, 1917–1927*. Chicago: University of Chicago Press, 1994.

Rossiter, Margaret L. *Women in the Resistance*. New York: Praeger, 1986.

Rousseau, Renée. *Les Femmes rouges*. Paris: Albin Michel, 1983.

Rousso, Henry. *La Collaboration*. Paris: MA Éditions, 1987.

——— . *Le Syndrome de Vichy: 1944–198.* . . . Paris: Seuil, 1987; rev. ed., 1990. English edition: *The Vichy Syndrome: History and Memory in France since 1944*. Cambridge, MA: Harvard University Press, 1991.

Roux, Catherine. *Le Triangle rouge*. France-Empire, 1969.

Ruffin, Raymond. *Résistance P.T.T.* Paris: Presses de la Cité, 1983.

Sauvy, Alfred. *La Vie économique des Français de 1939 à 1945*. Paris: Flammarion, 1978.

Saywell, Shelley. *Women in War*. Markham, Ont.: Penguin, 1985.

Schank, Roger. *Tell Me a Story: A New Look at Real and Artificial Memory*. New York: Scribner's, 1990.

Schoenbrun, David. *Soldiers of the Night*. New York: New American Library, 1981.

Scott, Joan Wallach. *Gender and the Politics of History*. New York: Columbia University Press, 1988.

Simone et ses compagnons. Paris: Éditions de Minuit, 1947.

Sineau, Mariette. *Des Femmes en politique*. Paris: Economica, 1988.

Slitinsky, Michel. *La Résistance en Gironde*, 2nd ed. Bordeaux: Cahiers de la Résistance, 1970.

Le Souvenir, la Résistance, la Déportation. Students of the Collège public Sainte-Apolline, Courdimanche, Val-d'Oise, under the direction of history teachers Jean-François Couriol and Jean-Pierre Dubreuil. Versailles: CRDP, 1992.

Sowerwine, Charles. *Sisters or Citizens? Women and Socialism in France since 1876.* Cambridge, U.K.: Cambridge University Press, 1982.

Steel, James. *Littératures de l'ombre.* Paris: Presses de la Fondation Nationale des Sciences Politiques, 1991.

Steinberg, Jonathan. *All or Nothing: The Axis and the Holocaust 1941–1943.* London: Routledge, 1990.

Sullerot, Evelyne. *Les Françaises au travail.* Paris: Hachette, 1973.

———. *Histoire et sociologie du travail féminin.* Paris: Gonthier, 1968.

Sweets, John F. *The Politics of Resistance in France (1940–44): A History of the "Mouvements Unis de la Résistance."* DeKalb, IL: Northern Illinois University Press, 1976.

———. *Choices in Vichy France: The French under Nazi Occupation.* New York: Oxford University Press, 1986.

Szpiner, Francis. *Une Affaire de femmes, Paris 1943, Execution d'une avorteuse.* Paris: Éditions Balland, 1986.

Tartière, Drue. *The House near Paris.* New York: Simon and Schuster, 1946.

Témoignages: Le Crime contre l'esprit. Paris: Éditions de Minuit, 1945.

Terrenoire, Elisabeth. *Combattantes sans uniforme: Les Françaises dans la Résistance.* Paris: Bloud and Gay, 1946.

Teyssier-Jore, Raymonde. *Le "Corps Féminin."* Paris: France-Empire, 1975.

Thébaud, Françoise. *Quand nos grand-mères donnaient la vie: La maternité en France dans l'entre-deux-guerres.* Lyon: Presses Universitaires de Lyon, 1986.

Tillion, Germaine. *Ravensbrück.* Paris: Seuil, 1973; rev. 3d ed., 1988.

Tillon, Charles. *On chantait rouge.* Paris: Laffont, 1977.

Todorov, Tzvetan. *Une tragédie française: été 1944: scènes de guerre civile.* Paris: Seuil/L'Histoire Immédiate, 1994.

Toklas, Alice B. *The Alice B. Toklas Cook Book.* New York: Harper & Brothers, 1954.

Torrès, Tereska. *Les années anglaises: Journal intime de guerre 1939–45.* Paris: Seuil, 1981.

Triolet, Elsa. *Le premier accroc coûte deux cents francs.* Paris: Denoël, 1945. English edition: *A Fine of Two Hundred Francs,* with a new Introduction by Helena Lewis. London: Virago Press, 1987.

Une Histoire des femmes, est-elle possible? Paris: Rivages, 1984.

De l'université aux camps de concentration: Témoignages strasbourgeoises. Strasbourg, France: Presses Universitaires de Strasbourg, 1989.

Vagliano, Hélène. *Hôtes de la Gestapo.* Paris: Malakoff, 1946.

Vagliano-Eloy, Sonia. *Les Demoiselles de Gaulle, 1943–1945.* Paris: Plon, 1982.

Veillon, Dominique, ed. *La collaboration: Textes et débats.* Paris: Librairie Générale Française, 1984.

———. *La Mode sous l'occupation: Débrouillardise et coquetterie dans la France en guerre (1939–1945)*. Paris: Payot, 1990.

———. *Le Franc-Tireur*. Paris: Flammarion, 1977.

Vercors (pseud. Jean Bruller). *La Bataille du silence: Souvenirs de Minuit*. Paris: Presses de la Cité, 1967.

Verny, Françoise. *Le plus beau métier du monde*. Paris: Olivier Orban, 1990.

Vielzeuf, Aimé. *La Résistance dans le Gard (1940–1944)*. Nîmes: A. Vielzeuf, 1979.

Vistel, Alban. *Héritage spirituel de la Résistance*. Lyon: Lug, 1955.

Vomécourt, Philippe de. *An Army of Amateurs*. New York: Doubleday, 1961.

Wake, Nancy. *The Autobiography of the Woman the Gestapo Called "The White Mouse."* Melbourne: Macmillan of Australia, 1985.

Weitz, Margaret Collins. *Femmes: Recent Writings on French Women*. Boston: G. K. Hall, 1985.

———, ed. *Mémoire et Oubli: Women of the French Resistance*. Special volume of *Contemporary French Civilization*, vol. 18, no. 1 (1994).

Werth, Alexander. *France 1940–1955*. Boston: Beacon Press, 1966.

Wieviorka, Olivier. *Nous entrerons dans la carrière: De la Résistance à l'exercise du pouvoir*. Paris: Seuil, 1994.

Wilhelm, Maria de Blasio. *The Other Italy: The Italian Resistance in World War II*. New York: W. W. Norton, 1988.

Wilkinson, James D. *The Intellectual Resistance in Europe*. Cambridge, MA: Harvard University Press, 1981.

Wright, Gordon. *The Reshaping of French Democracy*. Boston: Beacon Press, 1948.

———. *France in Modern Times*, 2nd ed. New York: Rand McNally, 1974.

Yalom, Marilyn. *Blood Sisters: The French Revolution in Women's Memory*. New York: Basic Books, 1993.

Young, Gordon. *The Cat with Two Faces*. New York: Coward-McCann, 1957.

Zeitoun, Sabine. *Ces enfants qu'il fallait sauver*. Paris: Albin Michel, 1989.

Zeldin, Theodore. *France 1848–1945*. Oxford, U.K.: Oxford University Press, 1979.

Zlatin, Sabine. *Mémoires de la "Dame d'Izieu."* Paris: Gallimard, 1992.

Zuccotti, Susan. *The Holocaust, the French, and the Jews*. New York: Basic Books, 1993.

Articles

Annales: Histoire—Science Sociale. Vol. 48, no. 3, mai-juin 1993 (special edition devoted to the history of the Jews in occupied France).

Barot, Madeleine. "La CIMADE et les camps d'internement de la zone sud, 1940–1944," *Églises et chrétiens dans la Deuxième Guerre mondiale*. Lyon: Presses Universitaires de Lyon, 1982.

"Ces Français qui ont été formidables," *L'Evénement du Jeudi*, no. 301 (August 9–15, 1990).

"Commemorating 50 Years of Women's Suffrage," *French Politics and Society*, vol. 12, no. 4 (Fall 1994).

Coutrot, Aline. "La Politique familiale de Vichy," in *Le Gouvernement de Vichy, 1940–1942*. Paris: FNSP, 1972.

Derogy, Jacques. "Cette France qui a sauvé ses Juifs," *L'Evénement du Jeudi*, no. 301 (August 9–15, 1990).

"Les Échos de la mémoire," *Pourquoi*, no. 255 (June/July 1990).

Eck, Hélène. "French Women Under Vichy," in *A History of Women: Towards a Cultural Identity in the Twentieth Century*, Georges Duby and Michelle Perrot, gen. eds., Françoise Thébaud, ed. Cambridge, MA: Belknap Press of Harvard University, 1994.

"Les Femmes dans la Résistance," *Le Nouveau Choisir*, no. 67 (1985).

Halls, W. D. "Catholicism Under Vichy: A Study in Diversity and Ambiguity," in H. Roderick Kedward and Roger Austin, eds., *Vichy France and the Resistance: Culture and Ideology*. London: Croom Helm, 1985.

Gray, Francine Duplessix. "When Memory Goes," *Vanity Fair* (Nov. 1983).

"Histoire orale et histoire des femmes," *Bulletin de l'Institut d'Histoire du Temps Présent*. Paris: CNRS, supplement no. 3 (1982).

Hoffmann, Stanley. "Aspects du régime de Vichy," *Revue Française de Science Politique* (January–March, 1956).

———. "The Effects of World War II on French Society and Politics," *French Historical Studies*, no. 1 (April 1961).

Institut d'Histoire du Temps Présent, *Bulletin Trimestriel*, no. 23 (March 1986).

Kline, Rayna. "Partisans, Godmothers, Bicyclists and Other Terrorists: Women in the French Resistance and Under Vichy." *Proceedings of the Western Society for French History*, no. 5 (1977).

Kaufmann, Dorothy. " 'Le Témoin compromis': Diaries of Resistance and Collaboration by Edith Thomas," *L'Esprit créateur*, vol. 33, no. 1 (1993).

"Le Mouvement syndical dans la Résistance," *Cahiers de l'Institut C.G.T. d'Histoire Sociale*, no. 12 (November 1984).

Noguères, Henri. "Egalité et participation des femmes et des hommes dans la Résistance," in *Les Femmes dans la Résistance: Actes du colloque tenu à l'initiative de l'Union des Femmes Françaises*. (Monaco: Éditions du Rocher, 1977).

Offen, Karen. "Body Politics: Women, Work and the Politics of Motherhood in France, 1920–1950," in *Maternity and Gender Policies: Women and the Rise of the European Welfare States, 1880–1950s*, Gisela Bok and Pat Thane, eds. London: Routledge, 1991.

Pollard, Miranda. "Women and the National Revolution," in H. Roderick Kedward and Roger Austin, eds., *Vichy France and the Resistance: Culture and Ideology*. London: Croom Helm, 1985.

"Que faire de Vichy?" (special issue), *Esprit* (May 1992).

"Questions à l'histoire orale," *Cahiers de l'IHTP*, no. 4 (June 1987).

"Résistants et Collaborateurs," *L'Histoire*, no. 80 (1985).

Rossiter, Margaret. "Le Rôle des femmes dans la Résistance en France," *Revue d'Histoire*, no. 155 (July 1989).

Sainclivier, Jacqueline. "Sociologie de la Résistance: Quelques aspects méthodologiques et leur application en Ille-et-Vilaine," *Revue d'Histoire de la Deuxième Guerre Mondiale*, 117 (January 1980).

Schwartz, Paula L. "*Partisanes* and Gender Politics in Vichy France," *French Historical Studies*, 16, no. 1 (spring 1989).

Veillon, Dominique. "Résister au féminin," *Pénélope*, no. 12 (spring 1985).

Vidal-Naquet, Pierre. "Réflexions sur les trois Ravensbrück," *Voix et Visages*, no. 218 (January–February 1990).

Vildé, Boris. "Journal et lettres de prison 1941–42," *Cahiers de l'IHTP*, no. 7 (February 1988).

Weitz, Margaret Collins. "As I Was Then: Women in the French Resistance," *Contemporary French Civilization*, vol. 10, no. 1 (1985).

———. "Lucie Aubrac: Femme Engagée," *Contemporary French Civilization*, vol. 15, no. 1 (1991).

———. "Geneviève de Gaulle: Refusing the Unacceptable," *Contemporary French Civilization*, vol. 18, no. 1 (1994).

Wright, Gordon. "Reflections on the French Resistance," *Political Science Quarterly*, vol. lxxvii, no. 3 (September 1962).

Other sources of articles: *Bulletin de liaison de l'Association des Médaillés de la Résistance Française; Voix et Visages, Bulletin de l'ADIR; Bulletin de l'Institut Charles de Gaulle; Notre Musée: Bulletin de l'Association pour la création d'un Musée de la Résistance*.

Conferences

"Women and the French Resistance" Harvard and Suffolk Universities, Cambridge, MA, November 13–16, 1992.

"L'Année 1942 et les Juifs en France," Ecole des Hautes Etudes et Sciences Sociales/Section d'Etudes Hébraiques et Juives de l'INALCO, Paris, June 15–17, 1992.

"Les échos de la mémoire," La Ligne/Sécretariat d'Etat chargé des Anciens Combattants et des Victimes de Guerre, Paris, June 15–16, 1992.

"Le Régime de Vichy et les Francais," CNRS/IHTP, Paris, June 11–13, 1990.

"Simone de Beauvoir/Sartre," Harvard University, Cambridge, MA, February 27–28, 1987.

"Women and War" Harvard University, Cambridge, MA, January 8–10, 1984.

"Journée d'Étude sur la Résistance," CNRS/IHTP, Sorbonne, Paris, 1983.

"The Jews in Modern France," Brandeis University, Waltham, MA, 1983.

"Oral History," Columbia University, New York City, 1983.

"Women Surviving: The Holocaust," Institute for Research in History, New York, March 20–21, 1983.

La Propagande sous Vichy. Exhibition at Musée de l'Histoire Moderne, Invalides, Paris, June 1991. Catalogue published by BDIC la Découverte, Paris, under direction of Laurent Gervereau and Denis Peschanski.

Index